BILL
ENJOY!

Joseph

W9-AXV-325

CHART OF SEVERN RIVER, ANNAPOLIS ROADS, AND THE ADJACENT WATERS OF THE CHESAPEAKE BAY

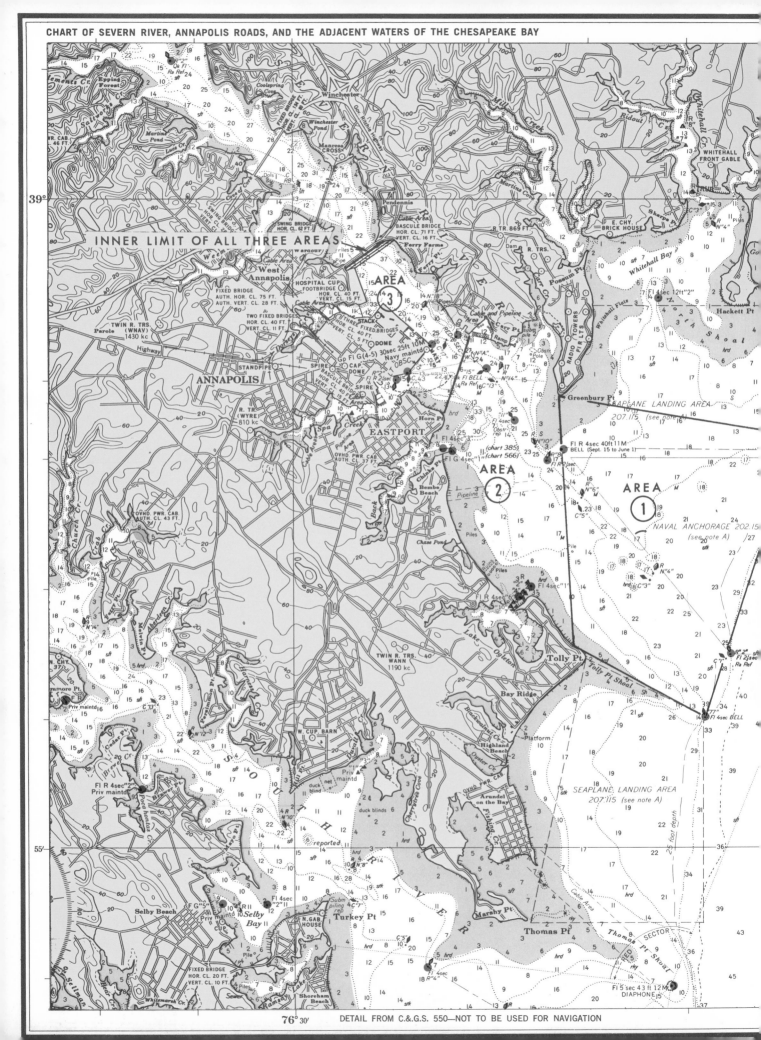

INNER LIMIT OF ALL THREE AREAS

AREA 3

AREA 2

AREA 1

ANNAPOLIS

EASTPORT

Bay Ridge

Tolly Pt

SEAPLANE LANDING AREA 207.115 (see note A)

NAVAL ANCHORAGE 202.15 (see note A)

SEAPLANE LANDING AREA 207.115 (see note A)

Thomas Pt

Turkey Pt

Selby Beach

SAIL AND POWER

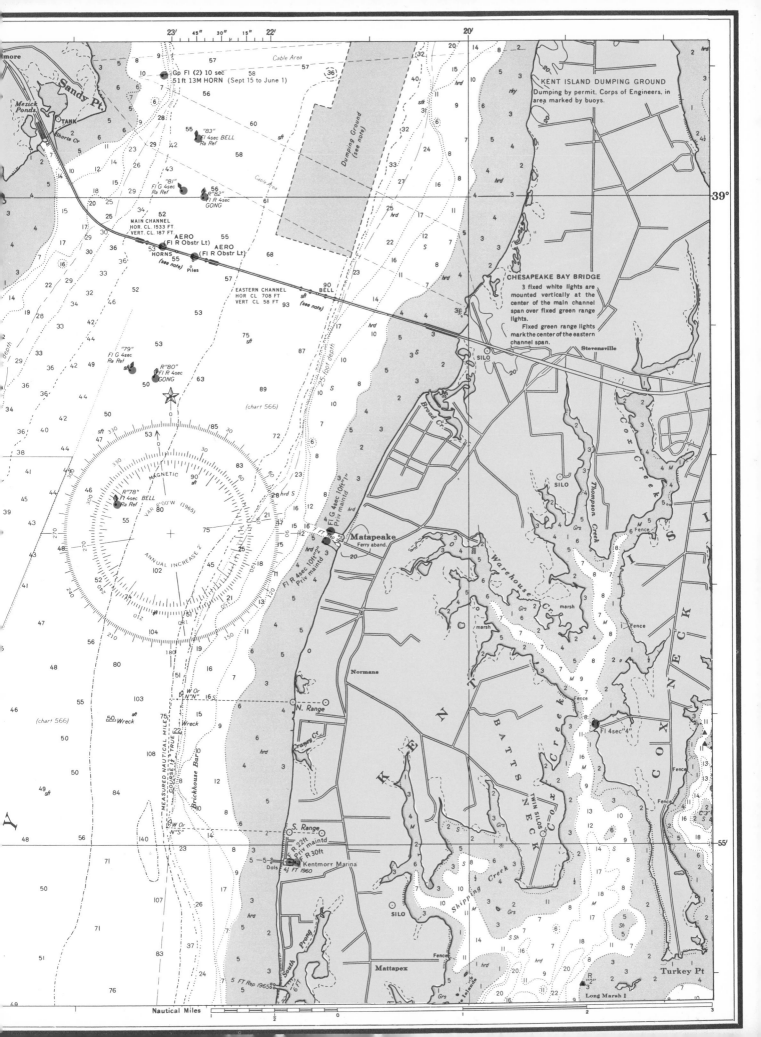

SAIL AND POWER

*A Manual
of Seamanship for
the United States
Naval Academy*

Richard Henderson
and
Bartlett S. Dunbar
Lieutenant, U.S. Navy

Illustrated by
Richard Henderson

UNITED STATES
NAVAL INSTITUTE
ANNAPOLIS
MARYLAND

COPYRIGHT © 1967
by United States Naval Institute, Annapolis, Maryland
Library of Congress Catalogue Card No. 67-22491
Second Printing, August, 1968

PRINTED IN THE UNITED STATES OF AMERICA

For war, the sail is as anachronistic as is the horse. Yet at the U.S. Naval Academy, where young men are concerned with learning about war at sea, the sail is thought to be a useful tool for teaching. This is not merely because sails once propelled men-of-war; it is no use teaching a missileman to shoot the crossbow. It is because the sailing vessel has this remarkable characteristic: she demands the utmost of devotion and competence from her master and crew; given anything less she will inevitably get them into trouble, perhaps mortal trouble. If a man can accept that he must be devoted to his ship and that he must know her needs, then he is setting the right course toward becoming a professional seaman.

Devotion to the vessel cannot be taught. That is simply an absolute requirement levied by the sea, and it must be met by each of us in his own way. Competence, on the other hand, certainly can be taught, and this book contains all the basic facts of seamanship, so that if it is closely studied, and if its procedures are practiced until they can be performed under a variety of weather conditions, then its users could be considered competent. Increased competence comes with more years of sailing, more years of learning from each maneuver.

Mastery? That is a word you will not hear much from the experienced seaman. He knows that the highest devotion and the greatest competence may be pitifully inadequate in the face of the relentless violence of the sea. He knows that the ocean can at any time take his physical safety and let it hang in the balance to be maintained or denied by some power beyond his control.

Without this element of danger, sailing would be less fun. The pleasures of making a boat go fast and maneuvering her smoothly using only the wind and current are satisfying enough in themselves, but they seem heightened by the constant demand for careful alertness that the boat's environment exacts. The sail produces a great challenge and a great opportunity. If a man can meet the challenge in a small boat under sail, he will certainly be able to cope with the essentials of a powerboat and will possess vital prerequisites for handling large vessels.

Good sailing to you. Here's wishing you a fair breeze and a following sea!

Authors' Preface

The primary purpose of this book is to familiarize and instruct the U.S. Naval Academy midshipmen in the essentials of small-boat handling and seamanship under sail as well as under power. In addition, the authors hope that the book will cause the midshipman to realize the unique opportunity he has to participate in a most extensive sailing program that includes instruction and competition in every kind of boat from dinghy to ocean racer. Obviously, the fundamentals of handling small craft under power should be mastered before ship handling is attempted; thus familiarity with the various powerboats used at the Naval Academy is an important part of a midshipman's training.

While some may argue that training in sail is not essential, there is no question that it is highly desirable. There is nothing like sailing to bring one into close contact with and to develop a real love for the sea. In addition to improving and broadening skills in boat handling and seamanship, sailing helps build resourcefulness, general nautical knowledge, the ability to make quick decisions, team spirit, and the ability to give and take orders. Furthermore, sailing and racing under sail encourage an understanding and sensitivity towards the wind, tide, and waves which are, after all, the seaman's environmental elements.

Many people have been helpful and encouraging to the authors in their preparation of this book. They wish especially to thank the following: Captain Jacob J. Vandergrift, Jr., U.S. Navy; Lieutenant Commander Bruce McLaughlin, U.S. Navy; Lieutenant Paul Dodson, U.S. Navy; Lieutenant (junior grade) Stuart A. Finlay, U.S. Naval Reserve; Lieutenant W. G. Furnholm, U.S. Navy; and Chief Warrant Officer M. Kerekesh, U.S. Navy. In addition, the authors wish to thank Mr. Henry Regnery, president of the Reilly and Lee Company, for permission to use many drawings from the book, *Hand, Reef, and Steer*.

Richard Henderson

Bartlett S. Dunbar
LIEUTENANT, U.S. NAVY

4 April 1967

Table of Contents

Chapters One through Ten are the work of Richard Henderson; Chapters Eleven through Fourteen were written by Lieutenant Bartlett S. Dunbar, U. S. Navy.

SAIL AND POWER

CHAPTER ONE

Nomenclature

Correct nautical language is a prime prerequisite to boat handling. Sailor's language is not an affectation, but a traditional and functional means of communication. Improper use of nautical terms by a sailor is not only lubberish, but it is in bad taste, and furthermore it can result in dangerous misunderstandings.

Since the boating novice is apt to be confused by an initial overdose of nautical terms and nomenclature, this chapter will serve merely as an introduction to the subject. More terms will be introduced in subsequent chapters, and all these terms are indexed at the end of the book. When the reader is first introduced to a new term in the text, the term will be italicized and explained or defined, in the text. The reader should familiarize himself with a new term the first time it is used because definitions are seldom repeated.

To begin with, boats are thought of as being feminine, and they are referred to as *she* or *her.* A boat's front is her *bow* or her *fore* part, and her back end is her *stern* or *after* part. When we move towards the bow we say we are going *forward,* but moving towards the stern, we are going *aft.* When one object on a boat lies farther aft than another object, we say the first object is *abaft* the second. Facing forward, the left side of a boat is the *port* side, while the right is the *starboard* side. It may be helpful for the beginning sailor to remember that port has the same number of letters as left. *Amidships* is the middle of a boat, halfway from side to side or from bow to stern. *Athwartships* means across a boat, as opposed to *fore and aft,* from bow to stern. The *thwarts* or seats in a rowboat run athwartships, but the *keel* or main structural member at the bottom of a ship runs fore and aft.

Figure 1 shows the system used for expressing *bearings* or directions in which objects are

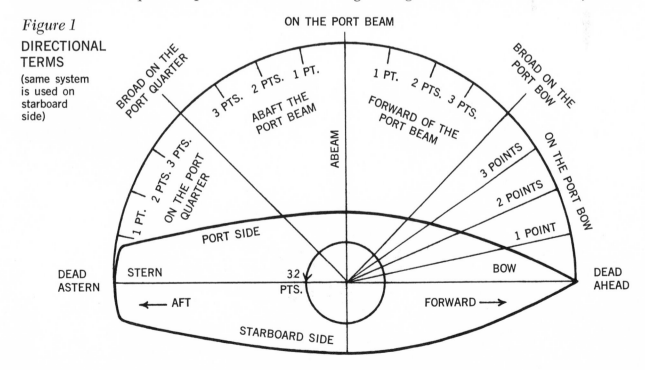

Figure 1

DIRECTIONAL TERMS

(same system is used on starboard side)

ON THE PORT BEAM

BROAD ON THE PORT QUARTER

3 PTS. 2 PTS. 1 PT.

ABAFT THE PORT BEAM

1 PT. 2 PTS. 3 PTS.

FORWARD OF THE PORT BEAM

BROAD ON THE PORT BOW

ABEAM

1 PT. 2 PTS. 3 PTS.

ON THE PORT QUARTER

3 POINTS

2 POINTS

1 POINT

ON THE PORT BOW

DEAD ASTERN

STERN

PORT SIDE

32 PTS.

BOW

DEAD AHEAD

AFT

STARBOARD SIDE

FORWARD

observed from a boat. If an object lies *on the port beam* it is said to be *abeam*, at right angles to the keel (on the port side in this case). Should the object lie halfway between *dead ahead* and abeam, it is *broad on the bow*, or *broad on the quarter* if halfway between abeam and *dead astern*. As the diagram shows, the distance around the boat is divided into 32 *points*, 8 points from dead ahead to abeam, and 8 points

more to dead astern, or a total of 16 points halfway around the boat. If a buoy or some other object bears between dead ahead and broad on the bow, we say it bears one, two, or three points on the bow. If it bears between broad on the bow and on the beam, it is one, two, or three points forward of the beam. From abeam to broad on the quarter, the object bears one, two, or three points abaft the beam; while from

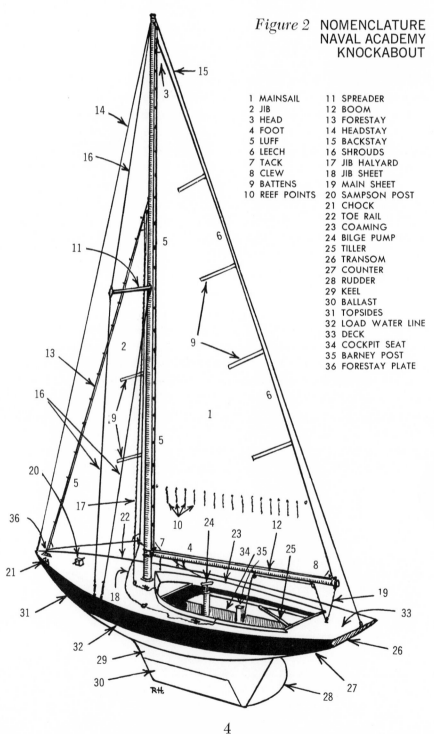

Figure 2 NOMENCLATURE
NAVAL ACADEMY
KNOCKABOUT

1 MAINSAIL	11 SPREADER
2 JIB	12 BOOM
3 HEAD	13 FORESTAY
4 FOOT	14 HEADSTAY
5 LUFF	15 BACKSTAY
6 LEECH	16 SHROUDS
7 TACK	17 JIB HALYARD
8 CLEW	18 JIB SHEET
9 BATTENS	19 MAIN SHEET
10 REEF POINTS	20 SAMPSON POST
	21 CHOCK
	22 TOE RAIL
	23 COAMING
	24 BILGE PUMP
	25 TILLER
	26 TRANSOM
	27 COUNTER
	28 RUDDER
	29 KEEL
	30 BALLAST
	31 TOPSIDES
	32 LOAD WATER LINE
	33 DECK
	34 COCKPIT SEAT
	35 BARNEY POST
	36 FORESTAY PLATE

broad on the quarter to dead astern, it bears one, two, or three points on the quarter. This is explained in the diagram.

Figure 2 deals with boat nomenclature. The boat illustrated is a Naval Academy knockabout, a 26-foot *day sailer* (without any living accommodations and intended for short-range sailing), having a *ballasted* or weighted keel. When we step on a boat we *board* her or *go aboard*. If we should drop or throw something over the side, we throw it *overboard*. Any part of the boat which extends beyond or is attached outside of the *hull*, the main body of the boat, is said to be *outboard*. If the object is inside the hull or near the boat's center it is said to be *inboard*.

When we board a knockabout we step on her *deck*, the flat surface at the top of her hull. Where the deck joins the *topsides* or upper sides of the hull, there is a low *toe rail* to prevent the *crew*, those who man the boat, from sliding overboard when the boat is *heeled*, tipped by the force of the wind when sailing. On small open boats (without decks), the extreme top of the sides is called the *gunwale* (pronounced gun'l). The large opening in the deck abaft the mast which accommodates the *helmsman*, one who steers the boat, is called the *cockpit*. The fore-and-aft benches in the cockpit are called *seats*.

The knockabout is *sloop*-rigged with one *mast* (vertical pole) supporting two sails, the *mainsail* and *jib*, as shown in the illustration. The mainsail's *foot* or bottom is secured to the *boom*, a horizontal pole hinged at its forward end to the mast with a fitting called the *gooseneck*. Poles used to spread sails are called *spars*. The sails are *hoisted* or pulled up the mast with *lines* (ropes) called *halyards*. They are pulled in or let out with lines called *sheets*. Halyards and sheets collectively are called *running rigging*, while the wire ropes which hold the mast upright and keep it straight are called *standing rigging*. Those wires which support the mast fore and aft are called *stays*. The *permanent backstay* is at the stern, and the *head stay* (outer stay) and *forestay* (inner stay) are at the bow. The wires which give lateral support are called *shrouds* and they attach at the rail to metal straps called *chainplates* and on the mast to metal straps called *tangs*.

The helmsman of a knockabout steers with a *tiller*, a wooden stick or handle which attaches to the *rudder*, a flat, underwater plate hinged to the *after* (back) end of the keel. The flat after part of the stern is called the *transom*, while the overhanging part of the stern below the transom is called the *counter*. Around the cockpit there is a low railing called the *coaming* which helps keep water from washing into the cockpit. The coamings on each side of the cockpit converge and meet just abaft the mast. Here they are raised slightly higher, and they are often referred to as *washboards* or *splashboards*. On the bow we find a *Sampson post* to which a docking line, anchor line, or towline may be fastened. These lines are led through the bow *chocks*, shown in the diagram, to prevent the lines from *chafing*, or rubbing the rail.

At the bottom of the cockpit there are *floorboards* on which the crew stands. Floorboards are not to be confused with *floors* or *floor timbers*, which are constructional members bolted to and running athwartships across the top of the keel. These members often tie in with the *ribs* or *frames*, the framework pieces which rise from the keel upwards, and to which the boat's planking is fastened. Beneath the floorboards is the *bilge*, the inside bottom of the boat which often contains, but should be kept clear of, bilge water. The place at which the bottom of a round-bottom boat curves upward to become its sides is called the *turn of the bilge*. On a V-bottom boat the bottom and sides join at a definite angle, and this is called the *chine*. Constructional parts for wooden hulls are shown in Figure 3.

On *cruising boats*, those having cabins, or roofed-over shelters with living accommodations, the floorboards are usually referred to as the *cabin sole*. *Bulkheads* are the athwartships walls with or without doorways. They divide a cabin for privacy, but their primary purpose is to stiffen and strengthen the hull. They are essential on fiberglass boats that customarily have few, if any, ribs. In the cabin there are *bunks* or *berths* (beds), the *galley* (kitchen), and *head* (toilet). The part of the cabin which sticks up above the deck is the *cabin trunk* or *deckhouse*.

Figure 3 HULL CONSTRUCTION

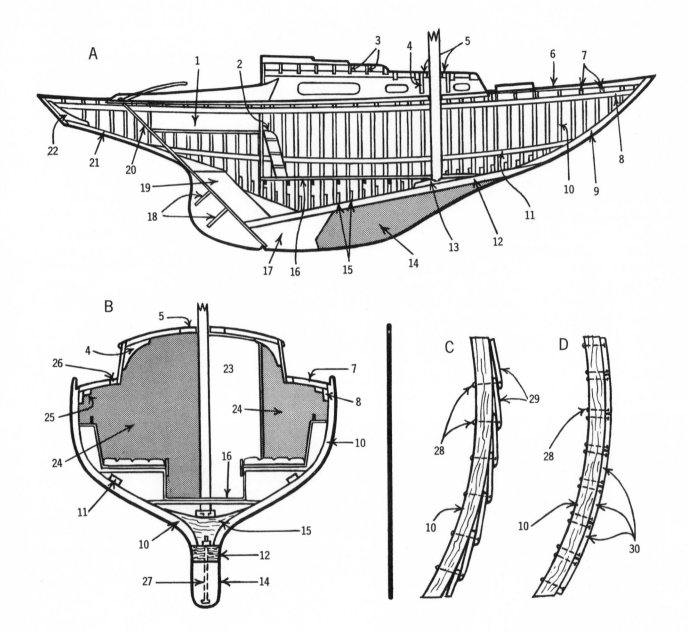

1	COCKPIT WELL	9	STEM	17	FALSE KEEL	25	DECK SHELF
2	COMPANION LADDER	10	RIB OR FRAME	18	RUDDER STRAPS	26	CARLIN
3	CABIN BEAMS	11	BILGE STRINGER	19	DEADWOOD	27	KEEL BOLT
4	HANGING KNEE	12	KEEL	20	RUDDER STOCK	28	FASTENINGS
5	MAST PARTNERS	13	MAST STEP	21	HORN TIMBER	29	CLINKER PLANKS OR LAP-STRAKE
6	RAIL	14	BALLAST KEEL	22	STERN KNEE		
7	DECK BEAMS	15	FLOOR TIMBERS	23	DOORWAY	30	CARVEL PLANKING
8	CLAMP	16	CABIN SOLE	24	BULKHEAD		

If the after end of the trunk is raised, it is often called the *doghouse. If* there is no cabin trunk, we say the boat is *flush-decked.* Holes or openings through the deck or cabin trunk which may be closed with covers are called *hatches.* The large hatchway through which we enter the cabin is called the *companionway,* and we climb down the *companion ladder.* We say we are going *below,* never downstairs. Small windows in the cabin which may be opened or closed are called *portholes.* Those that cannot be opened are called *port lights.*

Figure 4 shows thirteen frequently used terms which describe the shape or dimensions of a hull. The *load water line* (L.W.L.) is the line on which the boat floats. The hull is submerged below this line. *Tumble home* is the inward curving of the sides, while *flare* is the outward slant of the sides, usually at the bow. *Deadrise* is the vertical distance of the upward slant of a boat's bottom. If the bottom is flat,

she has no deadrise. *Entrance* is the forward part of the immersed hull, while the *run* is the after part which sweeps upward towards the stern. *Forefoot* is the immersed part of the bow, between the load water line and the fore end of the keel. *Draft* is the distance measured vertically from the L.W.L. to the deepest part of the keel's bottom. We say that a knockabout, for instance, *draws* four feet. *Sheer* is the horizontal curve from bow to stern along the rail. With *conventional sheer* the *freeboard,* height of the rail above the water, is lower amidships than at the bow or stern. Some boats, however, have a *straight sheer,* in which freeboard is constant, or a *reversed sheer,* where the freeboard is highest amidships. *Beam* is the maximum width of a boat. The rest of the terms in Figure 4 should be self-explanatory.

Today's most common sailing *rigs* (the system or arrangement of masts and sails) for *yachts* (pleasure boats) are shown in Figure 5. All these

Figure 4 DESCRIPTIVE TERMS FOR THE HULL

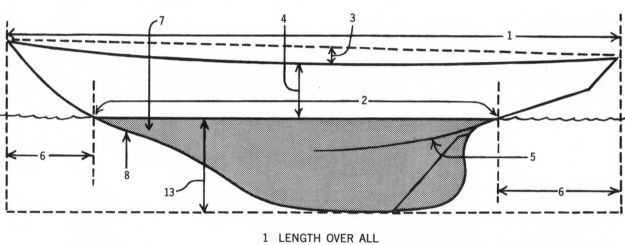

1 LENGTH OVER ALL
2 LOAD WATER LINE
3 SHEER
4 FREEBOARD
5 RUN
6 OVERHANGS
7 ENTRANCE
8 FOREFOOT
9 DEADRISE
10 FLARE
11 TUMBLE HOME
12 BEAM
13 DRAFT

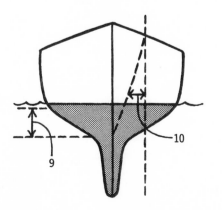

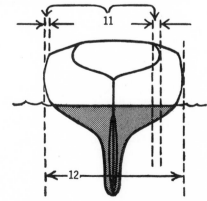

7

Figure 5 COMMON FORE & AFT RIGS

A. MAINSAIL B. JIB C. FORESAIL
D. FORE STAYSAIL E. MIZZEN

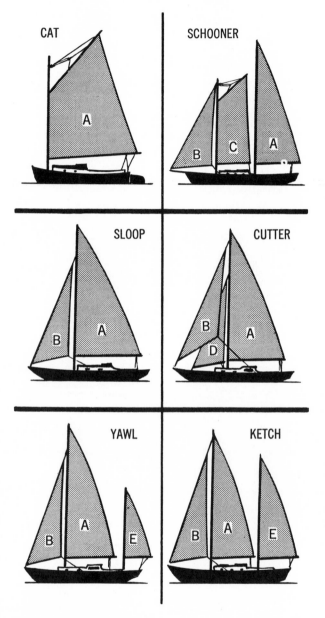

rigs are called *fore-and-aft* rigs as opposed to *square* rigs. The latter have sails, approximately square-shaped, that hang from *yards,* horizontal spars running athwartships which may be swung fore and aft to a limited extent only. Fore-and-aft sails may be pulled into a true fore and aft position and their forward edge is attached to a mast, stay or semi-fixed location. All the sails shown in Figure 5 are *Marconi*

or *jib-headed* except the mainsail (pronounced mains'l) of the *cat boat* and the *foresail* (pronounced fors'l) of the *schooner.* The *heads* (top edges) of these sails are attached to a *gaff,* a spar that may be hoisted *aloft* (high off the deck), and thus these sails are said to be *gaff-headed.* The cat boat has her mast *stepped* (put in place) far forward, and she carries no jib (the foremost sail). Like the cat boat, *cutters* and *sloops* are single-masted, but they carry jibs. The cutter's mast is stepped much farther aft than the sloop's, and the cutter often carries a *forestay-sail* (pronounced forstays'l) in addition to her jib. *Yawls, ketches,* and *schooners* each have two masts, although the last may have more than two. Yawls and ketches are quite similar, except that a ketch's *mizzen* (the aftermost sail) is much larger and farther forward than a yawl's. Notice that the schooner's mainsail is aftermost.

Figure 6 shows three traditional boat types which are often seen in the Annapolis area. Technically, the terms *bugeye, skipjack* (no relation to the small Skipjack-class boats used at the U.S. Naval Academy), and *log canoe* refer to hull types, but the distinctive rigs illustrated are associated with each type. These boats have an early origin and are peculiar to the Chesapeake Bay. The log canoe's ancestry goes back to the early Indian dugout canoe made from a single log. Even present log canoes, built from several logs, are very narrow and need *spring-boards* or *hiking boards,* which may be extended beyond the sides to support the weight of their crew in order to hold the canoes upright. They carry an enormous spread of sail in light airs.

Bugeyes and skipjacks are work boats used for oyster dredging. The former are growing scarce, but the latter are still plentiful. The bug-eye evolved from the log canoe. Originally it was built from several logs fastened together, but later conventional plank-on-frame construction was used. Usually, the bugeye has a sharp stern with a platform atop called a *patent stern.* Its rig consists of three sails named similarly to a schooner's sails, jib, foresail, and mainsail. These are supported by two masts sharply *raked* (leaning aft).

Unlike the bugeye, the skipjack has a V-bot-

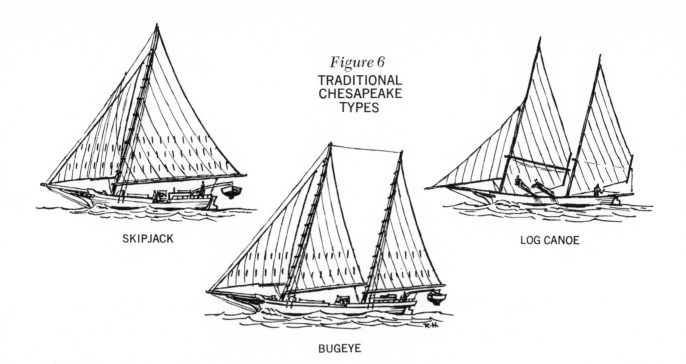

Figure 6
TRADITIONAL
CHESAPEAKE
TYPES

SKIPJACK

LOG CANOE

BUGEYE

tom with *hard* chines (sharp at the turn of the bilge). It is sloop-rigged, with a single, sharply raking mast. Like the bugeye, a skipjack has a fairly long *bowsprit*, a fixed pole extended over the bow, and a graceful *clipper bow*, a concave curve of the bow as seen in profile, similar to the old clipper ships. Currently working skip-jacks vary from 40 to 60 feet in length on deck.

Although a great deal of nomenclature and terminology has not been covered in this chapter, what has been presented seems an ample amount for a beginner. Details of sails, rigging, and boat fittings, as well as other nautical expressions, will be presented in later chapters.

CHAPTER TWO

Elementary Seamanship

Seamanship is a very broad term used to cover a variety of subjects, including general boat-handling, steering and maneuvering, managing a vessel under adverse conditions, and marlinspike seamanship, or knots, splices, and general ropework. This chapter is merely an introduction to the subject for the novice boatman. More advanced seamanship and other areas of the subject will be introduced in later chapters.

Small-Boat Safety

The beginning sailor should be constantly conscious of safety. Boating is a relatively safe activity, but hundreds of people drown every year as a result of careless seamanship. To begin with, every sailor should be able to swim well. He should be able to float with clothes on for at least five minutes.

Personal gear should include a knife and boat shoes, the latter with soles especially designed to grip a slippery deck (see Figure 7). A knife is not only extremely useful for numerous small jobs around a boat, but it might be needed to cut a line in an emergency. The sailor's knife usually has a locking marlinspike, which is handy for splicing and can be inserted into the eye of a shackle screw for tightening or loosening (see Figure 7).

Small open boats should carry Coast Guard approved life preservers, at least one for each person on board, an anchor and anchor line; a

large bailer or bucket for bilge water removal, and oars with oarlocks or a paddle. In addition, a small day sailer should have a *chart* (nautical map) of the local area, tools (at least a screwdriver and pliers), horn or whistle, spare parts (shackles, pins, etc.), a small compass, extra line, waterproof tape, twine, lubricating oil, sponge, and a flashlight.

Many small boats, particularly certain *dinghies* (small, open rowing or sailing boats, often used as tenders to and carried aboard larger vessels), have little initial stability. Boarding one of these boats should be done with caution. To some extent, stability can be judged by looking at the hull form. A flat-bottomed skiff or a beamy dinghy with flotation tanks on either side should be fairly stable or *stiff,* as sailors often say, but a boat with a narrow bottom and slanting sides, the dory form, will tip quite easily, or be *tender.* Never board any kind of small boat by stepping on her gunwale, and never jump aboard. Keep your weight amidships as much as possible. Avoid standing up in a small boat, and don't overload her. When carrying

Figure 7 BOAT SHOES AND KNIFE

folding marlinspike

several people or a heavy load, judge the condition of the sea and weather for wind strength and size of waves so that ample freeboard can be left to prevent water from sloshing in. A boat should generally be trimmed so that she is slightly lower at the stern than at the bow.

Basic Rowing

With the increasing use of the outboard motor for small boats there seems to be a diminishing interest in and emphasis on the skill of

Figure 8 ROWING

A

BLADE VERTICAL

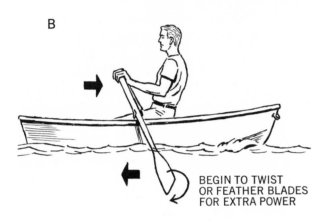

B

BEGIN TO TWIST
OR FEATHER BLADES
FOR EXTRA POWER

the blades leave the water at the conclusion of step B, they should be almost flat or horizontal.

A common mistake made by beginners is raising the oars with the blades vertical, which usually results in the oarsman being splashed with spray, or in dipping the blades in the water with them being turned flat or horizontal. This often results in the oarsman losing his balance and falling over backwards, since the blades will not *catch* or have any resistance against the water.

Another sure way of recognizing a beginner is to see him use the "paddlewheel stroke." This is when the oarsman lifts the blades up high in the air and then sinks them down unnecessarily deep in the water so that the oar blades describe great circles like windmill sails. Actually, the blades should be sunk only deep enough to get a good bite in the water, and on a calm day they should be lifted only a few inches above the surface.

When carrying one or more passengers in a dinghy, see that the boat is properly *trimmed,* so that she is not excessively down by the bow or the stern. This sometimes involves moving the oarlocks to another thwart; but it makes a tremendous difference in the ease with which the boat may be rowed.

Turning a rowboat is accomplished by pulling harder on one oar than on the other. A quick turn can be made by dragging one oar or even reversing the stroke direction of the oar while the other one is driving the boat ahead. Backing down is done by reversing the stroke direction of both oars. When landing alongside a vessel or pier, do not land bow first but turn the boat (into the wind if possible) so that you land side to side. *Ship* or take in your oar on the side that will face the vessel or pier in plenty of time. The other oar may be dragged with the blade held vertically to make the boat turn. When within several feet of landing, *ship your oarlock* which faces the side of the vessel or pier. Failure to do this has caused many gouges in the topsides of boats. Keep the outboard oar in use to hold the boat steady until all passengers have disembarked. Before leaving the boat, be sure both oars and oarlocks are shipped.

Rowing in the conventional manner requires

rowing. However, handling a boat with oars is one of the basics of good seamanship, and no one can call himself an accomplished boatman until he has learned to row well. Of course, this skill is acquired not only by instruction but by regular practice.

The simple principle of the rowing stroke is shown in Figure 8. In step A the oarsman with arms extended in front of him and the oar handles held side by side, dips the oar blades into the water. In step B he pulls the oar handles towards his chest and leans backwards slightly. This action causes the blades to move aft, which naturally makes the boat move ahead. At the end of this power stroke, the blades are lifted from the water and are then brought back to the position shown in step A.

Notice in step B that the blades enter the water almost vertically, but as they are pulled aft, they are twisted somewhat, which adds much to the power and effectiveness of the stroke. This is called *feathering* the oars. When that the oarsman face aft; thus, a final word of advice is that he should constantly turn his head around to look where he is going. To facilitate holding a straight course, try, if possible, to line up a near object aft with a distant object aft so that you have a range along which you may sight.

Capsizing and Righting

Although with proper care capsizing can be avoided, all small dinghies and boats with *centerboards* (a fore-and-aft board or plate that can be lowered through a trunk or well on the centerline to increase the boat's lateral resistance, as in Figure 28) are subject to turning over. Most boats capable of being capsized and all small rowing or sailing boats at the U.S. Naval Academy have built-in flotation to prevent sinking after a capsizing or swamping. The cardinal rule after turning over is to *stay with the boat*. Even if you are an excellent swimmer, hang onto your capsized boat and don't strike out for a "nearby" shore. Distances can be deceptive when you are in the water, wind and current are hard to predict, and you have a much better chance of being spotted when you are with your boat.

To recover from a capsizing, the overturned boat must be *righted* or turned upright, and then she can be bailed out. A small non-sailing dinghy will sometimes *turn turtle* or completely upside down. However, she can usually be righted easily if you lean backwards while gripping the bottom or keel with your fingers and, at the same time, exert pressure downwards at the gunwale with your knees or feet. A sailboat is usually more difficult to right because the weight of her mast and wet sails must be lifted up out of the water. Most sailboats will lie on their side with the sails resting on the water's surface, but some with extreme beam or excessive flotation or metal masts which can fill with water may have a tendency to turn turtle. Try not to let any sailboat turn bottom side up because in this position she is very difficult to right, and she is subject to damage. If the water is shoal, her mast may get stuck in the mud. To avoid turning turtle, stand on the centerboard immediately after capsizing. If another crew member is present, have him attach a float, a life preserver for instance, to the masthead. This float should be made fast to the halyard, in such a way that the float may be hauled down after the boat is righted and bailed out.

As soon as possible after capsizing, don life jackets. Some small boats carry Coast Guard approved kapok cushions in lieu of life jackets. These cushions may be worn over the chest and stomach with one handle strap around the neck and the other around a leg so that the hands are left free. Don't put one of these cushions on your back as it will tend to float you face down. Although cushions are legally allowed as life preservers, they are inferior to life preservers which are designed for no other purpose.

Not long after capsizing, equipment will begin to float out of the cockpit and start to drift away. Gather up this equipment and lash it or otherwise secure it to the boat, but do not swim any great distance away from the boat in pursuit of a floating object. The bailing bucket should have a *lanyard* (short rope) in order that it may be tied to the boat.

Figure 9 shows the procedure for righting a small sailboat. Lowering the sails will make the operation much easier. They should be loosely *furled* and *stopped*, rolled or bundled up and tied to the boom, and also the mainsheet should be pulled tight to prevent the boom from falling down off the deck. Lower the centerboard if it is not already down and climb up on it. Stand on the centerboard with your feet near the boat's bottom to prevent the board from breaking, and then lean backwards while holding on to the boat's rail or gunwale. With sails down, the boat should roll back upright. Since the water-filled boat will have little stability, she may want to keep rolling beyond the vertical and capsize again in the opposite direction. Once she is upright, it is a matter of splashing, rocking, or bailing the water out of the cockpit with a crew member on each side to counterbalance. If the boat has ample flotation the crew member on the windward or upwind side can climb aboard and bail much more effectively. If you are alone you may be able to board the boat by climbing over her stern. Should a rescue craft come along, try to right your boat before ac-

Figure 9 RIGHTING AFTER CAPSIZING

If float (life preserver for example) is fastened to masthead to prevent boat from turning upside down, secure float to halyard so that it can be pulled down after boat is righted.

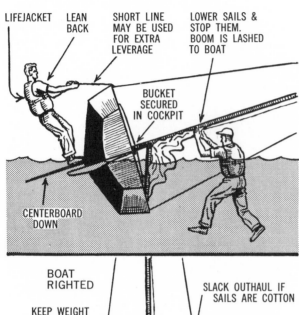

LIFEJACKET · LEAN BACK · SHORT LINE MAY BE USED FOR EXTRA LEVERAGE · LOWER SAILS & STOP THEM. BOOM IS LASHED TO BOAT · BUCKET SECURED IN COCKPIT · CENTERBOARD DOWN

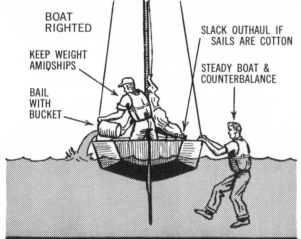

BOAT RIGHTED · KEEP WEIGHT AMIDSHIPS · BAIL WITH BUCKET · SLACK OUTHAUL IF SAILS ARE COTTON · STEADY BOAT & COUNTERBALANCE

cepting help, because a boat coming alongside a capsized sailboat can damage the rigging and get a floating line caught in her propeller. However, if the water is very cold, immediately board the rescue craft, before your boat is righted. The rescue craft should never attempt to tow a capsized boat until she has been righted. More will be said on the subject of rescue from a motor boat in the chapter entitled "Sailboats Under Power."

Basic Marlinspike Seamanship

Rope is almost constantly in use on all boats, particularly sailboats, and so learning to knot and handle it is of prime importance. Every sailor should know at least the basic knots shown in Figure 10, and he should learn to make a *whipping* and an *eye splice* shown in Figures 11 and 12. Of course he should also know how properly to make fast to a cleat and to coil lines (general term for light ropes used on a boat). These operations are shown in Figures 13 and 14.

A variety of fibers are used for making rope: manila, hemp, linen, sisal, and coir, but presently the most popular rope fibers are the synthetics, nylon and dacron. These are exceptionally strong, very resistant to chafe, and will not rot. Nylon is excellent for anchor or tow lines because it is quite elastic, but this characteristic makes it poor for most other uses. Dacron has very little stretch so it is very good for sheets and halyards.

A BUOYANT BOAT CAPSIZED

A crew member has climbed onto the centerboard immediately to prevent the boat from turning turtle. Notice that he has put his weight close to the boat's bottom to avoid bending or breaking the board. The jib is furled around the jibstay which will simplify righting. Lowering and stopping the mainsail will further simplify the job.

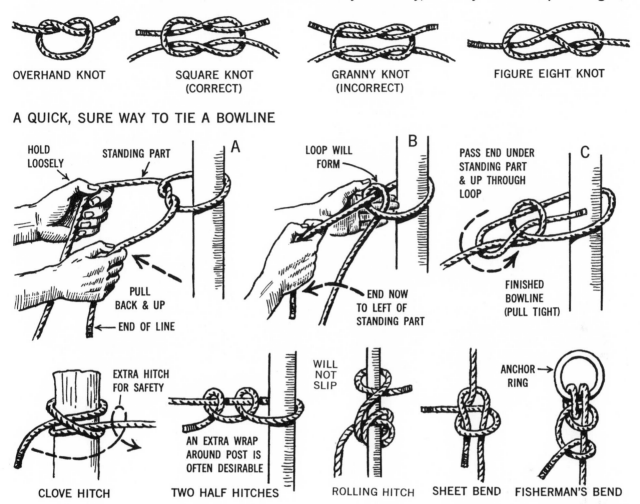

Figure 10 KNOTS, HITCHES, & BENDS

(All knots are shown tied loosely for clarity, but they should be pulled tight.)

OVERHAND KNOT

SQUARE KNOT
(CORRECT)

GRANNY KNOT
(INCORRECT)

FIGURE EIGHT KNOT

A QUICK, SURE WAY TO TIE A BOWLINE

HOLD LOOSELY   STANDING PART   A

PULL BACK & UP

END OF LINE

LOOP WILL FORM   B

END NOW TO LEFT OF STANDING PART

PASS END UNDER STANDING PART & UP THROUGH LOOP   C

FINISHED BOWLINE (PULL TIGHT)

EXTRA HITCH FOR SAFETY

CLOVE HITCH

AN EXTRA WRAP AROUND POST IS OFTEN DESIRABLE

TWO HALF HITCHES

WILL NOT SLIP

ROLLING HITCH

SHEET BEND

ANCHOR RING

FISHERMAN'S BEND

In cleating a line it is customary to start off with a round turn on the cleat and then to follow this with criss-cross wraps, as shown in the diagram. Finishing off with a hitch as shown in B (Figure 14), assures that the line will not jump off its cleat. However, this is sometimes a dangerous practice if the line has to be released in a hurry because it will often swell and jam when wet. Synthetic lines are not as likely to swell, but it is a good practice never to hitch a sheet which might have to be released quickly unless a slippery hitch (shown in the diagram) is used.

The knots illustrated in Figure 10 are self-explanatory. They are shown tied loosely for clarity but should be pulled tight. The bowline is a useful knot, as it will never jam.

Whipping consists of wrapping the end of a line with twine to keep it from unraveling. There are several methods of doing this, but the one illustrated, called *needle whipping*, is probably the most permanent. It requires a heavy sailmaker's needle and twine. It consists of a series of round wrappings of the thread followed by diagonal weavings of the thread following the *lay* or twisting of the rope strands. This is explained in Figure 11.

There are several kinds of splices but the *eye splice* illustrated is probably the most useful. The first series of tucks or interweavings of the strands (A, B, and C in the diagram) is the most difficult. Step C often gives the beginner the most trouble, but difficulty can be avoided if it is kept in mind that the strands are always

15

Figure 11 WHIPPING

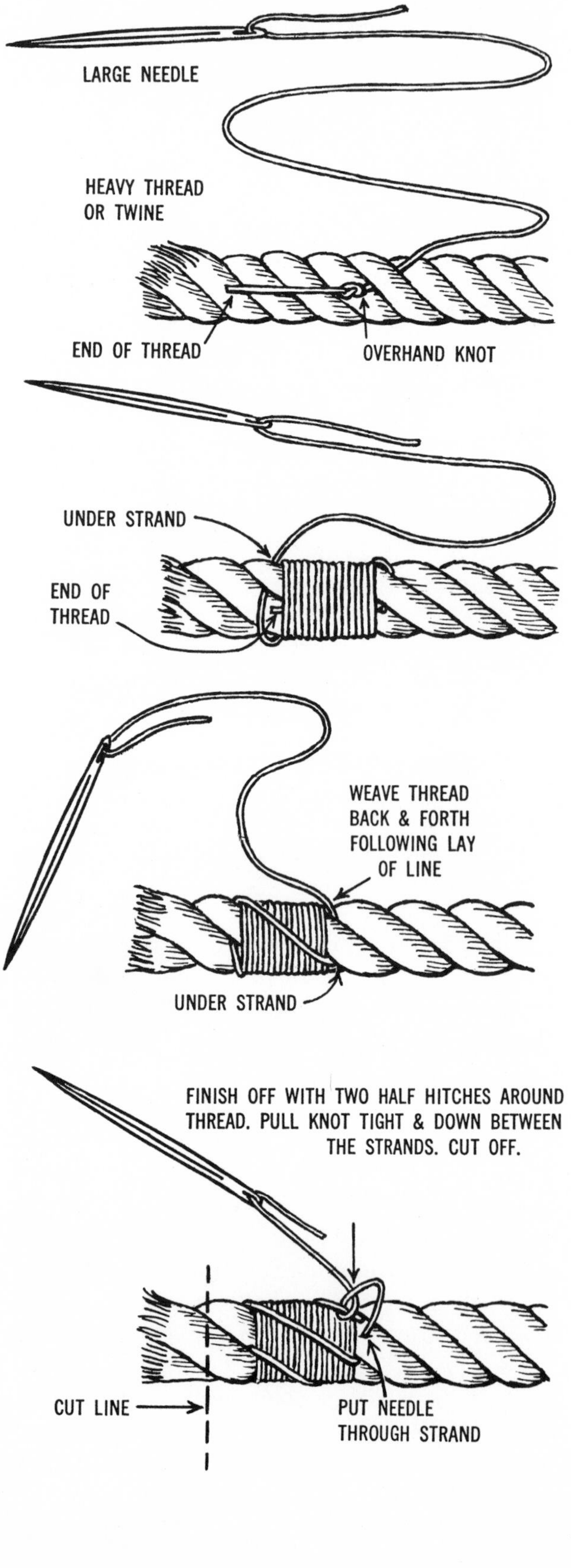

LARGE NEEDLE

HEAVY THREAD
OR TWINE

END OF THREAD

OVERHAND KNOT

UNDER STRAND

END OF
THREAD

WEAVE THREAD
BACK & FORTH
FOLLOWING LAY
OF LINE

UNDER STRAND

FINISH OFF WITH TWO HALF HITCHES AROUND
THREAD. PULL KNOT TIGHT & DOWN BETWEEN
THE STRANDS. CUT OFF.

CUT LINE

PUT NEEDLE
THROUGH STRAND

Figure 12 EYE SPLICE
(the first series of tucks)

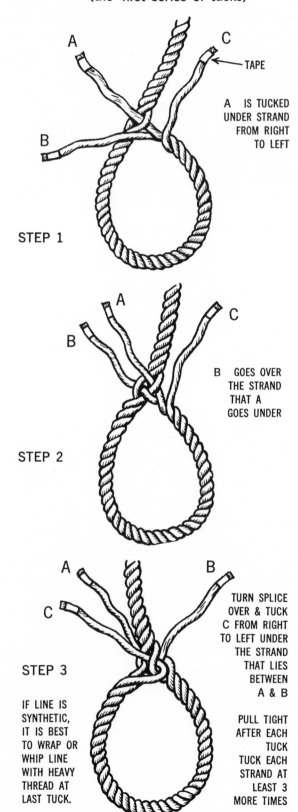

A

C

TAPE

A IS TUCKED
UNDER STRAND
FROM RIGHT
TO LEFT

B

STEP 1

A

B

C

B GOES OVER
THE STRAND
THAT A
GOES UNDER

STEP 2

A

B

C

STEP 3

TURN SPLICE
OVER & TUCK
C FROM RIGHT
TO LEFT UNDER
THE STRAND
THAT LIES
BETWEEN
A & B

IF LINE IS
SYNTHETIC,
IT IS BEST
TO WRAP OR
WHIP LINE
WITH HEAVY
THREAD AT
LAST TUCK.

PULL TIGHT
AFTER EACH
TUCK
TUCK EACH
STRAND AT
LEAST 3
MORE TIMES

16

tucked from right to left. In step C the entire splice is turned over, but strand C is still tucked from right to left. In making the tucks, be sure that no two strand ends go through the same strand openings. A splice in a synthetic line should have at least four series of tucks. After the first series, the next are a simple weaving operation where A, B, and C each go over their neighboring strand and under the following strand. Before turning in the last series of tucks, the splice should be tapered. This is done by cutting about half the fibers out of each strand prior to tucking them. After the last tuck, pull each strand end tight and cut it off flush with the rope. To give it a smooth, finished appearance, roll the splice under your foot. Ragged whiskers may be burnt off with a match.

Anchoring

One of the basic skills required of a seaman is the ability to anchor a boat properly. Anchoring and handling *ground tackle* (anchors and related gear) is a lengthy subject, and only the rudiments will be touched on here.

Figure 13 BELAYING ON A STANDARD CLEAT

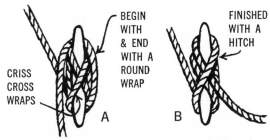

CRISS CROSS WRAPS

BEGIN WITH & END WITH A ROUND WRAP

A

FINISHED WITH A HITCH

B

Method B may be used on a halyard but a sheet should never be hitched unless a slippery hitch is used.

SLIPPERY HITCH

TO MAINSAIL

PULL TO UNTIE

Figure 14 COILING LINES

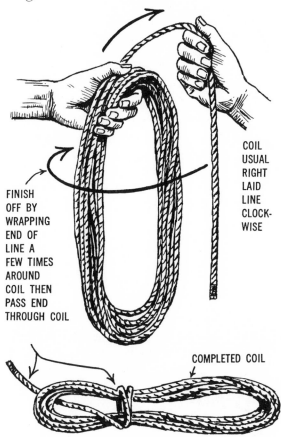

COIL USUAL RIGHT LAID LINE CLOCKWISE

FINISH OFF BY WRAPPING END OF LINE A FEW TIMES AROUND COIL THEN PASS END THROUGH COIL

COMPLETED COIL

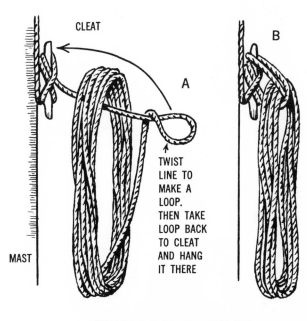

CLEAT

A

B

MAST

TWIST LINE TO MAKE A LOOP. THEN TAKE LOOP BACK TO CLEAT AND HANG IT THERE

HANGING A COILED HALYARD

17

Figure 15 ANCHORS

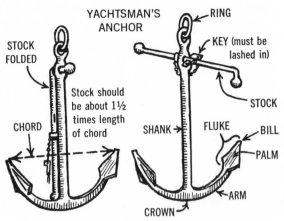

YACHTSMAN'S ANCHOR

STOCK FOLDED

RING

KEY (must be lashed in)

Stock should be about 1½ times length of chord

CHORD

STOCK

SHANK

FLUKE

BILL

PALM

ARM

CROWN

Wide palms for mud or soft sand bottoms. Sharp, narrow palms for hard sand, rock, weed, gravel, or shell.

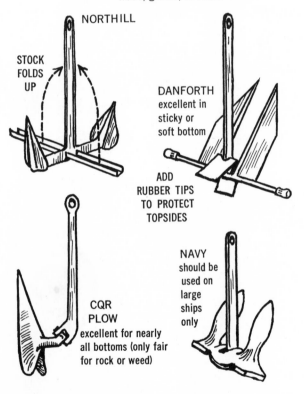

NORTHILL

STOCK FOLDS UP

DANFORTH excellent in sticky or soft bottom

ADD RUBBER TIPS TO PROTECT TOPSIDES

CQR PLOW excellent for nearly all bottoms (only fair for rock or weed)

NAVY should be used on large ships only

Figure 15 shows anchor nomenclature and a group of the most commonly used, non-permanent anchors. These are the kinds which are put over temporarily and, when not in use, are pulled up and usually stowed on the forward deck. Permanent anchors such as the mushroom type are often left on the bottom for years and are used for offshore moorings. Of the anchors shown in Figure 15, only the Navy anchor is

unsuitable for a small boat. It is designed to be pulled into the hawse pipe of a large ship. Occasionally it is seen on a boat, but in the small size, it is little more effective than a concrete block. The yachtsman's anchor is subject to fouling if the boat swings in a complete circle around her anchor so that the line wraps the exposed fluke (see Figure 16). The Danforth anchor is a popular anchor in the Annapolis area for it is especially effective in soft sand and sticky mud. One must be sure, however, that this anchor does not merely lie on the bottom, but that it digs in thoroughly by putting a strain on the line.

The holding power of an anchor depends on two principal factors aside from its design: its weight and the *scope,* or length, of its anchor line. The greater the anchor's weight and the longer the scope, the greater the holding power. As a general rule, the most effective length of scope is six or seven times the depth of water where the boat is anchored. A simple rule of thumb for weight is one-half pound per foot of over-all length for a light anchor and one pound per foot of over-all length for a heavy anchor. Of course, this rule depends on the type of anchor. Danforth and plow anchors generally need not be as heavy as the yachtsman's type.

When preparing to anchor, stand in the bow with the neatly coiled anchor line shackled or tied with a fisherman's bend to the anchor ring

Figure 16 FOULED ANCHOR

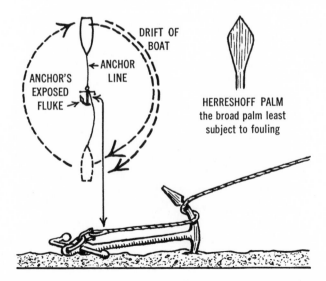

DRIFT OF BOAT

ANCHOR LINE

ANCHOR'S EXPOSED FLUKE

HERRESHOFF PALM the broad palm least subject to fouling

18

(see Figure 10). Then the boat is headed into the wind, and when she has stopped all forward motion, gently lower the anchor into the water. Never throw it in, for it can easily foul its line. When the anchor's crown strikes bottom, let the boat drift backwards and *pay out* or *veer* (let out) scope gradually, keeping a slight tension on the line until the anchor flukes can bite into the bottom. Then *snub* the line, stop it from running out by taking a turn around the bow cleat. This should cause the flukes to dig in deeply and make the anchor hold effectively.

When raising or *weighing* the anchor, pull in on the line until it lies straight up and down. At this time, there is a minimum of scope and the anchor has little if any holding power. Then a hard tug up on the line will pull the anchor's head up and break the flukes out of the bottom.

If the anchor is difficult to break out, additional force may be applied to the line, once it is straight up and down, by taking a turn or two on the cleat and swaying on the line. Taking a turn and swaying on the last few inches of line to bring it truly up and down is a most persuasive technique against a recalcitrant anchor. Or the anchor may be sailed out by heaving in to up-and-down, belaying, and setting a headsail and backing it to blow the bow off. With the anchor line straight up and down, any motion of the boat applies tremendous force to the line.

Sufficient scope is important for holding power because when the line makes a small angle to the bottom (when it is nearly parallel to the bottom), this causes the anchor to dig in. However, in many of today's crowded harbors, it is not always possible to let out all the scope one might desire. It is of the utmost importance to have *swinging room,* or room to clear other anchored boats no matter what direction the boats are swung by the current or wind. Small boats should be anchored in shallow water so that they will need relatively little scope to achieve the aforementioned ideal (6 or 7 to 1) scope to depth of water ratio. If large boats cannot veer sufficient scope due to crowded conditions, their heavy anchor should be used. When veering scope be sure to take into consideration and allow for the rise or fall of the

tide. After anchoring, take bearings on various stationary objects so that these may be checked later to see if the anchor is holding.

If the bottom is rocky, it is often wise to rig a *tripping* line, a line tied to the anchor's *crown* (see Figure 17), so that the anchor can be broken out flukes first in the event it becomes jammed between two rocks. The free end of the trip line is often buoyed (attached to any floating object) and left overboard to float directly above the submerged anchor. Then if the anchor cannot be pulled up with its *rode* (anchor line) in the conventional manner, it can be pulled up with the trip line.

Figure 17 TRIP LINE

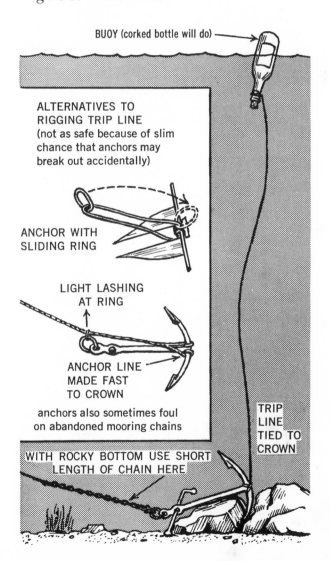

BUOY (corked bottle will do)

ALTERNATIVES TO RIGGING TRIP LINE (not as safe because of slim chance that anchors may break out accidentally)

ANCHOR WITH SLIDING RING

LIGHT LASHING AT RING

ANCHOR LINE MADE FAST TO CROWN

anchors also sometimes foul on abandoned mooring chains

WITH ROCKY BOTTOM USE SHORT LENGTH OF CHAIN HERE

TRIP LINE TIED TO CROWN

Elementary Steering

Small boats are usually equipped with tillers for steering and large boats have steering wheels. A tiller usually turns the rudder directly, its length providing leverage, while a wheel often has a worm gear or is rigged in some other way to give the *helmsman* (steersman) a mechanical advantage. As a rule, tillers are

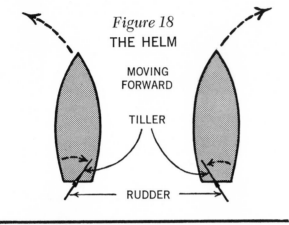

Figure 18
THE HELM

MOVING
FORWARD

TILLER

RUDDER

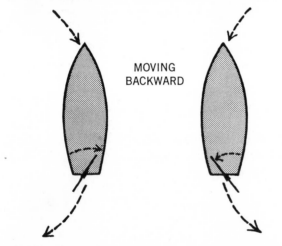

MOVING
BACKWARD

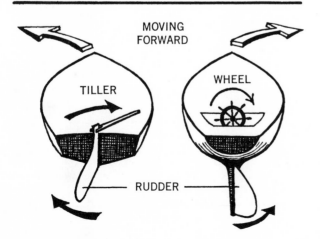

MOVING
FORWARD

TILLER

WHEEL

RUDDER

quicker and more sensitive, while wheels are more powerful and require more movement to make the boat respond.

Figure 18 shows how the turning of the *helm* (wheel or tiller) affects the turning direction of the boat. A helmsman turns his wheel in the direction he wants his boat's bow to turn when moving ahead. This is similar to steering an automobile. But with a tiller the reverse is true. The helmsman pushes the tiller in the opposite direction from that in which he wants his bow to turn. When moving backwards the stern follows the direction in which the rudder is turned.

An important point the helmsman should always keep in mind is that the rudder is effective in turning the boat only so long as the boat is moving ahead or backwards. The more *way* she carries, or the faster she moves, the more effective is the rudder. Steering a boat under power with single or twin screws and also the fine points of helmsmanship under sail will be discussed in subsequent chapters.

Shoal Water

A good seaman always attempts to familiarize himself with the waters in which he sails. Knowledge of local topography, water depths, landmarks, the location of shoals, channels, and channel markers are readily obtained from government charts. Every boat above the size of a small dinghy should carry a chart of the area in which she sails.

A study of local charts will not only give proper orientation, but will prevent needless groundings. It is especially desirable to avoid running aground in a deep-keel boat. Centerboard boats usually can be freed quite easily by raising the board, provided care is taken to see that the boat is not blown farther onto the shoal, but keel boats are more difficult to get off. If a keel boat is driven hard aground it is usually a wise practice to lower all sails, until the situation is studied and the exact shape of the shoal is obtained from the chart or from soundings taken around the boat or from a dinghy, if available, so that the boat will not be driven farther aground. Then if the boat is headed in the right direction, sail may be hoisted and sheeted in to cause heeling and to drive her off.

There are several methods of freeing a boat. If she is small she might be simply poled off. If she has power she might be backed off or driven ahead after the vessel has been turned the right way. Placing all crew members on the bow often lifts the keel off the bottom. Of course, heeling the boat by sail, by putting crew on one side, or putting a man on the end of the main boom after it has been swung out over the water, help decrease the boat's draft. An effective method of freeing a vessel is by *kedging*. This means that an anchor is carried out some distance from the vessel by wading or in a dinghy and then the anchor line is hauled on until the vessel is moved. If all these methods fail, it becomes necessary to wait until the next high tide or to wait for a tow from a power boat. Remember that a power boat can damage a boat that is hard aground in trying to tow her off.

The end paper shows a chart of the Annapolis area. Notice the shoal off Greenbury Point and particularly the shoal off Horn Point. The latter area especially has claimed many grounding victims. Shoals and channels are marked with buoys or channel markers. Figure 19 shows the principal types of unlighted, soundless, navigational aid buoys. It will be noted that they are painted solid or in combinations of red, black, and white. The age-old expression for understanding channel markers is *Red, Right, Returning*. This simply means that when returning to the harbor, you leave a red marker on your right or starboard side. Of course, the reverse is true when leaving the harbor. The red is left to port. Figure 19 shows *mid-channel* and *junction* or *obstruction* buoys also. The former mark the middle of a channel and should be passed close by on either side. Junction or obstruction buoys can be passed on either side but should be given a wide berth. As shown in the illustration, the topmost band of color indicates the preferred channel.

Local Weather

In the Annapolis area during the summer months, the most frequent wind direction is from the south or southwest. This area is fre-

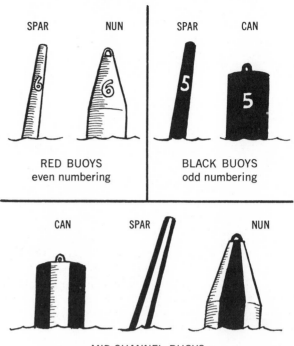

Figure 19 U. S. BUOY SYSTEM
unlighted buoys without sound

SPAR NUN SPAR CAN

RED BUOYS
even numbering

BLACK BUOYS
odd numbering

CAN SPAR NUN

MID-CHANNEL BUOYS
black and white vertical stripes

PREFERRED CHANNEL LIES TO PORT (RETURNING)

SPAR NUN

PREFERRED CHANNEL LIES TO STARBOARD (RETURNING)

SPAR CAN

JUNCTION OR OBSTRUCTION BUOYS
red and black horizontal bands

NOTE: In addition to the above federal markers there are Intracoastal Waterway markers (along the Atlantic and Gulf coasts) and state markers within certain state areas (such as crowded inlets and lakes). However these marker systems are generally compatible.

Intracoastal Waterway aids to navigation are distinguished by a special yellow border or other yellow mark. On this waterway, black markers are on the port and red markers on the starboard side of the channel entering from north and east and traversed to south and west respectively.

State "Regulatory Markers" use international orange geometric shapes with a white background on a sign or buoy.

Figure 20 CLOUDS

CIRROCUMULUS "mackerel sky" (over 20,000 ft.) can predict approach of warm front in unstable air

ALTOSTRATUS (about 19,000 ft.) gray sheet often warns of approaching warm front

CUMULONIMBUS "thunderhead" (thunderstorm cloud)—can reach height of cirrus

CIRRUS "mares' tails" (over 25,000 ft.) if thick often advanced forerunners (24 hours or more) ahead of a front

CIRROSTRATUS (over 20,000 ft.) whitish sheet often causing halo around sun—can warn of approaching warm front

ALTOCUMULUS (over 12,000 ft.) like sheep—can warn of cold front in unstable air

STRATOCUMULUS (about 8,000 ft.) dark globular rolls

CUMULUS (over 4,000 ft.) fair weather unless extreme towering up

NIMBOSTRATUS (about 3,000 ft.) dark rain cloud

STRATUS (about 1,500 ft.) gray sheet

quently under the influence of the *Bermuda high,* a region of high barometric pressure near Bermuda, whose winds rotate around the high in a clockwise direction. This brings warm, moist, southerly winds up the Chesapeake Bay. Warm weather is often relieved by highs dropping down from Canada. These usually bring cool, dry, gusty northwest winds. Low pressure cells with their cyclonic or counterclockwise rotation bring bad weather. These travel, as does the entire weather system in the middle latitudes, from west to east. When these lows pass to the north of Maryland, they cause only brief periods of stormy weather and this is usually accompanied by *veering* winds (changing clockwise) which brings clear northwesters. But when the low pressure cells pass to the south of Maryland, the wind *backs* (changes counterclockwise) from south to northeast and often there is a lengthy period of stormy, rainy weather. This is known as the "northeaster," and it will usually last for two or three days, perhaps longer.

Figure 21 shows storm warning signals which are displayed at most boating centers or weather stations and, of course, at the Naval Academy. These warnings should be heeded. Even if conditions look clear at the moment, it is likely that the bad weather will soon arrive. Sometimes boats are taken out when the small craft warning is up, but this should be done only with great caution and never by a beginner sailing alone.

The greatest weather hazard in the Annapolis area is the frequent midsummer thunderstorm. These are most likely to occur in the late afternoon of a hot day; and they will generally come from the west. Fortunately, they can usually be spotted a long way off because they have a very distinctive and awesome cloud form, the *thunderhead* or *cumulo-nimbus.* This is illustrated in Figure 20. Cumulus clouds, the white, puffy, "cotton wool" type of clouds, indicate fair weather, but look out when one of these clouds

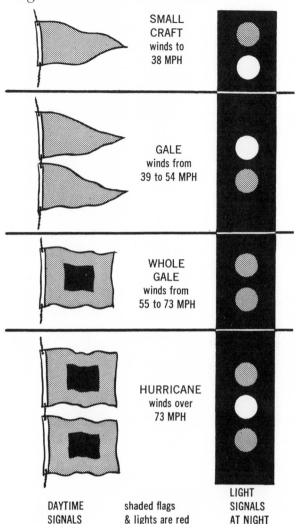

Figure 21 STORM WARNINGS

SMALL CRAFT
winds to 38 MPH

GALE
winds from 39 to 54 MPH

WHOLE GALE
winds from 55 to 73 MPH

HURRICANE
winds over 73 MPH

DAYTIME SIGNALS — shaded flags & lights are red — LIGHT SIGNALS AT NIGHT

shows extreme vertical development. It could develop into a thunderhead. When a cumulus cloud has built up to such altitudes that its top fans out into ice crystals forming what looks like an anvil top, and when the cloud's bottom half begins to turn dark, it has turned into a full-fledged thunderhead, and you could well be in for a blow.

If you are far away from home base, take sails down, and anchor in plenty of time. These storms can be severe, but usually they don't last.

CHAPTER THREE

Theory of Sailing

This chapter will describe merely the general fundamentals of sailing, such as the points of sailing, general sail positions, turning maneuvers, and elementary aerodynamics. Practical details, specific procedures, and the fine points of steering will be discussed in the next chapter.

Points of Sailing

A sailboat's directional heading with respect to the wind is called her *point of sailing*. There are five basic points of sailing: *beating, close reaching, beam reaching, broad reaching,* and *running.* These are illustrated in Figure 22 along with the approximate sail position for each point of sailing. When the wind is from dead astern to approximately two points on the quarter (see Figure 1), the boat is running. When the wind comes from two points on the quarter to approximately one point abaft the beam, the boat is broad reaching. With the wind abeam the boat beam reaches; but with the wind ahead of a half point forward of the beam until the wind bears approximately three points forward of the beam, the boat close reaches. When the average boat sails with the wind broad on her bow, she is beating. As the wind comes from farther ahead, the sails begin to flap or *luff*, and they become increasingly ineffectual until the boat is *head to wind* (headed directly into the wind) at which time they are totally ineffectual. A sail that is not luffing is said to be *full* (full of wind). The terms *luffing*

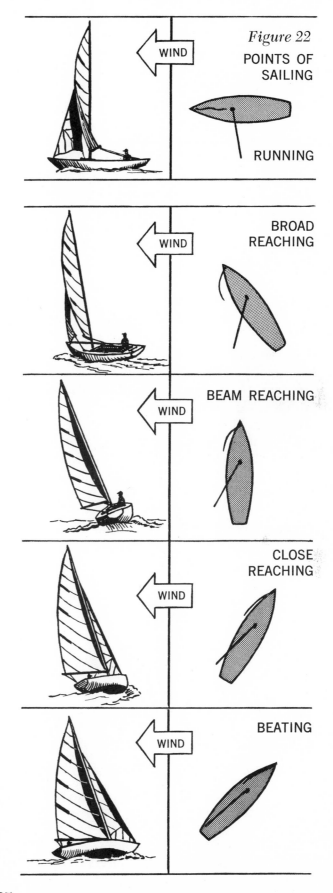

Figure 22
POINTS OF SAILING

RUNNING

BROAD REACHING

BEAM REACHING

CLOSE REACHING

BEATING

or *full* can be applied to the boat herself, as well as to individual sails.

The sail positions shown in Figure 22 are achieved by adjusting the sheets which pull the sails in towards the boat's centerline or allow them to swing out to a more athwartships position. When the sheets are pulled in, the sails are said to be *trimmed*, but when the sheets are let out they are said to be *cracked, started, eased,* or *slacked,* to use the terms in increasing order. The word *trim* is also used to indicate whether or not a boat's sails are in exactly the right position for a given point of sailing, a vital factor for speed, as for example, "Her sails are well trimmed," or "She is trimmed too flat."

In Figure 22, the topmost boat is shown running. She is also said to be sailing *before the wind, off the wind* (also applied to reaching), *sailing free* (with sheets eased), or sailing with *a fair wind.* The illustration shows her jib hanging limply because the wind is from nearly dead astern, and the mainsail is *blanketing* the jib or blocking off its wind. The jib might be made to *draw* (fill with wind) if it were *wung-out* or pushed out on the opposite side from the mainsail. The boat then would be said to be sailing *wing and wing.* Notice in the illustration that the *main boom* (mainsail's boom) is let out so that it is almost athwartships. When a boat is running with the wind nearly dead astern, her

boom is let out as far as it will go without chafing against the aftermost shroud. As the boat is gradually turned towards the wind, her sheets are slowly trimmed until, when beam reaching, her jib and main boom are about halfway in, roughly 135° to the wind or 45° to the boat's centerline. When close reaching, the sheets are trimmed still closer, somewhere between the beam reaching position and about 10° from the boat's centerline.

On various points of reaching, especially when beam reaching or sailing slightly further away from the wind, boats usually achieve their highest sailing speeds. Some boats having planing hulls lightweight and with flattish bottoms will gain considerable speed by *planing* or lifting up on their bow waves and skimming over the top of the water rather than plowing through the water like a boat with a *displacement hull* (a deep, heavy hull). At most times when boats are traveling at their highest speeds, sails must be trimmed a little flatter than normal. This is due to the *apparent wind* which is explained in Figure 23. Since the boat in the diagram is moving ahead at 4 *knots* (nautical miles per hour), she causes a 4-knot wind from directly ahead. The *true wind* or actual wind is a 9 knots from slightly forward of the beam; thus the apparent wind is a resultant of these two forces (boat-speed wind and true wind), which in this case is blowing at 11 knots from broad on the bow. Sails should always be trimmed to the apparent wind. To put it very simply, the faster a boat travels (unless dead before the wind), the closer her sheets are trimmed. This becomes evident especially when the true wind is nearly on the beam.

When beating, a boat's sails are trimmed quite flat. Very generally speaking, this is to within about 10° or less of the boat's centerline. The average modern boat intended for day sailing or cruising-racing can be made to sail to within about 45° of the wind. Strictly cruising types will not sail quite this close, but some racers will sail closer than this. Progress directly to *windward* (upwind) is accomplished by making a series of *tacks* or zigzag courses towards the windward destination. On the zig course, the sails lie to one side of the boat, and on the zag

Figure 23 APPARENT WIND

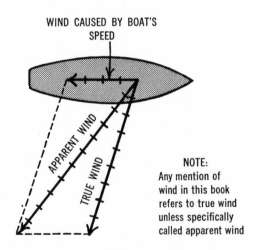

WIND CAUSED BY BOAT'S SPEED

APPARENT WIND

TRUE WIND

NOTE:
Any mention of wind in this book refers to true wind unless specifically called apparent wind

If true wind is 9 knots and boat speed is 4 knots, then apparent wind is 11 knots.

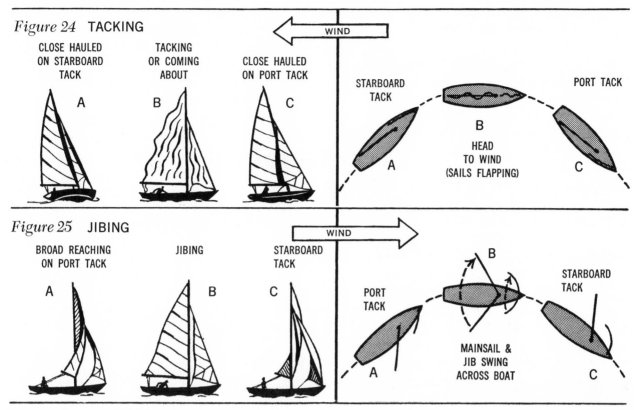

Figure 24 TACKING

CLOSE HAULED ON STARBOARD TACK — A

TACKING OR COMING ABOUT — B

CLOSE HAULED ON PORT TACK — C

WIND

STARBOARD TACK — A

HEAD TO WIND (SAILS FLAPPING) — B

PORT TACK — C

Figure 25 JIBING

BROAD REACHING ON PORT TACK — A

JIBING — B

STARBOARD TACK — C

WIND

PORT TACK — A

MAINSAIL & JIB SWING ACROSS BOAT — B

STARBOARD TACK — C

course, they are held by the wind to the boat's opposite side. With the sails on the port side and the wind blowing from the starboard side, the boat is said to be on the *starboard tack,* but she is on the *port tack* when the wind comes from the port side and the sails lie to starboard. Obviously, with an average boat that can *point* or head up to within 45° of the wind, the highest heading on the starboard tack will be at right angles to the highest heading on the port tack. Other terms for beating are *sailing close-hauled, sailing to windward, tacking, on the wind* or *hard on the wind,* and *by the wind. Full and by* means beating, with the emphasis on keeping the sails full rather than on heading as close to the wind as possible.

Turning Maneuvers

There are two ways a boat can turn from one tack to the other. First, she may *luff* or *head up* into the wind and continue turning through the eye of the wind until her sails fill on the other tack. This is called *coming about* or *tacking.* Secondly, she may *bear off* or head away from the wind until the wind is dead astern and then continue turning until the wind suddenly

swings her sails across to the boat's opposite side. This is called *jibing* or *wearing ship.* To put it simply, a tack is an upwind turn with the bow swinging across the wind, causing the sails to flap; but a jibe is a downwind turn with the stern crossing the wind and the sails suddenly filling on their opposite sides and swinging across the boat. These turns are illustrated in Figures 24 and 25. Specific procedures involved in tacking and jibing will be discussed in the next chapter.

Prior to making the final tack when beating towards a windward destination, there arises the question of exactly when to tack in order to arrive at the mark in the quickest time without sailing any extra distance or having to make additional tacks. If the boat can be brought about at the proper moment so that she is pointed directly at the windward mark on her final tack, she is said to be *fetching* or *laying* the mark. This final approach tack which brings the close-hauled boat directly to the mark lies on an imaginary line called the *fetch line* or *lay line.* This is explained in Figure 26. If the helmsman tacks his boat too soon, before reaching the fetch line, then he has *under-stood* the mark (he

Figure 26 FETCHING THE WINDWARD MARK

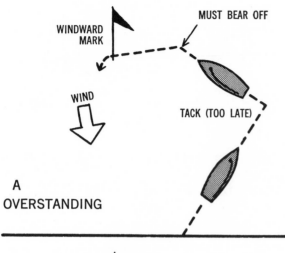

WINDWARD MARK

MUST BEAR OFF

WIND

TACK (TOO LATE)

A OVERSTANDING

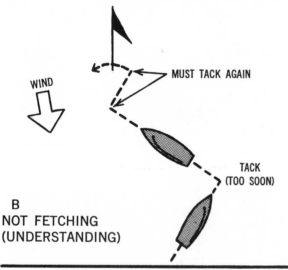

WIND

MUST TACK AGAIN

TACK (TOO SOON)

B NOT FETCHING (UNDERSTANDING)

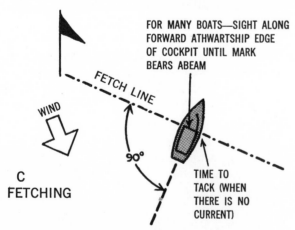

FOR MANY BOATS—SIGHT ALONG FORWARD ATHWARTSHIP EDGE OF COCKPIT UNTIL MARK BEARS ABEAM

FETCH LINE

WIND

90°

TIME TO TACK (WHEN THERE IS NO CURRENT)

C FETCHING

FETCH LINE (or LAY LINE)—A boat pointed at and fetching a mark is on her fetch line. TO TAKE ADVANTAGE OF WIND SHIFTS, DO NOT SAIL UP TO FETCH LINE UNTIL FAIRLY CLOSE TO MARK.

is heading *below* it) and must tack twice again. On the other hand, if he waits too long before tacking or sails beyond the fetch line, he has wasted time and distance. In this case he has *over-stood* the mark (he can head *above* it). Assuming that the boat can sail to within 45° of the wind, then the proper time to tack is when the mark bears abeam or lies at right angles to the boat's centerline if there is no *current* (flow of water). The foregoing discussion has been concerned with only the final windward tack when approaching a mark. Planning windward courses and the general strategy of beating will be discussed in Chapter 9, "Basic Racing."

Aerodynamics of Sailing

It is not difficult to understand how a boat sails before the wind. To quote a sailors' old saying, "Even a haystack will sail downwind." But understanding how a boat can sail against the wind is not so easy. The force which drives a sailboat to windward is similar to the force which gives lift to an airplane's wing or to be more exact, a glider's wing. The sail is actually an airfoil stood on end. The airfoil characteristic is achieved by building a fore-to-aft curve into the sail which we call *draft* or *camber*. This curve is parabolic, having its greatest amount of curvature near the *luff* or forward edge of the sail, but the curvature flattens out or becomes straighter near the *leech*, the after edge of the sail. An explanation of how draft is built into a sail will be given in Chapter 5.

When a boat reaches or beats to windward, the air flows around her sails from luff to leech or from front edge to back edge. As the wind meets the luff it splits to form an airflow to windward of the sail and another flow to *leeward* of the sail (on its downward side). The molecules of air on the leeward side have the greater distance to travel around the sail, and they increase their speed as they race back to join the windward airflow molecules at the leech. As a result of this difference between windward and leeward flow speeds, the pressure is lowered on the sail's leeward side. This is in accordance with a principle of physics known as Bernoulli's principle, which tells us that in

28

fluid motion wherever the velocity of flow is high, the pressure is low. When the pressure is lowered on a sail's leeward side, a suction pull is created which acts at right angles to the sail (see Figure 27). If the boat is close-hauled, most of this suction pulls the boat to leeward and a small amount pulls her forward. However, all boats intended for windward sailing are designed to resist making *leeway* or being blown sidewise but to resist as little as possible being pulled forward; thus, for the most part, the suction pull can only draw the boat ahead.

Resistance to making leeway or *lateral resistance* is supplied by one of the means illustrated in Figure 28. All Naval Academy boats are equipped with either keels, centerboards, or dagger boards which may be raised or lowered as shown in the diagram. Figure 29, which compares a child on a sliding board to a boat close reaching, perhaps gives the simplest explanation of how lateral resistance forces the boat ahead.

Figure 27 LEE SIDE SUCTION

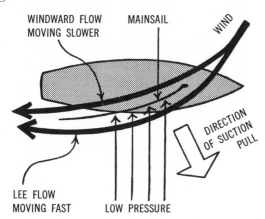

Up to this point we have been discussing the aerodynamic forces acting on a single sail, but the addition of another sail in close proximity to the first has a considerable influence on these forces. A correctly trimmed jib set just ahead of a mainsail creates a narrow space, often called a *slot*, between the jib's leech and the mainsail's luff. Much of the airflow passing to leeward of the mainsail must first pass through this slot. The wind accelerates as it is squeezed through the constricted slot, and this has the effect of

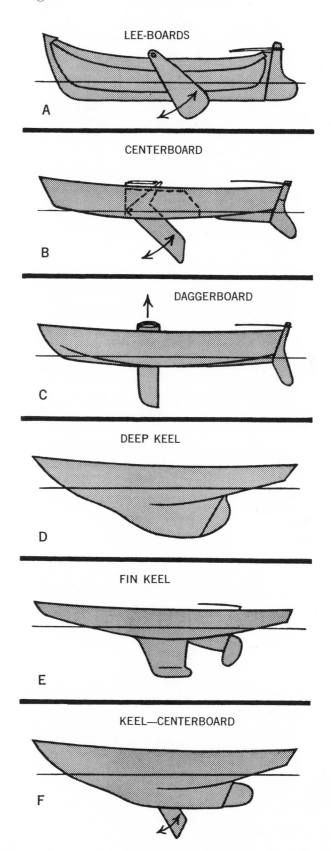

Figure 28 LATERAL RESISTANCE

29

Figure 29 FORCES WHEN SAILING UP WIND

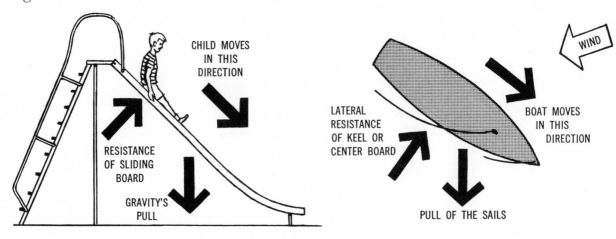

further lowering the pressure to leeward of the mainsail and thus further increasing the suction pull on that sail (see Figure 30). With the proper adjustment in width, the jib slot acts as a venturi, similar to the nozzle of an ordinary garden hose that may be adjusted to squirt a narrow but fast-moving stream of water. Thus we can see that a jib's effectiveness is not due entirely to its additional sail area, but also to its beneficial influence on the mainsail. If, however, the jib is trimmed incorrectly so that the slot is too wide, much of the venturi effect will be lost; or if the jib is trimmed too close with the slot too narrow, the airflow will be deflected against the mainsail's luff causing it to bulge and shake. Figure 31 shows the result of a jib being trimmed too close. In this case the jib

is said to be *backwinding* or *backing* the main, and its beneficial effects have been destroyed. The fine points of jib trimming will be discussed in Chapter 5.

A simple demonstration of the venturi effect and Bernoulli's principle is shown in Figure 32. Water (or any fluid) is forced through a large pipe which is pinched in at its middle. The flow speeds up as it passes through the constricted area. There are three pressure gauges, two at the pipe's widest diameter and another in the pipe's constricted region. The diagram shows that when the flow accelerates due to the venturi effect it lowers the pressure in accordance with Bernoulli's principle. In this demonstration we can see that we are dealing with very real forces and not simply vague theories.

Figure 30 VENTURI EFFECT OF JIB SLOT

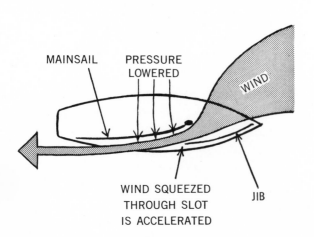

Figure 31 JIB BACKWIND

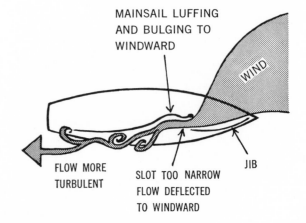

Sails alter the direction and velocity of the wind flow. They may do this in a beneficial way so as to give maximum drive to a boat, or they may do it in a harmful way so that they lose their drive or disturb the wind of other sails in close proximity. We have seen examples of disturbed air in the blanketed jib of Figure 22 and the backwinded mainsail of Figure 31. *Backwind* is the turbulent air which flows off a sail's leech and is deflected to windward. The blanket or *wind shadow* is the resulting turbulence and partial absence of air when the wind is blocked off or a *lee* is formed by a sail or other object. More will be said about disturbed air in Chapter 9, "Basic Racing."

Sails can only reach maximum effectiveness when they have the proper shape, especially draft, and when they have the correct *angle of incidence* (angular position to the wind). Figure 33 shows two close-hauled boats sailing about 45° to the wind. On one boat, the main sheet is not trimmed close enough and its luff extends too far to leeward so that the wind blows directly on its lee side causing it to luff or flap. In this case, the sail is said to be *luffing*, and the forward component of the suction pull is partially destroyed. The other boat in the diagram shows the other extreme, that is trimmed too flat. In this case, the sail is partially *stalled*. Instead of the leeward airflow being relatively smooth it becomes turbulent, and *eddies* or reverse currents are formed to leeward of the

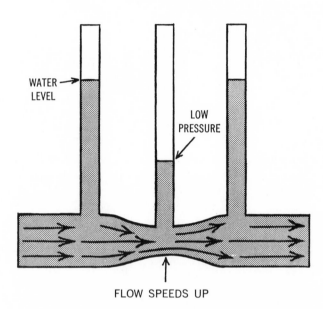

Figure 32 BERNOULLI'S PRINCIPLE

WATER LEVEL

LOW PRESSURE

FLOW SPEEDS UP

leech. The most effective angle of incidence lies somewhere between the stalling and luffing angles, and, of course, this depends on the heading of the boat and the trim of her sails. We shall investigate this in the next two chapters.

Figure 33 LUFFING & STALLING

AIR FLOW

WIND DIRECTION

LUFFING
due to insufficient sail trim or from pointing too high

AIR FLOW

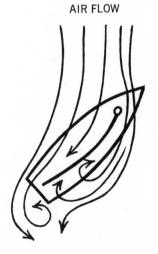

STALLING
due to trimming the sail too flat

CHAPTER FOUR

Helmsmanship and Maneuvering Under Sail

The fine points of sailing can only be learned thoroughly with practice and experience; however, the actual handling of a boat under sail should be preceded and accompanied by a study of the basic principles in maneuvering, helmsmanship, and sail trim. With preliminary book study, the beginner can hasten his learning and avoid many pitfalls.

Wind Direction

In Chapter 2 we examined the simple rudiments of steering with a tiller or wheel. Obviously, this is a prime prerequisite of sailing. Another prerequisite is the determination of wind direction. Just as you can't control a boat's heading without knowing how her steering gear works, you can't control the boat or properly trim her sails without knowing from what precise direction the wind is blowing.

Wind direction can be detected by careful observation of the water's surface. Small ripples will move in the direction the wind is blowing. However, do not be misled by the movements of larger waves. Quite often the larger waves are controlled by a previous wind, and their movement doesn't indicate the direction of a new wind which has recently *shifted* or changed its direction. The present wind must be determined by watching the movement of the smallest ripples.

Other signs of wind direction are flags flying; smoke from ships, chimneys, or cigarettes; and the heeling as well as the sail trim of other boats. If anchored by the bow, boats and ships will lie with their bows pointed directly into the wind unless their heading is controlled by a strong current. The most effective means of determining wind direction and observing momentary shifts is by making use of wind indicators, shown in Figure 34. The *masthead fly* and *wind sock* illustrated are carried at the top of the mast where they are either permanently secured or are hoisted into position when needed with a flag halyard. *Telltales* are short pieces of yarn, thread or ribbon tied to the shrouds about seven feet above the deck. These are easy to watch and respond instantly to even the lightest breeze. It must be borne in mind, however, that wind indicators on a moving boat do not show the true wind, but only the apparent wind.

Sight is not the only means of determining wind direction. Most experienced sailors develop a sensitivity to the feel of the wind. They can detect slight shifts and velocity changes by feeling the breeze on their cheeks, necks, arms, or hands. Of course, this method is particularly valuable when sailing at night. More will be said of this in Chapter 10.

Sailboat Maneuvering at Dock or Anchorage

The fine points of sailing should be tried and practiced in open water, where there is *sea room*

Figure 34 WIND INDICATORS

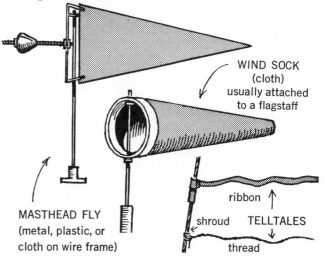

WIND SOCK (cloth) usually attached to a flagstaff

MASTHEAD FLY (metal, plastic, or cloth on wire frame)

ribbon

shroud   TELLTALES

thread

33

(ample room for maneuvering) for holding a fairly long *board* (tack or leg to windward). But before reaching open water, a boat must be sailed from her dock or mooring which nearly always involves tight maneuvering in crowded anchorages or other constricted areas. It is therefore very important to understand the basic principles of sailboat control. This involves *gaining way* (picking up speed), *killing way* (slowing down), turning, and holding a straight course.

Before getting *under way* (starting to move), a boat should be headed into the wind so that when her sails are hoisted, they will merely flap and not drive the boat ahead before she is ready to get under way. If she is at a mooring (permanent anchor), she is probably already lying head to wind, but if she is made fast to a dock or pier, she will probably have to be swung into the wind by *casting off* (releasing) her stern line. This is shown in Figure 35. After the sails are hoisted and the boat is ready to leave, she is shoved straight back with the rudder *amidships* (held straight or on dead center). When she is well clear of the dock, the rudder is put over to the right or left to swing the bow in the opposite direction (since the boat has sternway), as illustrated in Figure 35 (also see Figure 18, The Helm). The sails will begin to draw because the boat will turn so that the wind is broad on the bow. Putting the helm over too soon will result in the boat gaining headway

too soon, which might cause her to strike the dock before she can be turned away from it. After the boat has stopped drifting backwards, the helm is turned the opposite way because the boat will begin to move ahead as her sails fill. Notice in the diagram that the jib is *backed* or pulled in by its windward sheet so that it is trimmed from the wrong side. This will cause the bow to fall off, away from the wind very rapidly. When the boat has gained headway and if she is clear of the dock, the windward jib sheet is released and the jib is trimmed on the boat's proper side.

The same procedure is followed when a boat leaves a permanent mooring. The mooring line is simply cast off and left afloat. Getting under way when anchored involves the same basic principles. Sail is hoisted while the boat is head to wind, the anchor is hauled in until the line lies straight up and down, then the anchor is broken out and hauled aboard, the jib is backed to make the bow fall off in the desired direction, and then the sheets are trimmed in on their proper side as the boat gains headway.

There are just a few times when it might be advisable to hoist sail down wind instead of when head to wind. These might occur in a very constricted docking area or if a strong current swung the boat's stern into the wind when anchored or moored. In these cases it is often best to drift with the wind or current or sail away under jib alone until the boat is clear of docks and obstructions, and then head as close to the wind as possible before hoisting the mainsail. Currents are seldom strong enough to cause serious problems in the Annapolis area.

Leaving the windward side of a dock under sail presents a problem usually. The boat must be moved so that she is headed into the wind when sails are hoisted. She might be moved by *warping* (moving her with lines) or kedging with the anchor, or by paddling if the boat is small and the wind is light. No matter how she is moved, her bow should be fairly near the wind. If she cannot be brought directly head to wind, great care should be taken to see that booms do not strike anything on the dock and that sheets do not catch on dock *pilings* (posts) or cleats.

Figure 35 LEAVING A DOCK

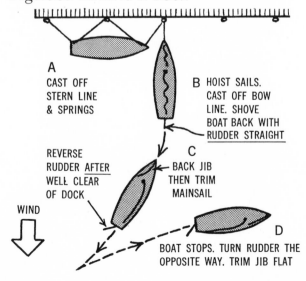

A
CAST OFF
STERN LINE
& SPRINGS

B HOIST SAILS.
CAST OFF BOW
LINE. SHOVE
BOAT BACK WITH
RUDDER STRAIGHT

REVERSE
RUDDER AFTER
WELL CLEAR
OF DOCK

C
BACK JIB
THEN TRIM
MAINSAIL

WIND

D
BOAT STOPS. TURN RUDDER THE
OPPOSITE WAY. TRIM JIB FLAT

Figure 36 shows the proper approach when landing at a dock under sail. Notice that in all five situations the boat is turned into the wind and held there with sails flapping until headway is lost. This maneuver is called *shooting*, and it is also used when anchoring, picking up a mooring, or landing alongside another boat. Helm control is very important when shooting for a dock or mooring. If the wheel or tiller is turned suddenly and to its full extent, the boat's *way* or momentum is partially killed because a rudder rapidly jammed to one side acts somewhat like a brake. If it is desired to make a long shoot, the helm is eased over slowly, and the boat carries a lot of way or coasts a long distance before coming to a stop. A boat's weight or displacement will have a great bearing on how much way she carries also. A heavy boat, such as a Luders yawl, will carry way for a very long distance compared to a light boat, such as a Naval Academy Skipjack. The exact distance a given boat will shoot under any given conditions will vary greatly and can only be determined by experience.

A boat's momentum also depends on how fast she is moving and on conditions of wind and water. In a strong wind and rough water, a boat will carry less way. Strength and direction of current must be noted, because naturally this will affect the boat's speed greatly.

Since the latter part of a "shoot" will be at very slow speeds, any current will affect the maneuver out of all normal proportion. A boat with a favorable current under her seems to shoot forever. Many an otherwise well-planned maneuver has been spoiled because it was only when the boat slowed down in a shoot that a small but significant current announced its presence to a surprised skipper by taking over the situation. Even the best of sailors sometimes misjudge a boat's shooting speed and distance. When this happens, if the boat is carrying too much way, do not attempt to land at the dock or pick up the mooring, but bear off, sail away, and try the approach again. Notice in Figure 36 that the shooting boats are never aimed directly at the dock, but they are landed almost parallel to the dock or in such a manner that they can easily be turned away from the dock at the

Figure 36 APPROACHING A DOCK UNDER SAIL (in weak current)

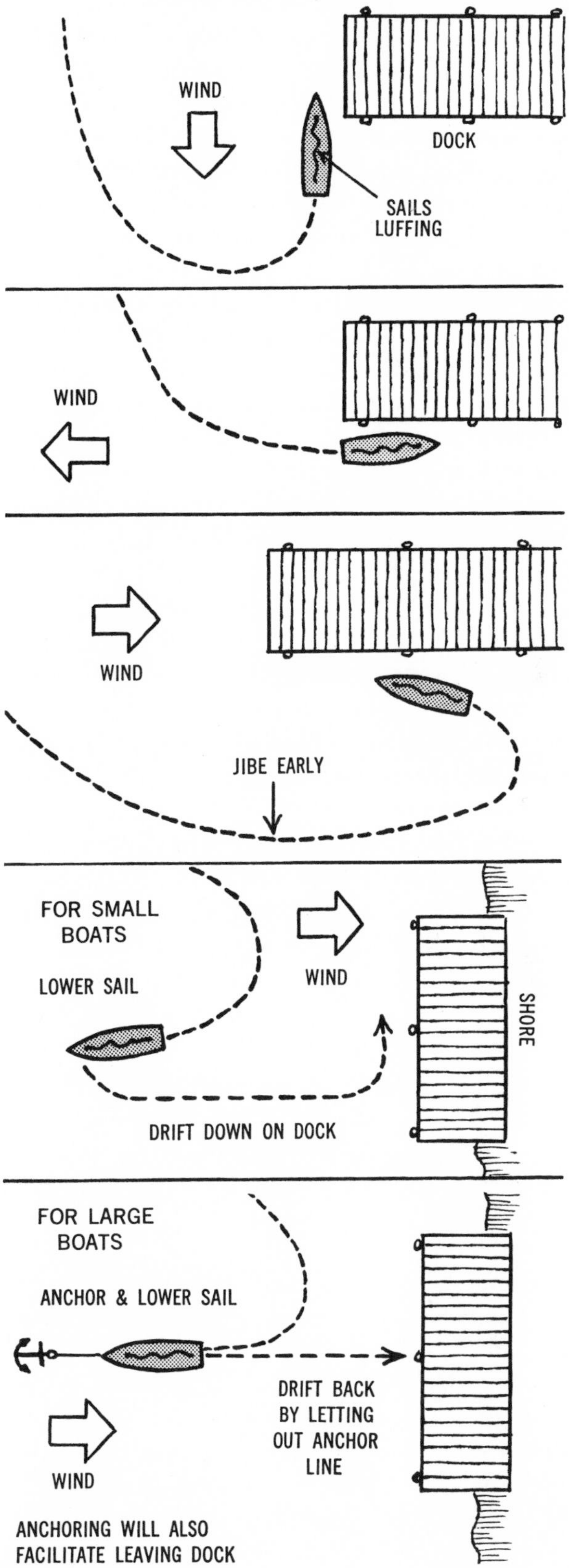

WIND

DOCK

SAILS LUFFING

WIND

WIND

JIBE EARLY

FOR SMALL BOATS

LOWER SAIL

WIND

SHORE

DRIFT DOWN ON DOCK

FOR LARGE BOATS

ANCHOR & LOWER SAIL

WIND

DRIFT BACK BY LETTING OUT ANCHOR LINE

ANCHORING WILL ALSO FACILITATE LEAVING DOCK

35

last minute if they are carrying too much way. Occasionally it is necessary to make a direct, right angle approach in the dock's middle so that the landing must be made bow first. This can be very dangerous in a large, heavy boat, and it should be avoided if possible. If unavoidable, however, a very slow approach should be made. It is better to have the boat stop short than carry too much way. If she stops short without quite reaching the dock, a crewman stationed on the bow might be able to throw a line to someone standing on the dock. In a small, light boat a fast landing, with too much way, is not quite as serious, though it is certainly most unseamanlike. A crewman can sit on the foremost part of the bow facing forward with a leg on each side of the jib stay so that he can *fend* off (push off) with his feet just before the bow makes contact with the dock. Falling short and having to make another try is far preferable to risking damage to the boat and injury to the crew.

There is another basic method of slowing a boat down to land at a dock or pick up a mooring besides shooting into the wind. This is to slack the sheets while on some point of sailing between close-hauled and a beam reach. A close reach is the optimum. With sheets slacked and sails luffing all over on a close reach, no power is being applied to the boat, and she will lose headway. If more headway is desired during such a maneuver, the sheets need simply be trimmed back in. The amount they are trimmed back in will correspond to the amount of power applied to the boat. By alternately trimming in and slacking out the sheets to achieve the desired amount of luff, precise speed control can be attained, and the boat can be eased slowly up to a dock or mooring buoy.

The reason why a close reach is the optimum heading for this maneuver is that wind shifts can then be responded to merely by adjusting the trim of the sails, while maintaining the same heading. By contrast, if the boat were luffing along close-hauled, and the wind shifted more ahead during the maneuver, the option of trimming in for more power would be lost, and the only way to gain headway would be to head off, which would take the boat away from the

course desired to her dock or buoy. If, on the other hand, the boat were luffing along on a beam reach, and the wind shifted aft more, then the option of continuing to luff the sails would be lost, and the only way to slow down would be to head up, again heading the boat away from her desired maneuvering course. Significant wind shifts are common in harbors, where this kind of maneuvering is likely to be done.

The following basic principles of sailboat maneuvering should always be kept in mind:

• For maximum *steerageway* or rudder control, keep way on the boat. Remember that the rudder is only effective when the boat is moving.

• Quick rudder action will slow a boat, but slow rudder movement will enable the boat to carry way for a long distance.

• Heading into the wind and/or releasing sheets so that the sails' flap will stop headway.

• Sails are hoisted or lowered when the boat is heading into the wind.

• When maneuvering a centerboard boat, see that the centerboard is all the way down, otherwise she will make leeway, especially at low speeds.

• When making a sharp turn, allow for some stern skid. During such a turn the bow turns in one direction and the stern skids somewhat the opposite way. This is important to bear in mind when landing alongside a dock or another boat. Stern skid is more apparent on flat-bottomed centerboarders.

• When headway is lost after unsuccessfully shooting for a dock or mooring, back the jib to make the bow fall off in the desired direction. If the boat has no jib, wait until she drifts backwards, and then reverse the rudder as explained in Chapter 2 under "Elementary Steering."

• If the boat has too much way on when shooting for a mooring, she can be slowed by pushing her main boom forward so that it goes *aback* or fills from the wrong side.

• Maneuvering in constricted areas should be done under a *balanced* sail plan. This means that the boat should neither have too much sail forward nor too much aft, but a sail plan that will permit the easiest possible steering. Balance will be discussed in the next chapter.

• Remember that fast-moving, heavy boats in smooth water carry a lot of way when shooting, but slow-moving, light boats in rough water and high winds carry little way.

• Remember that even a small current will be the biggest single factor affecting a boat's speed at the very low speeds of getting under way or landing.

• The speed of a boat may be controlled precisely by putting her on a close reach and adjusting the sheets to luff the sails to produce the desired power. Variations possible are from no power to the full power available with the given wind strength.

Windward Helmsmanship

After having cleared the crowded waters of the anchorage or mooring area, we can concentrate on sail trim and helmsmanship. Our purpose is efficiency, to steer the boat and to adjust her sails so that she is traveling her fastest on the most advantageous course.

Sailing to windward, we are concerned with sailing the boat as close to the wind as possible but at her best possible speed on this point of sailing. If we sail her too close, her sails will begin to shake at the luffs, and we will feel her begin to slow down. On the other hand, if we bear off too far, the boat will pick up speed, but we will not gain as much distance to windward as she could. Beating is always a delicate balancing of these two factors, *pointing* (heading as close as possible to the windward objective) and *footing* (sailing through the water as fast as possible). When we sail too high so that we accentuate the gain to windward at a sacrifice of speed we are said to *pinch,* but when sailing too low, at a good speed but at a sacrifice to windward gain, we sail too *full.* Usually, under normal conditions, the best windward course lies somewhere between pinching and sailing too full. Making a boat do her best to windward is always an interesting challenge. Since the conditions of wind and sea that produce the challenge change continuously, the problem of getting to windward never loses its appeal. Even

Figure 37 WIND PUFFS

A puff is a sudden increase in the wind's velocity usually within a small area and of short duration.

EFFECT OF A PUFF ON APPARENT WIND

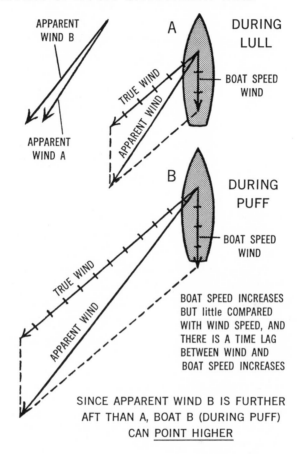

SINCE APPARENT WIND B IS FURTHER AFT THAN A, BOAT B (DURING PUFF) CAN POINT HIGHER

THE RADIATING PUFF OR CATSPAW

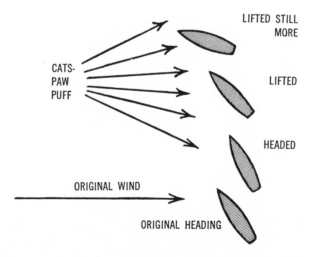

the most seasoned sailor must constantly solve it afresh.

Some winds are relatively steady, but most winds constantly vary in direction and velocity. A temporary increase in velocity over a limited area is known as a *puff,* and it can be seen as a dark patch of ripples darting across the water's surface. Most puffs allow a boat to point higher because they cause the apparent wind to blow from more off the beam. This is explained in Figure 37. Some puffs are the radiating type, often called *catspaws,* which are also shown in the diagram. This type will force the helmsman to bear off when he first feels the puff, but then he is *let up* or allowed to point increasingly higher as he sails through the puff.

The wind nearly always fluctuates in direction as well as velocity. When the breeze blows from farther ahead (more from the bow) and forces the helmsman to bear off, this change in wind direction is called a *header,* but when it blows from farther aft (more on the beam) enabling the helmsman to point higher, it is called a *lift.* Fluctuations in direction can be detected

immediately by watching the masthead wind indicator and particularly the telltales on the windward shrouds. When they swing more abeam the helmsman should point up, but when they swing more ahead he must bear off. This is illustrated in Figure 38.

The skilled, experienced helmsman uses all of his senses when sailing a boat to windward. In addition to watching the telltales, he watches the luffs of his sails. When they begin to flutter or luff in normal winds or sailing conditions, he is generally sailing too high and must bear off. The experienced helmsman also watches for puffs on the water on his windward bow. If the water darkens with ripples from a puff, he is ready to head up when the boat first feels its effect. The sense of hearing is used by listening to the sound of the bow wave. A clearly audible bow wave indicates that the boat is moving at her best speed, while only a slight murmur of the wave suggests that perhaps the helmsman is pinching slightly or perhaps the sheets could be better trimmed for more speed. A good helmsman also uses his sense of balance as well as his

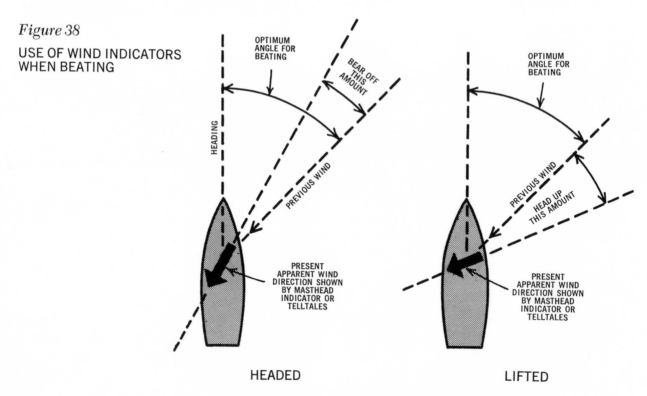

Figure 38

USE OF WIND INDICATORS
WHEN BEATING

HEADED

LIFTED

The optimum angle is the angle between apparent wind
and the boat's most efficient heading when beating. A
slow boat has a wider angle than a fast boat.

vision to detect a change in the boat's angle of heel. When beating, a boat should be heeled to leeward at least slightly, but the heel should not be excessive. For the average boat, if the lee rail begins to *bury* (dip in the water), the boat is being heeled too far. This can result in loss of speed and even a capsizing in a centerboard boat. Excessive heeling can be controlled in two ways, by heading up or pointing higher, or, as a last resort, by slacking the main sheet so that the mainsail begins to luff.

Perhaps the most important sense used by the skilled helmsman is the sense of feel or touch, often called the *tiller touch*, though, of course, it applies to steering with a wheel also. This is sailing "by the seat of the pants" or sensing when the boat is going to windward at maximum efficiency. Of course, such a sense can be acquired only after a good deal of practice. The average, properly balanced boat will have a slight *weather helm* or tendency to turn into the wind in moderate breezes (this will be discussed in the next chapter). The weather helm will exert a light pull or pressure against the helmsman's hand. This pressure will increase as the wind freshens and heels the boat, or it will decrease when the wind slackens and causes a smaller angle of heel. In the former case, the helmsman should relax his pressure on the helm and let the boat point up until he senses that she is beginning to lose speed or when her sails start to luff. In the latter case, however, when the helm pressure slackens, he should bear off slightly to see if the boat will pick up a little speed.

Good helmsmanship to windward is really a matter of experimentation. The helmsman should alternately point up or prod the wind to see if she won't sail just a little higher without slowing down, and then, as soon as she shows signs of slowing down, bear off a little to see if she won't sail a little faster.

Figure 39 illustrates how the helmsman uses all his senses when beating to windward. Notice that the illustration shows a useful visual sign which has not been discussed, the sagging of the jibstay. Ordinarily the jibstay should be set up tight for best efficiency to windward, but it will always sag off to leeward slightly. When

Figure 39

AIDS TO HELMSMANSHIP THROUGH THE SENSES

WATCH SAG OF JIB STAY

WATCH & LISTEN FOR SHAKING SAILS AT LUFFS

WATCH TELLTALES

WATCH AND FEEL ANGLE OF HEEL

FEEL PUFFS ON FACE

WATCH FOR PUFFS ON WATER

LISTEN FOR MORE OR LESS SOUND FROM BOW WAVE

FEEL BALANCE OF HELM (WEATHER OR LEE HELM). IN LIGHT AIRS USE ONLY TWO FINGERS ON TILLER OF SMALL BOAT.

the boat is sailing full and by, the sag will be most pronounced, but when she is being pinched the stay will be almost straight. Thus if there is considerable sag the helmsman should point up somewhat, but with little or no sag he should fall off a little. This aid to the helmsmanship should not be relied on in rough water because as the boat pitches (rocks fore and aft), the mast will move forward and aft somewhat, causing the jibstay to slacken and tighten correspondingly.

When sailing into a *chop* (a short, steep sea) the helmsman should sail his boat full and by, because wave action tends to kill headway. The boat must be given enough power to drive through the waves. Likewise, in very light airs, the boat should not be sailed extremely close to the wind. She should be kept footing to minimize leeway and to take advantage of a stronger apparent wind. In a moderate breeze, however, most boats can be sailed *fine*, or quite close to the wind. Rudder action in light airs

39

Figure 40 CLEATING THE MAIN SHEET

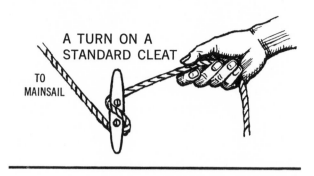

A TURN ON A STANDARD CLEAT

TO MAINSAIL

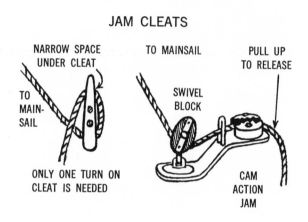

JAM CLEATS

NARROW SPACE UNDER CLEAT

TO MAINSAIL

PULL UP TO RELEASE

TO MAIN-SAIL

SWIVEL BLOCK

ONLY ONE TURN ON CLEAT IS NEEDED

CAM ACTION JAM

should be slow and gentle, but in moderate breezes the helm of a small boat can be turned quite rapidly to respond to lifts and headers. With large, heavy boats a slower action must be used. Remember that excessive rudder angles have a braking effect.

In a strong or puffy breeze, the helmsman should be ready to release his mainsheet at a moment's notice. In a small, capsizable center-boarder, the mainsheet should be held in hand. If its pull is too great, a turn may be taken around a cleat as shown in Figure 40. On larger boats jam cleats may be used (see Figure 40). It is perfectly permissible to cleat the mainsheet on a large keel boat which will not capsize, but, as you will recall from Chapter 2, it is a danger-ous practice to hitch the mainsheet on a cleat, unless a slippery hitch is used. As previously mentioned, wind may be spilled from the sails by luffing up, and naturally this method of righting an excessively heeled boat should be used before the mainsheet is released so that distance can be gained to windward. Sheets

should be slacked only as a last resort. Keeping a boat *on her feet* (as upright as possible) by luffing up sharply in the puffs is known as *feath-ering*. By using this technique, a skillful small-boat sailor can gain a much greater distance to windward than can a sailor who merely slacks his sheets to keep upright.

To summarize, here is a list of tips for the windward helmsman:

• Watch the water for puffs. Head up in them. In the radiating type, bear off when first entering the puff then head up.

• Watch the telltales for wind direction changes. Head up when they swing farther abeam, and bear off when they swing farther ahead.

• Watch the luffs of sails. When they begin to flap, the boat is usually being pinched. There are two exceptions to this. In a heavy breeze, the mainsail can be trimmed less flat than usual so that it carries a slight luff for the purpose of preventing excessive heeling. Secondly, when carrying a large, overlapping jib, a certain amount of backwind can be expected, and this can cause the mainsail to luff slightly.

• Use your senses of hearing, balance, and visual signs, such as jibstay sag, as aids to good helmsmanship.

• Develop a tiller touch by concentrating on sensing when the boat is travelling her best through the feel of varying pressures on the helm. Of course, the tiller touch should be used in conjunction with all of the aforementioned audible and visual signs which can aid the helmsman.

• Constantly experiment to see if you can't sail your boat higher without reducing her speed.

• Be conscious of rudder action. Large boats should be turned more slowly than small ones. In light airs turn the boat slowly, with a gentle touch. In moderate to heavy breezes, a quicker action should be used in responding to headers and lifts. In heavy breezes, feather up sharply to prevent heeling. Slack sheets only as a last resort.

• Sail full and by in rough seas and light airs, but point high in smooth waters and moderate winds.

Tacking

The rudiments of tacking and the problem of when to tack to fetch a windward mark were discussed in the last chapter. Now we will deal with the specific procedures and helmsmanship involved in coming about.

Figure 41 shows a typical small centerboard sloop being tacked. Most Naval Academy boats do not have the kind of backstays illustrated. Those shown are called *running backstays* or *runners*, and every time a boat is tacked the stays must be changed, with the windward one being set up *taut* (tight) and the leeward one being slacked off. If the boat is not equipped with these stays, then, obviously, tacking her is a much simpler procedure. Navy yawls carry running backstays at times, and this will be discussed in Chapter 7.

In any kind of boat which carries a crew, certain commands should be given by the helmsman so that the crew can know what to expect and can carry out his or their duties at the proper moment. The first command should be *"Stand by to come about."* This is especially important in a large boat because it alerts the crew and gives them time to get to their proper stations. Details on tacking a large boat will be given in Chapter 7. The next command is *"Ready about,"* and this is promptly followed by *"Hard a-lee,"* or *"Helm's a-lee."* The latter expression is said when the helm is actually moved. The tiller is pushed to leeward or a-lee (a wheel, of course, is turned to windward), and this naturally turns the bow into the wind. When the boat is head to wind, all crew members should keep their heads low and watch out for booms or flogging *fittings* (boat hardware) that could hit someone. Crew weight is usually shifted to the new windward side unless there is a very light air. Notice that in Step 3 of illustration A, the leeward jib sheet is not released until the boat is almost head to wind. It is a very common mistake to release the jib sheet too soon. This results in loss of boat speed and less distance gained to windward when making the turn.

After the boat turns through the eye of the wind, the jib should be trimmed in immediately for two reasons. First, it is easier to trim before it completely fills with wind, and secondly, the trimmed jib will help pull the bow around onto the new tack. After the tack has been completed, the boat will have lost some way, therefore the helmsman should bear off to slightly below his normal windward course in order to get her moving again. It often helps to *crack* or slightly slack the mainsheet momentarily until speed is regained. As the boat picks up speed,

Figure 41 TACKING PROCEDURE

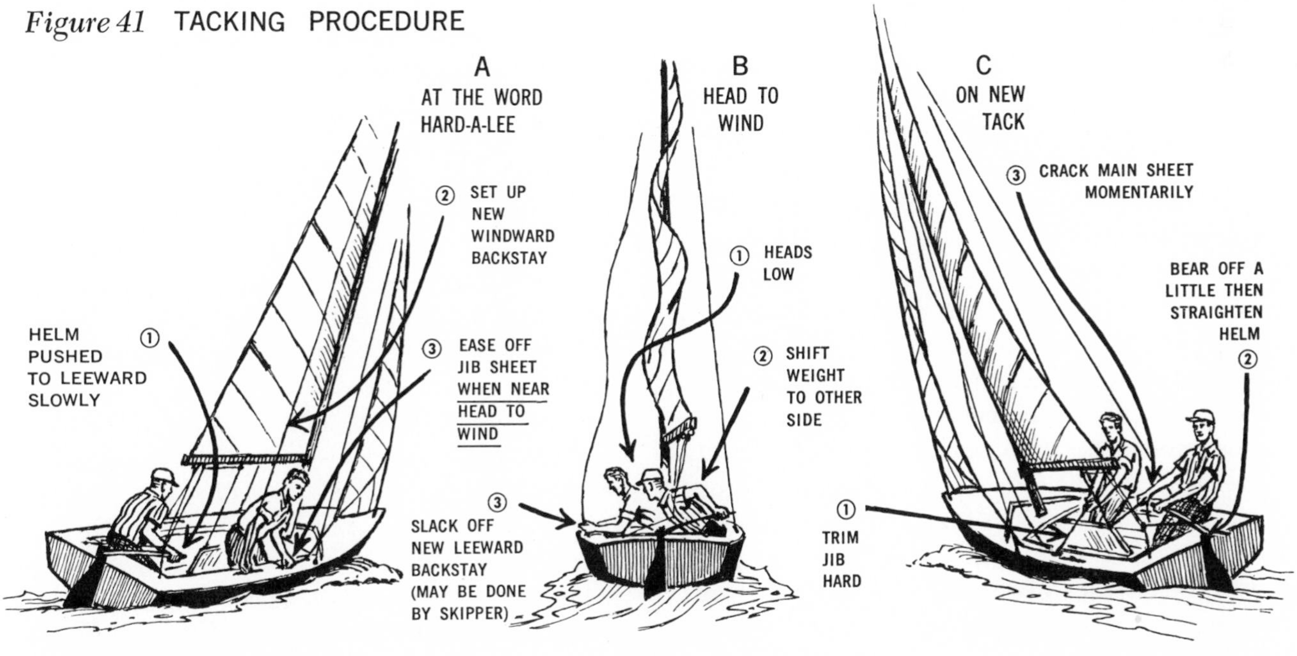

A
AT THE WORD HARD-A-LEE

HELM PUSHED TO LEEWARD SLOWLY ①

② SET UP NEW WINDWARD BACKSTAY

③ EASE OFF JIB SHEET WHEN NEAR HEAD TO WIND

③ SLACK OFF NEW LEEWARD BACKSTAY (MAY BE DONE BY SKIPPER)

B
HEAD TO WIND

① HEADS LOW

② SHIFT WEIGHT TO OTHER SIDE

① TRIM JIB HARD

C
ON NEW TACK

③ CRACK MAIN SHEET MOMENTARILY

BEAR OFF A LITTLE THEN STRAIGHTEN HELM ②

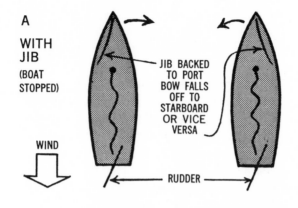

Figure 42　IN STAYS

A

WITH
JIB
(BOAT
STOPPED)

JIB BACKED
TO PORT
BOW FALLS
OFF TO
STARBOARD
OR VICE
VERSA

WIND

RUDDER

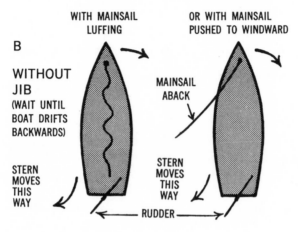

WITH MAINSAIL
LUFFING

OR WITH MAINSAIL
PUSHED TO WINDWARD

B

WITHOUT
JIB
(WAIT UNTIL
BOAT DRIFTS
BACKWARDS)

MAINSAIL
ABACK

STERN
MOVES
THIS
WAY

STERN
MOVES
THIS
WAY

RUDDER

the helmsman can begin to head up and trim in the mainsail.

Immediately prior to tacking, the helmsman should see that his boat is moving at her best close-hauled speed, for if the boat is tacked without sufficient way, she is liable to get *in stays* or *in irons*. This means that so much way is lost when the boat is head-to-wind that she is unable to complete the tack. In such a predicament, the boat drifts helplessly backwards with her sails flapping. Figure 42 shows how to recover after being in stays. If the boat has a jib, the jib may be backed, and this usually is sufficient to cause the bow to be blown off, away from the wind. In a cat-rigged boat, however, the helmsman must wait until the boat gains sufficient stern way so that the rudder may be used. The mainsail may be pushed to windward as shown in the illustration to accelerate the backward speed. Of course, the stern will follow the direction of the rudder when moving backward.

Proper rudder action is important to avoid getting in stays. If the rudder is jammed hard over, it will act as a brake and kill headway. On the other hand, if the rudder is turned too slowly, the boat may not have enough momentum to carry her through the resulting long, slow turn. As said before, have ample way on your boat before bringing her about. When tacking in a rough sea, wait for a relatively smooth spot before tacking, and be sure to trim the jib flat after passing through the eye of the wind.

Downwind Helmsmanship

Getting the best performance from a boat that is broad reaching or running requires nearly as much skillful helmsmanship as getting the best windward performance. It might be said that sailing downwind requires rudder action which is almost directly opposite to that used when sailing to windward. The windward helmsman bears off in the lulls and heads up in the puffs, but the downwind helmsman bears off in the puffs and heads up in the lulls. This is illustrated in Figure 43 which shows how a boat is properly worked to leeward. The boat in the diagram will surely reach the leeward mark before a boat which merely follows a straight course. The reason for this lies in the fact that reaching is a faster point of sailing than running; thus, during a lull, the helmsman heads up from a running course to a broad reaching course in order to keep his boat moving despite the decrease in wind. During the puffs, he bears off to almost a dead run because he has sufficient power from the puff to retain his speed. Also his boat will be less subject to speed-retarding heeling forces when the wind is from nearly dead astern. Furthermore, by heading far off during the puffs, the helmsman sails slightly below his course for the leeward destination and so compensates for the high heading he sailed during the previous lull.

Working to leeward is a constant weaving back and forth during the puffs and lulls to maintain boat speed. This principle applies when sailing slightly below a beam reaching course, because as we approach a beam reach, the boat speed increases. In moderate to heavy

42

winds when we sail higher than a beam reach speed begins to decrease. In light airs, the best speed often occurs near the close reaching point of sailing. Thus it should be kept in mind that when sailing lower than a beam reach in moderate to heavy breezes or lower than a close reach in light airs, *the helmsman bears off in the puffs and heads up in the lulls.*

Sailing for longer than very brief periods with the wind from dead astern should be avoided if possible. As previously said, a dead run is a slow point of sailing, and when the wind is dead astern, the after sails will have a blanketing effect on the forward sails causing a definite reduction in boat speed. A means of avoiding this predicament is to use the procedure called *tacking downwind.* It is illustrated in Figure 44. Instead of running directly for the leeward mark, the boat shown in the illustration broad reaches towards the mark on one tack and then jibes over and broad reaches toward the mark on the other tack. Quite often the extra distance sailed to reach a destination is more than compensated for by additional speed gained in broad reaching. It is easy to overdo this strategy, however, and to sail too high so that the extra speed does not make up for the extra distance sailed. Generally, a safe rule to follow is to sail as far off as possible yet still keep the forward sails *drawing* or filled with wind. In puffy weather, of course, this strategy should be used with the previously mentioned "working to leeward" technique. Quite often, when tacking down wind, the boat can be headed (with her forward sails drawing well) closer to her desired course on one tack than on the other tack. In such a case, the helmsman should first take the tack which allows him to head closer to his destination. More will be said on this when we discuss racing tactics in Chapter 9.

Aside from the consideration of boat speed, there is another reason to avoid running with the wind flat aft or from dead astern. Since the wind is usually shifty or slightly oscillating in direction, a boat sailing dead before the wind is subject to a shift from the "wrong side," or a shift which blows from the leeward side instead of the windward side. When this happens the boat is said to be *running by the lee.* To put it

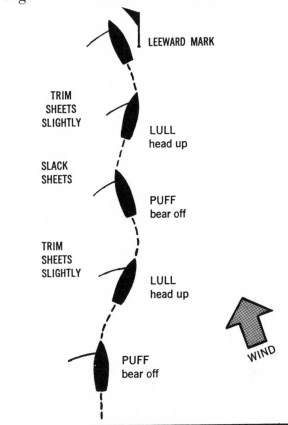

Figure 43   WORKING TO LEEWARD

LEEWARD MARK

TRIM
SHEETS
SLIGHTLY

LULL
head up

SLACK
SHEETS

PUFF
bear off

TRIM
SHEETS
SLIGHTLY

LULL
head up

WIND

PUFF
bear off

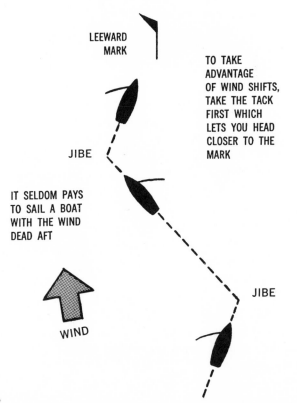

Figure 44   TACKING DOWN WIND

LEEWARD
MARK

TO TAKE
ADVANTAGE
OF WIND SHIFTS,
TAKE THE TACK
FIRST WHICH
LETS YOU HEAD
CLOSER TO THE
MARK

JIBE

IT SELDOM PAYS
TO SAIL A BOAT
WITH THE WIND
DEAD AFT

JIBE

WIND

43

Figure 45
JIBING
PROCEDURE

A
AT THE WORD
"STAND BY TO
JIBE"

① HEAD OFF
DIRECTLY
BEFORE THE
WIND

② ADJUST
JIB
SHEETS
FOR NEW
TACK

B JUST BEFORE JIBING

① MAIN SHEET HAULED IN
BOAT HELD BEFORE
THE WIND. BELAY
MAIN SHEET WITH
TURN ON CLEAT
EXCEPT IN LIGHT AIR

④ BOAT TURNED
ON TO NEW
TACK

② BACKSTAYS
SHIFTED
FOR NEW
TACK

③ HEADS
LOW
WEIGHT
SHIFTED

C AT THE WORD "JIBE-HO"
BOOM SWINGS ACROSS
(Jibe completed from
starboard to port tack)

① STRAIGHTEN HELM.
SLACK MAIN SHEET
QUICKLY. THEN STEER
ON TO NEW COURSE

② TRIM JIB
FOR NEW
COURSE

another way, when a boat, sailing with the wind flat aft, turns to leeward as though to jibe but does not jibe, she is sailing by the lee. Of course, she can only turn to leeward a limited extent before she is forced to jibe, but from a dead run to the point where her sails go aback and force her to jibe, she is by the lee. This is a dangerous point of sailing because, since the boat is on the verge of jibing, there is a possibility she might have an accidental or unintentional jibe. More will be said about this in the next section when we discuss the technique of jibing.

Jibing

It is very important to understand the principles involved in jibing, because if improperly executed, a jibe can be a somewhat dangerous maneuver. This is because a heavy boom swinging suddenly and unexpectedly across the boat, can strike a crew member, cause damage to the rigging, or cause a centerboard boat to capsize. However, a properly executed jibe is a completely safe maneuver. It should be respected but never feared.

As previously stated, a jibe is a downwind turn from one tack to the other. When the sails cross from one side of the boat to the other, they do not flap as when tacking, but they fill from the lee side and swing over rapidly.

When it is blowing so hard that a jibe would be dangerous, an alternative method of getting the boat on the other tack is to bring her up close-hauled, tack, and then head off to the desired course.

Figure 45 shows the proper procedure for jibing a small sloop. As with tacking, certain commands should be given prior to jibing in order to alert the crew. The helmsman first calls out, *"Stand by to jibe."* At this warning, the crew get to their proper stations and prepare to duck their heads to avoid being struck by the boom. The helmsman steers off dead before the wind. The sheets may have to be slacked to effect this maneuvering, especially if the wind is blowing hard and the boat is reaching. Once dead before the wind, he or a crew member begins to haul the mainsail in by its sheet. It is important that the sheet is pulled in as far as it will come before the boat is turned onto the new tack. A crew member changes the jib sheets, casting off the cleated sheet and cleating the windward sheet which will be on the leeward side after the jibe has been completed. If the wind has much strength, it is necessary to avoid having both jib sheets cast off simultaneously, even for an instant, or the jib may blow out ahead and its flogging may quickly snarl the sheets. If the boat has running backstays, of course, these must be changed so that the leeward stay on the new tack will be slack.

When the helmsman is ready to turn onto the new tack, he calls out, "*Jibe-ho.*" This warns the crew that he is jibing at that moment. The crew duck their heads and shift their weight to the new windward side if the boat is a small one, while the helmsman steers slowly off to leeward until the main boom swings over. At this point the helmsman should straighten up his helm or steer almost dead before the wind until the mainsail is slacked off rapidly to the position in which it should be for running. It is a common mistake, when it is blowing, to round up into the wind too quickly after jibing. This has led to the capsizing of many centerboarders. In a fresh breeze the mainsail must be slacked all the way off before rounding up. Unless this is done, the boat is exposing her beam to the wind with flattened sheets which will cause extreme heeling, and furthermore she is heeled by the centrifugal force of her turn towards the wind. Immediately after jibing, most boats will have a natural tendency to turn into the wind. The helmsman must counteract this tendency by straightening his helm or even reversing it momentarily in order to hold his boat before the wind until the sheets are slacked.

When jibing in a fresh breeze, the main sheet should have a turn around its cleat as illustrated in Figure 40, because otherwise, the force of the boom crossing over the boat might cause the sheet to run through the hands of the one who is tending it. *Shortening sheet,* or pulling it all the way in, is particularly important when jibing in a strong wind. If the main sheet is not shortened prior to jibing, the boom can swing up high in the air and result in what is called a *goosewing jibe.* This is illustrated in Figure 46.

Figure 46 GOOSE WING JIBE

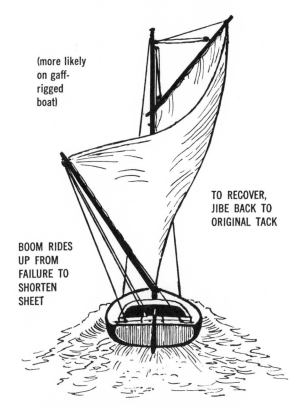

(more likely on gaff-rigged boat)

TO RECOVER, JIBE BACK TO ORIGINAL TACK

BOOM RIDES UP FROM FAILURE TO SHORTEN SHEET

NOTE: IF ROLLING SEVERELY WHILE RUNNING, A BOAT WITH LOW FREEBOARD AND LONG BOOM MIGHT NEED HER BOOM'S END SLIGHTLY LIFTED WITH TOPPING LIFT TO PREVENT DIPPING BOOM IN WATER. THIS MAY INCREASE TENDENCY TO GOOSE WING.

Notice in the illustration that the lower half of the sail has jibed over while the upper half has not. The proper way to recover from this predicament is to jibe back onto the original tack. A goosewing jibe can always be avoided if the sheet is properly shortened or some other means, such as a *boom vang,* is used to hold the boom down when jibing. The boom vang is a tackle or line attached to the boom for the specific purpose of holding it down. The boom vang will be dealt with further in the next chapter when we discuss sails and sail trim.

As previously said, an improperly executed jibe can result in a mishap. The most common mistakes which cause poorly executed jibes and the means of avoiding these mistakes are listed as follows:

• *The accidental or unexpected jibe.* This can result in personal injury or damage to the rigging from the boom flying across the boat.

To avoid accidental jibes, *do not sail excessively by the lee.* When sailing nearly dead before the wind, *watch the telltales* or masthead indicator for a wind shift which puts you by the lee. Also *watch the luff of the mainsail* for the first sign of its beginning to fill from the leeward side, and especially *watch the jib* because it will nearly always jibe before the mainsail. When the jib swings over, head up so that the wind comes from more on the windward quarter. When running before a following sea which tends to make the boat *yaw* (turn from side to side) rig a jibing *preventer.* This is merely a line or lashing to hold the boom forward in the event of an accidental jibe.

• *The goosewing jibe.* This can result in damage to the sail and rigging.

To avoid, shorten sheet. Be sure the main sheet is pulled all the way in before the boom swings across. *Use the boom vang* if your boat has one that fastens to or near the base of the mast (see Figure 52). Set it up tight to prevent the boom from lifting. To recover from a goosewing, jibe back to the original tack.

• *The broaching jibe.* When a running boat suddenly makes an involuntary turn towards the wind so that she lies beam to the wind, she is said to *broach to.* This turn can be caused by a yaw-producing sea rolling under her quarter while simultaneously the bow is buried in another sea. Most boats are particularly susceptible to broaching to immediately after jibing when they develop the aforementioned strong tendency to turn into the wind. The dangers of a rapid turn towards the wind after jibing are that the boat will heel excessively due to the centrifugal force of the turn and the fact that the boat lies beam to the wind and waves, her most vulnerable position to heeling forces. Excessive heeling can cause the shipping of water, a capsizing, or the breaking of the main boom if it *trips* (if its end dips into the water).

To avoid broaching to, *reduce sail* when the seas are steep and the wind is heavy. Take in the aftermost sails first. *Move the crew aft.* Their weight will keep the stern down and keep the rudder submerged for better helm control. If the boat is a centerboarder, she will be running with the board nearly all the way up when the waves are not steep, because in this position, the board offers little resistance and allows the fastest hull speed. However, in rough water or when the boat develops a tendency to yaw or broach to, *lower the centerboard* slightly. This will help prevent broaching to. *Immediately after jibing, reverse the helm momentarily* in order to counteract the strong tendency most boats have to turn into the wind. *Slack off the mainsheet quickly after jibing. Be sure the mainsheet is clear* and does not foul. Keep the wind aft until the mainsheet is slacked. *Prevent heeling to leeward* by slacking the mainsail and moving the crew weight to windward. Heeling increases the tendency to turn into the wind. *Trim in the jib flat* when the boat shows a tendency to broach to. A flattened jib will help hold the bow off before the wind.

Jibing in light airs usually presents no problems. Quite often the sheet tender can gather the mainsheet into a bunch and use a direct pull on the boom when he pulls it across the boat, rather than pulling on only a single rope of the mainsheet tackle. In bunching the sheet, he obviously sacrifices power for speed, but this is perfectly permissible in light airs provided care is taken to see that the sheet does not foul.

46

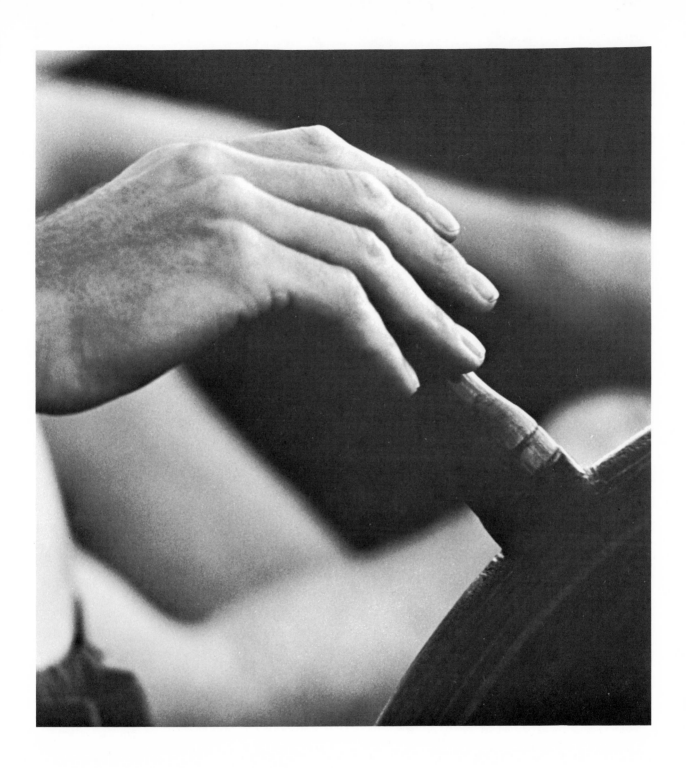

CHAPTER FIVE

Sails and Rigging

Classification of Modern Sails

Yacht sails may be grouped into three general classifications: *working sails, storm sails,* and *light sails.* The first group includes mainsails, mizzens, and moderate-sized jibs or forestaysails of moderate weight which are carried most of the time for ordinary or everyday sailing. Storm sails are small, extra heavy sails used in heavy weather. These include the *storm trysail,* a small triangular sail, usually not attached to the boom, which is set in place of the mainsail, and the *spitfire,* or small, heavy, storm jib. Light sails are racing sails made of lighter-weight cloth than that used for working sails. The most common light sails are *Genoa jibs, spinnakers, drifters, spinnaker staysails,* and *mizzen staysails,* or *mizzen spinnakers,* which are actually balloon-like mizzen staysails. All but the last of these sails are illustrated in Figure 47.

The well-known Swedish yachtsman, Sven Salén, is given credit for inventing the Genoa jib. It was first shown to the sailing world at a regatta in Genoa, hence its name. The Genoa, or *Jenny,* has a long foot which overlaps the mainsail. It is an effective sail for reaching and beating to windward because of its great area and the strong venturi it creates due to its overlap. It comes in various sizes and weights and is carried when racing in all breezes, except perhaps the very lightest airs, up to strong winds.

The spinnaker is a balloon-like, triangular sail carried when the true wind is abaft the beam. It is made from very light cloth and is an essential sail for racing. The spinnaker can be tricky to handle, trim, and steer by; therefore Chapter 8 will be devoted entirely to it.

The drifter or *ghoster* is a lightweight jib for reaching in very light airs. It is cut high at the clew so that it will fill easily in the lightest airs and so that it can be sheeted to the main boom as shown in the illustration. It is often cut fuller or with a deeper belly than a Genoa, and the drifter's leech or after edge is nearly straight, without having concave curvature as is the case with a Genoa's leech.

The spinnaker staysail is a balloon-like forestaysail of lightweight cloth which is set beneath the spinnaker as illustrated. In a good breeze, a well-designed spinnaker will rise or lift so that its foot or bottom edge is high above the deck. The spinnaker staysail, sometimes called the *cheater,* simply fills in the gap under the lifted spinnaker.

The mizzen staysail, of course, is carried only by boats having mizzens, yawls or ketches. It is set forward of the mizzen and is sheeted to the mizzen boom. This sail will be discussed in Chapter 7. The mizzen spinnaker is set identically, but its shape is that of a spinnaker.

Sail Materials

Nearly all of today's sails are made from synthetic cloth. In almost all respects the synthetics are superior to cotton, the most commonly used natural fiber cloth for sails. Presently, the most suitable synthetic for most sails is dacron (known as Terylene in England). This cloth is highly resistant to rot, mildew, and stretch. In addition, it is smooth, relatively non-porous, and it needs little, if any, gradual breaking-in, as is necessary with new sails made of cotton. A new cotton sail must be handled gently. At first, it must be used in light breezes only, and it must never be stretched extremely tight on its mast or boom until it has been used for a considerable length of time. A new dacron sail, however, can be stretched reasonably tight and can be carried in all but the strongest winds. It

Figure 47 LIGHT SAILS

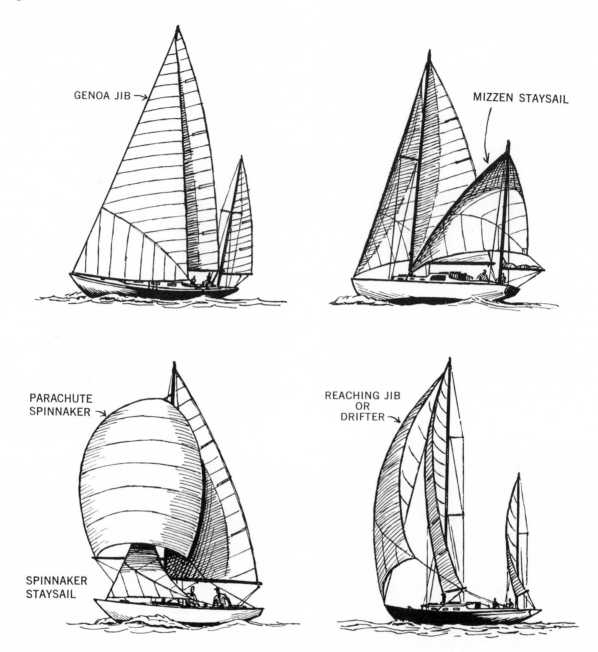

should set properly, have the correct shape, and almost fit its spars the first time it is used. In time, its luff and foot may grow slightly longer from being constantly stretched tight, but the lengthening will be very slight compared to a cotton sail.

The other most commonly used synthetic sail cloth is nylon. This has most of the major advantages of dacron, except one. Nylon is not resistant to stretch. In fact, it is highly elastic, a characteristic which is very bad for all sails except certain downwind sails, such as the drifter and spinnaker. The big advantage in nylon for these sails is that it is very strong and is made in very light weights, as light as three-quarters of an ounce per yard. Elasticity of sail cloth is detrimental to any sail that is carried to windward, especially in strong winds, because the sail stretches out of shape and loses its proper curvature. However, for balloon-like, downwind sails this loss of shape is not really harmful, and it is more important to use lightweight cloth which is definitely advantageous in light airs.

Cut and Draft of Sails

Two typical modern sails, a jib and mainsail, with their nomenclature and details of their fittings are shown in Figure 48. The mainsail is *cross-cut* with its *cloths,* the narrow panels of material, running at right angles to the leech of the sail. This minimizes *bias stretch* (stretch which is diagonal to the direction of cloth weave) at the leech where it is particularly harmful. The jib shown in the illustration is *miter-cut* with the cloths at right angles to the leech and the foot, meeting at a diagonal seam, called the *miter seam,* which bisects the angle at the *clew* (the sail's after corner).

Modern cross-cut mainsails almost always have a *roach* or convex curve to the leech which adds to the sail's area. This requires that the leech be fitted with *battens,* strips of wood or plastic shown in Figure 48, which hold out the leech, preventing it from curling inward. These battens fit into cloth pockets sewn to the leech. Two methods of securing battens in their pockets are shown in the illustration. There is another variation of the offset pocket which has the opening at the side of the pocket instead of above the pocket on the leech.

As previously mentioned, sails must be made with a luff-to-leech curvature called draft, or camber, in order that they function as efficient airfoils. Correct draft is perhaps the prime requirement of a high-performance sail. Draft is built into a sail by either or both of two principal methods. The usual method is to give the foot and luff a slightly convex round. When these edges are stretched along a straight mast, stay, or boom, curvature is thrown into the material abaft the luff and above the foot. The second method of building draft into a sail is to taper slightly the cloths of a cross-cut sail at the luff and the leech. In other words, every cloth panel will be narrower at each end than it is near the middle. It seems that this latter method is being used more and more as improvements are made in the *stability* (resistance to loss of shape) of the newer sailcloths.

Figure 49 shows the draft curves of some typical sails. Good and bad cambers are shown for comparison. In general, a correct draft curve should have its points of maximum draft anywhere from one-third of the distance from the luff to the leech to almost halfway from luff to leech. The latter draft will work better in light airs and when sailing downwind. For upwind sailing, a draft curve should be flat in its after section. From the middle of the sail to the leech, the curve should gradually flatten until it is almost a straight line at the leech. For downwind sailing, the leech area should have a little more curve. However, if a sail having excessive draft in the leech is trimmed in for beating, the lee-side suction pull in the after part of the sail will tend to pull the boat backwards because this suction force acts approximately at right angles to the surface of the sail.

The efficient upwind sail should not have excessive draft nor should the draft be too far forward, because when the boat is sailing close hauled, the wind will blow against the leeward side of the draft curve and cause the sail to luff prematurely. This is especially true for a mainsail set abaft a jib and particularly if the jib overlaps the mainsail. A jib tends to deflect the leeward airflow towards the lee side of the mainsail. Draft curves should be considerable for light airs or in a rough sea, but less for a strong breeze that is not accompanied by a steep chop. In other words, it is usually desirable to have a flat sail for a breeze and a full sail for light airs or rough water. Unless a boat is equipped with two *suits* (sets) of working sails, one for light weather and another for heavy weather, her sails should be made for average conditions and with consideration for all points of sailing. For this kind of sail, draft should be average, with the maximum amount of draft (the distance, measured at right angles from a straight line running between luff and leech, to the deepest part of the curve) being about one-tenth of the sail's width (from luff to leech) at a height of slightly lower than halfway up the mast. This maximum draft's fore-and-aft location should lie forward of the halfway point between luff and leech but no farther

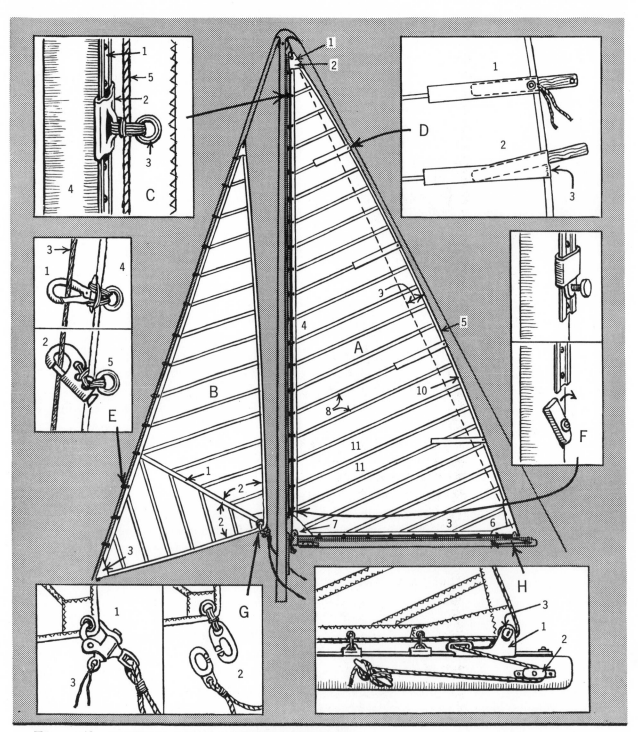

Figure 48   WORKING SAILS & RELATED FITTINGS

A MARCONI CROSS-CUT
   MAINSAIL
   (1) head (2) headboard
   (3) foot (4) luff (5) leech
   (6) clew (7) tack (8) seams
   (9) roach (10) tabling
   (11) cloths

B MITER-CUT JIB
   (1) miter seam
   (2) angle between foot
       and miter seam is equal
       to angle between leech
       and miter seam
   (3) corner patch

C SAIL SLIDE OR CAR
   (1) track (2) slide (3) grommet
       small shackle may be used to
       secure slide to grommet.
   (4) mast (5) bolt rope

D BATTENS & BATTEN POCKETS
   (1) conventional type with lanyards
   (2) offset pocket sewn closed at (3)

52

forward than a third of the luff-to-leech distance abaft the luff (see A in Figure 49).

Although draft is built into a sail, the curvature may be altered slightly by making certain adjustments to the sail. Of course, with only one suit of working sails for average conditions, the slight alterations in draft can be tremendously helpful in adapting the suit to varying wind conditions and different points of sailing. The principal draft-altering adjustments are: stretching or loosening the luff or foot of a sail, bending the mast, changing the angle of trim with the sheet, and use of the boom vang. There are one or two special draft-changing devices, such as zippered or laced foot pockets which may be opened to increase draft or closed to decrease draft. However, these devices will not be discussed, because at the present time, they have not been used enough for valid conclusions to be drawn concerning either their operation or their effectiveness.

The simplest and most often neglected draft alterations are the luff and foot adjustments. The foot is adjusted by tightening or slacking the *outhaul*, the line or device which pulls the clew out on the boom (see Figure 49). Tightening the outhaul stretches the sail's foot and in general flattens the sail, especially just above the foot. The outhaul is usually tightened in a breeze and when sailing to windward, but slacked in light airs and when sailing downwind.

The luff is adjusted by either the halyard or the *downhaul*, a line or tackle attached to the forward end of the boom which can pull it down. Of course this requires a sliding gooseneck (a gooseneck fitting which slides on a track) in order that the fore end of the boom can move up and down on the mast. The *tack* or forward corner of the sail is attached to the top of the gooseneck; so naturally when the gooseneck is pulled down, the tack will move down and stretch the sail's luff. Tightening the halyard with the downhaul cleated accomplishes the same thing as tightening the downhaul, except that the halyard adjustment has more effect on the upper part of the sail. Many racing boats have black bands painted around the top of their masts to indicate maximum hoist. Class rules or handicap rules forbid that the *head* (top) of a sail be hoisted above the bottom of the black band. Therefore, in such a case, it is customary to hoist the head to its highest legal position and then to make all luff adjustments with the downhaul. Luff adjustments alter the fore-and-aft position of the draft. Stretching the luff tight will move the draft forward, and slacking the luff moves the draft aft. In heavy winds the draft is usually blown aft due to the stretch of the sail cloth; thus, it is wise to tighten the luff. In light airs, however, the luff should be quite slack especially when sailing downwind. It is a common mistake to overtighten the luff of a dacron sail when the wind is light. In most breezes except heavy winds, the luff should be stretched just tight enough to smooth out the horizontal wrinkles along the luff.

The other methods of altering sail draft will be discussed later in this chapter. Draft changes made with mast bend will be dealt with briefly when we discuss rigging, and draft alterations through sheet trim and use of the boom vang will be dealt with in the next three sections.

E JIB HANKS (two types)
   (1) snap hook (2) piston hank
   (3) head stay or jib stay
   (4) jib (5) grommet

F SLIDE STOPS (two types)
   to keep slides or cars from
   sliding off track when you
   wish to lower mainsail but
   not remove it from mast

G JIB CLEW SHACKLES
   (two types)
   (1) snap shackle
   (2) Brummel or Inglefield hooks
      (hooks interlock when
      placed at right angles
      to each other)
   (3) lashing cord (spring-loaded pin
      on snap shackle should be lashed
      in because it can open when
      jib flaps violently)

H OUTHAUL FITTING
   (1) outhaul slide
   (2) cheek block (3) clew pin

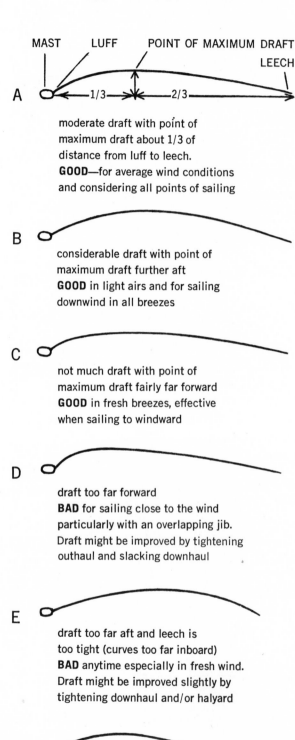

Figure 49 SAIL DRAFT AND
LUFF AND FOOT ADJUSTMENTS

MAST   LUFF   POINT OF MAXIMUM DRAFT
LEECH

A   ◀——1/3——▶◀——————2/3——————▶

moderate draft with point of
maximum draft about 1/3 of
distance from luff to leech.
GOOD—for average wind conditions
and considering all points of sailing

B

considerable draft with point of
maximum draft further aft
GOOD in light airs and for sailing
downwind in all breezes

C

not much draft with point of
maximum draft fairly far forward
GOOD in fresh breezes, effective
when sailing to windward

D

draft too far forward
BAD for sailing close to the wind
particularly with an overlapping jib.
Draft might be improved by tightening
outhaul and slacking downhaul

E

draft too far aft and leech is
too tight (curves too far inboard)
BAD anytime especially in fresh wind.
Draft might be improved slightly by
tightening downhaul and/or halyard

F

leech too slack
BAD at all times especially in
light airs

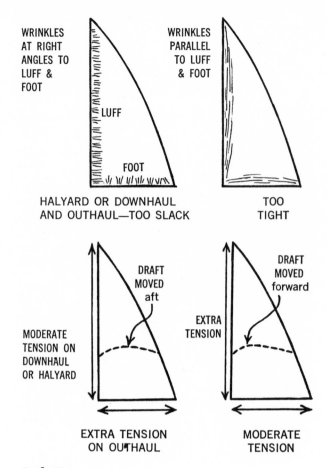

WRINKLES
AT RIGHT
ANGLES TO
LUFF &
FOOT

LUFF

FOOT

HALYARD OR DOWNHAUL
AND OUTHAUL—TOO SLACK

WRINKLES
PARALLEL
TO LUFF
& FOOT

TOO
TIGHT

MODERATE
TENSION ON
DOWNHAUL
OR HALYARD

DRAFT
MOVED
aft

EXTRA TENSION
ON OUTHAUL

DRAFT
MOVED
forward

EXTRA
TENSION

MODERATE
TENSION

Sail Trim

A sail is trimmed with its sheet. Let us review
briefly the general sail positions for each point
of sailing. When running, a sail is let all the way
out; when beam reaching, it is about halfway
out or somewhat closer; when broad reaching,
the sail should lie somewhere between the running and beam-reaching positions; when close
reaching, it should lie between the beam-reaching position and its closest point of trim; and
when beating the sail should be trimmed in almost as far as it will come. These are only approximate positions. Exact positions will depend
on the strength of the breeze, the design of the
boat, the cut of her sails, the boat speed, and the
size of the seas.

As said in Chapter 3, sails are always
trimmed to the apparent wind. The faster a
boat travels, especially when she is beam reaching, the closer her sheets must be trimmed.
When she is beating, the difference between the
true and apparent wind will not be very great
in either direction, but there will be a great

difference in velocity. On this point of sailing the boat speed is added to true wind which increases the apparent wind speed. When running, however, the boat speed wind is subtracted from the true wind to give a decreased apparent wind. There is no directional change in the apparent wind when a boat runs dead before the wind; therefore in all breezes on this point of sailing the mainsail should be let out until the boom almost touches the after shroud. When trimming sails, always refer to the telltales or wind indicator, because these give the apparent wind direction.

The simplest way to obtain proper trim on a reach is to slack the sheets until the sail begins to luff, then the sheet is pulled in until the sail stops luffing. It is usually better to err on the side of trimming the sails too far out than too far in. A sail that is trimmed too far in will stall, as explained in Chapter 3, and, in addition, causes extra heeling. A sail that is trimmed too far out, although not correct, at least will be in such a position that the suction pull, on the sail's leeward side, has a more favorable angle with the boat's centerline to pull her ahead instead of sideways. It is usually advantageous to keep the sail *on edge*, so that it is just on the verge of luffing. This is when the sail is most effective. In order to do this while holding a straight course on a reach, the sheets must be tended constantly. Especially when racing, the sheets should be *played* or adjusted for every wind shift and every puff or lull.

On the beat, sail trim is not changed so often as when reaching. This is because the helmsman changes his course more often to conform with changes of wind direction and velocity. However, when there are great variations in wind speed, sheets should be slacked slightly during the lulls and tightened during puffs. There are two exceptions to this rule. In heavy breezes when the boat is *overburdened* (carrying too much sail), the mainsheet should be eased so that it carries a slight luff. The other exception is that when sailing into a rough sea which tends to slow the boat, sheets should be started, and as said in the last Chapter, the helmsman should bear off slightly to keep the boat footing.

Sheet Leads

When we consider sail trim, we must not only consider the in-and-out adjustment of the sheet, but also the location of its *lead*. A sheet lead is usually a *block* (pulley) on the deck or rail through which the sheet is led. Most leads are mounted in such a way that their location (fore and aft and/or athwartships) can be changed slightly to give the sheet the most favorable angle of trim for various sailing conditions. This altering of location is usually accomplished by the block being attached to a slide on a track, although sometimes a lead block slides on a low, athwartships metal bar called a *traveller* or *horse*.

Figure 50 shows correct and incorrect leads for working jibs. Notice that the fore-and-aft location should be at a point where neither the foot nor leech is stretched excessively tight. A tight leech, caused by a lead which is too far forward, almost closes the upper venturi slot between the jib and the mainsail thereby restricting the air flow, and the leech deflects the flow into the lee side of the mainsail producing harmful backwind. A loose leech, on the other hand, opens the slot aloft too much so that the space between the jib's leech and the mainsail's luff is too wide thereby harming the efficiency of the venturi. A correct jib lead is placed so that neither the jib's leech nor the foot is stretched excessively tight when the sail is trimmed in flat. It is often very helpful to gauge the fore-and-aft lead position by its relationship to a projection of the jib's miter seam as shown in Figure 50. The correct lead position for most working jibs lies slightly forward of the point where the miter seam projection strikes the deck. When the sheet of the average close-hauled jib is properly led, the sail will first begin to luff along the general area just above the miter seam (see Figure 50). If the jib's luff begins to shake below the miter seam, the lead is usually too far forward; but if the luff shakes aloft near the sail's head, the lead is too far aft. When reaching, with the mainsail slacked off, it sometimes pays to move the jib lead slightly further aft than its normal position for beating. This is done to help prevent the upper mainsail

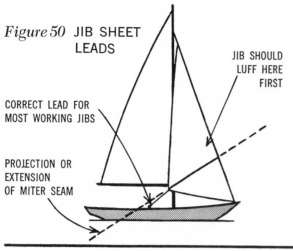

Figure 50 JIB SHEET LEADS

JIB SHOULD LUFF HERE FIRST

CORRECT LEAD FOR MOST WORKING JIBS

PROJECTION OR EXTENSION OF MITER SEAM

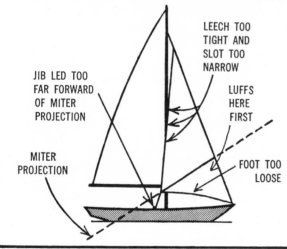

JIB LED TOO FAR FORWARD OF MITER PROJECTION

MITER PROJECTION

LEECH TOO TIGHT AND SLOT TOO NARROW

LUFFS HERE FIRST

FOOT TOO LOOSE

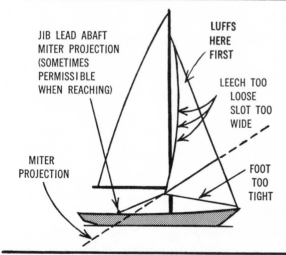

JIB LEAD ABAFT MITER PROJECTION (SOMETIMES PERMISSIBLE WHEN REACHING)

MITER PROJECTION

LUFFS HERE FIRST

LEECH TOO LOOSE SLOT TOO WIDE

FOOT TOO TIGHT

ATHWARTSHIP LEAD FOR BOATS OF AVERAGE BEAM (WIDER BOATS USE WIDER ANGLE)

LEAD

CENTER LINE

12°

JIB SHEET

from being backwinded by the jib.

In addition to the fore-and-aft sheet lead, we must consider the athwartships position, or how far inboard or outboard the lead is located. On many fast, narrow racing boats the jib lead should be placed about ten degrees out from the boat's centerline, but for the average day-sailer with moderate beam, twelve degrees is a more realistic angle (see Figure 50). Actually, this angular measurement should be used only as a guide. The exact athwartships point of trim should be decided upon only after experimentation. It should be located as far inboard as possible without causing the jib to backwind the mainsail when the sails are trimmed in flat for beating.

The Genoa jib is nearly always led from an adjustable slide on a track which is mounted on the boat's rail; thus there is no athwartships adjustment but only a fore-and-aft choice for the lead position. This jib lies outside the shrouds; when the average Genoa is trimmed in flat for beating, its foot lies snugly against the shrouds while its upper leech lies an inch or less from the end of the *spreaders* (the struts which hold the shrouds away from the mast). Of course, the Genoa lead position will vary according to the size and shape of the particular jib, the position of the shrouds, the length of the spreaders, and the position of the life lines around the boat. Most authorities say that the lead should be located slightly abaft the miter projection (see Figure 51), however, some Genoas are more effective when the lead lies at the point where the projection strikes the rail or even slightly forward of this point. As previously said, a little more backwind can be expected from a Genoa than from a working jib, therefore, with a Genoa, it is not usually harmful to carry a very slight shake in the lower luff of the mainsail, especially in a fresh breeze.

As with a working jib, when the Genoa's lead is too far forward, the leech becomes tight; but when the lead is too far aft the leech becomes loose. It is usually better to favor the loose leech, because the tight leech will cause excessive backwind. However, a leech which is too loose will often develop an annoying flutter. Some authorities say that a leech flutter does no real harm; nevertheless, it should be minimized or stopped if possible. Sliding the lead forward slightly will help. If your Genoa has a *leech line* (a light adjustable line sewn into the leech), this can be tightened slightly to help eliminate the flutter. However, great care should be taken not to over-tighten the leech line, as this can cause a tight, curling leech which can be very harmful aerodynamically.

Quite often chafing problems arise from constant sailing with a Genoa. If the spreader ends touch the sail, it should have a *reinforcing patch* (an extra piece of cloth sewn over the weak or rubbed area) on the spot which is rubbed. This is especially true if the spreaders touch a sail seam because the stitching will soon chafe through. Also the spreader ends should be wrapped with felt or some soft material. The Genoa foot will usually rub on the shrouds, therefore the outboard and forward shrouds should be equipped with *shroud rollers*. These are split tubes of wood or plastic which are taped closed on the shrouds in order that the tubes can turn or roll and minimize chafe to the jibs or sheets (see Figure 51). Rollers will also speed up tacking because there is less friction

when the jib wipes across the shrouds as the boat turns through the eye of the wind.

Mainsheet leads can only be adjusted athwartships because this sail is attached to a boom, and so there would be little point in having a fore-and-aft adjustment. When beating in light airs the mainsheet lead should be kept near the centerline of the boat. This will permit the boom to lift a little which will give the sail maximum draft. At the same time, of course, the sheet should be eased. When beating in a fresh breeze, the mainsheet should be moved to a position farther outboard where the sheet can pull the sail down as well as in. This will tend to flatten the sail and give it a more desirable draft for a good breeze. One word of caution, however, don't lead the mainsheet very far outboard when carrying a Genoa, because this will tend to close the slot and increase jib backwind.

The Boom Vang

The boom vang, sometimes called the *kicking strap,* has been mentioned, and it is illustrated in Figure 52. This is an important device for shaping and controlling the mainsail. Its fundamental purpose is to pull the boom down, preventing it from riding up when the sheet is eased. When the boom rides up or lifts, the leech curves or sags off and the sail becomes twisted causing the bottom area to be trimmed closer than the top area. This is shown in Figure 52. With the vang set up, however, the leech becomes straighter and the head and foot of the sail lie almost in the same plane. The boom vang is most effective when reaching in a fresh breeze because this is when the boom will have the greatest tendency to lift. The lighter a boat's boom, the tighter should be the vang adjustment to hold the boom down.

The value of a vang during a jibe has already been pointed out. It will ensure against a goosewing. Some large boats with cabin trunks, however, cannot carry a vang secured at the base of the mast as shown in the illustration because the boom vang will foul the cabin top or because of interference with deck gear. In such a case the vang must be fastened off center to a through-bolted fitting to leeward on the side

Figure 51 GENOA LEAD AND SHROUD ROLLER

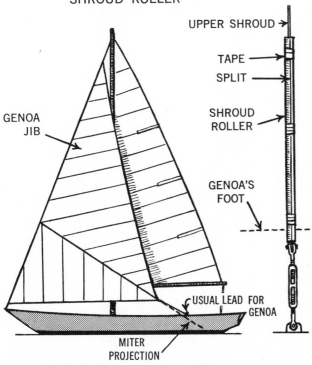

GENOA JIB

UPPER SHROUD

TAPE

SPLIT

SHROUD ROLLER

GENOA'S FOOT

USUAL LEAD FOR GENOA

MITER PROJECTION

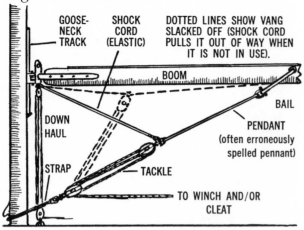

Figure 52 BOOM VANG

GOOSE-NECK TRACK

SHOCK CORD (ELASTIC)

DOTTED LINES SHOW VANG SLACKED OFF (SHOCK CORD PULLS IT OUT OF WAY WHEN IT IS NOT IN USE).

BOOM

DOWN HAUL

BAIL

PENDANT (often erroneously spelled pennant)

STRAP

TACKLE

TO WINCH AND/OR CLEAT

NOTE: THIS TYPE OF VANG REQUIRES A VERY STRONG GOOSENECK WHOSE TRACK SHOULD BE BOLTED TO MAST. BOATS WITH LIGHT ALUMINUM BOOMS REQUIRE GREATER USE OF THE VANG.

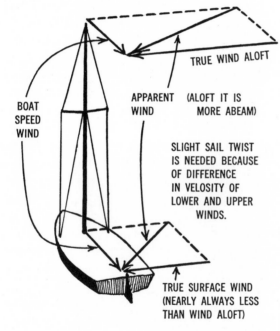

TRUE WIND ALOFT

BOAT SPEED WIND

APPARENT WIND

(ALOFT IT IS MORE ABEAM)

SLIGHT SAIL TWIST IS NEEDED BECAUSE OF DIFFERENCE IN VELOSITY OF LOWER AND UPPER WINDS.

TRUE SURFACE WIND (NEARLY ALWAYS LESS THAN WIND ALOFT)

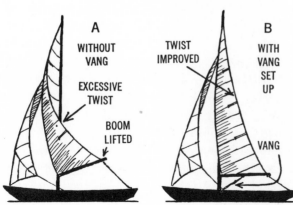

A
WITHOUT VANG

EXCESSIVE TWIST

BOOM LIFTED

TWIST IMPROVED

B
WITH VANG SET UP

VANG

deck. When this is necessary, the vang must be adjusted every time there is a change of sheet trim. Obviously, this kind of vang must be removed before jibing.

It is often advantageous to carry the vang set up tight when beating in a good breeze. The vang will sometimes bend a limber boom down near its. middle to help remove draft and on many boats it will help tighten the jibstay which is definitely advantageous when beating. If the boat has a fixed, non-adjustable, mainsheet lead, a vang rigged to the side deck will help pull the boom outboard and give the same effect as could be achieved with an adjustable traveller. The vang is often carried in fairly light breezes when the sheets are slacked in order to tighten the leech and remove sail twist, but usually it should not be carried to windward in light airs. At this time the mainsail should have maximum draft, and the vang will tend to flatten the sail. Figure 52 shows that a slight twist in a sail is desirable because the wind near the head of a sail usually has a greater velocity than at its foot. This causes the apparent wind aloft to be farther aft. Nevertheless, most sails, when trimmed for reaching in anything but light airs, have far too much twist and need at least some tension on the vang.

Handling and Care of Sails

Although sail construction and fitting details often vary with different boats, the procedure for *bending* sails (putting them on) is basically the same for all boats. When bending on a jib or staysail, we start with the tack, which is fastened to the *stem head fitting* (a metal fitting with eyes at the top of the stem) or some other eye fitting at the lower end of the jib stay. The tack is secured with a *shackle* (a U-shaped fastener) which is usually closed with a screw or twist pin or spring-loaded piston (see the *snap shackle* in Figure 48). The jib is usually hooked to its stay with *piston hanks* or *snap hooks* (see Figure 48) unless it is *set flying* (set without being hooked to a stay). When snapping on the hanks or hooks, we start at the sail's tack and work towards the head being sure that the hanks all face the same way so that they are not

58

twisted. Then we shackle on the halyard to the head and attach the sheets to the clew. After the sheets are run through their lead blocks, figure-eight knots should be tied in the very ends of the lines to prevent them from accidentally being pulled back through the blocks.

On most boats the mainsail is held to the mast and boom by one of two means: slides on a track (shown in Figure 48), or with grooved spars. When the spars are grooved, the sail's *bolt rope* (a rope sewn to the edge of the luff and foot) is fed into the boom groove as the clew is pulled aft, and then the bolt rope is fed into the mast groove as the sail is hoisted. In some cases, small plastic cylinders are fastened to a sail's luff or foot and these are fed into the grooves. In any event, in bending on the luff of a mainsail, it is obviously necessary to start with the head and work down towards the tack. Also it is necessary to work from clew to tack when bending on the foot. The last edge of the sail (luff or foot) to be bent should first be run through the hands to see that the sail is not twisted before the bending is completed. Next the battens should be inserted. They should be shorter than their batten pockets by an inch or more. A sail equipped with batten pockets should not be used without the battens being inserted. Before hoisting the mainsail, be sure to set up the *topping lift* (the line which supports the boom when the sail is not hoisted). Failure to have the boom lifted up high when the sail is being hoisted or lowered may result in deck gear or a crew member being struck by the boom, and also it can over-stretch the sail's leech. After the sail is entirely hoisted, the topping lift is slacked off so that it gives no support to the boom.

Although dacron sails are tougher and can stand more abuse than the cotton sails of former days, dacrons are still vulnerable to certain mistreatment. Chafe is often a problem with synthetic sails because the stitching does not sink down into the cloth but lies on the surface where it is susceptible to being rubbed. Any area of a sail which is constantly chafed should be protected with a reinforcing patch. Sun rot is also a problem, especially with nylon. Sails which are left bent on should be furled, *stopped* (tied with cloth straps called *stops* or elastic shock cord), and protected with *sail covers* (specially fitted cloth covers which are lashed or snapped around the furled sail and its boom). Sail covers should not be lashed entirely closed at the bottom, because lack of air inside the cover will encourage mildew, even on synthetic sails.

When furling a sail, pull the entire sail over to one side of the boom. Grab the leech of the sail and pull it aft so that the battens lie flat or parallel to the boom. Then bundle up the loose sail and neatly roll it up on top of the boom. After the roll is as tight as you can get it, secure it to the boom with stops. Before the sail is covered, slack off the outhaul. This is especially important if the sail is made of cotton.

If the sails are taken off and bagged be sure the battens are removed as they can be broken or permanently bent inside a bag. Don't bag a wet sail. Let it dry first. Sails can be dried by hoisting them while moored, but only if the breeze is very light. The violent flapping and flogging of sails in a wind can be very harmful to them. Cotton sails are extremely susceptible to shrinkage when wet, thus it is very important to slack their outhauls and halyards or downhauls when they get wet.

When sailing is done in salt water, sails should be washed fairly frequently to remove salt crystals which become lodged in the material. A salt-caked sail usually does not set well because the salt absorbs any moisture in the air even on a seemingly dry day. Sail washing should be done fairly gently and never with a detergent.

One of the greatest sources of damage to a sail is the cotter pin. This is a thin, bent metal pin that is put through a hole in a threaded screw fitting to prevent it from becoming unscrewed (see Figure 56). Cotter pins have sharp ends which can easily snag and tear a sail. All these pins should be thoroughly wrapped in waterproof adhesive tape, and they should be inspected regularly to see that they remain taped. Another frequent source of sail damage is from cigarette or pipe ashes. Synthetic sails will not burst into flames, but they can be holed from sparks very easily.

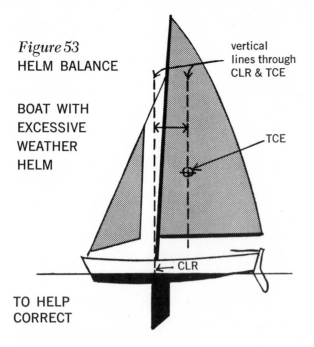

Figure 53
HELM BALANCE

BOAT WITH
EXCESSIVE
WEATHER
HELM

vertical
lines through
CLR & TCE

TCE

CLR

TO HELP
CORRECT

1 PREVENT HEELING TO LEEWARD
2 MOVE WEIGHT AFT
3 RAISE CENTERBOARD SLIGHTLY
4 RAKE MAST FORWARD
5 TRIM JIB SHEET (PULL IT IN) OR SET LARGER JIB
6 REDUCE AREA OF MAINSAIL OR HAVE IT RECUT
   TO REDUCE DRAFT (SEE FIG. 49) NEAR AFTER EDGE

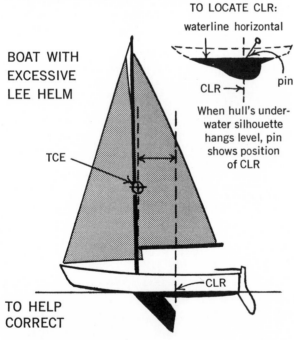

BOAT WITH
EXCESSIVE
LEE HELM

TCE

CLR

TO LOCATE CLR:
waterline horizontal

CLR →
pin

When hull's under-
water silhouette
hangs level, pin
shows position
of CLR

TO HELP
CORRECT

1 HEEL TO LEEWARD
2 MOVE WEIGHT FORWARD
3 LOWER CENTERBOARD
4 RAKE MAST AFT
5 EASE (SLACK) JIB SHEET OR SET SMALLER JIB
6 ENLARGE MAIN AND/OR TIGHTEN ITS
   LEECH (AFTER EDGE)

Balance

As previously mentioned, helm balance has to do with the ability of a boat to hold a straight course when her helm is left alone. If she tends to head up into the wind, she has a *weather helm;* but if she heads away from the wind, she has a *lee helm.* A boat's helm balance primarily depends on the relationship of the *center of effort* (CE) of her sails to the *center of lateral resistance* (CLR) of her underwater profile. The point at the geometric center of the side view of a sail is commonly referred to as the center of effort, and a combination of the center of effort of each sail concentrated at a single point or the center of effort of the entire sail plan is often called the *total center of effort* (TCE). The CLR is the central point on the hull's underwater side at which the boat can be pushed sideways (at right angles to her centerline) without turning. The fore-and-aft position of the CLR may be found by cutting from cardboard the silhouette of the immersed hull and hanging it in a level position from a pin, as shown in Figure 53. Almost all boats are designed with the TCE slightly "leading" or ahead of the CLR because it has been found that this gives the best average balance when considering all conditions of sailing. The amount of lead is generally from three to twenty per cent of the boat's waterline length.

Although the fact that the TCE is forward of the CLR would apparently produce lee helm, several other forces acting on the boat tend to produce weather helm. For example, the curvature of a boat's sails result in the part of the sail abaft the CE presenting a broader angle to the wind than does the part of the sail forward of the CE. This means that the after portion of a sail exerts more turning force on the boat than does the forward portion. Thus the boat tends to turn into the wind, or have a weather helm.

Also, weather helm usually increases as a boat is heeled. The greater the angle of heel, the more weather helm. Of course, this will vary with individual designs. A hull with fairly balanced ends (symmetrical underwater, with the bow sections similar to the immersed stern sections) will develop only a slight increase in weather helm when heeled, but a hull with a sharp entrance and flat run will have a strong tendency to turn into the wind when heeled. Every boat should be designed or *tuned* (properly adjusted) to carry a slight weather helm in all but the lightest breezes. A slight weather helm makes it easier for the helmsman to feel his boat, and also it is a built-in safety device; because, if the helmsman should happen to leave or lose his grip on the helm, the boat will automatically round up into the wind where she will lose headway and gain stability.

Furthermore, it has been found that a slight weather helm when beating actually boosts a boat to windward. If a rudder which is attached to the trailing edge of a keel, is held at an angle of from three to six degrees from the boat's centerline, depending on the design, the keel-rudder combination will act as a hydrofoil and create a lateral lifting force. Of course, too much weather helm can be very harmful because a rudder which is held over too far will partially stall and create a great amount of drag. When this happens the rudder acts partially as a brake.

Improper balance is seldom extreme in a one-design class boat or boats designed by recognized naval architects, and these include all Naval Academy boats, but many individual boats have minor helm faults which can be corrected by various minor adjustments. These are shown in Figure 53. Most of the adjustments, raking the mast, raising or lowering the centerboard, moving crew weight, and setting larger or smaller sails forward or aft, change the boat's balance by changing the relation of the CLR to the TCE, as can be seen in the diagram.

There is a possibility, however, that one or two of these adjustments may be harmful to the boat's speed even though her helm is improved. For example, setting a smaller jib in light air to help correct a lee helm, might cause a loss of speed. Therefore, care should be taken to see that helm balance is not improved at the expense of over-all performance. The first correction to be made when a boat is improperly balanced, is to change the angle of heel. The severe weather helm often experienced when sailing in a blow is due mainly to an extreme angle of heel. This can be lessened by hiking or putting the crew as far as possible to windward and also by carrying a slight luff in the mainsail while the jib is trimmed flat.

The last balance correction listed in Figure 53 (correction #6) mentions the tightening or slacking of the mainsail's leech. A tight leech will increase weather helm, while a loose leech will decrease weather helm. Drastic changes in the leech can only be made by a skillful sailmaker, and even then, the changes may not be completely successful. Improving a sail's leech by recutting should be attempted only as a last resort to improve an original faulty draft. Slight, temporary changes in the leech can be made by adjustments to the boom vang. Tightening the vang will tighten the leech, but slacking the vang will slack the leech. Sometimes an overly tight leech can be eased by manually stretching it when the sail is unbent.

Figure 54 shows how balance should be maintained when sail is reduced for heavy weather. As the diagram explains, there are various methods of shortening sail and these will vary according to the boat's rig. *Reefing* is the method of reducing a sail's area by lashing its lower area to its boom or by winding its foot around the boom. It should also be remembered that reefing the mainsail not only reduces the angle of heel, but also moves the CE of that sail forward. Thus reefing reduces weather helm in two ways. These procedures will be discussed in Chapters 6 and 7. The purpose of Figure 54 is to illustrate that the sail areas on either side of the TCE should be fairly equal when sail is reduced. In actual practice, however, most boats should carry more sail forward of the TCE as the wind increases in order to compensate for the excessive weather helm caused by extreme heeling.

Standing Rigging

A boat's rigging can be divided into two categories: running and standing. Running rigging refers to the movable lines or wires used to set or adjust sails, and this rigging includes halyards, sheets, downhauls, outhauls, and topping lifts. Standing rigging, on the other hand, is

61

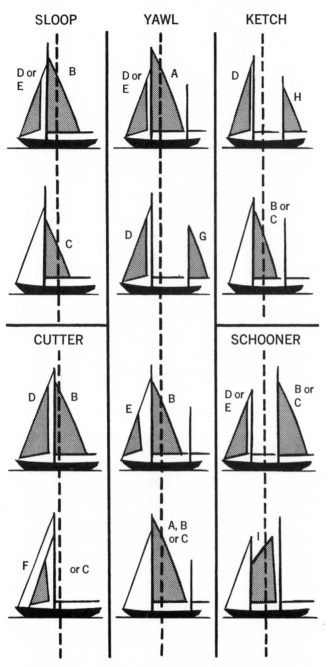

Figure 54 BALANCE WITH REDUCED SAIL

SLOOP YAWL KETCH

CUTTER SCHOONER

BROKEN LINES ARE TCE UNDER FULL SAIL

A. full mainsail B. reefed main C. deeply reefed main D. jib
E. storm jib F. staysail G. mizzen H. reefed mizzen I. foresail

1×19 construction wire (one solid strand of 19 wires) which is particularly resistant to stretch.

Figure 55 illustrates two basic standing rigging plans with suggestions for tuning or adjusting the shrouds and stays. There are many standing rigging variations, but boats A and B in the diagram, representing the *Masthead* and *Seven-eighths* rig, illustrate typical modern rigs of a simple form, and they show the basic principles of tuning which can be applied to nearly all boats. Specific variations or departures from the norm, if any, will be pointed out when each individual Naval Academy boat is discussed.

Tuning the standing rigging can be a complicated and sometimes controversial procedure. A detailed study will not be attempted here but simply an introduction to the generally accepted rules. A common-sense rule is to adjust the shrouds so that the mast is held up vertically, at right angles to the deck near the partners, when the boat is viewed from her bow or stern. When the boat heels, of course, the mast will be supported by the windward shrouds only, and they will tighten, which will cause the leeward shrouds to slacken considerably. In this case, the mast will not be exactly at right angles to the deck, but it should be nearly so. From this same view (from the bow or stern), the mast should be kept straight. This requires that the lower shrouds be kept slightly more slack than the upper shrouds, because the latter are longer, pass over a spreader, and therefore have more stretch when the boat heels. Lateral bends and "S" curves in a mast can be very harmful to the set of its sail.

Another fundamental of tuning is to keep the jibstay or head stay taut. This is essential to good windward performance. In order to keep these forward stays taut, then naturally, the permanent backstay must be kept taut to counteract the pull of the forward stays; and if the boat has running backstays, which pull directly behind the jibstay, these must be kept taut alternately when beating. Jumper stays on a seven-eighths rig (shown on boat B) should be kept taut if it is desired that the mast be kept straight when it is viewed from the side.

It has already been mentioned that there are certain occasions when masts are intentionally

more or less fixed, and this includes various stays and shrouds which support the mast and control its bending. On modern boats this rigging nearly always consists of wire rope, usually

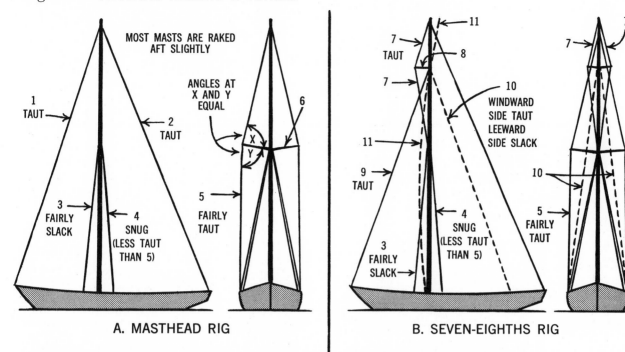

Figure 55 STANDING RIGGING & TUNING

MOST MASTS ARE RAKED AFT SLIGHTLY

ANGLES AT X AND Y EQUAL

1 TAUT

2 TAUT

3 FAIRLY SLACK

4 SNUG (LESS TAUT THAN 5)

5 FAIRLY TAUT

6

X
Y

A. MASTHEAD RIG

11

7 TAUT

8

7

10 WINDWARD SIDE TAUT LEEWARD SIDE SLACK

11

9 TAUT

3 FAIRLY SLACK

4 SNUG (LESS TAUT THAN 5)

5 FAIRLY TAUT

7

7

10

B. SEVEN-EIGHTHS RIG

1 HEAD STAY 2 PERMANENT BACKSTAY 3 FORWARD LOWER SHROUD 4 AFTER LOWER
SHROUD 5 UPPER SHROUD 6 SPREADER 7 JUMPER STAY 8 JUMPER STRUT
9 JIB STAY 10 RUNNING BACKSTAYS 11 MAST BOWED TO FLATTEN SAIL FOR HEAVY WINDS

bent aft in order to alter draft. This is common practice with certain small-boat classes. The principle behind this bending or flexing of spars is shown by the bent mast (indicated by the dotted line) in Figure 55. When a mast is bent so that its top bends aft and its lower portion, below the jibstay point of attachment, bows forward, then the sail is stretched fore and aft abaft the luff, and this flattens the draft. Boats with "bendy" rigs carry very full mainsails on straight spars in light airs or rough seas, but sail with bent spars in a good breeze to reduce the draft. If the boat is equipped with jumper stays and a permanent backstay, the former can be slacked while the latter is tightened to achieve a bend. In some very small boats with limber masts and few stays, bending the mast may be accomplished simply by tightening the boom vang or sheet.

Mast bending works very well in many cases, but there should be a few words of warning. Sails must be specially cut for flexible spars. If the sail is cut for a straight mast, it will often be badly distorted if carried on a bent mast. A mast should rarely be bent in light airs as this is when full draft is needed. Also, it is usually not wise to attempt bending a mast which has a head stay to the masthead (shown on boat A in Figure 55), because of difficulties in pulling the masthead aft without putting a compression bend in the mast, changing the normal set of the jib, and having a slack head stay and upper shrouds because the top of the mast will be lower when it is bent. As a general rule, it is wise not to attempt bending the spars of any large cruising-racing yacht. The result could be the loss of a mast.

Standing rigging is adjusted with turnbuckles (see Figure 56). Once the shrouds are adjusted correctly, they should be left alone for most of the sailing season with only an occasional tightening if the rigging stretches; therefore shroud turnbuckles should be locked with cotter pins as shown in the diagram. Don't forget to wrap the cotter pins with tape. Stay turnbuckles, however, might need more frequent adjustment;

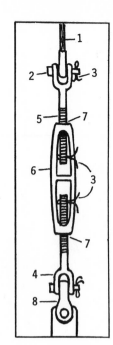

Figure 56

TURNBUCKLE
(1) shroud (2) clevis pin
(3) cotter pin (should be
    wrapped in tape)
(4) clevis (5) threads
(6) barrel (turn to tighten stay)
(7) some turnbuckles have
    locknuts here instead of
    cotter pins
(8) toggle (should be on large
    boats at head stay to prevent
    metal fatigue at clevis)

therefore it is often wise to use lock nuts at the top and bottom of the turnbuckle barrels to prevent them from becoming unscrewed accidentally (see Figure 56). Head stays and jibstays often have a lot of lateral movement due to the side pressure of a jib or staysail; thus it is important that, on large boats at least, these stays are fitted with *toggles* as shown in the diagram. A toggle is a small fitting with a pin which makes a moveable joint between the bottom of the turnbuckle and its eye, stemhead fitting, or other point of attachment. Without a toggle, the lower jaws of a turnbuckle are subject to breakage through metal fatigue.

The question of how tight to set up the rigging is an often debated one. Rigging that is too loose allows the mast to jump around and move too much in a seaway, but on the other hand, rigging that is too tight often seems to kill a boat's speed, and it puts unnecessary strain and stress on the hull. Almost everyone agrees that the jibstay or head stay should be taut for windward sailing, but these should not be so taut that they put great strain on the stem or that they put compression bends in the mast. When tightening up the head stay, sight up the mast track on the after side of the mast to see that no bend is developing. Sight from aft forward and also from the side.

For most boats, shrouds should not be any tighter than they have to be to hold the mast nearly at right angles to the deck (when viewed from the bow or stern) when the boat is heeled. In other words, the mast should not be allowed to lean too far to leeward. As for the amount of rake in a mast (the amount it leans fore and aft when viewed from the side), most boats are designed to carry a slight rake aft. This usually makes the mainsail hang better (provided the after end of her boom is not too low) and it also causes the jibstay to stand better, allowing a minimum of sag. The question of rake, however, will depend primarily on the balance of the boat as mentioned in the last section. If the boat has too little weather helm or a lee helm, her mast should be raked fairly far aft; but with too much weather helm, the mast should be almost vertical and in some rare cases, raked slightly forward of the vertical.

A few last words of advice about rigging: a spreader should be adjusted so that the angles between the shroud and spreader above and below are exactly equal (see Figure 55). Failure to do this can cause the spreader to slip which could result in the loss of the mast. Get in the habit of checking fittings for cracks, wear, or fatigue. Particularly, check lock nuts which often seem to come loose. Avoid, or at least be very cautious about making rigging adjustments while under way. Rigging on the leeward side is normally quite slack when a boat is heeled, and it is easy to adjust it too tight which can destroy the proper tune and put a great strain on the boat.

A Summary of Sail Adjustments

In this chapter, a fair amount has been said about sail shaping and adjusting; therefore a summary of the main points in outline form may be helpful. This will list the various adjustments for sailing to windward (beating) or off the wind (running and reaching) in different conditions of wind and sea.

In light airs or in rough seas, maximum draft is desirable. (Keep boat heeled slightly to leeward.)

- Slack outhaul and ease downhaul slightly
- Ease sheets and lead mainsail from centerline of boat for light airs but farther outboard in rough seas
- Ease boom vang
- Keep mast straight
- Keep jibstay moderately taut.

In a moderate breeze with smooth water, draft should be reduced.

- Tighten outhaul and downhaul
- Flatten sheets and lead main slightly outboard from centerline
- Boom vang moderately taut
- Mast may be bent slightly if rig is flexible
- Jibstay taut.

In a strong breeze with fairly smooth water, flatten draft, avoid a tight leech, and keep boat from heeling excessively.

- Tight on downhaul and fairly tight on outhaul, unless seas are rough
- Ease main but flatten jib
- Lead main farther outboard

- Boom vang tight
- Mast bent if rig is flexible
- Jibstay taut.

In light airs, full draft with most draft farther aft is desirable.

- Slack outhaul and downhaul
- Ease sheets to point of luffing when reaching
- Jib leads might be moved slightly farther aft
- Boom vang only slightly taut unless boom is very light
- Keep mast straight
- On some boats the backstays may be eased.

In a strong breeze, slightly less draft desirable.

- East outhaul and downhaul
- Carry slight luff in main if there is a strong weather helm
- Keep boom vang tight, but be ready to release it if the boom should start to dip in the water
- Keep mast straight and particularly free from compression bends
- Don't slack backstays.

CHAPTER SIX

Small Sailboats

In the preceding chapters we discussed general principles of sailboat handling, but obviously there are variations of rig, sails, and hull within each specific class of boat. Thus, moving from the general to the particular, we shall now discuss the principal small-boat classes used at the Naval Academy: the knockabout, the Skipjack, and the Shields classes.

It is interesting to compare these boats, because each represents a slightly different concept of small, class-boat sailing. The knockabout is an old, heavy-displacement, ruggedly-built, ballasted keel design that is unsophisticated but *smart* (quite fast and maneuverable) and reliable. The Shields is also a ballast-keel boat, but is a modern racing type, sensitive, sophisticated, and designed to excel in windward performance. The Skipjack, on the other hand, is a high-performance, light-displacement, modern, racing dinghy. Knockabouts make good trainers for the basic rudiments of sailing and preliminary big-boat handling. Shields boats are good trainers for keel-boat racing, light-sail handling, and for developing helmsmanship and a fine "tiller touch." Skipjacks are good trainers for centerboard boat seamanship, racing, and special techniques, such as planing and sailing with flexible spars.

Knockabout Sloops*

The knockabout has been shown in Figure 2. As can be seen in the illustration, she is a sloop-

*This description applies specifically to the wooden knockabouts, but only generally to the fiberglass knockabouts.

rigged day sailer, half-decked with an open cockpit. This kind of cockpit drains directly into the bilge, but the boat is equipped with a large, fixed bilge pump for the removal of rain water or spray which often accumulates in the bilge. (Some boats of this size or larger have *self-bailing* cockpits, with the floor level above the waterline and through-the-hull drains.)

Despite her large rig, the knockabout is a stable boat, for she has ample beam and 1,580 pounds of iron ballast attached to her keel. She is nearly impossible to turn over, and she is fitted with flotation tanks which would prevent her from sinking in the event that she should become filled with water. Of course, a knockabout can be heeled over, held down and swamped if she is not handled properly. In a fresh, puffy breeze, knockdowns must be expected, but if the boat is not let right up, especially in rough water, she may ship enough water to affect her stability. Such a predicament is extremely unlikely if the knockabout skipper follows common sense rules for heavy-weather sailing, that is if he reefs or shortens sail, luffs up in hard gusts, and slacks sheets when the rail buries. An effective feature for comfort and safety is the high coaming around the knockabout's cockpit which helps keep waves from sloshing in when the boat is heeled.

The dimensions of these sloops are 26 feet length over-all, 18 feet on the load water line, 7 feet beam, and 4 feet draft. The knockabout hull is conventional wood construction and is fitted with a nonflexible wood mast and boom. The mainsail's sail area is 249 square feet and the jib has 89 square feet, a large rig by modern standards but suitable for the boat's heavy displacement. Lines for the knockabouts were first drawn in 1929, and they were built in naval shipyards between 1935 and 1952. There are 30 of these boats at the Naval Academy. (See Figure 57.)

Knockabout sails are bent on in the conventional way with the jib hanked to the forestay and the mainsail's luff attached to the mast with slides on a track. However, the mainsail is *loose-footed*, that is to say the foot is not attached to the boom except at the tack and clew. Loose-footed mainsails are particularly sensitive

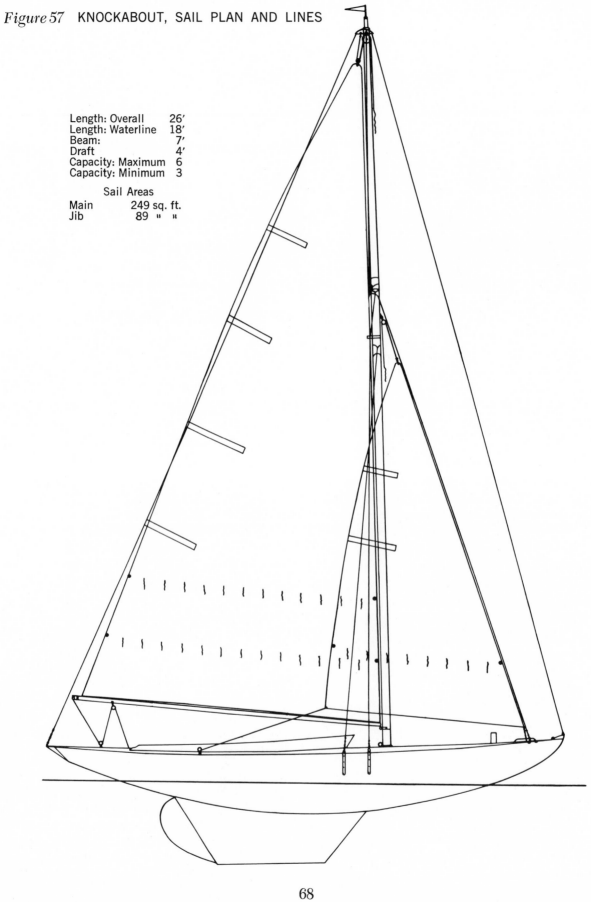

Figure 57 KNOCKABOUT, SAIL PLAN AND LINES

Length: Overall   26'
Length: Waterline   18'
Beam: 7'
Draft   4'
Capacity: Maximum   6
Capacity: Minimum   3

Sail Areas
Main   249 sq. ft.
Jib   89 " "

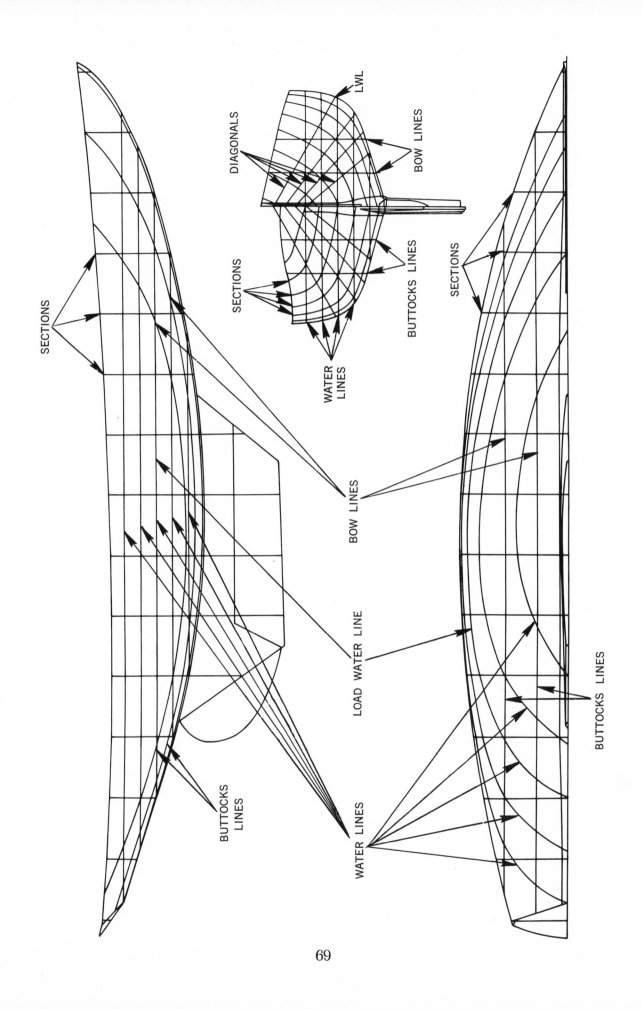

SECTIONS

SECTIONS

DIAGONALS

LWL

BOW LINES

BOW LINES

SECTIONS

BUTTOCKS LINES

WATER LINES

BOW LINES

LOAD WATER LINE

BUTTOCKS LINES

WATER LINES

BUTTOCKS LINES

69

to outhaul adjustments, and a common mistake is to overtighten the outhaul. Knockabouts especially, being heavy boats, need a lot of draft in their sails for maximum drive. Thus, the outhaul should be slack enough to allow a draft depth of about one foot for average conditions. In other words, when the sail is full and drawing, the point of maximum camber at the sail's foot (near the middle of the boom) should be about 12 inches from the boom. Of course, when it is blowing hard, the outhaul can be adjusted tighter to reduce the draft. Be sure that the outhaul is at least fairly taut before the sail is hoisted, and be sure the boom is supported by a topping lift or by hand while hoisting so that an unnecessary strain will not be put on the sail's leech.

The knockabout's halyards lead through blocks on the deck on either side of the mast (main to starboard and jib to port), and they *belay* (make fast) to a cleat just forward of the cockpit. Sail can be hoisted and lowered without leaving the cockpit. However, in order to hoist the sails very taut, it is usually necessary to *swig* or *sway* them up. This is a certain method of pulling on a halyard which may be used by one or more men and which may be described as follows when done by one man: After the sail is hoisted as taut as possible by pulling in on the halyard, a turn is taken on the cleat. Then the halyard is led forward to the mast without releasing the strain, and is held with one hand. With the other hand the halyard is grasped above the lead block and pulled out from the mast at right angles to the direction of the mast. Then body weight is put on the halyard and it is brought back to the mast while slack is taken in around the cleat. With two men, one can swig while the other takes in the slack. Knockabouts do not have sliding goose-necks with downhaul adjustments, therefore luff tension must be controlled with the halyard. When hoisting sail, watch the sail and look aloft to see that the battens do not foul the rigging and that everything up the mast is clear. Before getting under way be sure that the sheets are clear and that there are figure-eight knots in the ends of the jib sheets to prevent them from running through the lead blocks. Knockabouts do not carry light sails, and the rig is not flexible. The rigging should be tuned to hold the mast straight. Working sails are of dacron.

Although they are not quite as maneuverable as the Shields and particularly the Skipjacks, knockabouts can be considered quite maneuverable. With their fairly short keels (short from fore edge to after edge) and with ample rudder areas, these heavy sloops can turn quickly and within a fairly small radius. However, it is important to keep good headway at all times for effective rudder control. Knockabouts balance reasonably well under mainsail alone, and if given at least some breeze, they will sail under jib alone except when beating. Of course, they are least maneuverable under jib alone, especially in light airs.

On account of her heavy weight, a knockabout *forereaches* (carries way when shooting) a considerable distance; thus a dock, mooring, or *dolphin* (mooring post) should be approached with definite headway but at low speeds. At the Naval Academy, the knockabouts are kept moored to a seawall which faces somewhat north of northeast in the Santee Basin. Careful planning is required to get under way and land at these berths. Of course, exact procedure will vary according to the strength and direction of the wind. The boats are moored with their sterns in and bows out from the seawall. They are moored by a heavy adjustable bow line, which is referred to as the outhaul mooring line, and a fixed stern line, referred to as a *stern fast*. This mooring arrangement is shown in Figure 58. The outhaul line runs from the boat's bow bitt through a large block on a dolphin about 60 feet out from the seawall and from this block back to the seawall where it is made fast to a large iron ring. In order to board a knockabout, her stern must be pulled in to the seawall. This is done by hauling in on the stern fast as the outhaul is eased (slacked off but with tension on the line). Immediately prior to getting under way, all halyards and sheets should be carefully checked to see that they won't foul when sails are hoisted; and halyards as well as the sheets should have figure-eight knots in their ends.

When getting under way with the wind from astern, the jib may be hoisted first, and the

Figure 58   ARRANGEMENT FOR MOORING KNOCKABOUTS

This photograph shows the dolphins, outhaul mooring lines, stern fasts, and manner of securing the lines to iron rings on the sea wall. Sails are being bent on prior to getting under way.

knockabout may be run out from her berth under jib alone. The stern fast is unsnapped and left on the seawall and the outhaul mooring line is coiled up and left on top of the dolphin as the boat moves past. The helmsman should keep the boat headed directly out at right angles to the seawall until well clear of the dolphins, and then he should round up toward the wind while the mainsail is hoisted.

Whenever the mainsail is being handled, that is hoisted, lowered, or reefed, the *topping lift* (line leading from the end of the boom to a point high on the mast and back to the deck, used to hold the boom up when the sail is down) should be set up, the boom removed from the crutch, and the crutch stowed. On a boat with no topping lift, a crew member must hold the boom during sail handling.

If the wind is abeam or from ahead, a knockabout should be propelled from her berth by a simultaneous push and pull before sail is hoisted. A crew member on the stern should push from the seawall as a crew member on the bow

pulls on the outhaul. When there is a strong head wind, a great deal of force should be exerted to propel the boat well clear of the dolphins so that sail can be hoisted before she drifts back towards the seawall. Of course, the outhaul is coiled and left on the dolphin as the boat moves out of her slip. Remember the basic principles of heading into the wind when hoisting sail, hoisting the aftermost sail first (the mainsail in this case), and backing the jib to make the bow fall off in the desired direction.

When returning to her berth (see Figure 59), the knockabout should be landed at her dolphin bow first and at a slow speed. If the wind is from ahead or blowing from the seawall, the boat is luffed into the wind with sails shaking some distance from the dolphin in order to kill headway. In this situation, it is generally advisable to lower the jib prior to landing in order to help slow the boat, give better visibility to the helmsman, and give more freedom of movement to the man on the foredeck. If the wind is on the beam or abaft the beam when the boat is headed

71

Figure 59 KNOCKABOUT MOORING

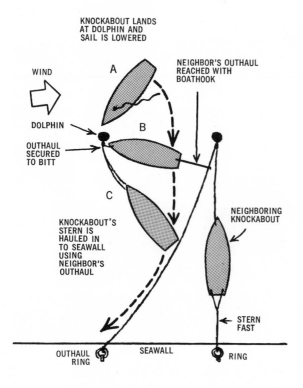

KNOCKABOUT LANDS
AT DOLPHIN AND
SAIL IS LOWERED

NEIGHBOR'S OUTHAUL
REACHED WITH
BOATHOOK

WIND

DOLPHIN

OUTHAUL
SECURED
TO BITT

A

B

C

KNOCKABOUT'S
STERN IS
HAULED IN
TO SEAWALL
USING
NEIGHBOR'S
OUTHAUL

NEIGHBORING
KNOCKABOUT

STERN
FAST

OUTHAUL
RING

SEAWALL

RING

directly towards the seawall, it is best to sail to windward of the dolphin, luff up and lower the main, and then sail downwind under jib alone toward the dolphin. If it is not blowing hard, the jib may be dropped just before reaching the dolphin, but if it is blowing hard, the boat should be sailed downwind toward the dolphin *under bare poles* (with all sails down). Remember that a knockabout will not go to weather under jib alone, so stay to windward of the dolphin.

After the crew on the bow has caught the dolphin and taken the coiled-up outhaul line, he belays it to the Sampson post. Then all sail is lowered. The proper orders are: "Let go the main (or jib) halyard; douse the main (or jib)." The boat is then pushed into her slip on the port side of her dolphin. A crew member on the stern reaches for the neighboring boat's outhaul line with a *boat hook* (a pole with a blunt hook at its end), and then the knockabout is turned around end for end so that her stern is brought back to the seawall. The stern fast is secured, and the boat has then assumed her original moored position. Before leaving the boat, bat-

tens are removed from the sails, sails are bagged and stowed under the forward deck to keep them dry, lines are belayed and coiled, and the bilge is pumped dry.

In heavy weather, a knockabout's sail area may be reduced by reefing. The need for reefing should be determined by a careful evaluation of weather conditions before getting under way, because it is much easier to reef before sail is hoisted and in the calm waters of a mooring area. There are no hard and fast rules for when to reef, but generally a knockabout should be reefed when the wind blows over 18 knots (see Beaufort Scale, Appendix E). This will depend somewhat on the experience of the skipper. A novice skipper should reef sooner than a veteran sailor with previous knockabout experience. If it should breeze up after a knockabout has left her mooring area, the skipper should slack his mainsheet and carry a moderate luff in the mainsail. But if the boat still buries her rail and takes a lot of spray over the washboards into the cockpit, it is definitely time to reef.

Figure 60 shows a properly reefed sail. Notice that before the sail is reefed there is a row of eyelets with lanyards (short lines) hanging from them. These are called *reef points*, and they hang down on each side of the sail. In line with the reef point eyelets at the luff, there is a reinforced hole in the sail called the *luff cringle* and at the leech a similar hole called the *leech cringle*. When reefing the sail, these cringles are lashed down to the boom with short, stout lines called *earings*. Each knockabout is supplied with a clew and tack earing. The luff cringle should be lashed down before the leech cringle is pulled aft. The clew earing must not only hold the leech cringle down, but the line must pull the cringle aft as well. The earing should run from the cringle aft through the clew outhaul fitting (or some other reeving point at the boom's after end), and then the line is led forward to the cringle again. The sail is hauled aft until it is tight along the boom, and then the leech cringle is lashed down to the boom with the remaining end of the earing. After both cringles are lashed, the loose lower part of the sail below the reef points, which is called the *bunt,* is rolled up neatly and placed on top of the boom where it is tied with the reef points. Notice in Figure 60 that the reef points are not tied around the boom, but they pass between the boom and the sail. Were they tied around the boom, unequal tension on different reef points could cause harmful stretching or even tearing of the sail.

If reefing is done while under way, the mainsail should be entirely lowered. The topping lift is set up, the boat is luffed into the wind, and the sail is lowered. This requires that the boat be a sufficient distance from the *lee shore* (downwind shore) before the operation is begun so that considerable leeway can be afforded while the reef is being tied in. The boat can be made to jog along under jib until the reef is tied in. While reefing, the boom should be in its crutch and the mainsheet must be *bowsed down* (pulled tight) to hold the boom in place.

Shaking out (untying) a reef is usually easier than tying one in. This is one reason why it is better to reef before getting under way when there is doubt as to the need for reducing sail.

Figure 60 CONVENTIONAL REEFING

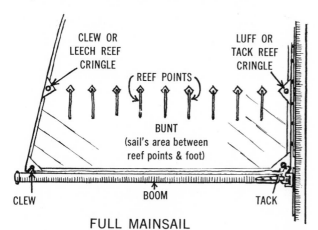

FULL MAINSAIL

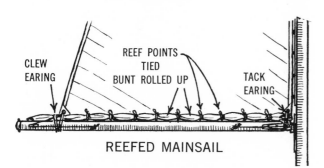

REEFED MAINSAIL

Should it be found, when under way, that conditions don't warrant a reef, it is not difficult to shake it out. This can usually be done without lowering the sail. First the topping lift is set up. Then the reef points are untied, the clew earing is cast off, and finally the tack earing is unlashed. The helmsman then luffs slightly and another crew man stands by the halyard to hoist the sail up hard as soon as the tack earing has been let go. More will be said on the subject of reefing in the following chapter about the Luders yawls.

Knockabouts should be sailed with a minimum of three in the crew (the skipper plus two crew members) or a maximum of six. The sloops are provided with six life jackets and a ring buoy. Naval Academy regulations for knockabout sailing are explained in Appendix D.

Skipjacks

The Skipjack is a typical, modern, high-performance planing dinghy. Her dimensions are 14 feet, 7 inches in length over-all, 5 feet, 3 inches beam, 300 pounds displacement, and she is sloop-rigged with 125 square feet of sail. Her hull is fiberglass and the spars are aluminum. These boats were designed and built by Newport Boats, Gloucester, Virginia, and the Naval Academy presently owns 26 of them.

A Skipjack is illustrated in Figure 61. There are two transom bailers, one on either side of the rudder. These are small, round holes covered by hinged flaps. The flaps are held closed by a piece of shock cord and a lanyard that is fastened to a jam cleat within reach of the helmsman. The Skipjack is very buoyant, and her cockpit floor is above the water level; thus when water accumulates in the cockpit, the bailers can be opened to let the water run out.

Being an unballasted centerboarder, the Skipjack obviously can capsize; but having ample foam flotation under her gunwales, she will float high on her side when overturned. In addition, there is foam in the mast to help keep the boat from *turning turtle.* Righting a Skipjack is quite easy. Usually it is not necessary to lower sail. The bow is brought around near the wind and a crew member climbs on the centerboard.

This photograph of a Skip-jack sailing in a moderate breeze shows the skipper and crew with their feet well under the hiking straps. This will enable the men to lean far backwards for effective hiking during strong gusts. Notice the skipper handling the mainsheet with one hand and the tiller extension with the other. Note that the extension is kept nearly at right angles to the tiller. The crew is reaching inboard with his right hand to help haul in the mainsheet.

Figure 61 THE SKIPJACK

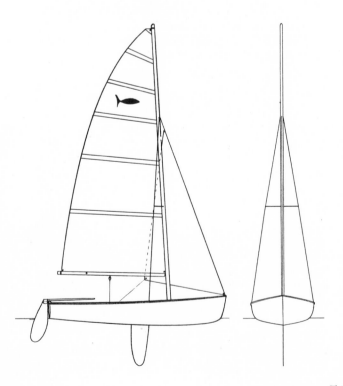

The crew counterbalance each other and scramble over the sides or stern after the boat is righted. Bailing is not necessary with the self-draining cockpit. (See Chapter 2 for the basics of capsizing and righting.)

As with any small centerboard dinghy, the Skipjack depends on crew weight for much of her stability. The boat is provided with *hiking straps* (web straps secured inside the boat on the bottom) in order that the crew and skipper may put their feet under these straps and lean far out to windward when the boat heels excessively. The inboard edge of the side decking is rounded for comfortable hiking, and the helmsman is provided with a *tiller extension* (a bar that pivots from the end of the tiller), which allows him to steer while sitting far out to windward. The tiller can be adjusted fore and aft to a limited extent by sliding it through the head of the rudder. A pin in the after end of the tiller keeps it from sliding out of the rudder head. Hiking should be an almost instinctive reaction for the small centerboard dinghy sailor. These boats should be kept as nearly flat (without heel) as possible except in very light airs when they should be heeled slightly to leeward.

The Skipjack is nearly always rigged as a sloop, but she may be converted to a cat rig (sometimes called *una-rig*) if the mast is stepped forward and the jib is dispensed with. The boat is provided with several choices of fore and aft positions for the mast step. Ordinarily, when sloop-rigged, the mast is stepped in the aftermost position, but if permanently cat-rigged,

74

the mast is stepped in the extreme forward position. If temporarily sailing under mainsail alone, however, it is not necessary to restep the mast. The boat will balance reasonably well under mainsail alone with the mast stepped aft.

Skipjacks use the bendy or flexible rig. Standing rigging consists of merely a jibstay and, at each side, a single shroud which is secured at the gunwale about one foot abaft the mast. These shrouds are held from the mast by spreaders which are hinged to move fore and aft to a limited extent. The rigging should be carried quite slack. Mast bend is achieved with the boom vang and mainsheet. Bowsing these down will pull the top of the mast aft and bow the lower part of the mast forward to flatten the sail. The vang consists of a tackle, the upper block of which is fitted with a wire and a small swaged cylinder. This cylinder fits into a keyhole slot on the underside of the boom about two feet abaft the mast. The lower block of the boom vang is attached to a ring at the base of the mast. With this particular type of vang, cleating is not necessary. The hauling part or *fall* of the tackle is hauled up to tighten the vang, and then it is pulled down to lock or jam the line. Notice that the mainsheet is led from a bar traveller crossing the cockpit nearly amidships. This gives the helmsman good control over the sheet, and it can flex the boom in its middle to help remove sail draft. However, an amidships traveller means that athwartship lead adjustment should be considerably less than if the traveller were located under the boom's after end. Furthermore, to hold the boom near the boat's centerline when beating in light airs, it is often necessary to move the lead slightly to windward of the centerline. When beating in a fresh breeze, the traveller should be adjusted so that the boom's end will lie approximately over the corner of the transom.

A fairly unique feature is the Skipjack's full-length mainsail battens. These are flexible slats of fiberglass which run from leech to luff. Their purpose is to hold out an extra large roach and to allow some draft change through batten adjustment. The deeper a batten is inserted, the greater the sail's draft. The end of each batten has several holes through which a metal snap

pin on the leech is inserted. For average conditions, the pin is inserted through the fourth hole from the batten's end, leaving three holes exposed. In a light breeze, the batten could be inserted further, while in a strong breeze, it might not be inserted as far. When the sail is unbent, the battens are not removed. The sail is simply rolled from head to foot, or vice versa.

The mainsail's clew outhaul consists of a simple lashing, and the boom is fitted with a downhaul to alter tension on the luff. Halyards are wire and rope combinations. After sail is hoisted, the wire parts of the halyards carry the full sail-supporting loads. The halyards do not belay to a cleat, but are secured by locking one of several small cylinders swaged to the wire under a slotted hook on the mast. When the jib is properly hoisted, the wire sewn into the luff of the sail takes the full load and causes the jib stay to go slack. In order to get the jib halyard taut, it is often necessary to make a loop in the halyard a foot or so above the mast step and then to stand on this loop until the appropriate swaged cylinder is pulled down to the slotted hook on the mast. Jib leads have a fore-and-aft adjustment only, and usually the correct adjustment lies near the center of the short track located on the side deck.

The sloop-rigged Skipjack carries a two-man crew (skipper plus a crew member). Team work is required to sail any boat effectively, but this is especially true with this type of boat in a breeze. The crew does most of the hiking and shifting of his weight for the purpose of correcting the angle of heel so that the skipper can be in the most comfortable and convenient position to concentrate on his helmsmanship. The skipper hikes or moves his weight inboard only if it is really necessary. The boat should be kept at a more or less consistent angle of heel. During a puff the crew should hike, but during the lulls he should move inboard or even to leeward in light airs. In heavy winds, of course, both skipper and crew must hike to keep the boat flat.

Duties of the crew are: to trim the jib, tend the centerboard, adjust the vang and downhaul, hike, shift his weight fore and aft to affect hull trim, keep a lookout for other boats, and be alert for any maneuvering situations that should be called to the skipper's attention. The jib should be trimmed flat most of the time when beating except in light airs and in rough seas at which times it should be eased. Cam-action jam cleats are provided for the jib sheets. The sheet is belayed by pulling it down into the cams, but a tug upward will release it quickly. The centerboard is lifted with a tackle which may be adjusted from either side of the boat. The board is held down by a stout rubber cord. When running, the board is pulled all the way up, but when beating it is usually all the way down. On a reach, the board should not be down any farther than is necessary to prevent the boat from making excessive leeway. Opinions differ somewhat as to the proper board adjustment when jibing a light dinghy in a breeze. Most authorities agree that the board should not be all the way down because these boats have a tendency to trip on their board, which will encourage a capsizing. Many consider it dangerous to carry the board all the way up because of side slipping and the tendency of the boat to roll and yaw in a heavy seaway. As a general rule it is the best policy, when jibing in a breeze, to carry the board about a quarter of the way down or slightly farther up.

Duties of the skipper are: to steer, handle the mainsheet, instruct the crew as to sail adjustment when necessary, look around frequently to keep a lookout and size up maneuvering situations, operate the bailer when necessary, and of course, make the major decisions during a race or in an emergency. When steering with the tiller extension, the extension arm must be kept almost at right angles with the tiller, because if the angle becomes extremely obtuse (the extension arm tending to make a straight line with the tiller), then the tiller might be unintentionally flipped in the wrong direction. The mainsheet should always be held in hand unless it is temporarily jammed in the cam-action jam cleat in such a way that the sheet may be released instantly with an upward pull. The skipper should always hold the helm in one hand; so, of course, this leaves only one hand for tending the sheet. This becomes awkward when it is necessary to trim the mainsail in very much. It

is sometimes necessary for the skipper to hold the sheet in his teeth while he slides his hand up the rope for a higher grip when the sail is being pulled in. In a fresh breeze it is often desirable for the crew to help with this operation. The helmsman's hands should usually be in constant motion slacking or trimming the mainsheet and/or moving the tiller to weave the smoothest course through the waves and to respond to puffs or lulls. When beating in a moderate breeze the tiller should not be jammed over violently but it should be moved quite rapidly. In light airs, of course, a slower, smoother tiller action is used.

Planing in a small dinghy is an exhilarating experience. At this time the boat lifts up and breaks away from her speed-retarding wave system. Requirements for planing are a strong breeze and a light displacement hull having a flat run aft. Following seas are often very helpful. A plane is usually attained most easily when sailing between a broad and a beam reach. To get on a plane the helmsman waits for a puff, heads up slightly if sailing low, and quickly trims in his mainsheet. As the boat begins to heel and pick up speed, he bears off but may have to trim in his sheets, because the apparent wind has been drawn forward due to the increased boat speed. At the same time the skipper and crew should hike out to keep the boat flat. Don't forget the rule for sailing to leeward: head up in the lulls and off in the puffs. Crew weight should be moved aft during a plane. This is particularly true when the bow begins to dig into the waves. The stern should not be allowed to bury, however. The boom vang is set up tight to remove sail twist, and the centerboard should usually be nearly all the way up when planing. Keep the jib full. On the other hand, the mainsail may be allowed to luff slightly when planing in a strong wind. A planing Skipjack is shown in Figure 62.

Skipjacks may be reefed by a simple *roller reefing* arrangement. The boom is pulled aft so that it disengages from a square plug at the gooseneck and then the boom is rotated by hand so that the foot of the sail is wrapped around the boom similar to a window shade. Roller reefing will be discussed in more detail

Figure 62 A SKIPJACK PLANING

Notice that the crew have their weight well aft to keep the bow up and that they are hiking to keep the boat flat. The boom is bowsed down with the vang, and the sails are being watched to see that they remain full as the apparent wind draws ahead when the boat picks up speed.

when we describe the Luders yawls in the next chapter. Skipjacks are seldom reefed, however, because they can be sailed effectively under mainsail alone, and when racing they usually need maximum sail off the wind for planing purposes. It seldom pays to reef on a short upwind leg of a race course because of the time involved in the reefing operation. In such conditions, the boats can nearly always be kept flat by letting the main luff and by feathering. In a really strong breeze, races are quite often cancelled.

At the Naval Academy, Skipjacks are kept out of water on *cradles* (wooden supports) built on *floats* (floating docks). The boats are pulled out of the water bow first and launched stern first. Most of the rigging preparation for sailing

should be done while the boat is afloat. It can be harmful to the hull to climb aboard a Skipjack while she is on the cradle.

The Shields Class

In 1963, five Shields class sloops were donated to the Naval Academy by Mr. Cornelius Shields, one of America's most famous yachtsmen. This class was designed by Sparkman and Stephens to specifications suggested by Mr. Shields. Since Mr. Shields was an organizer, founder, and champion of the well-known International One-Design class, it is not surprising that the Shields sloops bear a resemblance to the Internationals. The Shields boats are built of fiberglass by the Chris-Craft Corporation. Their dimensions are 30 feet, 2½ inches, length over-all, 20 feet on the waterline, 6 feet, 5¼ inches beam, and 4 feet, 9 inches draft. They carry 360 square feet of sail on aluminum spars.

Figures 63 and 64 illustrate Shields sloops. Notice that her standing rigging plan is basically similar to the seven-eighths rig shown in Figure 55, except that the Shields does not carry jumper stays or struts. It is interesting that the original rigging plans for the Shields called for jumpers, but evidently it was felt later that the boat did not need these extra stays. Obviously, the simplest rig that can control the mast effectively is the best. Superfluous rigging causes tuning complications, windage, and extra weight aloft, which is harmful to a boat's stability. Also the elimination of jumper stays allows a jib which is slightly longer on the luff when this is considered desirable.

This sloop rig might be termed semi-flexible. The spars are not bent nearly as much as the Skipjack's, but the Shields mast is bowed in a breeze to some extent. This bowing is accomplished by tightening the permanent backstay, which may be adjusted from the cockpit. Instead of having a turnbuckle, as have the jib stay and shrouds, the backstay runs through the after deck, and it is attached to a tackle which lies under the deck and may be controlled from the cockpit's after end. It is customary to tighten the backstay when beating to windward in a breeze, but to slack it when running. The single

Figure 63 SHIELDS SLOOP, SAIL PLAN

THE SHIELDS ONE-DESIGN CLASS

LENGTH OVER ALL	30 FEET, 2½ INCHES
LENGTH WATER LINE	20 FEET
BEAM	6 FEET, 5¼ INCHES
DRAFT	4 FEET, 9 INCHES
SAIL AREA	360 SQUARE FEET

pair of lower shrouds are usually carried quite slack for two reasons: to keep the mast straight laterally and, since the lowers are slightly abaft the uppers, to allow the mast's middle to bow forward when the backstay is tightened. The mast should be raked aft very slightly. If a plumb line were dropped from the after side of the mast head, the plumb bob should lie about six inches abaft the base of the mast at the deck.

Sails are of dacron, and they are fitted with conventional short battens. No means of reefing is provided. When sailing in a fresh breeze, it is necessary to ease the mainsheet and let the mainsail luff slightly, or, in a strong breeze to drop the mainsail and sail under jib alone. The mainsheet is a tackle at the boom's after end. It does not have a sliding lead but trims from a fixed point. Jib sheets have leads on tracks which allow athwartships as well as fore-and-aft adjustments. Halyards and sheets are provided with winches for extra power; winches will be discussed in more detail in the next chapter.

Halyards are controlled from the forward end of the cockpit, with the main halyard and winch under the deck, while the jib halyard is on the port side above the deck. Lines belayed on deck at the forward end of the cockpit include the halyard, lift, and downhaul for the spinnaker. (Spinnaker handling will be discussed in Chapter 8.) The boom is equipped with a powerful vang, and this is especially important for sail shaping, because the Shields has a large mainsail and a lightweight boom. The boom is also fitted with an adjustable downhaul.

A Shields sloop is delightful to sail, especially on the wind in a moderate breeze. With her short keel and cutaway forefoot, she turns rapidly and has a sensitive helm. When properly tuned, she balances well with just a slight weather helm when moderately heeled. She responds to every touch of the tiller and can be worked to windward effectively using the technique discussed in Chapter 4. Although she is not nearly as heavy as the knockabout, she gives a feeling of power when beating against a chop, and her narrow hull knifes through the waves without appreciably being slowed by them. Her moderately light weight and large

Figure 64 THE SHIELDS SLOOP COMPANION BEATING TO WINDWARD

The jumper struts and stays shown in this picture are no longer in use. It appears as though the skipper is watching intently his masthead wind indicator. This is very helpful to good helmsmanship, but telltales placed low on the shrouds are usually just as effective and prevent the helmsman from getting a crick in his neck.

sail area make her a good performer in light air, despite the fact that she carries no Genoa jib. On account of her ample keel ballast, she is quite *stiff* (resistant to extreme heeling) in a breeze. She will heel fairly easily to a certain point, but then rapidly gains in stability. Although it is possible (but not likely) for her to swamp, she is unsinkable. Flotation tanks fore and aft and in the bilge are said to be sufficient to buoy up the swamped boat with as many as thirteen people aboard, although normally she carries only three or four crew members.

Shields sloops are moored in a similar manner as the knockabouts (see Figure 65), and roughly the same basic problems are faced when getting under way or landing. The Shields are somewhat more maneuverable, carry less way, and handle better under jib alone than do the knockabouts. Neither class has self-draining cockpits, but the

Figure 65 THE MOORING ARRANGEMENT FOR THE SHIELDS SLOOPS
Notice such details as the boom vang, halyard lead blocks at the base of the mast, and absence of mainsheet traveller.

Shields are equipped with cloth cockpit covers which are set, when the boats are left moored, for the purpose of keeping out rain water.

Rules of the Road

On today's crowded waterways, it is extremely important to know the rules which govern boat traffic. There are separate rules for boats under power, and these will be explained in Chapter 11; but in this section, we will discuss sailboat rules. A sailboat has the right of way over a power boat except when the former is overtaking the latter. Also a sailboat must keep clear of boats fishing with nets, lines, or trawls.

Figure 66 shows the rules which cover converging situations for a sailboat meeting another sailboat. These are the Inland Rules, for U. S. waters. When on the high seas, vessels operate under International Rules, which are quite different in some respects from the present Inland Rules. The Inland Rules were developed in the days of square-rigged sailing ships that were handicapped when beating to windward; therefore these rules favor the close-hauled boat. International Rules, however, have been modernized, and these will be discussed in Chapter 10, when we discuss sailing offshore. Obviously, Inland Rules, shown in Figure 66, are used on the Chesapeake Bay. Under the

80

Steering and Sailing Rules of the Inland Rules, when two sailing vessels are approaching one another so as to involve risk of collision, one of them shall keep out of the way of the other as follows, namely:

- A vessel which is running free shall keep out of the way of a vessel which is close-hauled.
- A vessel which is close-hauled on the port tack shall keep out of the way of a vessel which is close-hauled on the starboard tack.
- When both are running free, with the wind on different sides, the vessel which has the wind on the port side shall keep out of the way of the other.
- When both are running free, with the wind on the same side, the vessel which is to the windward shall keep out of the way of the vessel which is to the leeward.
- A vessel which has the wind aft shall keep out of the way of the other vessel.

Another situation not covered under the preceding rules would arise if a sailboat overtakes another sailboat on the same tack and the same point of sailing when neither is to windward of the other. In this case, the overtaken boat is privileged or has the right of way. The overtaking boat is burdened and must keep clear. In any converging situation the privileged boat must hold her course until there is no longer any danger of collision. If a sailboat is equipped with an auxiliary engine, the only time she is considered a sailboat is when she is propelled by sail alone.

Common sense and courtesy should be exercised at all times on the water. A sailboat skipper should never demand his right of way when converging with a large ship in constricted waters. In fact, International Rules and Inland Rules strictly forbid sailboats to hamper large power vessels in a narrow channel. Boats which are not racing should attempt to stay out of the way of boats which are racing, even though the former have the right of way. Rules for racing are quite different from the present Inland Rules of the Road. Racing rules apply only to boats racing among themselves. Obviously, these rules don't apply to boats not racing. Racing rules will be taken up in Chapter 9.

Figure 66 RIGHT OF WAY SITUATIONS FOR BOATS UNDER SAIL

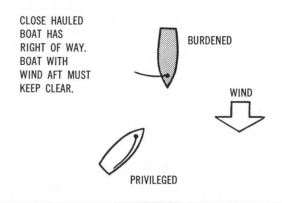

CLOSE HAULED BOAT HAS RIGHT OF WAY. BOAT WITH WIND AFT MUST KEEP CLEAR.

BURDENED

WIND

PRIVILEGED

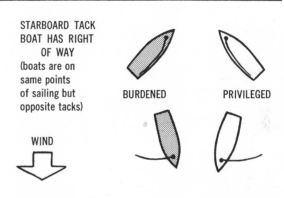

STARBOARD TACK BOAT HAS RIGHT OF WAY (boats are on same points of sailing but opposite tacks)

BURDENED

PRIVILEGED

WIND

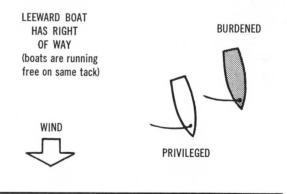

LEEWARD BOAT HAS RIGHT OF WAY (boats are running free on same tack)

BURDENED

WIND

PRIVILEGED

OVERTAKING BOAT MUST KEEP CLEAR EVEN IF OVERTAKEN BOAT IS UNDER POWER

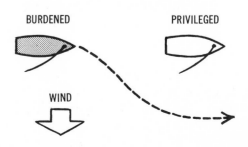

BURDENED

PRIVILEGED

WIND

CHAPTER SEVEN

Luders Yawls

In addition to having a fleet of small sailing craft, the Naval Academy owns and maintains twelve nearly identical 44-foot Luders yawls. These offer an excellent and unique opportunity for training in large ocean-racing sailboats. These boats carry a full complement of light sails, and they may be used as a class (racing against each other), or they can compete against comparable boats of different designs under a handicap system. A safe and seaworthy design, the Naval Academy yawls have been raced in many ocean races, even across the North Atlantic.

These yawls were designed for the Naval Academy in 1939 by the Luders Marine Construction Company of Stamford, Connecticut. The original twelve boats, the last of which were completed in 1943, were built of wood. Since 1963, however, the wooden yawls are being gradually replaced with fiberglass versions. Although hull forms and rigs are nearly identical, there are certain differences between the wooden and fiberglass yawls. For instance, the wooden boats are engineless, while the fiberglass boats are fitted with diesel power; the old boats have wooden spars, while the new ones are fitted with aluminum masts and have improvements in the rigging, some of which will be discussed later; accommodations below have been changed considerably, and the new boats carry slightly more keel ballast than the old boats. Eventually, all wooden yawls will be replaced by fiberglass yawls.

The dimensions of the Luders yawls are as follows: length overall, 44 feet, 2½ inches; length water line, 30 feet, 1 inch; maximum beam, 10 feet, 10½ inches; draft, 6 feet, ⅜ inch; mainmast height from deck to masthead, 52 feet, 3 inches; displacement (light) (fiberglass), 22,260 pounds; keel ballast (fiberglass), 9,850 pounds; keel ballast (wood), 9,000 pounds; and working sail area (main, mizzen, and forestaysail), 722 square feet.

Figure 67 shows a Luders yawl under sail. The shape of the Luders hull may be seen in Figures 68 and 69. The interior layout for the fiberglass yawls is shown in Figure 70, and that for the wooden yawls in Figure 71. The sail and deck plan for the fiberglass yawls is Figure 72.

Yawl Rigging

Figure 72 also shows the rigging of the Luders yawl. The rig is basically a masthead plan with a headstay and an opposing permanent

Figure 67 THE LUDERS YAWL UNDER SHORTENED SAIL

The yawl **Frolic** close hauled under the well balanced rig of mainsail and forestaysail. The photo was taken in about 1953. Since then anchor windlasses (shown on her foredeck) have been removed. The forestaysail halyard needs setting up, the main topping lift wants some slack, and the mizzen might be furled a bit more securely.

backstay on the mainmast. At a distance of about fifteen feet down from the *truck* (top of the mast) on the mast's fore side a forestay is attached. The forestay has two functions: to support the forestaysail, of course, and also to help prevent fore-and-aft bending below the headstay. Runners (running backstays) are attached to the mast at the same point to prevent the mast from bowing forward at the forestay's point of attachment. Originally the yawls were designed to carry jumper stays and struts to eliminate the need for running backstays, but jumpers would have interfered with the tacking of large headsails; and so it was decided that runners would be used.

Figure 68 &69 HULL OF THE FIBERGLASS LUDERS YAWL, **FEARLESS**

This photograph, together with the lines, shows a successful compromise between an able, seakindly, fairly heavy displacement hull and one that is easily driven. The slack bilges (having a gradual, as opposed to a sharp curve) and moderate deadrise lessen wetted surface for speed and give an easy motion in a seaway. These factors make for a boat which will heel quite easily initially, but that will become increasingly stiff as her ample keel ballast becomes effective at higher angles of heel. The keel is of sufficient length to give good directional stability, but it is sufficiently cut away forward to reduce wetted surface and to assure reasonably quick helm response. The keel is also of ample draft to assure good performance when beating to windward, and the deep draft allows the keel ballast to be placed low where it is most effective. With their long graceful overhangs, moderate freeboard, graceful sheer, and sleek underbody, the Luders yawls are among the most aesthetically pleasing of sailing yachts.

Actually these stays are not used at all times but only when it is blowing hard enough to bend the mast or when the forestaysail is set. Likewise, the forestay is not usually set up in a light to moderate breeze. When not in use, it is released from its deck fitting by a lever and is brought aft, slack, and clipped to the shrouds. In this position, it will not interfere with the tacking of a large Genoa jib. The aluminum masts are stiffer than the wooden ones; therefore on the new yawls, forestays and backstays are usually not needed except when a Genoa is carried in a fresh breeze. The need for these stays varies with individual boats. Some masts are more limber than others. The proper time for setting up these running stays should be determined by sighting up the mast. If it is bowing more than very slightly, set them up. Don't take a chance on breaking the mast.

At their lower ends the running backstays have *whips* (a tackle in which only one block is

used. See Figure 72). One end of the whip has an eye which fits on a hook secured to the deck, while the whip's other end is adjusted with a lever (on the wooden yawls) or a winch (on the fiberglass yawls). When the runners are in use, naturally the one to leeward is slacked, while the one to windward is tightened with its lever or winch. However, when the runners are not in use, the eye ends of the whip are released from their hooks and the stays are brought forward, slack, and are secured to the after shrouds. The shrouds are provided with snap shackles for holding the runners.

The mizzenmast on a wooden yawl is provided with a backstay that is set up with a *pelican hook* (a hinged hook that is held closed with a sliding ring). A mizzen backstay is usually not set up unless the mizzen staysail is carried in a moderate breeze. This sail has a strong tendency to pull the mast forward. Of course, the backstay must be released when tacking or

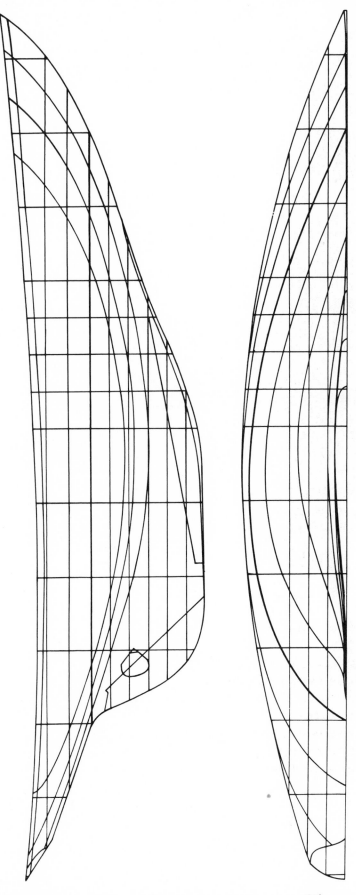

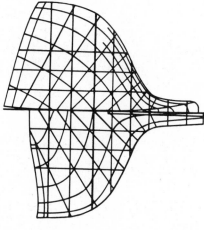

LENGTH OVERALL: 44 FEET 2½ INCHES
LENGTH WATER LINE: 30 FEET 1 INCH
BEAM EXTREME: 10 FEET 10½ INCHES
DRAFT: 6 FEET ⅜ INCH
MAST FROM DECK TO MASTHEAD: 52 FEET 3 INCHES
DISPLACEMENT (light):   22,260 POUNDS
BALLAST: WOOD   9,000 POUNDS
       FIBERGLASS   9,850 POUNDS

Figure 69 LUDERS YAWL, LINES

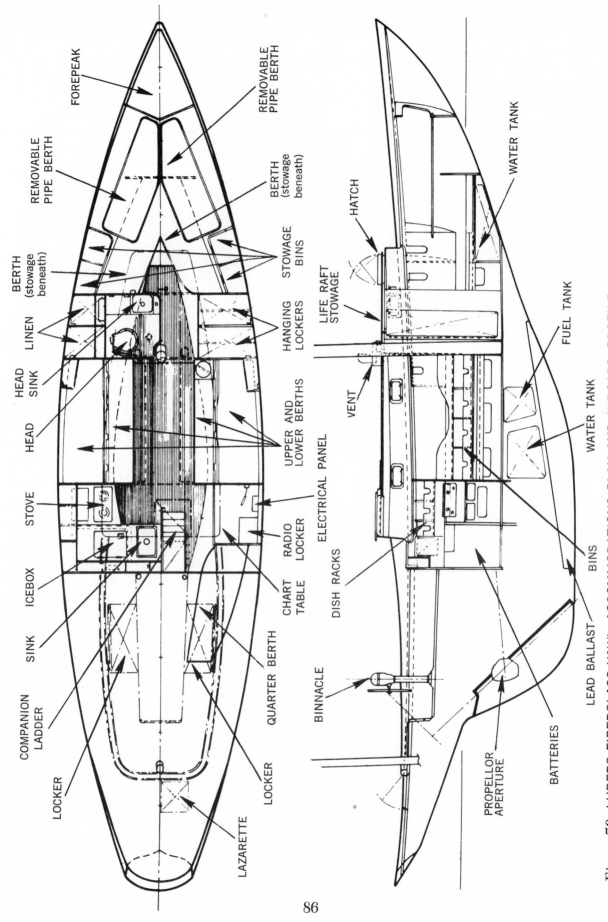

FOREPEAK

REMOVABLE
PIPE BERTH

REMOVABLE PIPE BERTH

BERTH
(stowage
beneath)

BERTH
(stowage beneath)

STOWAGE BINS

LINEN

HEAD
SINK

HANGING
LOCKERS

HEAD

UPPER AND
LOWER BERTHS

STOVE

ELECTRICAL PANEL

SINK

ICEBOX

RADIO
LOCKER

COMPANION
LADDER

CHART
TABLE

LOCKER

QUARTER BERTH

LOCKER

LAZARETTE

WATER TANK

HATCH

LIFE RAFT
STOWAGE

FUEL TANK

VENT

WATER TANK

DISH RACKS

BINS

BINNACLE

LEAD BALLAST

BATTERIES

PROPELLOR
APERTURE

Figure 70 LUDERS FIBERGLASS YAWL, ACCOMMODATIONS PLAN AND INBOARD PROFILE

86

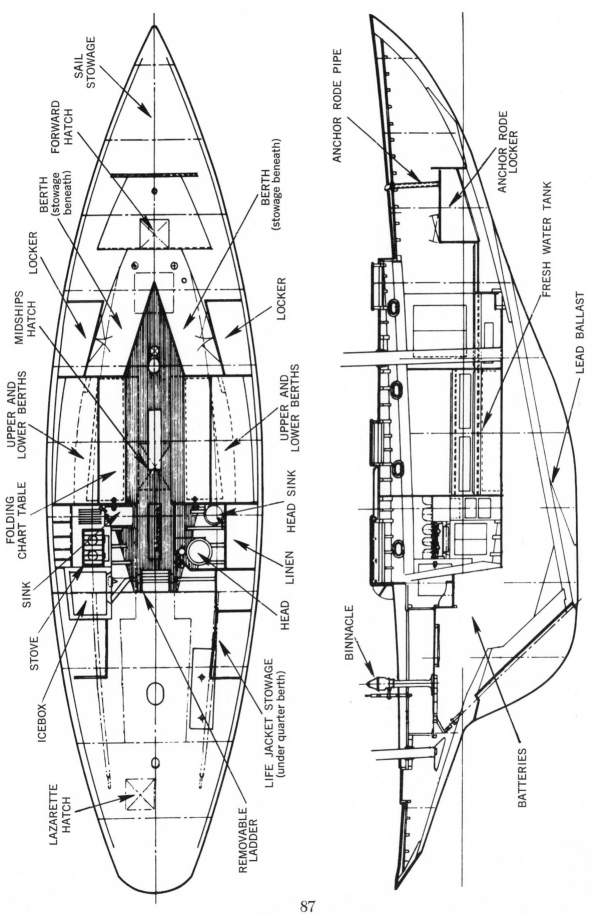

SAIL STOWAGE

FORWARD HATCH

BERTH (stowage beneath)

BERTH (stowage beneath)

LOCKER

MIDSHIPS HATCH

LOCKER

LOCKER

UPPER AND LOWER BERTHS

UPPER AND LOWER BERTHS

FOLDING CHART TABLE

HEAD SINK

SINK

LINEN

STOVE

HEAD

ICEBOX

LIFE JACKET STOWAGE (under quarter berth)

LAZARETTE HATCH

REMOVABLE LADDER

ANCHOR RODE PIPE

ANCHOR RODE LOCKER

FRESH WATER TANK

LEAD BALLAST

BINNACLE

BATTERIES

Figure 71 LUDERS WOODEN YAWL, ACCOMMODATIONS PLAN AND INBOARD PROFILE

87

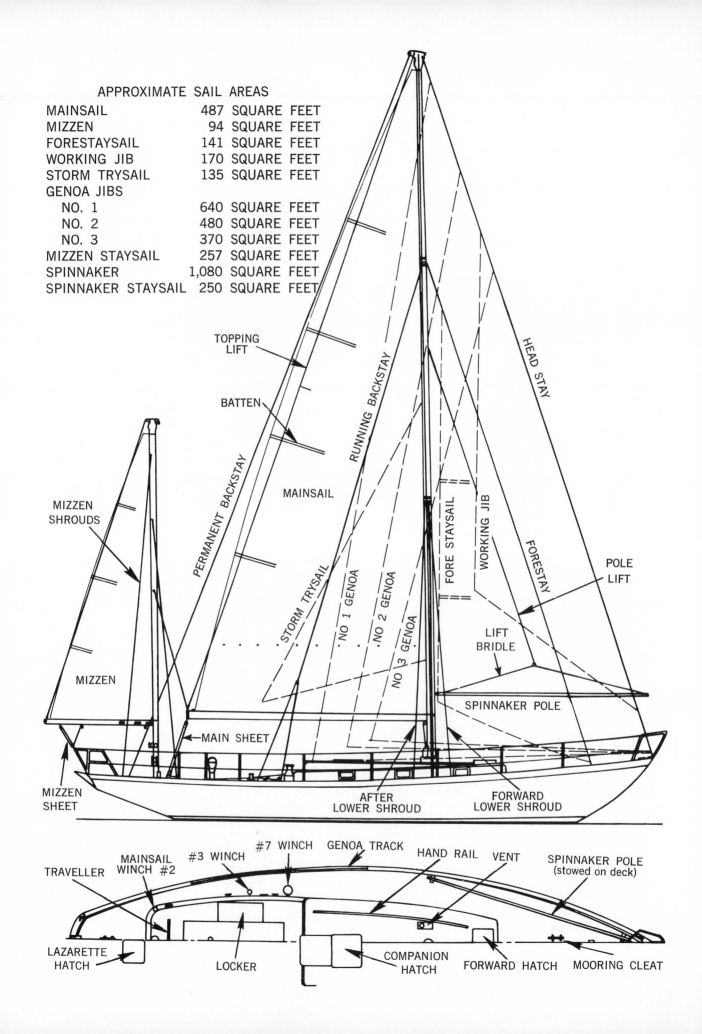

APPROXIMATE SAIL AREAS

MAINSAIL	487 SQUARE FEET
MIZZEN	94 SQUARE FEET
FORESTAYSAIL	141 SQUARE FEET
WORKING JIB	170 SQUARE FEET
STORM TRYSAIL	135 SQUARE FEET
GENOA JIBS	
NO. 1	640 SQUARE FEET
NO. 2	480 SQUARE FEET
NO. 3	370 SQUARE FEET
MIZZEN STAYSAIL	257 SQUARE FEET
SPINNAKER	1,080 SQUARE FEET
SPINNAKER STAYSAIL	250 SQUARE FEET

TOPPING LIFT

BATTEN

HEAD STAY

RUNNING BACKSTAY

PERMANENT BACKSTAY

MIZZEN SHROUDS

MAINSAIL

FORE STAYSAIL

WORKING JIB

FORESTAY

POLE LIFT

STORM TRYSAIL

NO 1 GENOA

NO 2 GENOA

NO 3 GENOA

LIFT BRIDLE

MIZZEN

SPINNAKER POLE

MAIN SHEET

MIZZEN SHEET

AFTER LOWER SHROUD

FORWARD LOWER SHROUD

TRAVELLER

MAINSAIL WINCH #2

#3 WINCH

#7 WINCH

GENOA TRACK

HAND RAIL

VENT

SPINNAKER POLE (stowed on deck)

LAZARETTE HATCH

LOCKER

COMPANION HATCH

FORWARD HATCH

MOORING CLEAT

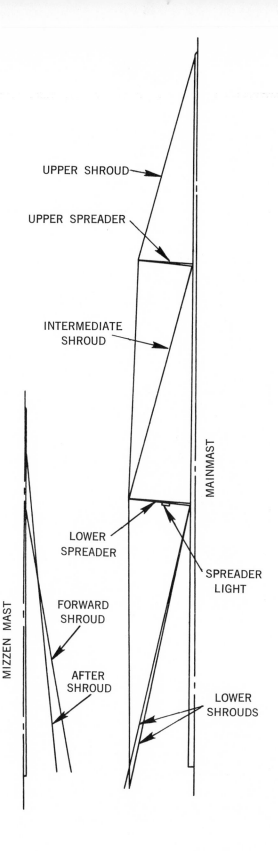

UPPER SHROUD

UPPER SPREADER

INTERMEDIATE
SHROUD

MAINMAST

LOWER
SPREADER

SPREADER
LIGHT

MIZZEN MAST

FORWARD
SHROUD

AFTER
SHROUD

LOWER
SHROUDS

Figure 72

LUDERS FIBERGLASS YAWL;
SAIL, RIGGING, AND HALF-DECK PLANS

jibing. Fiberglass yawls have the chainplates for the mizzen after shrouds located much farther aft than on the wooden yawls; therefore on the new boats, mizzen backstays are really not necessary. The mizzenmast is fitted with a jumper stay running over a strut; it keeps the top of the mast from bending aft.

Looking at the rigging plan from the bow or stern, we can see that the mainmast has two sets of spreaders and has intermediate shrouds as well as upper and two sets of lower shrouds. Although the rigging seems complicated, it involves merely the same tuning principles as were discussed in Chapter 5. The upper shrouds should be kept fairly taut, while the intermediates are slightly less taut, and the lowers are still less taut. The after and forward lowers are adjusted to keep the mast straight. Obviously, this is a masthead rig and the sails are cut for a straight mast; thus the mast should be kept straight, both fore and aft and athwartships at all times. The headstay and backstay should be kept quite taut for efficient windward sailing. In my opinion, it is a good idea to tighten these stays slightly before a race but to slack them off again after the race. This lets the boat relax and keeps the strain off her most of the time. The yawls are designed to carry their masts with a slight rake aft of about 26 inches, which gives them a proper, slight weather helm. Of course this may vary slightly with individual boats because of differences in trim and sails.

Most of the running rigging consists of ½-inch dacron sheets and a combination of wire and dacron for halyards. There are five halyards on the mainmast: one for the forestaysail and spinnaker staysail which runs through a block just below the point of attachment of the forestay, a main halyard, two masthead jib halyards running through mast sheaves (pulley set into the masthead as shown in Figure 73) on the fiberglass yawls, and a spinnaker halyard running through a block hung just above and forward of the point of attachment of the headstay. Also there is a spinnaker pole lift which runs through a block hung on the fore side of the mast some distance below the upper spreaders. All these lines belay at the base of the mast. The wooden yawls have a double purchase or tackle arrange-

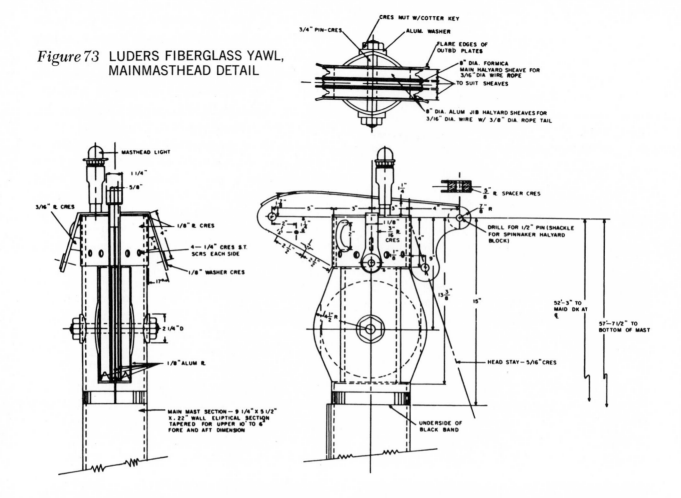

Figure 73 LUDERS FIBERGLASS YAWL, MAINMASTHEAD DETAIL

ment for their main halyards and a Number 2 ratchet main halyard winch on the mast. The halyard is wrapped three or four times around the winch after the sail is almost hoisted. The fiberglass boats, however, have a different main halyard arrangement. Their halyards are single wires which wind up on reel winches, similar in principle to fishing line reels. When the sail is hoisted, the entire halyard has been wound around the reel. The operation of winches will be discussed near the end of this chapter.

There is also a difference between the wooden and fiberglass yawls in their sheeting arrangements for most sails. On the former, there are adjustable forestaysail leads consisting of slides on tracks mounted on the side decks. On the new fiberglass boats, forestaysail sheets are led to one of two pad eyes on each side to which lead blocks are fastened. Both wooden and fiberglass yawls have main sheet travellers abaft the cockpit, but on the wooden boats, the

sheet runs along the underside of the boom to a block near the gooseneck, and then it is led back to a cleat and winch atop the cabin house near its after end on the starboard side. On the fiberglass boats, however, the sheet is controlled from the after end of the cockpit. The sheet tackle is arranged so that it may be adjusted from either side of the boat. There is a mainsheet winch and cleat on the starboard side and another winch and cleat directly opposite on the port side. Genoa sheets are essentially the same for all boats. These sheets lead outside the shrouds through blocks on adjustable slides that attach to tracks mounted on the rails. They are then taken to winches through a *turning block* (block used to change the direction of a line), as shown in Figure 74.

The mizzen running rigging includes the mizzen halyard, which has a Number 2 winch on the starboard side of the mast, and a mizzen staysail halyard, which has a similar winch on the mast's port side. On the wooden yawls, the mizzen sheet is double purchased and is provided with a Number 2 winch mounted on the lower, after side of the mizzen mast. The sheet's cleat is just below the winch. The mizzen staysail sheet is led through a block at the end of the mizzen boom and belays to a cleat on the boom.

Yawl Sails

Yawl mainsails are made of heavy dacron and have an area of 487 square feet. They are usually left furled and stopped on the boom when the boats are not in use. The sails are se-

cured to their spars with tracks and slides. The main boom's gooseneck may slide up or down on the mast, and all luff tension adjustments are made with the boom downhaul. The sail is hoisted until the top of the headboard (the plate in the head of the mainsail) is even with the bottom of the black band at the masthead, and then the downhaul is adjusted to give the proper luff tension appropriate to the wind velocity or a particular point of sailing. When sighting aloft to align the headboard with the black band, remember that you are sighting from directly beneath, and the extreme perspective will make it appear that the headboard is higher relative to the band than it really is. Once a main-

Figure 74

A FIBERGLASS LUDERS YAWL ON THE WIND

This close view of the **Fearless** working to windward full and bye shows the Genoa sheeting arrangement. Note that the sheet runs through the sliding lead block on the track on the rail, through a turning block abaft the lead block, and then forward to the large winch. To get extra power, the crew has then led the sheet across the boat to the weather winch. The helmsman is sitting to leeward where he can get a clear view of the jib. The slot is kept fairly wide to avoid backwind. Observe the dinghy in her chocks and secured by criss crossed straps. The mizzen might set a little better if its topping lift were slacked.

Figure 75 ROLLER REEFING

WORM GEAR

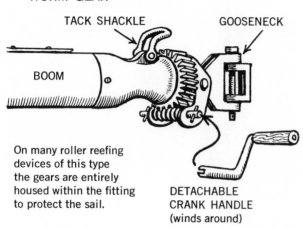

TACK SHACKLE

GOOSENECK

BOOM

On many roller reefing
devices of this type
the gears are entirely
housed within the fitting
to protect the sail.

DETACHABLE
CRANK HANDLE
(winds around)

sail is hoisted to its proper height, it is often possible to mark the halyard with a piece of tape which can be aligned with another tape mark on the mast for future reference. It is important to hoist the mainsail as high as possible for two reasons: in light airs there is usually more wind aloft, and the maximum distance between upper and lower black bands may be utilized fully to tighten the luff in a fresh breeze.

The clew outhaul on the main boom of the fiberglass yawls has an easy-to-operate screw gear and crank handle at the boom's after end for tightening or slacking the mainsail's foot. When not in use, the crank handle is folded into a housing well on the boom. The mainsail clew on any yawl should never be pulled abaft the forward edge of the black band at the boom's end. Never forget to *slack the outhaul* of any furled sail left bent on its boom. Before hoisting or lowering the mainsail, be sure that the boom topping lift (see Figure 72) is set up, and that it is slacked off when under way. Sailing with a taut topping lift is nearly always harmful to the set of a sail.

Mainsails on the wooden yawls are reefed in the conventional way, similar to reefing in the knockabouts. Of course the yawls do not have loose-footed mainsails as have the knockabouts, but the reefing procedures are essentially the same with the reef points passing between the sail's foot and the boom. Never tie the reef points around the boom (see Figure 60). Since some yawls are equipped with more than one row of reef points, it is very important, before hoisting sail, to check that all the tied reef points are from the same row. A sail could be seriously torn if some points were tied from the first row while others were tied from the second row. If a mainsail is not equipped with reef points but only a row of eyelets, then a long, continuous reefing line may be rove through the eyelets and around the foot of the sail (not around the boom). If a reef is taken in while under way, it is easier to lower the mainsail before reefing it, but this is not essential. To reef without lowering sail, set up the topping lift and sail close-hauled with a slight luff in the mainsail, ease the halyard until the luff cringle comes down to the boom, set up the tack earing and then the clew earing, tie in the reef points, and finally hoist the sail until the luff is taut and slack the topping lift.

The fiberglass yawls are equipped with roller reefing. With this reefing method, the mainsail is rolled up on its boom, which may be rotated with a gear and crank handle at the gooseneck. Figure 75 shows a worm-gear roller reefing mechanism similar to that used on the Navy yawls. For clarity, the illustration shows the gears exposed, but in actuality they lie within a metal housing so that the sail will not get caught in the gears. With roller reefing, sail is never lowered entirely before reefing. The halyard is simply eased off as the crank is turned. The bottom four slides on the mainsail are attached to the *jack line* (a small line on the sail's luff). Before reefing, the jack line is unrove from the slides allowing them to remain on the track when the sail is wound around the boom. If a deeper reef is required, the upper slides must be removed from the track, one at a time, when they are pulled down to the bottom of the track by the boom's rotation. It is nearly always necessary to have one or two crew members pulling aft on the sail's leech near the clew, in order that the roll be kept smooth all the way along the boom. The mainsheet is attached to a swivel fitting at the end of the boom. Someone should check to see that this fitting is swivelling smoothly as the boom is turned. When unrolling a reef, the procedure is reversed. The boom is turned in the opposite direction unwinding the sail, while the halyard is taken up and the slides are fed back onto the track and/or the bottom four slides are secured to the sail.

The mizzen on a Navy yawl is quite similar to the mainsail except, of course, that it is comparatively very small, with an area of 94 square feet. For this reason it is not provided with any means of reefing. The clew outhaul is a slide on a track controlled with a purchase, but the gooseneck is fixed, so luff tension must be controlled with the halyard. The mizzen's primary function is to act as a balancing sail. When the sail is sheeted in flat, weather helm is increased, but when the sheet is eased, weather helm is lessened. Because the mizzen is usually backwinded by the mainsail when sailing close hauled, some sailors feel that the mizzen is of little value on a beat. However, it actually has considerable value as a balancing sail, particularly in light airs, to give the boat a little weather helm. As said previously, this helm is important to give the keel hydrodynamic lift and especially to give the helmsman a "helm feel." In a strong breeze, when weather helm is excessive, the mizzen can be lowered, and this will nearly always relieve the boat's strong tendency to round up into the wind. One of the advantages of the yawl rig is that in a squall or gale the mainsail may be lowered and balance will be maintained under forestaysail and mizzen. Also, unless the boat is heeled excessively, reasonable balance can be had under mainsail and forestaysail, or even under mainsail alone, if it is desired that the jib and mizzen be lowered (see Figures 54 and 67).

The forestaysail is a fairly small (area, 141 square feet), heavy sail with battens, and it is hanked on to the forestay. It is the basic, working headsail on a yawl. Usually this sail is set in a strong breeze only, or when squalls threaten, or when a yawl is undermanned in a moderate breeze. The most usual sail combinations that include the forestaysail are as follows:

• Main, mizzen, forestaysail and a high-cut working jib hanked on to the headstay. This combination of sails forward of the mainmast is known as the *double head rig*, and it is some-

Figure 76 THE NUMBER ONE GENOA JIB

This picture shows the sail from two different views. Most Genoas have concave leeches (reverse roaches), because they are not fitted with battens. This leech curve is especially important with the Luders yawls in order that the leech will clear the upper spreaders. On the Resolute (starboard tack), the Genoa's foot seems to be stretched overly taut against the shrouds. This might be relieved by moving the lead further forward provided that the knot or splice in the sheet is not pulled into the lead block. In this light breeze, she might foot a little faster with the main sheet started an inch or two.

times carried when beating to windward in a fresh breeze. This combination can be very effective.

• Main and forestaysail, or reefed main and forestaysail, the latter especially a well balanced plan for a strong breeze.

• Mizzen and forestaysail for a gale or squall.

• Forestaysail alone in a strong gale. If the boat is heeled severely, this sail will balance the boat reasonably well even though it is well forward of the normal total center of effort (see Figure 54).

• Forestaysail set in combination with a Genoa jib, mainsail, and mizzen in squally weather, so that if a squall hits, Genoa and mainsail may be dropped quickly and the boat will be under a very short, balanced rig.

Light sails used on the yawls include three sizes of Genoa jibs, spinnaker (to be discussed in the next chapter), spinnaker staysail, mizzen staysail, and drifter. The large Genoa, called the number one Genoa, with an area of 640 square feet, is the "work horse" of a yawl in light weather. It supplies the principal driving power in a light breeze on all points of sailing, except when the wind is abaft the beam at which times the spinnaker comes into prominence. The number one is probably carried more often than any other sail except the main and mizzen. (See Figure 76.)

The number two is the next smaller size Genoa, and it has an area of 540 square feet. This is carried when the wind is too strong for the number one. It is hard to say exactly when jibs should be changed. This will depend on whether the boat is being raced or cruised, how many and how skilled are her crew, the cut and condition of the paticular jibs involved, and of course there is some variation in the stiffness of some yawls. To be very general, however, the number one should probably be replaced with the number two when the wind velocity is between 17 and 20 knots when the boat is racing.

When a boat begins to be overburdened with the number two Genoa, the number three should be used. This sail has an area of only 220 square feet. In a breeze which would warrant carrying this sail, perhaps 25 to 35 knots, there would be an option between the number three and the aforementioned double head rig. When reaching, especially in a race, the former might be preferable; but when beating, particularly into heavy seas, a low-cut Genoa often takes heavy spray and solid water against its foot and this could obviously damage the sail. Another factor to take into consideration is the trend of the weather. If it seems likely that the breeze will increase and develop into a gale, the double head rig will be preferable because the forestaysail is already set and the jib can be quickly doused if the wind becomes overpowering. When it comes to carrying only one headsail in a gale, the forestaysail is nearly always easier to manage than a long-tailed overlapping jib.

The drifter and spinnaker staysail have been discussed very briefly in Chapter 5. The former is a light-weather sail, and therefore it should have a lightweight sheet so that its clew will lift in the slightest zephyr. If it is cut high in the foot, its sheet should be led to a block on the end of the main boom when sailing between a beam reach and a close reach, in order that the sail be trimmed a maximum distance outboard (see Figure 47). Of course, when racing with the wind abaft the beam, the drifter is not carried because this is when the spinnaker is the most effective sail. These two sails should not be carried simultaneously, because they will interfere with each other's wind. Drifters are rarely carried on a beat except perhaps in the very lightest airs. On the wind, it is usually better to carry a lightweight number one Genoa, especially when there is a confused sea caused by power boat swells. The spinnaker staysail is carried simultaneously with the spinnaker because it is a low sail, designed to fill in the area beneath the spinnaker. This sail works best on a reach. It is usually blanketed too much by the mainsail to be effective when running (see Figure 47).

The mizzen staysail can be an effective sail on certain points of sailing; its area is 257 square feet, as opposed to the mizzen's 94 square feet. The most effective point of sailing for the mizzen staysail is the broad reach. When the wind draws abaft the quarter the sail begins to be blanketed by the mizzen, but when the wind draws forward of the quarter the staysail begins to backwind the mizzen. The mizzen staysail can almost never be carried on a dead run, and it can rarely be carried effectively on a beam reach. On this latter point of sailing, it not only backwinds the mizzen, but it is backwinded by the mainsail, and it also blankets the lower, after corner of the mainsail. The mizzen staysail is tacked down to a pad eye located on the windward side of the cabin top, or just inboard of the weather shrouds. Remember always to secure the tack to windward of the boat's centerline. The sail must be hoisted to leeward of the permanent backstay. Its sheet runs outside the mizzen shrouds, through a block on the end of the mizzen boom, and inboard (see Fig-

Figure 77 THE MIZZEN STAYSAIL

Although this yawl is able to carry her mizzen staysail, it is probably doing her little good, because the apparent wind direction is too far forward, and the sail is trimmed so flat that it is seriously backwinding the mizzen. Note that the upper spreaders are sagging dangerously. Each spreader should bisect its shroud angle (see Chapter 5).

ures 47 and 77).

As when trimming any sail on a reach, the mizzen staysail's sheet should be kept eased to the point where the sail begins to luff. In addition, there should be an ample slot between the leech of the staysail and the lee side of the mizzen. The clew of the staysail should never be pulled close to the mizzen boom when the mizzen is hoisted because of the problem with backwind. When pulling in on the staysail sheet, always watch the mizzen to see that it does not begin to bulge from the staysail's backwind. When this bulge occurs, the staysail's sheet must be eased or else the mizzen must be lowered. Occasionally it pays to lower the mizzen when it blankets the mizzen staysail or when the latter backwinds the former, because the staysail has the larger sail area. Once the mizzen staysail is basically well trimmed, it is often best to make fine trim adjustments with

the mizzen sheet. Since the staysail sheet is led to the mizzen boom, then obviously the mizzen sheet will also affect the staysail's trim. Making the adjustments with the mizzen sheet will keep the slot between staysail and mizzen wide, and also the staysail will be led the maximum distance outboard. When sailing close to a beam reach, be sure the staysail's luff is taut. When jibing, the mizzen staysail must be lowered and removed entirely before the main boom swings across. Then the staysail may be reset on the new tack, again with tack to windward and halyard to leeward. Don't forget to remove the mizzen backstay before jibing.

As said previously, the mizzen spinnaker is cut like a spinnaker but is set and sheeted like a conventional mizzen staysail. Unlike a conventional spinnaker set on the mainmast, the mizzen spinnaker is not equipped with a pole that holds the sail out to windward; therefore the mizzen spinnaker is particularly subject to being blanketed by the mizzen when the wind is far aft. On a run it often pays to lower the mizzen to avoid this blanketing. Although by tightening its luff the conventional mizzen staysail can be carried when sailing almost as high as a beam reach, the mizzen spinnaker, with its full cut, cannot be carried that close to the wind. In a fresh breeze, the mizzen spinnaker should be allowed to lift to the maximum extent. This means that the sheet and tack should be eased liberally. When the sail is well lifted, it also often pays to slack the halyard slightly to let the head of the sail move away from the mizzen's wind shadow.

Stowable Gear and Equipment

Before getting under way in a Navy yawl (or any boat), it is important to know the location of her gear and equipment. For obvious reasons, all stowable gear should be returned to its proper location. Heed the old expression, "a place for everything and everything in its place."

Figure 70 shows the accommodation plan of a fiberglass yawl. The arrangement of the wooden yawls is similar (see Figure 71), except that on these boats, the head is located aft on the starboard side, adjacent to the companion ladder.

Of course, the fiberglass yawls have much more practical and comfortable accommodations for the crew.

Locations for stowable gear are as follows:

• Life jackets are evenly distributed throughout the boat in order that they may be reached from anywhere regardless of the type of emergency that requires them.

• Two life rings are carried aft in holders attached to the mizzen shrouds. These rings should never be lashed in their holders.

• Sails are stowed forward under the foredeck in the wooden yawls, but in bins under the cockpit seats to port and starboard in the fiberglass yawls.

• Sheets are kept near the sail stowage area. In the wooden yawls, sheets are stowed in the labeled areas on either side of the mainmast. Genoa sheets are forward to starboard, spinnaker sheets aft to starboard, forestaysail sheets forward to port, and spare sheets and halyards aft to port. On the fiberglass boats, however, sheets are on the port side under the cockpit seat.

• *Snatch blocks* (removable, side-opening blocks) on the wooden yawls are stowed in drawers under the galley sink. When detaching a block from its pad eye, keep the sheet rove through the block until it is detached and has been moved inboard, so there is no possibility of dropping it overboard.

• Winch handles are stowed in drawers in the same area as the snatch blocks on the wooden boats. When under sail, if the handles are not in use, they are always kept in special holders in the cockpit.

• Snatch blocks and winch handles on the fiberglass boats are stowed in bins or drawers under the amidships bunks on the port and starboard sides.

• On all boats, reefing earings and sail stops are stowed in this same area, in the forward port drawers.

• These same drawers hold the tool kit, sail repair kit, and lead line.

• The fog horn is stowed in this area, although some yawls have it mounted on the cabin top.

• Flares and a first-aid kit are kept in the head, in lockers outboard against the hull.

• Fenders, a *fender board* (a plank hung over the side outboard of the fenders to protect the topsides when lying alongside a pier), a *bosun's chair* (a wooden seat used to haul a man up the mast), and certain cleaning gear is kept in the *lazarette* (space under the hatch on the after deck abaft the cockpit).

• Other cleaning gear is stowed in the galley.

• One Danforth anchor (about 40 pounds) is kept forward in the sail locker. An anchor line is stowed in the lazarette.

• A fire extinguisher is mounted in the galley and another is in the forward cabin. These are dry chemical extinguishers, and each crew member should be familiar with their operation. They should be checked frequently to be sure they are pressurized.

Each Luders yawl is equipped with one dinghy, a 7-foot, 9-inch, unsinkable, Dyer Dhow. The boats, which can be either rowed or sailed, are primarily for the sake of convenience in going to and from the yawls when they are anchored or moored offshore in various harbors away from home. However, the dinghies have a secondary safety purpose. Rules for ocean racing and even for racing on the Chesapeake Bay require that each yacht carry a dinghy or life raft, or both, and of course, these must be capable of taking off the entire crew in the event of an emergency. A Dyer Dhow can carry only three or four men, depending on their weight and the condition of the sea. The remainder of a yawl's crew are provided for with inflatable rubber life rafts, stowed on the cabin house, between the mast and the forward hatch.

When not in use, a Dhow is carried upside down on her yawl's cabin top. The dinghies are lashed to special *chocks* (wooden blocks specifically designed to hold a boat or other equipment in place so that it will not shift during an extreme angle of heel or in rough weather). Usually one continuous line, often the boat's *painter* (bow line), is used to lash a boat in her chocks. If the painter is used, it is run through the eye in either forward chock and then the line is passed over the boat's bottom to the after chock on the opposite side. Here the line is passed through the chock's eye, back over the boat's bottom, through the handgrip hole in the boat's skeg, and through the eye in the other after chock. The line is then passed over the boat's bottom to the forward chock on the opposite side, and here the line is secured with two half hitches. It is a wise precaution to finish off this knot with a slippery hitch (see Figure 14) for quick release in an emergency. As can be seen the lashing line will make a criss-cross pattern over the dinghy's bottom.

Oars, oarlocks, and a bailer should be lashed inside the dinghy.

A Dyer Dhow, weighing slightly less than 70 pounds, can easily be lifted aboard a yawl by two men. One man can lift the dinghy by her painter while another can lift her with a stern line made fast to the metal ring at her stern. An upward pull on these lines from a normal position on the yawl's deck at her rail above the dinghy, will not only lift the dinghy but tilt her over so that her lower gunwale can be rested on the yawl's rail. From here she can easily be lifted over the life lines, turned upside down, and placed on her chocks. When a dinghy is brought aboard in this manner, the yawl's topsides should be protected with fenders or lines draped over the side.

If a heavier boat is brought aboard, the main halyard can be used for lifting purposes. First a bridle is rigged from the stern ring to the bow ring, and then the halyard is shackled on to a loop in the center of the bridle. The bridle's loop should be in such a position that the boat is balanced or hangs horizontal when she is lifted clear of the water. Obviously, a great deal of power can be had with the halyard when it is put on a winch.

The Dyer Dhows are cat-rigged and are fitted with a removable rudder and dagger board. The boats have very small sails and are a bit sluggish in light airs, but in a moderate to fresh breeze they are quite responsive and great fun to sail. Yawl crews should rig and sail the dinghies whenever the opportunity arises, as they afford a good means of practicing the fundamentals of sailing (see Figure 78).

The Dhow's sail is attached to a spar which is hooked on to the top of a short mast. First the mast is stepped and then the sail is bent to the spar by sliding the sail's luff rope into a groove on the after side of the spar. Next the spar, with sail attached, is lifted up and hooked to the top of the mast. The sail is loose-footed and secures to the boom with a hook at the tack and a short outhaul at the clew. The boom's forward end has jaws which fit around the mast. The mainsheet is snapped to the traveller and rove through the sheet blocks.

The rudder is hooked to a vertical rod on the transom and the dagger board, stowed under the thwart, is slid down its well. Then the boat is ready to sail.

Figure 78 THE DYER DHOW

Crew weight is placed well so that the boat is not trimmed excessively by the stern. Notice that the mainsheet has fouled on its traveller on the fully shown boat.

Handling the Yawl Under Sail

Although it is possible to sail a Navy yawl *singlehanded* (with a crew of one), the Naval Academy requires that there be a minimum crew of four. When sailing with this minimum, one man obviously will be at the helm. Another man should be assigned to the cockpit area forward of the helmsman where he will tend the jib sheets and sheet winches. The third man should be assigned to the foredeck where he will tend to the mooring line, the halyards, and clear the jib if necessary when tacking. The fourth man should lend a hand either on the foredeck or in the cockpit. Sailing shorthanded requires careful planning ahead. The skipper should try to anticipate any difficulties that could arise as a result of having a small crew. A forestaysail or easy-to-handle jib should be carried in most cases.

The ideal racing crew for a Navy yawl generally numbers between seven and ten members (the new yawls have sleeping accommodations for nine). The yawls may be sailed with less than seven but not at maximum efficiency under all racing conditions, unless the crew are exceptionally skilled and experienced. When a crew numbers more than ten, some members are superfluous and they usually get in the way of each other and the working crew as well.

A crew should be divided into two groups, a foredeck crew and an after guard. The latter group is concentrated in or near the cockpit, and it consists of the skipper who is the principal helmsman, a relief helmsman who may tend the mizzen and mizzen staysail, a navigator who may double as a mainsheet tender or help with other sheets or backstays, and the winch men. The foredeck group has a foredeck captain or person in charge of all activities forward of the mainmast, and he has at least two assistants. This forward group is particularly busy when the spinnaker is set.

The wooden yawls are moored offshore on permanent anchors. It is usually much easier to leave and return to these moorings under sail than to leave a slip similar to those in which the knockabouts and Shields are kept. However, the yawl is a comparatively large, heavy boat, and there must be good coordination between her crew members. Fiberglass yawls are kept in slips, but they are not difficult to maneuver in or out of their slips with their auxiliary power. Operation of their engines and maneuvering under power will be discussed in Chapter 11.

Leaving and landing at a mooring under sail has been discussed briefly in Chapter 4, and of course the same basic principles apply to the Navy yawls. The skipper should size up the weather, estimate wind strength and direction, and determine which sails will be carried before boarding his yawl. This will prevent any apparent indecision on the skipper's part and allow him to give instructions to the crew immediately after going aboard. Any inexperienced crew should be checked out on their particular duties and on the operation of deck gear they will handle. The mizzen is hoisted first, and it is sheeted flat so that the boat is held head to wind. Next, the mainsail is hoisted; but prior to this operation, both running backstays should be secured forward against the shrouds so that the mainsail will not foul them. Before casting off the mooring line, the mizzen may be backed (pushed to windward). This will cause the stern to move in the direction opposite to the sail. In other words, if the mizzen is pushed to port the stern will move to starboard, and the bow will fall away from the wind to port. When the bow has fallen away slightly, the jib may be hoisted. Care should be taken that the jib does not get aback in the wrong direction. After the mooring line's eye is taken off its bitt, the eye may be taken to the windward side of the bow and walked a short distance aft to assure that the yawl will sail off in the desired direction. Then the mooring line is cast off, the jib is trimmed flat, or backed if necessary, and the mizzen is slacked until the yawl is on her proper course. Before casting off, be sure the halyards are coiled and all sheets are clear.

When picking up the mooring, the yawl is headed into the wind, of course. It is usually the safest policy to approach the mooring about two or more boat lengths to leeward of it on a beam or close reach at low speed with the sails luffing. If it is found that the speed is too slow, sails may be trimmed in a little; but if the speed

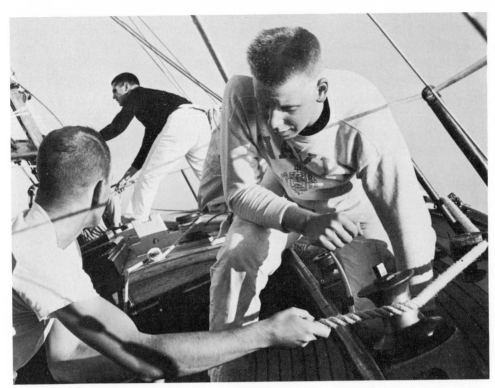

Figure 79

**STANDING BY
TO COME ABOUT**

Notice the difference between the sheeting arrangement and Genoa winch for the fiberglass yawl (Figure 74) and the wooden yawl shown here, which has the large winch aft. When the boat tacks, the man forward will help the jib around the mast and pull aft on the clew. The tailer is ready to put one or two turns around the winch, while the cranker is standing by with the winch handle. It would be preferable for the cranker to be facing forward so that he can watch the jib, provided he doesn't get in the way of the helmsman.

seems too fast, sheets can be slacked. When nearing the mooring buoy, the bow is turned slowly into the wind while all sheets are slacked. The mooring *pendant* (line) is picked up with a boat hook. If the boat should have slightly too much way, then the main boom may be pushed up to windward so that the sail will act as a brake. Be sure the runners are secured forward.

Another, but less desirable, mooring approach can be made directly downwind. The boat is sailed before the wind down to her mooring. She passes one or two boat lengths away from the buoy, leaving it on the windward side. When the buoy is less than half a boat length abaft the stern, the helm is put hard to leeward and the boat rounds up sharply coming to a nearly dead stop. Remember that a slowly turned rudder does little to kill speed, but a rudder jammed hard over acts as a brake.

It is usually best not to pick up a mooring with a Genoa jib set, because this sail restricts visibility and causes confusion on the foredeck when its long tail thrashes around as the boat heads into the wind. The mooring can be approached with a small jib or forestaysail set or without any headsail (under main and mizzen,

or mainsail alone). If the mizzen is set, its sheet must be slacked off to maintain balance. After the buoy is picked up, the mizzen sheet should be pulled in to hold the boat's bow to the wind. Sails, are doused from bow to stern, with the mizzen being the last sail lowered.

The procedures for tacking and jibing have been discussed in Chapter 4. It is important that all crew members understand the basic principles of these maneuvers, because maneuvering a Navy yawl requires teamwork. Before tacking, of course, the skipper alerts his crew to stand by to come about. The crew take their stations. If the Genoa is set, a tall man takes his position as far forward as possible on the bow where he straddles the headstay. One or two men should take a position along the foot of the sail to run the foot forward during the tack. A man stands by to release the jib sheet and set up the running backstay if it is in use. Two men stand by the windward Genoa sheet winch that will be used to bring the jib in on the new tack. Another man stands by to pull back on the jib's clew when it is first being trimmed in, and this same man can then release the leeward running backstay if it is set up. Be sure that every man has a station and knows his job. (See Figure 79.)

At the command hard-a-lee, the helm is put over. The jib sheet is slacked when almost head to wind, and it is eased off. It is not suddenly released, because this will noticeably slow the boat and kill her momentum. The skipper often tells the man on the sheet when to release it. If the runners are being used, the man who releases the sheet can set up the new windward backstay. Some authorities advise setting up the runner before the jib sheet is released, because at this time it is often possible to get the stay very taut. The men stationed at the foot of the Genoa carry it forward while the bowman gathers in the slack. If the forestay is set up, the jib must be fed through the space between the forestay and headstay. When the boat swings past the head-to-wind position onto the new tack, the jib will be blown through the space between the stays. The helmsman luffs his boat slowly until head to wind, and then he momentarily turns sharply in the same direction, so that the jib will quickly blow through the space. After this, the helm is again turned slowly to give the sheet trimmers maximum help in winching in the jib. Of course, if the backstays are not in use, and especially if the forestay is not set up, tacking is a much simpler job.

Figure 80 REEL WINCH FOR THE MAIN HALYARD ON A FIBERGLASS YAWL
The crank is fitted on the center projection for power. Notice the projection used for high speed and also the brake handle behind the middle of the crank.

Jibing involves essentially the same crew activity as tacking, except that not as many men are needed to handle the jib and two men are needed to tend the mizzen and main sheets. The man on the main sheet has an especially important job because the mainsail is quite large and its boom has considerable weight. He must be sure that, in a breeze, the sheet is pulled all the way in when the boom crosses over the boat's centerline, and he must never ease the sheet until the new leeward running backstay has been slacked. The helmsman does not actually turn onto the new tack until the mainsheet tender is ready and has the main boom amidships. At the word jibe-ho, the helmsman turns the bow to leeward so that the boom swings across onto the new tack.

It is important that all crew members be thoroughly familiar with the operation of winches. Members who are inexperienced should be given rudimentary winch instruction soon after boarding a yawl, because improper operation of a winch can be dangerous and cause injuries. As previously mentioned, main halyards on the fiberglass yawls are operated with reel winches, the kind that wind the entire halyard up on a drum. These have a hand brake at the bottom to lock and release the halyard. These winches are two-speed with two square projections onto which the crank handle is fitted. With the handle fitted on the center projection (at the axis of the drum) the winch speed is low but its power is high, but with the handle on the other projection (out from the axis of the drum) the speed is high and power is low. When the halyard is under a great strain the brake should be eased slowly. Never release the brake with the crank handle in place unless someone has a firm grip on the handle, because it can spin around and hit a person in the head or arm. (See Figure 80.)

Other winches on the yawls are conventional top-action (with handle at the top) ratchet or geared winches. With these winches, several turns of a sheet or halyard are wound around the winch and the winch is turned around with its crank handle while the line's tail (that part of the line between the winch and its free end) is pulled upon. A tension must be kept on the tail or else the line will slip on the drum. The man

Figure 81   GENOA SHEET WINCH IN OPERATION

The tailer (not shown) should keep the sheet low, almost at right angles to the winch axis, so that the crank clears the sheet when the crank is turned all the way around. If the turns begin to slip on the drum, the cranker will have to remove the handle quickly while the tailer puts another turn around the drum.

or men who pull on the tail are often called *tailers* and their job is *tailing the sheet*. With winches on the Navy yawls, and on nearly all American boats for that matter, *lines are wound around the winches in a clockwise direction.* (See Figure 81.)

The yawls are equipped with powerful geared winches for the Genoa. Good teamwork is required to trim this jib rapidly when tacking in a breeze. When the jib swings over and begins to fill after the boat has tacked, the Genoa sheet tailer winds two or three loops of the sheet clockwise around the winch; then he pulls in on the sheet, hand over hand, as quickly as he can before the jib completely fills. The helmsman should be bearing away very slowly. When the tailer no longer has strength to pull in the sheet by hand, he wraps another turn or two around the winch, and the cranker (the man who cranks the winch) inserts the crank handle. The cranker then cranks the winch, turning the handle all the way around making complete circles until he no longer has the strength for this, and then he ratchets with the handle, or moves it back and forth so that the winch turns spasmodically. Winch cranking can be a tiring task if tacks are frequent; so it is usually wise to have the cranker and tailer alternate or to have other crew members spell the cranker. If the line begins to slip on the drum as it is being winched in, the cranker must quickly remove the handle, while the tailer puts another turn or two around the drum.

The following are a few tips on handling winches: Handles are always removed when the winch is not being used. When winching in a sheet, never throw on too many turns at first, as they can override each other and jam. When easing off a winch under strain, carefully unwrap one turn at a time while keeping tension on the tail; then ease off slowly until most of the strain has been relieved. When taking turns off a ratchet halyard winch, keep tension on the tail in such a way that it is pulled at right angles to the drum axis or else at a slight angle toward the mast, otherwise the line is liable to slip off the drum. When winching in a jib after tacking, be sure the windward sheet is completely clear to run through its lead blocks. When winding a wire-to-rope splice around a winch (some halyards are part wire and part rope), see that the splice is not left bent around the winch (this can harm the splice and cause wire snags to appear through the rope. Crank the winch a little farther, until the splice clears the drum). Never stand or sit with your head near a winch handle while it is being cranked, because the handle could slip out of the operator's hand. Be very cautious about placing fingers near a winch drum under strain. Be particularly cautious with wire on a winch. And once again, don't forget that a line is wrapped around a winch in a clockwise direction.

When sailing a yawl off the wind, especially during a race, a main boom vang is often used. This consists of a tackle that fastens to a strap which is put around the middle part of the boom. The bottom of the tackle does not secure at the base of the mast but at various points on the side deck, depending on the trim of the sail. This type of vang is sometimes called a *go-fast*. The lower part of the vang should never be secured to the Genoa track as this could pull the track up, but the vang can be hooked to any through-bolt fitting, such as a pad eye or the base of a life-line stanchion. Naturally the vang must be removed before jibing.

When sailing a yawl (or any boat), a lookout must be kept at all times. Of course, this is primarily the helmsman's responsibility, but when a low-cut Genoa jib is set, it is very difficult for the helmsman to see off the lee bow. Therefore a lookout should be stationed to leeward where he can see under or around the jib. The lookout should make constant reports to the helmsman concerning the location of approaching boats or obstructions that lie in this "blind" sector.

Boarding and Securing Procedures

The following are rough check lists of what should be done after a yawl is boarded, before getting under way, and what should be done before securing or leaving her.

BEFORE GETTING UNDER WAY

• Check the bilge and pump it. See that the pump discharge valves are shut after using. (Salt water piping systems will be discussed in Chapter 11.)

• See that the head is almost dry and that its water intake valve is shut.

• See that halyards are clear aloft and that sheets are bent and led properly.

• Remove binnacle (the compass housing) cover and wheel cover and stow these below.

• Set up the topping lift and *strike* (take down) boom crutch. Stow this and the boat hook below.

• Bend on the desired jib and check to see that it is correctly bent.

• Break out winch handles and place in their proper holders.

• If aboard a fiberglass yawl, see that the engine's fuel and water valves are opened and that the main battery switch is on. (Engines will be discussed in Chapter 11.)

• Unstop furled sails and tighten their outhauls just before hoisting.

• See that all loose gear below is properly stowed and that all opening lockers are closed so that gear will not spill out when the boat is heeled.

• See that ports are shut unless it is a calm, hot day with clear weather.

- Be sure mooring pendants are properly secured on the bow cleat. It is well to put a short, stout lashing through the mooring pendant eye and the center part of the cleat, so that even should the eye jump off the cleat, it would be held by several turns of lashing.
- If on a mooring, put up the anchor light.
- If moored in a slip, secure the boat so that she lies straight fore and aft in the slip and as nearly as possible in the slip's center. Be sure that there is some slack in the mooring lines to allow for a change in tide, and that the lines are properly secured with tail ends coiled.
- Pull boarding plank in and leave it on the pier. Coil hose over proper rack.
- See that bent sails are properly furled, well stopped, and that outhauls are slacked. Tie down the heads of furled sails.
- See that sails are properly bagged and stowed. Wet or torn sails should be bagged and taken ashore to be dried or repaired.
- Halyards should be secured in such a manner that they do not chafe the rigging or mast. It is a good idea to pull them somewhat away from the mast by lashing them to the shrouds with short lengths of line, often called *gilguys*. They should be securely belayed to their proper cleats. The main halyard should be unshackled from the head of the mainsail and shackled into a rubber strop, provided for the purpose, which is led under the main boom at about its midpoint.
- The mainsheet should be taut enough to keep the boom from jumping out of the boom crutch.
- The mizzen topping lift should be set up enough to tilt the mizzen boom slightly upward, and then the mizzen sheet set up taut enough to keep the boom from swinging. A drooping mizzen boom makes the whole boat look droopy, while a topped up mizzen gives her a cheerful look.
- Lines should be coiled and, if not removable, should be hung up off the deck.
- All removable sheets, blocks, winch handles, and other gear should be stowed in their proper places.
- Set up runners, but not overly taut. No line should be pulled overly taut. Some allowance should be made for shrinkage in wet weather.
- Strike and stow ensign and burgee.
- Replace covers on the wheel and binnacle.
- See that the main electrical and other switches are off and that the engine is properly secured (if on a fiberglass yawl).
- See that the bilge and sink are dry and bilge pump discharge valve is shut.
- The head should be clean and the intake and discharge valves shut.
- The icebox should be drained, and all ice, food, and beverage should be removed. Prop open the icebox door.
- All lockers below should be opened to allow adequate circulation of air. All deck ventilators should be turned the correct way. The aft end of the companionway should be left open, but other hatches and ports should be shut, except the port in the head. The after end of the lazarette hatch should be propped open about three inches.
- Secure lower extension berths in outboard position.
- A yawl should be left shipshape and in a cleaner condition than when she was boarded.
- Remove all trash, sweep down cabin sole, clean out sinks, wipe off bunk cushions, and wash down decks. Use hoses and fresh water when available, but otherwise use a bucket and Bay water. If possible, hose down topsides to remove salt deposits. Stow cleaning gear.
- Note any discrepancies—negative reports are required—in the log and sign it (please print). Turn log in to Sailing Center.

Most of the essential information on the Luders yawls has been covered in this chapter, but other subjects related to these boats will be discussed later. Chapter 10, "Distance Racing," will cover emergencies such as man overboard and rigging failures. It will also discuss the shifting of headsails and heavy weather sailing. Chapter 11, "Sailboats Under Power," will cover yawl engines, piping, water, and electrical systems.

CHAPTER EIGHT

The Spinnaker

Description

The Luders yawls and Shields sloops are equipped with spinnakers. These sails are essential for racing and are often difficult to handle; therefore, this entire chapter will be devoted to them.

The spinnaker derives its name from the fact that an early version of the sail was first carried by the British yacht, *Sphinx*. It is said that rival crews called the sail a "Sphinxer" and sometimes referred to it as "Sphinx's Acre." These names soon evolved into our present term for the sail.

The modern racing spinnaker, the type carried on the Navy boats, is properly termed a parachute spinnaker. It is shaped like a ballooned isosceles triangle, the upper corner of which is called the head, and the lower corners of which are both called clews. When set, the sail is supported at these three corners only. Either clew may be fastened to the end of a boom called the *spinnaker pole,* which is carried on the side of the boat opposite to the main boom, and the clew on the pole would then actually be called the tack. The clews are interchangeable, that is, either may be used as the tack, depending on whether the sail is set to port or to starboard. Figure 82 shows a typical parachute spinnaker with its lines and fittings. The line attached to the tack and pole is called the *after guy* (or often just *guy*), while the line attached to the clew is the sheet. Of course, the head is supported by the halyard. Another line shown in the illustration is attached to the pole to hold it down and forward, and this line is called the pole *downhaul* or *foreguy.* Still another line shown in the illustration is the *pole topping lift,* or simply *lift,* and this holds the pole up.

Pole Adjustments

At its inboard end, the pole is attached to a slide on a track that is fastened to the fore side of the mast. The outboard end of the pole may swing forward until it touches the headstay or aft until it touches the forward shroud. The after guy controls the pole's fore and aft position. When beam reaching, the pole is carried all the way forward; when running, the pole is all the way aft; but when broad reaching, the pole is about halfway between the running and beam-reaching positions. These positions are illustrated in Figure 83. Notice that the pole is always about at right angles to the direction of the apparent wind. This holds true no matter what the point of sailing. Most spinnakers cannot be carried effectively when the true wind comes from forward of the beam or when the boat is on a point of sailing that is slightly higher than a beam reach.

The pole may be raised or lowered at either end. The height of the outboard end is controlled with the lift, and the inboard end is controlled with the adjustable slide on the mast track. Given a good breeze, a well-designed parachute spinnaker will lift, and it should be encouraged to do so. The pole should be carried as high as possible when the 'chute is lifting, but the tack should not be allowed to lift much higher than the clew. In other words, the tack and clew should be kept at about the same level, almost parallel to the deck or horizontal when the boat is unheeled. Then also, the pole should not be cocked up very much with its outboard end a great deal higher than its inboard end.

Proper up and down pole positions are shown in Figure 84. In a light breeze, the pole should make an approximate right angle with the mast with the inboard end at the highest position

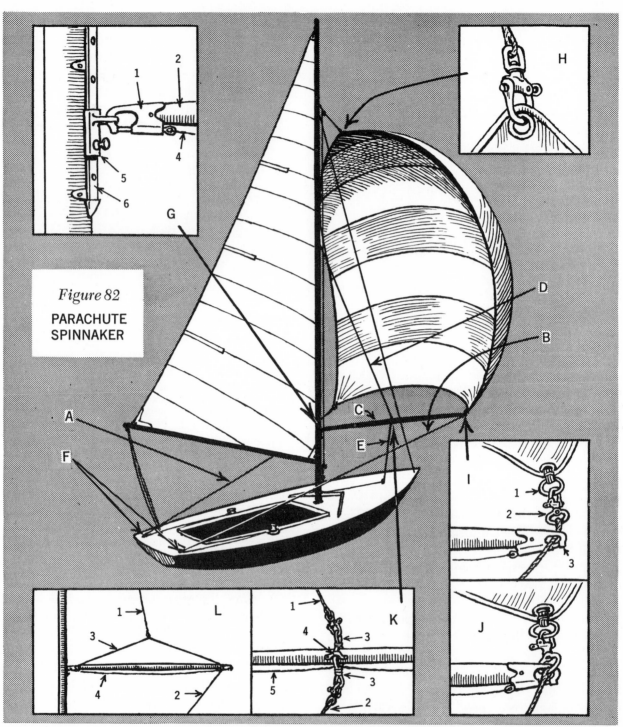

Figure 82

PARACHUTE SPINNAKER

A   SPINNAKER SHEET

B   GUY (sheet & guy
    lead outside shrouds)

C   SPINNAKER POLE

D   POLE LIFT

E   POLE DOWNHAUL

F   SHEET & GUY
    LEAD BLOCKS

G   POLE FITTING & SLIDE
    (1) pole fitting (at each
        end of pole)
    (2) pole (3) spring loaded pin
    (4) lanyard (pull to open pin)
    (5) adjustable slide
    (6) track (on mast's fore side)

H   SPINNAKER HALYARD SWIVEL
    SHACKLE (at each end of
    halyard)

I   SPINNAKER TACK
    (1) metal ring lashed to
        tack grommet (optional)
    (2) Swivel ring shackle
        (same arrangement
        at clew)
    (3) pole snapped on guy

J   ALTERNATE METHOD
    (pole snapped to ring
    on shackle)

K   MIDDLE OF POLE
    (1) lift (2) downhaul
    (3) wire or rope strop
    (4) eye strap
    (5) continuous lanyard

L   ALTERNATE METHOD
    (1) lift (2) downhaul
    (3) bridle (4) lanyard

Figure 83 FORE & AFT SPINNAKER POLE POSITIONS

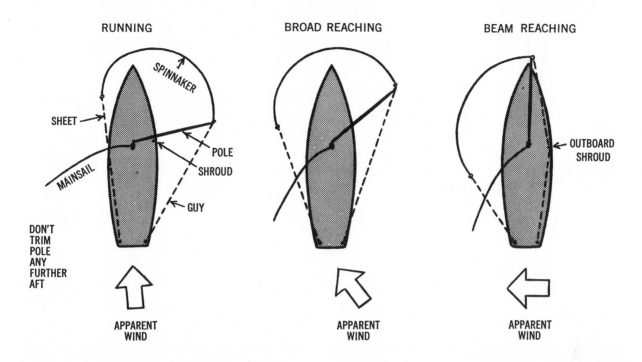

that will keep the tack level with the clew. In very light airs, the clew will not lift; therefore, the inboard pole end must be kept low. As the breeze freshens, the inboard end can be pushed higher up the mast until, in a moderate breeze, the pole is at the top of its track. If the clew is lifting sufficiently in this much breeze the pole can be raised with the pole lift until the outboard end is slightly higher than the inboard end. As the breeze continues to freshen, the pole's outboard end can be lifted until the pole comes in line with the angle of the after guy, as shown by position B in the diagram. In this position, the sail is lifted and the pull of the after guy doesn't exert an extra strain on the downhaul or the pole lift. Position A, shown in the diagram, is usually bad even when the spinnaker lifts in a strong breeze; because although the pole is lifted, its outboard end is too close to the mast, and an extra strain is put on the downhaul which already has a great deal of upward strain from the lifting 'chute. It is advantageous to keep the pole's outboard end away from the mast so that the spinnaker is held out in cleaner air, away from the blanketing effect of the mainsail.

The spinnaker pole may be rigged with its lift and downhaul in one of two ways. Both of these ways are illustrated in Figure 82. K in the illustration shows the lift rigged to the middle of the pole with the downhaul at the under side of the pole, directly beneath the lift. L in the illustration shows the downhaul rigged from the outboard end of the pole and the lift attached to the middle of a *bridle* or wire span running from one end of the pole to the other. A pole rigged by the first method, L, is usually somewhat easier to handle especially when jibing. This arrangement is often used on small boats and sometimes on fairly large boats in a moderate breeze. The other method, K, however, is most often used by large boats and in a strong breeze. With this arrangement there is less chance of breaking the pole. In a strong breeze, the spinnaker usually exerts a strong upward pull which can bend the pole up if the downhaul is secured in the pole's middle. This can be counteracted by putting the after guy into a forward lead so that the guy pulls on a greater angle down on the pole's outboard end; but usually the most effective way to stop the upward bending is to secure the downhaul to the

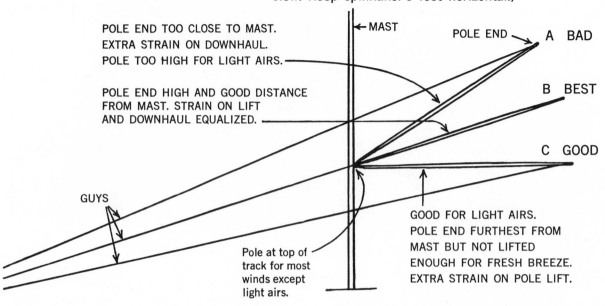

Figure 84 POLE LIFT ADJUSTMENTS (Tack should not be lifted above height of clew. Keep spinnaker's foot horizontal.)

POLE END TOO CLOSE TO MAST.
EXTRA STRAIN ON DOWNHAUL.
POLE TOO HIGH FOR LIGHT AIRS.

POLE END HIGH AND GOOD DISTANCE
FROM MAST. STRAIN ON LIFT
AND DOWNHAUL EQUALIZED.

GUYS

MAST

POLE END

A BAD

B BEST

C GOOD

Pole at top of
track for most
winds except
light airs.

GOOD FOR LIGHT AIRS.
POLE END FURTHEST FROM
MAST BUT NOT LIFTED
ENOUGH FOR FRESH BREEZE.
EXTRA STRAIN ON POLE LIFT.

pole's end. The bridle transfers the pull of the lift from the pole's middle to its end. No matter how a pole is rigged, it is wise to have the lift fastened directly above the downhaul. Most Navy spinnaker poles are rigged with the bridles, as shown by L in the illustration.

Setting the Spinnaker

It is generally considered that there are three ways to set a spinnaker: by stopping it, setting it from a turtle, or setting it from its bag. Actually, however, the latter two methods are practically the same. The turtle is a special container which holds the folded or bundled spinnaker on deck prior to hoisting. These containers are often quite varied in design, depending on the fancy of each particular skipper or foredeck captain. One type of turtle is shown in Figure 85. Notice that the three corners of the sail emerge from the container's top, which is held almost closed with a piece of elastic shock cord (sometimes rubber is used). Each corner is rigged to its proper line: the head to the halyard, the guy to the tack, and the sheet to the clew. Figure 85 shows the pole hooked onto the guy (the line itself), but the pole may be hooked

onto the ring of the swivel shackle as shown in Figure 82. The first method (the pole on the guy) is perhaps preferable for short races in sheltered waters, but the second method (the pole on the ring) is better for distance and offshore sailing because there is less chafe.

When setting the 'chute from its bag, the bag becomes a simplified turtle. About the only difference between the bag and the turtle is that the latter is more elaborate, and it is usually (though not always) designed to be secured forward of the headstay or jibstay as shown in Figure 85. Sometimes the turtle is equipped with snap hooks which snap on to the bow pulpit if the boat has one. When the spinnaker is set from its bag, however, it is usually secured to the foredeck abaft the headstay. The bag must have a lanyard at its bottom so that it can be lashed to the bow cleat or some other fitting on the foredeck. Figure 86 illustrates the usual manner of rigging the spinnaker bag. The sail's three corners hang out of the bag's top, which is closed with the bag's draw string and tied with a slip knot. Immediately prior to hoisting the spinnaker, the slip knot is pulled to release the sail. Notice that Figure 86 shows the jib hoisted. Usually, the jib is not lowered until after the spinnaker has been hoisted, at which time the jib is *quickly* dropped, so it will not blanket the spinnaker.

As Figure 86 shows, with dotted lines, that part of the halyard which fastens to the sail's head must lie to leeward of the jib. The hoisting part of the halyard is, of course, to windward of the jib, next to the mast. The halyard's end that snaps on the head must be put to leeward of the jib by running it aft, outside the shrouds, to the sail's leech. Then the halyard is put behind the leech and the halyard's end is worked forward under the foot of the jib until it is opposite the spinnaker bag where the end can be snapped onto the sail's head. Putting the halyard to leeward of the jib by running the line forward and around the headstay will often cause the halyard to make a wrap around the stay. More will be said about this later when we discuss spinnaker problems. Always look aloft to see that all is clear before hoisting the spinnaker.

It should be noticed in Figure 86 that the after guy runs around the headstay and to leeward of the jib tack where it is snapped onto the spinnaker's tack. If it is desired that the pole

Figure 85 A TURTLE (for medium size boat)

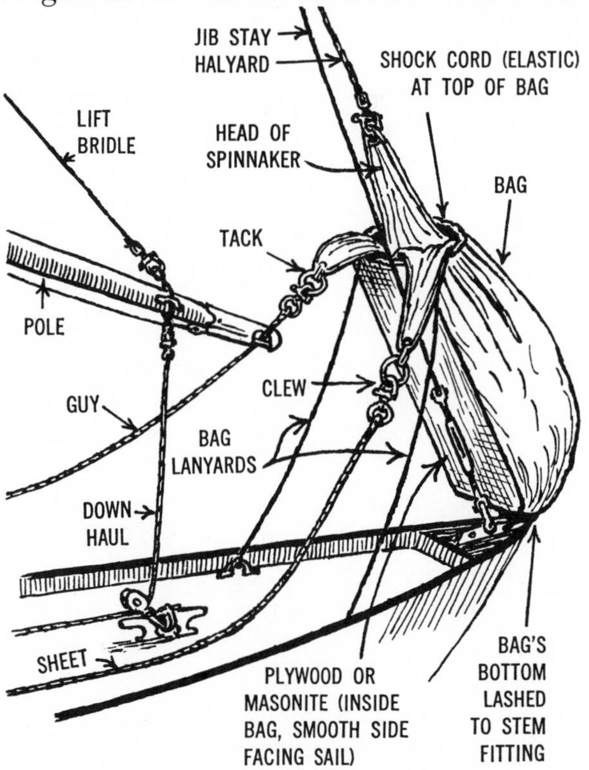

JIB STAY
HALYARD

LIFT
BRIDLE

SHOCK CORD (ELASTIC)
AT TOP OF BAG

HEAD OF
SPINNAKER

BAG

TACK

POLE

CLEW

GUY

BAG
LANYARDS

DOWN-
HAUL

SHEET

PLYWOOD OR
MASONITE (INSIDE
BAG, SMOOTH SIDE
FACING SAIL)

BAG'S
BOTTOM
LASHED
TO STEM
FITTING

SPINNAKER READY TO HOIST (POLE TO PORT)
Be careful that leeches are not twisted
around each other when sail is put into bag.
Spinnaker may be hoisted while jib is set, but
after spinnaker is up, jib should be lowered.

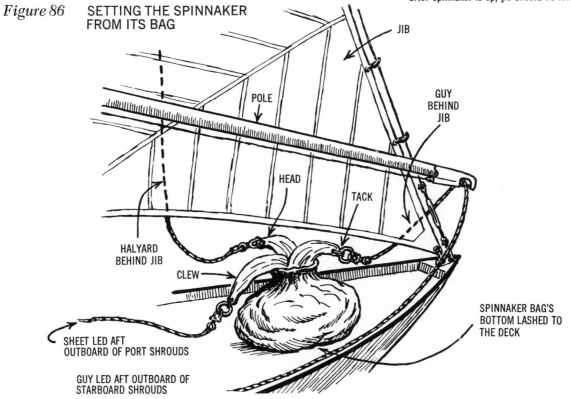

Figure 86   SETTING THE SPINNAKER
FROM ITS BAG

JIB

POLE

GUY
BEHIND
JIB

HEAD

TACK

HALYARD
BEHIND JIB

CLEW

SPINNAKER BAG'S
BOTTOM LASHED TO
THE DECK

SHEET LED AFT
OUTBOARD OF PORT SHROUDS

GUY LED AFT OUTBOARD OF
STARBOARD SHROUDS

be snapped to the guy's shackle ring, then the spinnaker's tack corner must be carried to leeward of the jib and around the headstay where the ring can be fastened to the pole's outboard end which is resting up against the headstay.

The sheet leads outboard of the lee shrouds and snaps into the clew.

On large boats with *life lines* (lines forming a safety railing around the outboard edge of the deck), it is especially important to check the sheet, guy, and halyard which are to leeward of the jib to make sure they are not fouled in the life lines. The spinnaker sheet, guy, and halyard are always led *over*, and never through, the life lines.

It is very important that the spinnaker be "made up" or properly prepared before it is stuffed into its turtle or bag prior to hoisting. This preparation consists of folding the two spinnaker leeches together before the sail is bagged so that the sail will not become twisted when it is hoisted. A simple method is to dump the loose sail on the cabin sole where it is protected from the wind; then starting at the head, each leech is located and folded one against the other. The man doing this works his way down towards the sail's foot, *flaking down* or folding the sail accordion style with the leeches together. When almost at the foot, the two clews are separated and pulled out in opposite directions. The loose bulk of the sail is stuffed into the bag followed by the folded leeches. The head and the two clews are left hanging out of the bag or the turtle's top with the head in the middle between the two clews. On large boats when the spinnaker is being hoisted, a man should "see" it out of the bag or turtle. He should let the spinnaker run through his hands or arms while looking aloft to see that the sail does not foul on a stay or spreader and that it does not become twisted. More will be said about this when we study spinnaker problems later in this chapter.

The remaining method of setting a spinnaker is to hoist the sail while it is rolled up and tied with light stops. After the sail is hoisted, the stops are then broken. This method is illustrated in Figure 87. In former days, before the advent of the turtle, stopping a spinnaker was the usual practice, but now this is not often done except on a big boat in a strong wind. In most instances, using a turtle or bag is simpler and quicker.

When a spinnaker is stopped its leeches are put together in much the same manner as when preparing the sail for a turtle. The sail should be stretched tight between its head and foot, and then the loose part of the sail between the leeches is rolled or bunched up so that it makes the appearance of a long, thin, sausage. A rolled sail is usually more difficult to break out than one that is bunched. The sail is then stopped tightly at about every two or three feet with rotten twine or light cotton thread which may be broken very easily. The tighter the twine is tied the easier it may be broken. It is usually a good practice to make "frog's legs" at the foot as shown in Figure 87. As can be seen, the lowest stops are not put around the two leeches but around the foot and leech so that each clew forms the end of a leg. It is important that the upper stop not be tied too close to the spinnaker's head because this stop is often difficult to break. Upper stops are usually tied with one turn, while lower stops may have two. The lower the stop, the more force can be applied to

Figure 87 A STOPPED SPINNAKER
(pull on sheet to break it out.)

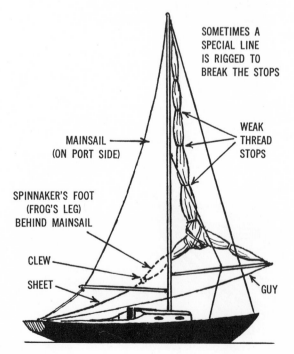

SOMETIMES A SPECIAL LINE IS RIGGED TO BREAK THE STOPS

WEAK THREAD STOPS

MAINSAIL (ON PORT SIDE)

SPINNAKER'S FOOT (FROG'S LEG) BEHIND MAINSAIL

CLEW

SHEET

GUY

110

it by a pull on the sheet.

Occasionally a special line is tied under the stops in such a way that the line may be pulled from the deck after the sail is hoisted to facilitate breaking the stops. Usually, however, a breaking line is not necessary. The leg stops can be reached and broken by hand, and a hard pull aft on the sheet will break the higher stops. When the stops begin to break, the wind will fill out the lower portion of the sail and help break the upper stops. The important thing in preparing a spinnaker for hoisting (whether it be in a bag, turtle, or stops) is to have the leeches running continuously together in order that the sail will not become twisted.

After the sail is hoisted, in a moderate or stronger breeze, ease the halyard slightly (about 12 to 18 inches) so that the head is blown slightly out and away from the mast. In light airs, however, the head should be as high as it can be hoisted.

Spinnaker Trim and Helmsmanship

One of two or a combination of two methods are used to sail with the spinnaker set. The first method is to trim the sail properly and leave it alone while the helmsman changes course to conform with changes in the velocity and direction of the wind. The second method is for the helmsman to hold a steady course while the spinnaker's trim is changed to match every change in the wind. On most top racing boats, however, a combination of these two methods is used.

When the first technique of sailing with a spinnaker is used, the helmsman must be able to watch the spinnaker's luff (the forward edge from masthead to the outboard end of the pole). When the sail begins to collapse, he must quickly alter course. When sailing between a beam reaching and broad reaching course, the helmsman bears off if the spinnaker starts to *break* (to luff, beginning to collapse). But if the boat is running and the spinnaker begins to collapse, it is often difficult for the helmsman to know which way to turn. The sail could be luffing on account of a wind shift that is more on the beam, or the sail might be blanketed by the

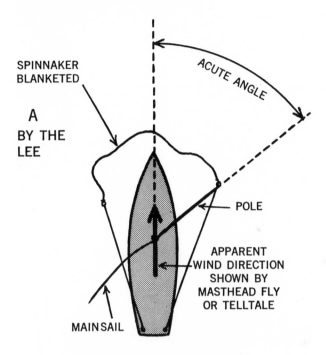

Figure 88
SPINNAKER HELMSMANSHIP

SPINNAKER BLANKETED

ACUTE ANGLE

A BY THE LEE

POLE

APPARENT WIND DIRECTION SHOWN BY MASTHEAD FLY OR TELLTALE

MAINSAIL

HEAD UP (turn to starboard)

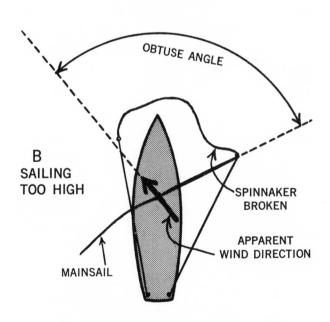

OBTUSE ANGLE

B SAILING TOO HIGH

SPINNAKER BROKEN

APPARENT WIND DIRECTION

MAINSAIL

BEAR OFF (turn to port)

Masthead flys often swing from side to side if boat is rolling severely. In such a case it is usually better to watch the telltales.

111

mainsail because of a shift which comes from astern and puts the boat by the lee (see Chapter 4). This can become a real problem even for an experienced sailor in a rapidly shifting wind. The best way to overcome the problem is to look at the windward telltales or a masthead wind indicator. These will tell which way the wind is shifting. The helmsman should remember that the pole should be kept at right angles to the apparent wind. Of course, the wind indicators will give the apparent wind direction; thus when an indicator makes an acute angle (less than 90 degrees) with the pole, the helmsman should *head up* to make the angle 90 degrees, but when the indicator makes an obtuse angle (more than 90 degrees) with the pole, he should *bear off* to make the angle 90 degrees. This is explained in Figure 88.

An experienced helmsman can often (but not always) tell what is causing a spinnaker to break by simply looking at the sail. If it suddenly shakes and begins to collapse all over, it is probably blanketed by the mainsail; but if the sail first curls or bulges in near the luff edge, then the sail is probably luffing because of being on a point of sailing that is too high for the sail trim. The helmsman can be aided by the feel of the wind on the back of his neck also. Nevertheless, many experienced sailors have caused a complete spinnaker collapse by steering the wrong way at the first sign of the sail's breaking. This can usually be avoided by referring to the wind indicators. In shifty conditions, it is sometimes wise to station a man near the telltales who can call their direction to the helmsman with the words "beamy" or "by the lee," or some such designation.

The second method of sailing with the spinnaker (changing the sail's trim for shifts while the helmsman holds a straight course) requires a lot of action and coordination on the crew's part, because the guy as well as the sheet must be constantly tended. The responsibility for preventing a spinnaker collapse lies primarily with the sheet tender instead of the helmsman. This method is rarely used unless the boat is being steered on a compass course at night or in a fog or if it is fairly certain that the course is the fastest one and the breeze is almost steady.

At most times it is best to use a combination of the two methods discussed, whereby the helmsman alters course to keep on the fastest point of sailing while a man stands by the sheet to prevent a collapse in the event of a sudden wind shift. With this technique, the fore and aft pole position is not often changed. The most frequent adjustments are with the helm and sheet. The helmsman should sail according to the principles discussed in Chapter 4. He should bear off in the puffs and head up in the lulls; and unless there is a good reason for not doing so, he should *moderately* tack downwind. It is nearly always harmful to run dead before the wind with the spinnaker set, because this is a slower point of sailing and there is the danger of the spinnaker collapsing from being by the lee. Of course, the helmsman should steer as low as possible but with the sails, especially the spinnaker, drawing at maximum efficiency. On a yawl, the mizzen staysail can be an effective guide to the helmsman. If he steers too low, this sail will collapse because of being blanketed by the mizzen. A simple rule of thumb for sailing a yawl downwind is to sail as low as possible without collapsing the mizzen staysail.

Principles for trimming the spinnaker sheet are essentially the same as for any other downwind sail. The sheet should be eased as far as possible without the sail beginning to bulge in at the luff. The sail should actually be carried "on edge," with the luff just beginning to curl. The man who tends the sheet is the key to successful spinnaker sailing. Since the wind and the boat's heading change almost continuously, he must follow with almost continuous experiments to try to ease the sheet more and more until the luff curls too much, then quickly trim in just enough to straighten the curl, then try to ease it out again, and keep on repeating this cycle. He must be stationed far enough forward so that he can watch the luff of the sail continuously. At times he may be able to put several turns around the winch with the sheet and then lead it forward to a position just forward of the main boom. At other times, on a large boat such as a Navy yawl, he may stand at the shrouds and reach outboard to the sheet to give it frequent inward tugs while another sheet trimmer

112

backs him up aft at the winch. If the man at the shrouds cannot reach the sheet with his hand, he may use a short piece of line looped over the sheet. This short line is sometimes called a *snatch line* or *jerking line*. The man at the shrouds should watch the luff continously and give the sheet a jerk when the luff edge begins to curl too much. In light airs, light sheets with lightweight shackles (or no shackle at all) should be used so that the clew will lift as high as possible. This sheet should be played by hand every moment.

The spinnaker sheet should be led as far aft as possible where it is a maximum distance outboard. On many boats this lead point is at the top corners of the transom, but on the Navy yawls and Shields the lead blocks are somewhat farther forward because these boats have such narrow sterns. When reaching, it sometimes pays to lead the spinnaker sheet through a block at the end of the main boom in order to move the lead outboard. This has been effectively done on the Navy yawls.

Jibing the 'chute

There are two principal methods of jibing a parachute spinnaker: the *end-for-end* method and the *dip-pole* or *free-wheeling* jibe. Since the 'chute is symmetrical with one leech and clew being identical to the other, the sail can merely be shifted bodily from one side of the boat to the other without turning it around leech for leech.

Figure 89 JIBING THE SPINNAKER

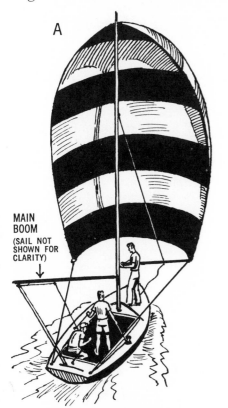

A

MAIN BOOM
(SAIL NOT SHOWN FOR CLARITY)

B

WINCH   WINCH

C

GUY ALTERNATE

HOOK FOR GUY

LIFT AND GUY SLACKED SLIGHTLY. FORE DECK MAN UNHOOKS POLE FROM MAST. On small boats one man can handle sheet & guy. Each line should be led to and snubbed on (wrapped around) a winch.

SHEET SLACKED SLIGHTLY. POLE END SNAPPED ON SHEET. POLE NOW ON BOTH CORNERS OF SAIL AND AT RIGHT ANGLES TO WIND. HELMSMAN HOLDS BOAT BEFORE WIND AND JIBES THE MAIN. On some small boats fore deck man can work in fore end of cockpit.

POLE UNHOOKED FROM FORMER GUY. NEW GUY (PORT SIDE) IS SLACKED. POLE END HOOKED TO MAST. NEW SHEET TRIMMED IN. On small boats, guy can be hooked down forward near shrouds (shown by dotted line) to hold pole down eliminating need for downhaul.

The first jibing method, end-for-ending, requires that the spinnaker pole be reversible, that there be identical fittings on each end of the pole. Actually, the vast majority of poles are made this way. Opinions vary as to which is the best method of jibing. But, generally speaking, end-for-ending seems to be more suitable for small boats, when jibing in a light breeze, when the lift and guy is rigged to the middle of the pole (as in K of Figure 82), and/or when jibing from a run on one tack to a run on the other tack. Dip-pole jibing is more often favored on large boats, when the inboard end of the pole is hard to reach and when the pole has a lift bridle and a pole-end downhaul (as in L of Figure 82), when jibing in a fresh breeze, and/or when jibing from a reach on one tack to a reach on the other tack. End-for-ending is most often done on the Shields sloops but dip-poling is usually done on the Navy yawls.

Figure 89 explains the end-for-end spinnaker jibe. The procedure is divided into three steps.

Figure 90 BELL FITTING FOR THE LUDERS YAWL

The pole end fits and locks into the bell, which is hinged to an adjustable slide on the track secured to the fore side of the mainmast. The lock release lever is shown on the side of the bell. The knob at the bottom of the slide pulls out to control a spring-loaded pin, which locks the slide in the desired position on the track.

In the first, Step A, the guy and lift are slacked slightly. The pole should be about horizontal and low enough to be within easy reach of the foredeck man. The inboard end of the pole is unhooked from the mast, and in Step B, this same pole end is hooked onto the spinnaker sheet or swivel shackle. At this point, midway in the jibe, the pole is attached to both lower corners of the spinnaker, the sail is directly ahead of the bow and is kept full, the pole is at right angles to the boat's centerline, the boat is headed directly before the wind, and the main boom has been pulled in amidships. In the final Step C, the pole end that was formerly the outboard end is detached from the sail and is hooked onto the mast while the new guy is being eased off and the new sheet is trimmed in as the boat turns onto her new course, and finally the lift is readjusted.

One advantage of this jibing technique is that it is usually not difficult to keep the spinnaker full and drawing during the entire operation. However, it is important that the helmsman turn from one tack to the other very slowly. He should hold her dead before the wind until he is sure that the foredeck personnel have everything under control and that the guy and sheet tenders are ready to slack and trim. Also, the mainsail should be held amidships and jibed very slowly in a light breeze; because if it is slacked too soon, it will blanket the spinnaker and perhaps cause the 'chute to collapse before it is properly trimmed for the new course.

A spinnaker pole of the type in Figure 82 should be rigged with a continuous lanyard or trip line which connects the pull pins of the pole-end fittings as shown in the illustration. With this arrangement, the foredeck man can release the sail from the end fitting by pulling the lanyard at any point on the pole.

Although it is customary to dip the poles of Navy yawls and they are usually fitted with lift bridles, the yawls can be jibed using the end-for-end method, and this can be very effective in a light breeze, especially when jibing from a run on one tack to a run on the other tack. The procedure is the same as shown in Figure 89 except that two men should be used to disconnect and connect the pole with the mast and another man is needed to help connect the new guy to the pole end and disconnect the former guy. The yawls are equipped with bell-shaped fittings on the spinnaker track slide (on the fore side of the mainmast). (See Figure 90.) The poles have tapered ends which fit into the bells and are locked in place with spring catches. As previously said, the poles have lift bridles, and the downhauls are attached to the outboard pole ends. When end-for-ending one of these poles, a minor problem is encountered in that after the jibe has been completed, the downhaul will be attached to the inboard end of the pole unless the line is shifted sometime during the jibe which, of course, is not desirable because it gives the busy foredeck crew an additional chore. A simple solution is to keep a downhaul fastened to each end of the pole.

A dip-pole jibe is shown in Figure 91. With this method, the outboard end of the pole is unhooked from the after guy or tack shackle, and the lift is slacked in order to lower (almost to the deck) the outboard pole end which is then passed under the headstay and across to the boat's other side where it is attached to the spinnaker's new guy or other clew. This method usually requires the inboard end of the pole to be slid up to the highest position on the mast track so that the pole will be short enough, when its outboard end is lowered, to clear the headstay. When dip-pole jibing, the spinnaker sheet and guy should be eased. The man who stands by the pole lift should trip the outboard end of the pole with the tripping lanyard, and perhaps another man will be needed to help remove the tack from the outboard pole end fitting. The pole is dipped by slacking the lift and it is swung inboard and ducked under the headstay. A man grabs the old sheet that will become the new guy and hooks it to the outboard end of the pole. Tension should be put on the new sheet immediately to prevent the sail from collapsing. At one point during this jibing procedure the spinnaker is, of course, completely detached from the pole. This is a crucial time and the helmsman must be careful not to put over his helm too suddenly before the pole is attached, the sheet trimmed, and the main boom is swung over. Also the mainsail should

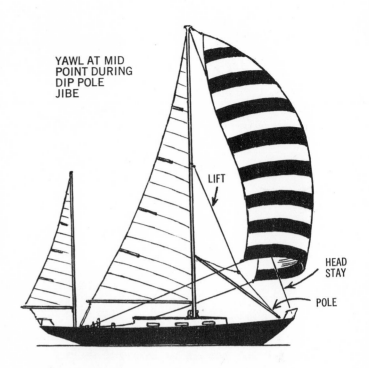

Figure 91 DIP POLE JIBING

YAWL AT MID POINT DURING DIP POLE JIBE

LIFT

HEAD STAY

POLE

POLE END RELEASED FROM GUY, LOWERED, PASSED UNDER HEADSTAY, AND HOOKED TO FORMER SHEET (NEW GUY)

not be slacked off so rapidly that it blankets the 'chute while it is guyed far forward and before the helmsman heads up onto his new course.

Dip-pole jibing is usually the best method in a strong breeze because the pole does not have to be removed and refitted to the mast, a considerable task in a blow. In heavy weather, on big boats especially, an extra pair of sheets can be bent to each spinnaker clew. This will greatly facilitate the handling of the sail because it gives extra lines to control the sail, and during the dip-pole jibe, the pole can be attached to the extra sheet when it is slack and inboard, within easy reach. This extra sheet to which the pole is fastened, then becomes the new guy after the jibe has been completed.

On small boats during a race, consideration should be given to keeping extra weight off the foredeck. To some extent this is even true with boats as large as the Navy yawls. When jibing, therefore, no extra crew should be on the foredeck, because this can have a harmful effect on

Figure 92

DOUSING THE SPINNAKER

The tack has been released from the pole end, and the sail is being handed under the lee of the mainsail. The crew is keeping the sail tightly muzzled so it cannot fill with wind, which is especially important when it is blowing hard.

the boat's fore and aft trim. On a Shields sloop one man should rig the spinnaker, getting it ready for hoisting. He may stand on the foredeck when jibing, but as far aft as possible, near the mast. End-for-end jibing, especially when done with a tripping lanyard on the pole, usually keeps weight on the foredeck to a minimum. There are conflicting schools of thought on whether the sliding pin on the pole-end fitting should be up or down. This is a matter of personal preference. The pole is usually easier to engage and disengage from the mast during an end-for-end jibe if the pin is down (as illustrated in Figure 82), but it is often easier to trip the end fitting with its lanyard to release the guy or tack if the pole is upside down with the sliding pin on top.

Handing the Spinnaker

Handing or taking in the spinnaker is not often difficult if the job is done properly and carefully, but poor helmsmanship and sailhandling during the lowering operation can mean trouble aplenty. In nearly all cases, the Genoa or some other jib is set before the spinnaker is taken down. This will provide continual sail power during a race, and the jib will help blanket the spinnaker and thereby make it easier to handle when it is being lowered. After the jib is hoisted, the guy is slacked all the way forward until the pole lies against the headstay or jibstay. Then the spinnaker's tack is released from the guy snap shackle so that the sail's luff flies free.

116

It is preferable that the boat be headed nearly dead before the wind when the tack is released in order that the spinnaker is blanketed to the greatest extent. At this point in the operation, a man or two is standing by the 'chute's clew and sheet. It is very important that the sheet's end is knotted so that it cannot run through its lead block in the event that the sail should get away from its sheet handler in a fresh breeze. In the event of a sudden knockdown to leeward, the spinnaker sheet should be released so that the sail spills its wind. Be sure the sheet is of sufficient length (twice the boat's overall length is the rule of thumb) in order that the sail will completely spill when the knot at the sheet's end jams in the lead block. When the men on the sheet are ready, a man on the halyard slowly lowers the sail. The sheet tenders, who are usually stationed abaft the main shrouds, pull in on the sheet and gather in the sail as it is lowered, either smothering the sail to keep it from blowing overboard or stuffing it out of the way (see Figure 92). It can often be stuffed under the fore end of the cockpit on a Shields sloop or down the companionway hatch on a Navy yawl. The halyard man must be sure he doesn't lower the spinnaker faster than it can be taken in; because otherwise, the sail will blow overboard and possibly scoop up water which could tear the sail and make it very difficult to haul it back aboard. In the rare instance that no jib is hoisted, the boat should be headed dead before the wind so that the spinnaker can be lowered in the lee of the mainsail.

A frequently encountered spinnaker lowering situation occurs when approaching a leeward turning mark during a race, when the next leg of the course is closer than a beam reach. The 'chute should be lowered in advance of reaching the mark. Unless sailing with an experienced crew who have worked together, it is far better to be too soon than too late getting the spinnaker off. If the mark can be approached on a broad reach, the Genoa can be hoisted early to substitute for the 'chute, and not a great deal of speed will be lost if the jib is not blanketed by the mainsail. When jibing around the mark, try to jibe early or else hoist the jib, lower the spinnaker, and then jibe. If the mark is rounded

sharply and the boat heads onto a close reach before the spinnaker has been lowered, the sail will blow quite far aft when its tack is released from the guy, and the dousing operation may be difficult because the 'chute will be partly out of the mainsail's wind shadow. In this case, the 'chute must be brought in under the after end of the main boom. On a yawl, great care must be taken to see that the sail does not foul the mizzen mast or its rigging. This has happened. When the 'chute is being lowered, it should be gathered in by the clew edge of the sail. Hand only one leech. If both leeches are pulled on, the sail will fill with wind and become very difficult to handle. The man lowering the spinnaker should always keep a turn of the halyard on its cleat or winch to be sure the sail will not get away from him.

Spinnaker Problems

In certain conditions of wind and sea, spinnakers can cause many problems even when they are reasonably well-handled. Many experienced offshore sailors feel that the modern 'chute is not a completely safe and seamanlike sail to carry at sea. However, there is no doubt that it is a very fast sail, and a boat racing without a spinnaker has little chance of doing well in a downwind race. Furthermore, troubles can be minimized with practice, careful sail handling, advanced planning, and a general knowledge of what to expect.

The most common spinnaker problems with brief suggested avoidances and/or solutions are listed as follows:

• *The hour glass*—This is a spinnaker twist about halfway between head and foot that prevents the middle of the sail from filling; but above and below the twist, the sail balloons out in such a way that it gives the appearance of an hour glass (see Figure 93). It is usually caused by improper preparation of the sail before hoisting. The best way to guard against the twist is to see that the *leeches of the sail are side by side* before hoisting when it is bagged, turtled, or stopped. Also, as said before, a man should see the sail out of its turtle or bag during the hoisting. He can often clear a twist before it develops by tugging

Figure 93 AN HOURGLASSED SPINNAKER
Crew members on the **Restless** are pulling on both leeches
in an attempt to make the swivel at the sail's head turn.
However, the twist is so low it is doubtful that this attempt
will succeed. The sail will probably have to be lowered to
clear it, or if the breeze is light, the tack and clew could
be detached and the lower half of the sail untwisted.

on a leech. In addition, the sheet trimmer should keep a tension on the sheet as the sail goes up. If an hour glass occurs near the spinnaker's head, the twist might be removed by tugging on the sheet or leech, because there is always a swivel at the head that might be turned to allow the sail to untwist. An hour glass near the middle or bottom of the sail will probably necessitate its lowering and untwisting by interchanging the tack and clew.

• *A fouled halyard*—Spinnaker halyard blocks are mounted on a swivel above the headstay (or jibstay with a seven-eighths rig). The halyard will either lie entirely on one side of the stay, or will straddle the stay (with one part of the halyard on either side of the stay). Some spinnaker halyards have snap shackles at both ends, but the usual 'chute halyard on a Navy boat has a shackle at one end of the line only. If a single-shackle halyard straddles the headstay and the shackle end of the line lies to leeward of the stay, then, as explained earlier, the leeward part of the halyard should be taken to leeward of the jib by passing the line aft around the jib's leech. *Do not pass the leeward part of a spinnaker halyard around the headstay to get it behind the jib,* because this will cause the halyard to wrap the stay. On the other hand, if this halyard's shackle end lies to windward of the stay, then the shackle end of the line must be taken forward where it is passed around the headstay to the jib's leeward side. Of course, it is then passed under the foot of the jib, and the shackle is snapped onto the spinnaker's head. With a double shackle halyard (a shackle on each end) straddling the headstay, one has a choice: to take the *leeward part* of the halyard *aft*, around the jib's leech, or take the *windward part forward* around the headstay. In the first case, the hauling part of the halyard is to windward of the headstay, and in the second case, the haul-

ing part is to leeward of the stay. The latter solution is better in the interest of chafe prevention when the spinnaker is carried for lengthy periods.

One method of simplifying halyard preparation is to fasten the halyard's shackle end (or both shackles on a double shackle halyard) to the bow pulpit ahead of the jib on a Navy yawl. It is then in a position to be easily rigged on either tack. However, it is not advisable to leave the halyard permanently hooked to the pulpit, because the whipping line will cause some windage and turbulence which will interfere with the jib's luff when beating to windward. The spinnaker halyard should be hooked forward only just prior to setting the 'chute.

Some good general rules for rigging the halyard are: *Determine well in advance of setting the spinnaker on which side the sail will be car-*

118

ried. Of course, this is determined by noting the wind direction and estimating what the spinnaker carrying course will be. Another vital rule is *always to look aloft just prior to hoisting the spinnaker to see that its halyard is clear*. See that the line is not wrapped around the headstay, and see that the block above the stay has properly swivelled.

• *Spinnaker knockdowns*—In a fresh breeze, it is not uncommon to see boats with spinnakers set take sudden knockdowns (extreme heelings) to either windward or leeward. (See Figures 94 and 95). Quite often these knockdowns will cause a loss of rudder control because the rudder will be acting in more of a horizontal than a vertical plane. A knockdown to windward can cause an accidental jibe, while a leeward knockdown can cause the main boom to break if it is broad off and vanged down. Either kind of knockdown can make the boat broach to or turn, out of control, broadside to the wind and seas.

The most seamanlike solution to this problem is to take the spinnaker off when there is real danger of a knockdown. However, in a race when competitors are carrying 'chutes successfully, it is desirable to carry the spinnaker as long as possible. It is often difficult to determine the exact time the spinnaker should be handed. To a large extent this will depend on the experience and skill of the crew and on the condition of the boat. By and large, however, when the boat is at hull speed, when she is yawing and rolling violently, or when there is a steep following sea, when extreme heeling commences, and/or when the helm is very hard to control, the spinnaker should be doused. Under these conditions the boat will be safer, handle much easier, and perhaps will not lose any speed carrying a poled-out Genoa jib. When poling out a jib, the spinnaker pole is rigged to windward, the jib is kept blanketed by the main, and then the jib's clew is hauled out to the pole's outboard end.

If caught by a sudden puff which causes a

Figure 94 SPINNAKER KNOCKDOWNS TO LEEWARD

This picture illustrates examples of the troubles that can be had when trying to carry spinnakers in too much breeze. Obviously both boats are overpowered, and they would have been safer—and would be sailing faster—with boomed-out jibs. The lead boat appears to have tripped on her main boom while it is vanged down. This could break the boom. The spinnaker pole has escaped its bell fitting and is flailing dangerously. The mizzen is trimmed in flat making it very difficult for the helmsman to bear off. The after boat should have slacked her spinnaker sheet and borne off. The mizzen staysail is doing no good and is only adding to the confusion.

119

Figure 95 A SPINNAKER KNOCKDOWN
TO WINDWARD

This is a well known picture of the Luders yawl **Flirt**
taken at the start of the 1958 Bermuda Race, off Newport,
R.I. Notice by the masthead fly that the yawl is sailing by
the lee. She should be sailing higher, almost on a broad
reach, and the spinnaker should be flattened in with its
sheet. The vang is insufficiently bowsed down, permitting
the boom to lift and the mainsail to wrap around the upper
spreaders. Here again there is too much breeze for the
spinnaker. With a boomed-out genoa the boat would be
under control and sailing faster.

knockdown to leeward when the spinnaker is
set, release the sheet to spill the wind from the
sail. Be sure, however, that the end of the sheet
is knotted so that it won't run out of its lead
blocks. It is often wise to rig two sheets, one
with a few feet of slack, so that when the taut
sheet is slacked, the loose sheet will take the
strain but still allow the spinnaker to go out
enough to spill its wind. With a knockdown to
leeward, the helmsman should try to bear off
immediately so that the boat will gain stability.

If caught by a sudden puff that causes a
windward knockdown, the sheet should be flattened quickly and the boat headed up, if possible. This kind of knockdown can be avoided by
overtrimming the spinnaker sheet and by not

sailing too low, by reaching instead of running.

• *Breaking the spinnaker pole*—Breaking a pole is not a common occurrence, but it does happen occasionally. As previously said, the lift bridle arrangement with the downhaul or fore guy secured to the pole's end is generally considered the strongest rig. However, with this arrangement, there is still a great compression load on the pole when it is guyed far forward because the after guy pulls almost straight aft.

One solution to this is the *reaching strut* which is often used by large boats on distance races but seldom on short, closed-course races. This strut is a short extra pole which is rigged to windward to hold the guy a few feet out from the windward shrouds. While the pole is guyed forward, the strut sticks out horizontally at a near right angle to the boat's centerline. The strut lies against the fore side of the forward shroud and it is usually lashed to the shroud. The length of the strut is equal to approximately three-quarters of the boat's maximum beam. The strut's inboard end hooks onto a pad eye or similar fitting on the mast, while the outboard end usually has a large sheave to accept the guy. Advantages of the strut are three-fold: to keep the pole from pressing too hard against the headstay, to reduce compression on the pole, and to prevent the guy from chafing against the outboard shroud. However, the strut does cause extra complications on the foredeck, and setting up and removing it require extra time; so it is not often used on short races in protected waters.

Whether or not the strut is used, care must be taken to see that the pole does not exert too much pressure against the headstay. The guy must be kept tight enough to hold the pole just off the stay even on a beam reach. In a strong wind the outboard pole end should be lowered slightly for two reasons: First, if the pole does hit the headstay, due to the guy stretching, the lateral strain will be near the pole's end where the spinnaker will not have the leverage to break the pole (by pulling it sideways against the stay). Secondly, by keeping the pole end low, the after guy will pull the pole down to help counteract the strong upward pull of the spinnaker. Of course, in winds less than those

which threaten to break the pole, the spinnaker should be allowed to lift for the greatest efficiency and drive, but in strong winds it is best to control and tame the 'chute somewhat by flattening it through over-trimming the sheet and lowering the pole.

• *The spinnaker wrap*—One of the most difficult troubles to clear up is the spinnaker headstay wrap. This is most likely to occur in a seaway when the spinnaker has collapsed, when its loose middle section lies against the headstay. Occasionally, a current of wind from the side will cause the loose folds of the sail to start spinning around the headstay. The boat's motion from the seas will often initiate or add to the twisting. This is most likely to happen if the sail collapses from sailing by the lee, during a jibe, or as the 'chute is hoisted without the jib being set. Of course, if the jib is kept up until after the spinnaker is hoisted and sheeted, then there is little chance of a wrap. The 'chute cannot wind around the stay as long as the jib is hoisted. For this reason many ocean racers carry *spinnaker nets* which are basically jibs made from big-mesh nets instead of cloth. In fact, the British often refer to spinnaker nets as *phantom jibs*. Nets vary greatly in design, but they are usually composed of the least number of lines or tapes that will do the job of preventing a wrap. Of course, a cloth jib should not remain hoisted because it will blanket the spinnaker.

Spinnaker nets are seldom used in short races or in protected waters because the nets take time to rig, and they are easy to tangle. Many small boats carry one or two *antiwrap lines* which are permanently rigged. An antiwrap line (usually of shock cord) is one permanently fastened to the mast at about a third or more of the mast's length down from the masthead (if the boat has a masthead rig). This line is slightly shorter than the distance from its point of attachment on the mast to the masthead. The other end of the line (the end not attached to the mast) is fastened to a sliding ring on the headstay. When no jib is set, the line hangs loosely between the mast and the stay where it will help prevent a spinnaker wrap; but when the jib is hoisted, the ring slides up to the top of the stay, and the line will be stretched tight against or near the fore side of the mast. Of course, effectiveness is increased if two such antiwrap lines are used.

With boats rigged like the Navy yawls, the forestay may be set up, and a jib halyard may be wound back and forth between the forestay and the headstay so that the halyard makes a kind of net. This is not recommended for short races but only on long spinnaker courses and when there is danger of a spinnaker wrap. At all other times when the spinnaker is carried, the forestay should be detached and secured to the shrouds. The foredeck should always be kept as clear as possible (stripped of anchors, boathooks, etc.) to minimize the possibility of lines becoming fouled.

Once the spinnaker becomes wrapped, it is usually very difficult to clear. The first action to take is to jibe over as soon as the wrap occurs, so that the wind current which caused the wrap will come from the opposite side. After jibing, the boat should be held almost dead before the wind. She should not be let up to a broad reach. This may cause the sail promptly to unwrap, but if not you are in for trouble. The sail might be unwrapped by taking the tack off the pole, bringing the tack and unsheeted clew together, and bodily unwinding the sail around the headstay. But if this doesn't work and the sail is badly wrapped, a man may have to go aloft in a bosun's chair to clear the twists.

Some general tips on spinnaker wraps are as follows: Try to avoid letting the sail collapse against the headstay, especially in a seaway. Keep the jib set until after the spinnaker is hoisted and trimmed. Try to keep the spinnaker full when jibing. After the jib has been lowered, unshackle its halyard and bring it aft to the mast; because if a wrap occurs, the sail can get pinched between the stay and halyard, and also the halyard may have to be used to hoist a man up in the bosun's chair. When there is danger of a wrap, keep tension on the spinnaker's sheet and/or pull on the leech, because anything that can be done to flatten the sail will be helpful. If the sail begins to wrap, a sharp change of course may stop it, but if not, jibe over and perhaps the sail will unwrap.

Summary

A brief summary of the main points in this chapter in list form may be helpful. Several of these points are illustrated in Figure 96. If any of the tips are not clear, they should be looked up in the preceding text where they are dealt with in more detail.

Spinnaker Tips:
• Plan ahead. Lay out sheet and guy, prepare the 'chute, and, set up pole with lift and downhaul well in advance of hoisting.
• Bag, turtle, or stop spinnaker with both leeches together.
• Look aloft before hoisting. Be sure halyard is not wrapped around the headstay.
• Be sure that the sheet, guy, and halyard are led over the life lines.
• Consider hooking spinnaker halyard on bow pulpit while getting the sail ready to hoist.
• Hoist spinnaker behind the jib whenever possible.
• Ease halyard slightly in a moderate or stronger breeze unless spinnaker begins to oscillate, in which case halyard should be *two-blocked* (hauled all the way up).
• Trim the sheet immediately after the 'chute is hoisted.
• Keep pole at right angles to apparent wind.
• Keep tack and clew at same level.
• Keep inboard end of pole high in a moderate breeze but low in a light air.
• Keep pole horizontal in a light air but cocked up slightly in a moderate breeze.
• Keep pole's outboard end low in a strong breeze.
• Keep spinnaker "on edge" with the sheet.
• Station the sheet trimmer where he can see the luff.
• Use a sheet snatch line in a strong breeze.
• Make maximum use of wind indicators when steering with the 'chute set.
• Avoid sailing low, or by the lee.
• Use a combination of course changing and sheet adjusting when sailing with the 'chute in a shifting breeze.
• Use the mizzen staysail as a guide to spin-

Figure 96

BEAM REACHING WITH THE SPINNAKER

The spinnaker being carried by the Luders yawl **Alert** is drawing well. Observe that the sail is well lifted, the clews are level, the pole is cocked only slightly above the horizontal, and the pole is about square to the apparent wind, as shown by the masthead indicator. This type of spinnaker, with the cloths running vertically, is no longer carried by the yawls.

naker steering.

• Jibe the mainsail slowly when the 'chute is being jibed.

• Consider dip-poling when jibing from reach to reach or in a strong breeze.

• Consider end-for-ending pole when jibing from run to run or in a moderate breeze.

• Keep excess crew off the foredeck.

• Slack the sheet during a spinnaker knockdown to leeward, and head off.

• Flatten sheet during a windward knockdown. Also head up and/or guy the pole farther forward.

• Lower 'chute in the lee of a jib.

• Cast off tack and hand the 'chute by one leech only.

• Keep a turn around the winch or cleat with the halyard when the 'chute is lowered, and lower slowly.

• Continue steering before the wind, if possible, until the 'chute has been entirely lowered.

• Keep the pole from bearing hard against the forestay.

• Consider using a reaching strut and/or some form of spinnaker net when distance racing in a rough sea.

• When beginning to lose helm control, douse the 'chute and pole out a jib.

CHAPTER NINE

Basic Racing

Although there are many excellent seamen who seldom race, there is little doubt that sailboat racing is a sport that sharpens and develops boat-handling skills, the ability to make quick decisions, good sailing habits, team work, organization, the power of concentration, and a desire to learn and improve. Volumes have been written on racing; thus we cannot hope to cover all the fine points of the subject in one chapter. However, a good deal of emphasis has already been put on a very important aspect of racing, that of getting the best speed and performance from a boat. This has included helmsmanship, sail trimming, crew duties, and sail handling. Therefore, a large part of competitive sailing has been dealt with. What remains to be covered may be roughly divided into three parts: starting, course tactics, and racing rules.

Introduction to Racing

When a group of sailboats race against each other as individuals (not as a team), there can be two forms of competition: handicap or class racing. The latter is boat-for-boat racing between nearly identical boats. In this case, the boat with the fastest *elapsed time* from start to finish, or the first boat over the finish line wins the race. In handicap racing, however, boats of different sizes and variations of type compete against each other. The larger, faster boats are given time handicaps. Under this system, each boat is given a *measurement rating* that attempts to predict her speed potential. This rating is assigned a time allowance in seconds per mile. To find the allowance a particular boat receives from a larger, faster one, the time allowances of the two boats are subtracted, and this difference is multiplied by the distance in miles of the particular race. The winning boat is the one with the best *corrected time,* or the best time for sailing the course after handicap corrections have been made.

The Skipjacks and Shields sloops are raced as a class; but the Navy yawls may be raced either as a class, when racing among themselves, or under a handicap system when racing against other boats of different sizes and designs. The yawls are rated under the Cruising Club of America (CCA) measurement rule for ocean racing. Under this rule each boat is assigned a rated length after certain vital dimensions and characteristics have been physically measured. These measurements include: load waterline length and the *sailing length* (approximate waterline length of the hull when heeled), beam, draft, displacement, sail area, stability, and propeller size and location. These various measurements are applied to the CCA rating formula, and this gives the boat's rated length which currently, in most cases, turns out to be near her sailing length.

Race courses are of two general types: the point-to-point course and the closed course. The former is literally from one geographic location to another. This type of racing may turn out to be a reach, beat, or run the entire way, or it may be some combination of these points of sailing depending on the wind direction with respect to the particular course. Certain aspects of this kind of racing will be discussed in the next chapter. Unlike the point-to-point course, the closed course has its start and finish in the same or approximately the same location. This type of race is deliberately planned to have a variety of points of sailing, and at least one beating leg is considered essential. Most closed courses are *windward-leeward, triangular,* or some combination of the two.

The simplest windward-leeward course has its first leg a near dead beat to a windward turning mark and then a run back to the starting point. Some windward-leeward courses have an initial short windward leg to the mark, then a long run to another mark to leeward of the starting line, and finally a short beat back to the starting area which then becomes the finish line. In a triangular course, three major marks are involved so as to make each leg of the course the side of a triangle. This kind of course is usually arranged so that one leg is a beat, another a run, and the other a reach. Combinations of windward-leeward and triangular courses make the *Gold Cup* and *Olympic* courses. The Gold Cup is a windward-leeward followed by a triangular course, and an Olympic is a triangle followed by a windward-leeward course with an extra windward leg. In all these cases the finish is in approximately the same location as the start.

A First Look at the Racing Rules

The principal racing rules in this country and those under which all Navy boats race are the North American Yacht Racing Union (NAYRU) rules. Among other information given by these rules, are the right of way principles for all converging situations. Remember that these are not rules of the road. The NAYRU rules govern boats racing among themselves only.

It is important for all racing skippers to know the rules. Of course, the newcomer cannot be expected to know all the fine points and the outcome of protest appeals that result from different interpretations of the rules, but all skippers should at least be thoroughly familiar with the main points expressed in Part IV of the NAYRU rules, which is "Sailing Rules When Yachts Meet—Helmsman's Rights and Obligations Concerning Right of Way." This and other parts of the rules are printed verbatim in Appendix C. Knowledge of these rules not only gives the racing skipper confidence to exercise his judgment and to make split-second decisions, but his knowledge considerably lessens the chance of a dangerous collision on the race course. Racing terms used in the rules are defined in Part I of the NAYRU rules and this is also printed verbatim in the appendix.

It is most important first to learn the Fundamental Rules, Numbers 36 and 37 in Part IV of the NAYRU rules; Number 36 is the *opposite tack rule*, and Number 37 is the *same tack rule*. Rule 36 is the most simple basic rule, and it states that: "A *port-tack* yacht shall keep clear of a *starboard-tack* yacht." There are but two exceptions to this rule. First, if you have crossed the starting line too early and must return to restart, you do not have the right of way even if on the starboard tack. This is expressed in Rule 44.1 (a). The second exception has to do with overlapping boats when rounding or passing a mark, and it is expressed in Rule 42.1 (a). We shall discuss the subject of rounding marks later in this chapter.

Rule 37 deals with boats converging when they are on the same tack. This states that: "1. A *windward yacht* shall keep clear of a *leeward yacht*. 2. A yacht *clear astern* shall keep clear of

Figure 97   OPPOSITE TACK RULE

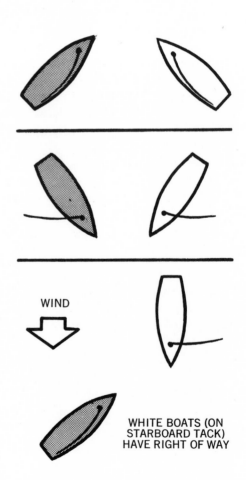

WIND

WHITE BOATS (ON STARBOARD TACK) HAVE RIGHT OF WAY

Figure 98 SAME TACK RULE

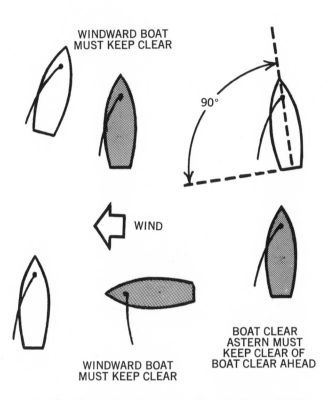

WHITE BOATS HAVE RIGHT OF WAY

WINDWARD BOAT
MUST KEEP CLEAR

90°

WIND

WINDWARD BOAT
MUST KEEP CLEAR

BOAT CLEAR
ASTERN MUST
KEEP CLEAR OF
BOAT CLEAR AHEAD

a yacht *clear ahead.* 3. A yacht which establishes an *overlap* to *leeward* from *clear astern* shall allow the *windward yacht* ample room and opportunity to keep clear, and during the existence of that *overlap* the *leeward yacht* shall not sail above her *proper course.*" In defining clear astern, clear ahead, and overlap, the rules say, "A yacht is *clear astern* of another when her hull and equipment are abaft an imaginary line projected abeam from the aftermost point of the other's hull and equipment. The other yacht is *clear ahead.* The yachts *overlap* if neither is *clear astern;* or if, although one is *clear astern,* an intervening yacht *overlaps* both of them. The terms *clear astern, clear ahead,* and *overlap* apply to yachts on opposite *tacks* only when they are subject to Rule 42, Rounding or Passing Marks and Obstructions. The term proper course is defined as follows: "A *proper course* is any course which a yacht might sail after the starting signal, in the absence of the other yacht or yachts affected, to *finish* as quickly as possi-

ble. The course sailed before *luffing* or *bearing away* is presumably, but not necessarily, that yacht's *proper course.* There is no *proper course* before the starting signal." (Words printed in italics in the quoted parts of the rule, are terms that are defined in Part I of the rule. For those terms not already defined, see Appendix C.) Examples of the opposite tack rule and the same tack rule are shown in Figures 97 and 98. More will be said about the racing rules later in this chapter.

The Start

The start is often the most difficult and unnerving part of a race especially for the novice skipper; but in a short race, getting a good start is tremendously important. Races have been won and lost at the start.

The starting line is an imaginary line between two points, usually a mark and a committee boat. The mark may be a fixed channel marker or buoy or a special mark, often a flag mounted in a small rowboat, temporarily put into position by the organization sponsoring the race. The committee boat may be any kind of craft with a mast from which flags and shapes (usually balls, cylinders, or cones) can be hoisted. Of course the boat must be large enough to accommodate several members of the race committee from the sponsoring yacht club. Usually, but not always, the starting line marker is placed so that it is passed on the same side as the course turning marks are passed. In other words, all marks are usually left on the same side. Course instructions are usually given in the form of a race circular mailed or handed to each contestant before the race, and often the course is given at a preliminary skipper's meeting or sometimes the course is posted with large signs on the side of the committee boat. In the latter case, the signs are often a combination system of single letters or numbers and the system is explained in the race circular.

The ideal starting line is one that is set approximately square (90 degrees) to the wind (if there is any variation, the left-hand end of the line should be set slightly closer to the first mark than the right-hand end. This variation should not exceed 10 degrees) with the first leg of the course (the direction to the first mark) being nearly a dead beat to windward. This is theoretically possible to achieve with a closed-course race, but it is usually not possible on a point-to-point course unless the wind happens to blow from exactly the right direction. Of course, the first mark may not always lie dead to windward, but the important thing is that the line be square to the wind. The object of such a line is that neither end of the line is favored, so that competitors will not be bunched or jammed together at one end. If the current or some other factor makes one end of the line more attractive, then the line should be slanted slightly away from the right angle to the wind in order to make both ends equally attractive. This principle holds true on reaching and running starts as well. It is highly desirable to have the starting boats evenly spread out along the line no matter what the point of sailing. Windward starts are preferable, because all the boats rarely arrive at the first mark at almost the same time, as so often happens with reaching and running starts.

Even on a closed course, the ideal starting line is often very difficult to set because of last minute wind shifts which cause the line to be slanted away from the 90 degree angle to the wind. In fact, even though the race committee makes a great effort to set a perfect line, more often than not, one end will be slightly more favored than the other.

The following system is customarily used to start a race: at precisely ten minutes before the start, a *warning* signal is given from the committee boat. This signal is given audibly, with a gun or whistle, and at the same time it is given visibly with the hoisting of a flag or shape. Exactly 4½ minutes later, the warning shape, which is usually white, is hauled down; and 30 seconds later another signal is given audibly and visibly with a gun or whistle and the hoisting of another flag or shape. This is called the *preparatory* signal and the flag or shape is usually colored blue. Four and one-half minutes later, the preparatory shape is hauled down; and 30 seconds after this, the *start* signal is given with the hoisting of the starting shape or flag, usually colored red, and the sounding of

the whistle or gun. Actually, the visual signal gives the exact time of the start, because a starting gun can misfire.

Racing skippers try to reach the starting line just as the starting signal is made. The ideal or perfect start is one that is made at the favored spot on the line, with the boat sailing at top speed and just touching the line as the signal is hoisted and the gun is fired. Of course, this is an ideal that is very difficult to achieve.

Choosing the favored spot on the line is one of the keys to successful starting. There is a simple rule for choosing the favored end when the line is not square to the wind. With the boat near the center of the starting line, luff up until the boat is headed directly into the eye of the wind, and the bow will point closer to one end of the line than the other. *The end that is closer to the boat's heading when she is head-to-wind is the favored end of the line.* This is illustrated in Figure 99. A boat making a well-timed start at the favored end is always ahead of boats making well-timed starts anywhere else on the line. In choosing the favored end, however, one has to be careful about a last minute wind shift which might favor the opposite end. If you are ahead but to leeward of a competitor, you gain if the shift is a header, but you lose if the shift is a lift. This can be seen in Figure 99.

Notice in the diagram, the starting boats are on the starboard tack. This is a fundamental rule. *Start on the starboard tack*, because you have the right of way and can force port tack boats about in converging situations. Of course, there are exceptions to every rule, and occasionally a perfectly timed port tack start will pay off. But there is no question that starting on the starboard tack is the safest policy, and it is most certainly recommended for beginners.

When choosing the favored starting spot on the line, there are factors to be considered other than what position will put you ahead of your competitors at that particular moment. The racing skipper must decide where he wants to go immediately after the start. He may, for example, wish to go offshore if the current is favorable and there appears to be a better breeze away from the land, or he may want to tack inshore to get into smoother water and to escape a foul current. If he knows where he wants to go, he must plan the kind of start that will allow him to reach his strategic course in the quickest time. For instance, if he starts to leeward on the starboard tack but wishes to stand inshore on the port tack, he might be boxed in or trapped by boats to windward that could prevent him from coming about. In this hypothetical case, it might be the better plan for him to take a late start to windward so that he could go over on the port tack immediately after crossing the line.

Another tremendously important consideration is where the starter should go to get clean, undisturbed wind. A boat's speed can be greatly harmed by the disturbed air (backwind and wind shadows) from other boats, and this is particularly true in the vicinity of a crowded starting line. A boat that makes a well-timed start at the line's favored end will usually get clean air. At the windward end of the line (when on the starboard tack of a windward start), a boat can usually get clear wind even if she gets a bad start, because she can promptly tack into undisturbed wind soon after crossing the line. If she gets a bad start at the line's leeward line, she may not be able to tack, but she may be able to bear off slightly and foot into clean air. Of course, if all the starting boats are headed, this will put the leeward boat in the most favored

Figure 99

FAVORED END OF THE
STARTING LINE

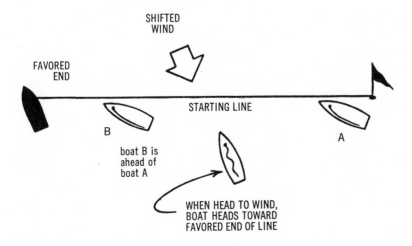

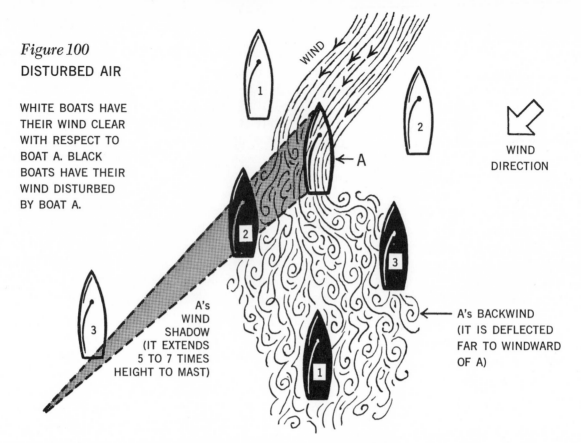

Figure 100
DISTURBED AIR

WHITE BOATS HAVE THEIR WIND CLEAR WITH RESPECT TO BOAT A. BLACK BOATS HAVE THEIR WIND DISTURBED BY BOAT A.

WIND

WIND DIRECTION

← A

A's WIND SHADOW (IT EXTENDS 5 TO 7 TIMES HEIGHT TO MAST)

A's BACKWIND (IT IS DEFLECTED FAR TO WINDWARD OF A)

position. In the event that the line is square to the wind and the starters are bunched at each end, there might be cleaner air in the middle; but when starting in the line's middle, it is usually difficult to bear off into less disturbed air and also difficult to tack for clean air.

Figure 100 shows just how a boat can disturb the air of other boats in her vicinity. The black boats in the diagram have their wind disturbed by boat A, while the white boats have their wind clear. Notice that black boat 3 is getting some backwind even though she is to windward of A. This is due to the draft curve of A's mainsail which deflects the backwind to windward. To clear her air, black 3 should pinch up in an attempt to work further to windward of A. Black boat 2, to leeward, is sailing in A's wind shadow. To clear her air, black 2 should try to drive off to leeward slightly with eased sheets until she sails out of the wind shadow. Black boat 1, dead astern of A, is getting backwind and also disturbed water from A's wake. The chances are that she cannot pinch up or drive off enough to clear her air without dropping far astern. Probably, her best alternative is to tack.

If her skipper wants to remain on the starboard tack, then he can tack again as soon as he gets into undisturbed air. White boat 1 in the diagram is in the most enviable position, because she is actually lifted slightly by the deflected air flowing to leeward of A's jib. White 1 is said to have a *safe leeward position*. Of course, she has her wind clear and is throwing backwind against the lee side of A's sails.

Once the starting spot on the line is selected, the next problem to cope with is how to hit the line with sufficient headway when the starting gun is fired. There might be considered five fundamental techniques for arriving at the line as the starting signal is made: (1) the timed start, (2) sitting on the line, (3) running the line, (4) the dip start, and (5) the barging start (see Figure 101). There are certain special occasions when any of these techniques or a combination of some of them might be used; but by and large, the timed start is generally the most effective and the safest.

The most commonly used method with this kind of start is known as the Vanderbilt system. This system suggests that you cross the line on

130

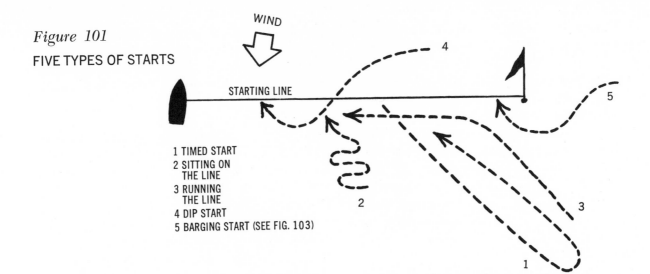

Figure 101

FIVE TYPES OF STARTS

WIND

STARTING LINE

1 TIMED START
2 SITTING ON
   THE LINE
3 RUNNING
   THE LINE
4 DIP START
5 BARGING START (SEE FIG. 103)

the port tack heading in the wrong direction (away from the first turning mark) while, as nearly as possible, beam reaching with very roughly 2 minutes to go before the starting gun. A timer, a crew with a stop watch, takes the time as you cross the line and notes the time remaining until the starting gun. You add the time it takes to turn (tack or jibe) to the time remaining and divide by 2. This figure gives the proper time to begin your turn to head back for the starting line. Theoretically, you should return to the line as the gun fires.

An example is shown in Figure 102. The boat crosses the line going the wrong way when there are 2 minutes and 20 seconds to go (until the start). The skipper estimates that it will take him 10 seconds to tack. He adds 10 seconds to 2

minutes, 20 seconds and divides by 2, which gives 1 minute, 15 seconds. He sails the boat on a steady course until there is 1 minute, 15 seconds to go, and then he tacks and heads straight back to the spot where he formerly crossed the line. In the absence of a current, interference from other boats, and if the wind is steady, he should reach the line at gunfire. This method usually works well when there are not a great number of boats racing. A crowded starting line can throw off the timing because of necessary course alterations.

The second starting technique, sitting on the line, is sometimes used when racing small, light dinghies, the Skipjacks, for instance. In this case, the starter approaches the line early, perhaps a minute before the gun, lets his sails luff

Figure 102   A TIMED START

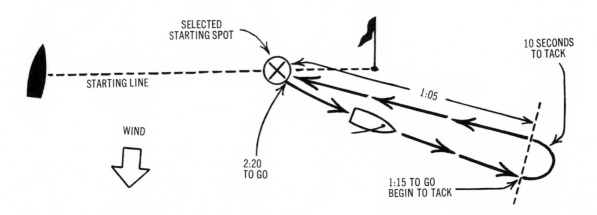

SELECTED
STARTING SPOT

STARTING LINE

WIND

2:20
TO GO

10 SECONDS
TO TACK

1:05

1:15 TO GO
BEGIN TO TACK

to kill speed, and then trims them in immediately prior to gunfire. This can be dangerous when right of way boats establish an overlap to leeward. This starting method is not recommended with large, heavy boats (Navy yawls, for instance), because they are slow to pick up speed after the sails are trimmed. Even in small boats that will accelerate rapidly, care must be taken that speed is not altogether killed, because then the boat has no rudder control. If there is open water around the boat using the sitting start, she might be sailed on a slightly weaving, up and down, course while her sheets are only slightly slacked.

The other three starting techniques should be used rarely and with great caution. When running the line a boat arrives at the line early and to windward of the desired starting spot. Her sheets are then eased, and she reaches along parallel to the line until just before the gun fires at which time her sheets are trimmed and she is headed up onto her proper course. This method has the advantage that the boat has good headway when she hits the line as the gun is fired. However, the method is dangerous because boats to leeward have the right of way. Never

attempt this unless there is plenty of open space to leeward; and if attempting it, always keep a constant lookout to leeward for converging boats. Also, run the line a safe distance away from the line.

The dip start can also be dangerous. In this case, you stay on the wrong side of the line and dip back across to the right side of the line just before the gun fires. This start is sometimes used when there is a strong foul current (flow of water against you) and when the other starters are late getting to the line. The dip starter must be very cautious and dip into a clear open spot, for he usually has no rights. This kind of start is certainly not recommended for beginners at a crowded start, especially in large boats.

The barging start is also dangerous. When a boat illegally barges, she attempts to force her way between the starting mark and another competitor as illustrated in Figure 103. However, it is perfectly legal to start on the wrong side of the danger line, as boats B are doing in the diagram, provided there are no boats close or overlapping you to leeward. The danger lines shown in the diagram represents the course to the first mark for a reaching start or the close-

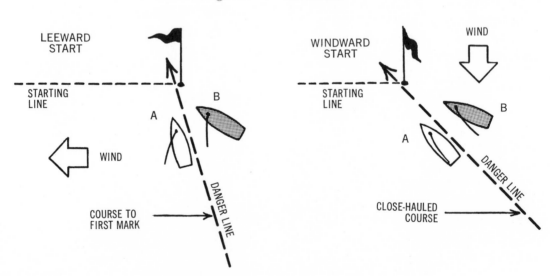

Figure 103 BARGING

In both cases B is barging illegally because she is trying to get room at the starting mark. A does not have to give room to B, but A cannot head above her course to the first mark (or her close-hauled course when beating) after the starting signal before she has crossed the starting line.

hauled course for a windward start.

In order to understand the barging start thoroughly, it is necessary to learn Racing Rule 42 which deals with rounding or passing marks or obstructions. Rule 42.1 covers various rounding situations when boats are overlapped, and Rule 42.1 (e) is the Anti-barging Rule. In most cases, when two boats are overlapped rounding or passing a mark, the outside boat must give the inside boat room to pass the mark on the correct side. An important exception is the Anti-barging Rule which says that the windward boat *cannot* claim room from an overlapping leeward boat. However, the rule goes on to say that the leeward boat may not sail above her course to the first mark on a reaching, or running, start or luff above a close-hauled course on a windward start after the starting signal has been made. Before the signal, the leeward boat may sail higher, and if she is close enough to the mark, she may squeeze out windward boats after the signal provided she doesn't sail above her close-hauled course or course to the next mark.

The following are a list of tips for getting good starts:
• Get to the starting area early (a half hour before your start or earlier if other classes are starting ahead of you).
• Study the race circular, wind, current and position of starting line.
• Luff head-to-wind to determine favored end of the line.
• Run the entire length of the line and time your run.
• Decide where you want to go after the start. (This should be based on such factors as wind, current, and where you think your competitors will go.)
• Try to determine the most probable area of undisturbed air. (This may be done by watching your competitors to see which end of the line they favor and by watching them make practice runs at preselected starting spots.)
• Stay close to the line especially in light airs.
• If other classes are starting ahead of you, watch their starts closely to see which boats profit and which do not in their various starting

tactics, but stay clear of them.
• Use a timed start in most cases.
• The timer should start his stop watch at the warning signal and call out the time remaining to the helmsman.
• If you are a little late for the start, properly trim your sails immediately, bear off slightly, and drive for the line.
• If it seems you will be a little too early slack sheets and/or luff up slightly to kill speed.
• Never kill speed to the extent that it affects helm control.
• Start on the starboard tack unless there is no doubt that you will be entirely clear on the port tack and if there should happen to be a great advantage to starting on the port tack.
• If the windward end of the line is favored on a windward starboard tack start, plan to start not exactly at the mark but a boat length or two to leeward of the line's windward end. In this position, there is little chance of your being forced into a barging position by boats to leeward.
• If the leeward end of the line is favored on a windward starboard tack start, plan to start not exactly at the mark but a slight distance to windward of the leeward end; because otherwise, a heading wind shift might keep you from fetching the leeward mark. Also, if the committee boat is at that end, you may, at the last moment, become trapped in what is often called the "coffin corner." A boat in this predicament cannot bear off at the last moment because she may hit the committee boat, and she cannot tack if there are boats close to windward because she will then be on the port tack with no rights, and Rule 41.1 says that a yacht tacking must keep clear of a yacht on a tack.
• If headed when approaching the coffin corner, do not try to pinch by the mark; but bear off, jibe around, and pass under the stern of the starboard tack boats.

The aforegoing discussion of starting has been primarily concerned with the windward start, the usual start for closed courses. The next chapter will deal with distance racing involving point-to-point courses, and so in this chapter there will be a little more said about the tactics of reaching and running starts.

133

Figure 104 CURRENT

To determine current's direction, watch buoys and fixed objects in water such as fish stakes. Buoys usually lean in direction of flow. Current causes buoys and fixed objects to make rippled wakes.

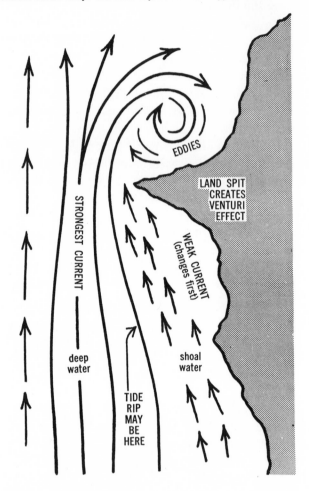

STRONGEST CURRENT

EDDIES

LAND SPIT CREATES VENTURI EFFECT

WEAK CURRENT (changes first)

deep water

shoal water

TIDE RIP MAY BE HERE

Basic Course Tactics

After the start, we are concerned with three general factors: boat speed, the fastest course, and the whereabouts of competitors. Of course, boat speed depends on what has already been discussed: helmsmanship, tuning, sail adjustment, and boat handling. The fastest course primarily depends on the wind and current if we discount the presence of other competitors. As the race progresses, competitors will have a definite influence on strategy, but to begin with there should be a basic preliminary plan, and this should mainly be based on wind and current. This section, therefore, will first touch on wind and current tactics and then on tactics relative to the competition.

Many sailors use the words current and tide interchangeably, but actually tide is the alternate, vertical rise and fall of water, while current is the horizontal movement of the water. Tidal currents are the currents caused by the tides. Before every race, the current should be looked up on *Tidal Current Tables,* which give the velocity of flow and the time of *slack water,* maximum *ebb,* and maximum *flood* in the general locality of your race. Slack water is no flow, while ebb means to flow outward and flood means to flow inward. Current tables should not be absolutely relied on because certain conditions of weather can throw them off. The flow of water should continually be checked visually, by looking at buoys, fish stakes, channel markers, anchored boats, crab or lobster pots, etc. Tall objects that are anchored such as spar buoys tend to lean in the direction of flow. Stationary objects in a strong current will leave a definite wake and appear as though they were moving through the water. Anchored boats in light airs will often swing to the current so that their bows will point in the direction from which the current is flowing. Incidentally, if we speak of a southerly wind we mean that the wind is blowing *from* the south, but a southerly current means that the current is flowing *towards* the south.

Figure 104 shows how land and bottom contours affect the current. In deep water and particularly in channels, the current flows fast, but the flow is slow in shallow water. However, the current changes first in shoal areas. If we have foul current (against us), then we should usually sail near the shore where the water is shallow, but if the current is fair (with us), we should probably go offshore where the water is deep. Of course, we also want to go where the current will first change to favor us. The current is often accelerated when it flows past a point, land spit, or constricted channel because of the venturi principle; and behind a point or spit there will often be eddies or contrary flows as shown in Figure 104. Tide rips are streaks of ruffled waters that usually mark the dividing line between a fast current and a slow current moving in the same direction or two currents moving in opposite directions. Usually it is wise to

134

stay out of the rip, but obviously you should stay to the favorable side of the rip.

When beating to windward against the current, try to take the tack that will allow the current to push against the lee side of your bow. This is called *lee-bowing* the current and will give the boat a push to windward. Sometimes a lee-bow current can be had by tacking into the mouth of a river when the river's current meets the main current (of the bay or principal body of water) at a wide angle. This is illustrated in Figure 105.

When sailing across a current, nearly at right angles to the current, allowance must be made for its sidewise push. If we continually aim our boat directly at the mark or destination, our course will resemble an arc, but if we steer above the mark (toward the direction from which the current is flowing), our course will be closer to a straight line. Obviously, the latter course is the shortest. Naturally, the stronger the current the higher above the mark we steer. This course can often be determined by ranging the mark against the shore. If the mark does not appear to move against the shore, the boat should arrive precisely at the mark.

Wind is far more difficult to predict than current. It is always a good plan to get the latest weather report before a short race and to obtain frequent weather reports during a distance race. But no one knows better than a sailor that these reports are not entirely dependable. Quite often the reports are accurate, but the weather does not follow the predicted timetable. An expected breeze may arrive eight hours later than expected, a front may arrive a day later than predicted, and so on. Also, something resembling the predicted weather may be taking place high above us, but there may be entirely different conditions at our location on the earth's surface. Forecasts of the general weather pattern are of far greater significance for the offshore, distance racer than for the closed-course, round-the-buoys racer. A two hours' difference between a predicted and an actual wind change may not be crucial during a race that lasts five days, but the same time lag will be crucial on a three-hour race. The short-distance racer is interested in the local weather over a limited period of time.

The local weather picture is very much influenced by the geography and topography of the land. The uneven heating of land and water give the diurnal and nocturnal land-sea breezes. In the daytime, on a hot summer's day, the land heats up considerably more than the water. This causes the hot air over the land to rise and leave a partial void which sucks in the cooler air from over the water; thus we have a sea breeze. On the other hand, after dark the land begins to cool, and the thermal activity is reversed with the warmer air over the water rising and the cooler land air being sucked towards the sea. In this case we have a land breeze. Sea breezes are most likely to be strong in the late afternoon on a clear, hot day after a cool night, while land breezes often occur late at night or in the early morning. Land and sea breezes are affected by such factors as the directional changes of the shore line, the clearness

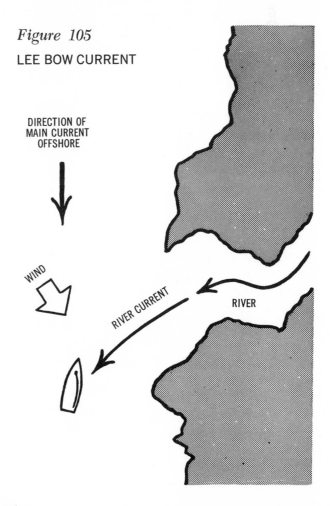

Figure 105

LEE BOW CURRENT

DIRECTION OF MAIN CURRENT OFFSHORE

WIND

RIVER CURRENT

RIVER

135

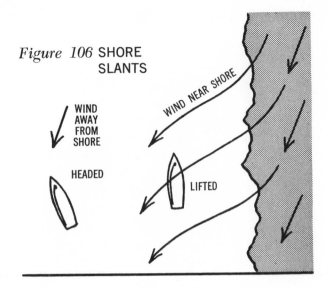

Figure 106 SHORE SLANTS

WIND AWAY FROM SHORE

WIND NEAR SHORE

HEADED

LIFTED

of the weather, and the surface of the land. Flat plains, beaches, pavements, and open fields heat up faster than wooded areas. The land and sea breezes usually do not dominate the prevailing winds but only exert an influence on them. For instance, if a south wind (the most frequent summer breeze in the Chesapeake area) has been blowing steadily and a sea breeze comes in from the east, the two winds will most likely combine to form a southeaster.

Away from the shore, a wind blowing diagonally to the longest dimension of an elongated body of water will generally shift direction so that it blows parallel to the body's longest dimension. Near the shore, however, the wind will often slant so that it blows more at right angles to the shore line. For example, the wind often blows directly down a river in its middle but makes an angle with the shore. This is shown in Figure 106. A boat beating near the shore can often get a lift from this shore slant as can be seen in the diagram. However, if the windward shore is high (with high banks or many trees) it should never be approached closely because of its wind shadow (see Figure 107). Even high lee shores should be approached with caution because the wind can rebound causing turbulence and even an adverse current near the shore. Needless to say, charts should be carefully examined before approaching any shore to avoid running aground. Wind shifts will often occur near the mouth of a river because of the wind bending to blow directly into

or out of the river. Crossing the river diagonally, the wind tends to shift so that it follows the course of the river.

In light airs look for streaks of wind on the water. The skipper should do this continually; so it is often a good idea to assign the puff-watching job to a capable crew member. When the wind is spotty, do not worry about sailing a direct course, but get into the breeze even if at first it appears you are going quite far off course to do so. Very often when the breeze is light, zephyrs will not come to you; so you must go to them.

In heavy winds look for smooth water on the windward leg. There is nothing that will slow a boat more than driving into a steep head sea. Usually the smoothest water will lie under the windward shore. Current will make a difference in the seas also. When a strong current sets against the wind, the seas become particularly steep.

When an imminent thunderhead is seen in the west on a hot, calm afternoon be prepared for the worst, but tack towards the cloud. Those boats closest to the squall when it hits will get the wind first. However, don't take chances with an ugly looking storm. Be ready to drop sails in an instant. If the storm appears to be a severe frontal type, if it is particularly dark and ragged and particularly if it has a preceding roll cloud and/or if weather reports have given warnings of severe thunderstorms, reduce sail

Figure 107 WIND & HIGH SHORES

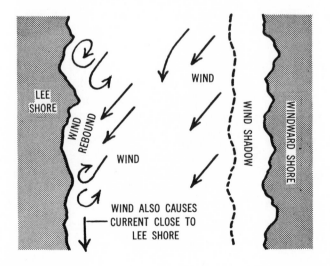

LEE SHORE

WIND REBOUND

WIND

WIND

WIND SHADOW

WINDWARD SHORE

WIND ALSO CAUSES CURRENT CLOSE TO LEE SHORE

and take all precautions. But head towards the storm.

Of particular importance to the racing sailor is an understanding of wind shifts. He cannot predict exactly when the wind will shift, but he can be in the right place to take advantage of a shift. Entirely steady breezes are rare. Of course, some are steadier than others. Winds which blow across the land are often shifty. In the Chesapeake Bay area, the southerly is generally the steadiest breeze, while northwesters are the least steady. However, even southerlies can fluctuate in direction to some extent.

The following are three general rules for beating in a shifty wind: (1) take the tack which brings you closest to the windward mark, (2) tack on each major header, and (3) don't sail out to the fetch line (or lay line) until close to the windward mark. The first rule is explained in Figure 108. It can be seen that the boat taking the close tack to the mark profits whether lifted or headed by a wind shift. If well lifted, the boat sailing the correct course can fetch the mark without tacking; and if headed severely, the boat tacks and can fetch on the opposite tack. Although the illustration shows how taking the close tack to the mark pays off when beating in shifty winds, the same principle applies when tacking downwind. Take the best sailing angle course (the downwind tack that lets the sails draw at maximum efficiency) which brings you closest to the mark. If the wind shifts so that it is flat aft, you can jibe and head directly for the mark on an efficient sailing angle; and if the wind shifts the opposite way (so that it is closer to the beam), you can head directly for the mark on an efficient angle without jibing.

Figure 108 also illustrates the second rule, tacking on major headers. This is clearly shown by the boat sailing the correct course in situation B. This strategy, however, will vary somewhat with the kind of boat that is being sailed. Small, light boats that pick up speed very quickly after tacking can be tacked far more often than large, heavy boats that are complicated to tack (the Navy yawls, for instance). With a large boat, a great deal of time is often lost tacking, so tacks should be limited. The

Figure 108 WINDWARD STRATEGY

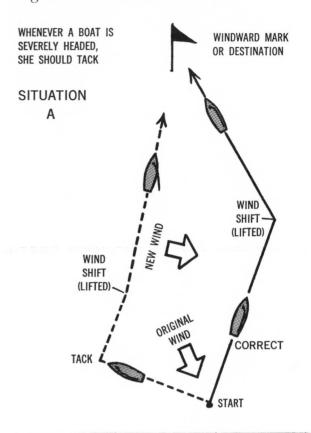

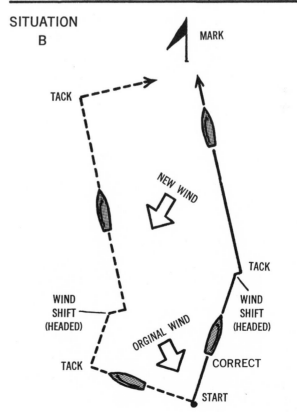

Figure 109 ROUNDING THE MARK

This photograph clearly shows the wakes of the yawls **Alert** (No. 2) and **Dandy** (No. 7) as they round a nun buoy. No. 2 is trying to blanket her rival, while No. 7 counters by luffing (the course to the next mark lies well off the port bow of both boats). If No. 7 had made a wider approach, then cut closer to the buoy's leeward side and afterwards headed as high as she could without breaking the spinnaker, she might have discouraged the blanketing tactics attempted by No. 2. Notice that No. 7 is able to keep her spinnaker full while No. 2 cannot, because No. 7's spinnaker tack has been slacked off so that it is a considerable distance from the end of the pole. This technique, however, is forbidden under both the CCA and NAYRU racing rules.

tacking-on-headers strategy still holds true for a large boat, but care should be taken to see that she is well into a major, definite shift before tacking.

The third tactical rule for beating in shifty winds warns against staying away from the lay line. If you sail out to the lay line far from the windward mark, any shift is bound to hurt you. When you are heading for the mark on the lay line, a lifting shift means that you have overstood the mark, and a heading shift means that you have wasted at least part of the time you spent reaching the lay line.

Although these aforementioned tactical rules apply most of the time, all rules have exceptions. For example, it might pay not to take the close tack to the mark first if this meant you had to sail in the backwind of boats ahead of you or if there were better wind and current on

the other tack. Before forming any final tactical judgment, look at the whole situation and take every influencing factor into account.

Up to this point our discussion of basic tactics after the starting gun has been concerned with sailing the fastest course as though there were no other boats in the race. The presence of competitors, however, creates tactical situations of a different sort which we might term competition tactics.

Most competition tactics involve *covering* situations. When one boat covers another, the covering boat keeps herself in a relatively advantageous tactical position with respect to the other. To cover another boat, you must be ahead or at least even with her. Actually there are two ways of covering a competitor, with a loose cover and a tight cover. The latter method has to do with keeping close to a competitor and maneuvering into a position where you can give her disturbed air, either backwind or wind shadow. The loose form of covering means that you simply try to stay in such a position with respect to your competitor that he gets no beneficial wind or current that you won't get also. Unless you have only one important competitor to beat (as in a match race or if you are tied in a series standings), it is generally wiser to use loose covering tactics; *because if you become preoccupied with one boat, the rest of the competition may leave you behind.* Loose covering tactics are based on a simple principle: *keep between your competitor and the next mark.* With this strategy, you will not do the competitor any particular harm unless he gets close enough to be affected by your disturbed air, but you will have reasonable assurance that you will be able to hold your lead position.

With a tight cover on a beat to windward, you try to attain the safe leeward position or else put your competitor in your wake where he will not only get disturbed air but will be affected by your wake. These tactics are quite often used with small class boats, but they are often not practical in large handicapped boats. In handicap races, the boats are not equal in speed or ability to point. Thus, if a leading boat were trying to tight-cover a faster more close-winded boat, the latter could not be held back; and if it were the other way around, with the faster boat ahead, she would simply leave the slower boat behind. In races involving small, light-displacement boats, it is common practice to tack under a competitor's lee bow so that the tacking boat attains a safe leeward position and can throw disturbed and deflected backwind against her opponent's sails. However, this is a dangerous maneuver with large, heavy boats because these are slow to gain headway after tacking. The rules forbid tacking too close to another boat (Rule 41.1); and furthermore, the boat that has not tacked will carry good momentum·and will probably pass right by the boat that has tacked just ahead.

Occasionally two boats become engaged in a tacking duel when the boat that is being covered tries to tack away from the covering boat. In this case, the covered boat attempts to break away from the leading boat's backwind by tacking, but the lead boat counters by tacking also in an attempt to blanket her rival and keep her covered. The leeward boat tacks again, and the windward boat also tacks again to cover. Such tacking duels come under the heading of becoming preoccupied with one competitor and should be avoided unless it is a match race (only two boats racing).

When a boat is being overtaken by a boat close to windward, the lead boat may luff to prevent the overtaking boat from passing (see Figure 109). The rules define luffing as, "Altering course towards the wind until head to wind." The maneuver is explained under Rule 38, Right-of-Way Yacht Luffing after Starting. This rule should be studied carefully in its entirety.

"Luffing Rights and Limitations" are given in the first part of the rule, 38.1. This says that, "After she has *started* and cleared the starting line, a yacht *clear ahead* or a *leeward yacht* may *luff* as she pleases, except that: A *leeward yacht* shall not sail above her *proper course* while an *overlap* exists if, at any time during its existence, the helmsman of the *windward yacht* (when sighting abeam from his normal station and sailing no higher than the *leeward yacht*) has been abreast or forward of the mainmast of the *leeward yacht*." The "mast abeam" line is illustrated in Figure 110. When the leeward boat

is ahead of the mast abeam line, she may luff, but behind this position, she cannot luff. Ordinarily, when a leeward boat luffs one to windward, the windward boat must respond by luffing also in order to avoid contact. However, if the leeward boat luffs when she is abaft the mast abeam line, the windward boat may not be able to luff without throwing her stern into the leeward boat's bow.

Competition tactics become very important at turning marks because this is where the competitors often bunch together. When you are converging with other competitors on a windward mark that is to be left to port, approach the mark on the starboard tack. The reason for this is obviously that the starboard tack boat has the right of way, and also if she can fetch the mark, she will not have to tack again whereas a port tacker will have to tack around the mark. When the mark is left to starboard, however, a port tack boat can often beat a starboard tacker around if the port tacker slows down slightly to allow her bow to be crossed by the other boat; because the starboard tacker must partially kill her way with an additional tack while the port tacker can simply drive for the mark. This is explained in Figure 111.

Figure 110   MAST ABEAM

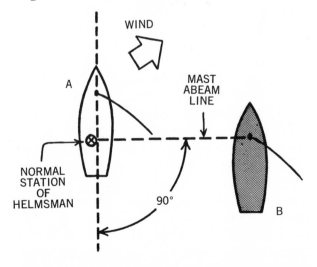

A is passing to windward of B. Before reaching this mast abeam position, B could have luffed. Now, or if A pulls further ahead, B cannot luff. If B is the faster boat and is attempting to pass to leeward of A, B cannot luff even if she draws ahead of the mast abeam line so long as this overlap exists.

In most cases when rounding a mark with other boats, try to maneuver to be on the inside at the mark so that you have the right of way. (See Figure 112). However, if you plan to squeeze into the inside position on a boat ahead of you, be very careful not to establish your overlap when the boat ahead is very close to the mark. Rule 42 deals with rounding or passing marks or obstructions, and this should be studied carefully. Rule 42.3 (a) says, "A yacht *clear astern* shall not establish an inside *overlap* and be entitled to room under Rule 42.1 (a) when the yacht *clear ahead:* (i) is within two of her own lengths of the *mark* or *obstruction,* except as provided in Rule 42.3 (b); or (ii) is unable to give the required room."

Figure 111 WINDWARD MARK
LEFT TO STARBOARD

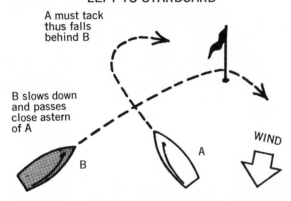

There is a definite technique to rounding marks. A turn which is too sharp will kill your boat's way; thus the turn should be fairly gradual. This is more true for big boats than for small ones. If you are not overlapped by other boats, do not approach the mark very closely when first beginning to make your turn, but cut close to the mark after the turn has been almost completed. This is important when turning onto a windward leg, in order that boats behind cannot sail up on your windward quarter in an attempt to go to weather of your backwind. You should try to keep boats following you, directly behind you or slightly to leeward. When turning onto a leeward leg, keep to windward of your close competitors so that you can blanket them. Be very careful not to touch the mark when passing or rounding it. The penalty for this is disqualification.

The following is a list of tactical and strategy tips to be used on the race course:

• Make use of the current tables.
• Observe current constantly during the race by watching buoys, stakes, marks, etc.
• Whenever possible take advantage of a lee-bow current.
• Stay in shoal water when the current is against you; and conversely, stay in deep water and channels when the current is with you.
• Try to take advantage of eddies and counter currents behind points or near river mouths.
• Stay where you get a favoring current for the maximum length of time, and stay where you get a foul current for the minimum length of time.
• Stay to the most favorable side of a tide rip.
• Allow for sidewise push when crossing a current.
• Do not always play the current at the expense of wind strategy. Unless the current is strong, it may be better to go where there is the best wind.
• Obtain marine weather forecasts before the race, but don't absolutely depend on the forecasts, especially during a short race.
• Look for the influence of a sea breeze during the afternoon of a hot, clear, summer day; look for the influence of a land breeze in the early morning.
• On calm days play the wind streaks. Go to them; don't wait for them to come to you.
• On a hot summer day, look in the west for rising cumulous clouds that could develop into thunderheads. If a thunderstorm develops, be cautious, but work towards the storm.
• When the wind blows diagonally across a shore, look for wind slants. Also look for slants near the mouth of a river.
• Do not sail too close under a windward shore because of the shore's wind shadow.
• Make a study of local weather. Take mental or actual notes of local conditions during each race. These conditions often repeat themselves.
• In a strong breeze and rough sea, look for a smooth lee near the windward shore.

Figure 112

SHIELDS SLOOPS AT THE WINDWARD MARK

No. 4 has an overlap and is entitled to buoy room. No. 7 has not established an overlap in sufficient time; so she has had to head up to keep clear of No. 4.

• In shifty winds when beating, take the close tack to the mark first.

• Tack on major headers.

• Do not sail out to the lay line until close to the windward mark.

• Do not tack more than is necessary, especially in a large boat.

• Constantly keep track of your competitors, particularly the best ones.

• Use loose covering tactics most of the time unless in a match race, or unless you are tied in a series.

• Keep between your competitors and the next mark whenever possible.

• In most cases, do not engage in tacking duels or prolonged luffing matches, especially when running or reaching.

• Keep your wind clear.

• If well clear of a competitor, consider tacking under his lee bow if you are sailing a small, light boat, but don't try this in a large, heavy boat.

• When beating, luff to prevent a boat from passing close to windward, but don't luff if you are abaft the mast abeam line.

• Approach a windward mark that is to be left to port on the starboard tack.

• Round a turning mark fairly slowly so that you do not kill your boat's speed.

• Do not sail close to the mark when first beginning to turn, but cut close to it after nearly completing the turn if turning onto a windward leg.

• Try to round a mark in such a way that competitors behind are placed in your backwind on windward legs and competitors abeam or ahead are in your wind shadow on running or reaching legs.

• Try for the inside position at a mark.

• Learn the racing rules.

• Stay out of trouble. Try to avoid crowds of boats jammed together; and anticipate conditions or maneuvers that could lead to a collision.

• Don't be a wild, tactical gambler. Play the percentages. If you are behind, don't split with the rest of the fleet on the wild hope that you might get a break when you are fairly certain you would be doing the wrong thing.

• If converging on the finish line with other boats, try to be on the starboard tack.

• Head for the closest end of the finish line.

141

CHAPTER TEN

Distance Racing

Distance racing and night sailing are, for the most part, done by seaworthy cruising-racing yachts, racing on a handicap basis, usually under the Cruising Club of America (CCA) rules. The Navy yawls participate in several night races on the Chesapeake Bay and quite a few ocean races. Among these are *The Skipper* magazine's race, the Gibson Island to Cedar Point Race, the Naval Academy Sailing Squadron race to Oxford, the Chesapeake Lightship Race, the Gibson Island to Cape May Race, the Cape May to Newport Race, the Newport to Bermuda Race, the Annapolis to Newport Race, the Marblehead to Halifax Race, the Buenos Aires to Rio de Janeiro Race, and the Transatlantic Race.

Safety at Sea

The primary consideration in any night or ocean race should be safety. It is easier than you might think to lose a man overboard at night in a rough sea, and if accidents happen offshore, prompt help is usually difficult to get.

Lists of required yacht equipment are compiled for most ocean races. Safety equipment on these lists includes such items as: fire extinguishers, a suitable first-aid kit with instruction book, double life lines with through-bolted *stanchions* (vertical posts supporting the life lines), bow and stern *pulpits* (metal railings), a *radar reflector* (folding, geometric shape made of light metal which is hoisted in the rigging), a suitable binnacle and light, running lights meeting legal requirements, flares and a *Very pistol* (flare-shooting gun), at least two large life rings equipped with water lights, whistles and dye markers, a properly buoyed, six-foot pole weighted so it will float upright and with a highly visible flag at the top, extra water, two compasses, two fog horns, two waterproof flashlights, two anchors, two chains or rodes, safety belts for each crew member, rafts or dinghies capable of taking off the entire crew, proper covers for all openings, navigation instruments, rigging cutters, a spare tiller or suitable auxiliary steering arrangement, etc. Of course, many of these items should be aboard your boat whether or not you are going to sea. Exact equipment requirements for an ocean race must be obtained from the sponsoring yacht club. Remember, however, that equipment required is not all the equipment needed. A great deal of preliminary planning should go into preparing for a long ocean race. Plans should be made to meet all possible emergencies, and a complete set of tools and spares for almost every part of the rig and fittings should be carried.

Some of the equipment listed above deserves brief comment. The large life rings should be placed in holders, usually on the life lines, near the helmsman, since there is always a man stationed at the helm. Never lash a life ring to its holder. The horseshoe life buoy is generally thought to be the best type (see Figure 113). The buoyed pole with a counterweight and flag is a very important item at sea where there are large waves, because the flag can be seen above the wave tops. The pole should be attached to a life ring, and if a man falls overboard, both pole and ring are thrown over the side instantly. The weighted pole will also tend to prevent the life ring from drifting excessively. It is often a good idea to attach a small *drogue* (a canvas, cone-shaped sea anchor) to a life ring that is not attached to a pole, in order to decrease drift. Obviously, water lights attached to life rings are essential at night. Electric water lights vary in design, but the usual type is equipped with a battery-powered light that shuts off when it is hung upside down. However, the light is buoyed and weighted in such a way that when it is thrown overboard, it rights itself and turns itself on (see Figures 113 and 114).

Safety belts are indispensable for the crew in rough weather at sea, especially at night. It is generally agreed that the best belt is one that fits on the chest and is equipped with shoulder straps. Attached to the front of the belt is a short, stout line with a large snaphook at its end. The belted crewman snaps the hook onto a convenient part of the rigging or life lines when he needs to work with both hands. The crew should always use safety belts when they leave the cockpit at night or when in a rough sea.

The radar reflector is very important at night and especially in fog. Its purpose is to warn large ships, or any radar-equipped vessel, of your presence. Obviously, the reflector is essential in or near shipping lanes.

The crew of an ocean racer should always be conscious of the watertightness of the hull. In bad weather or even in fair weather, a boat can be rolled over on her beam ends by a sudden squall. If ports, ventilators, and hatches are not closed and *secured,* the boat can quickly fill with water and perhaps sink. This has happened. *Sea cocks* (barrel-type valves in pipes where they go through the hull) on all through-hull openings should be shut in bad weather.

Figure 113 LIFE SAVING DEVICES

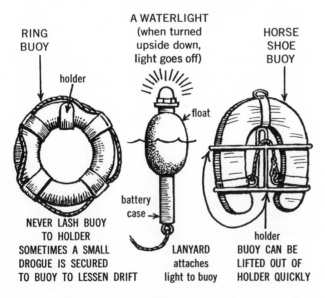

RING BUOY

holder

NEVER LASH BUOY TO HOLDER SOMETIMES A SMALL DROGUE IS SECURED TO BUOY TO LESSEN DRIFT

A WATERLIGHT (when turned upside down, light goes off)

float

battery case

LANYARD attaches light to buoy

HORSE SHOE BUOY

holder BUOY CAN BE LIFTED OUT OF HOLDER QUICKLY

NOTE: handy device is inflatable pocket life preserver pack.

Hinged cockpit seat locker lids should be latched shut, because during a severe knockdown, they can fall or float open. Portholes and hatches should be dogged down in bad weather, and vulnerable ventilators should be provided with a quick means of closing, even if they are only covered with small canvas bags.

Of course all stores and equipment should be properly stowed so that they cannot go adrift in any kind of a knockdown. It is especially important that heavy gear, and particularly any loose ballast in the bilge, is wedged in place or secured so that it cannot possibly shift position during the most severe heeling. Care should be taken to see that gear cannot fall against pipes, electric wires, or the handles of sea cocks.

Every man in the crew of an ocean racer should know where all the vital gear is stowed. He should also be thoroughly familiar with the operation of emergency equipment such as flares, fire extinguishers, and life-saving devices. He must know the proper and safe way to operate winches, and he must be thoroughly familiar with the rigging. A new crew member should study the halyards, sheets, leads, and cleat locations so that he can find them quickly in the dark.

Before sailing in an ocean race, a boat should be thoroughly surveyed and inspected. Most sponsoring yacht clubs require a superficial inspection, but most such inspections are far from complete. The hull should be checked for dry rot, seams carefully inspected to see that they are tight and well caulked, metal parts and fittings checked for fatigue or electrolysis, the fastenings of fittings should be checked, the nuts on keel bolts should be tightened, the sea cocks especially should be checked to see that they operate properly, and so forth. Electrical equipment, wiring, piping, water systems, and all mechanical gear must be checked.

The spars and rigging should receive particular attention. Look for hairline cracks or signs of wear and strain in turnbuckles, tangs, or any metal parts of the rigging. Look for the shifting of tangs, for bent bolts, worn pins, or any deformation of wood or metal. See that all tracks on the mast, deck, and rail are securely fastened. All tracks should be through-bolted wherever

Figure 114
CLOSE QUARTERS

This photo shows a close view of the yawl's stern pulpit, the ring buoys resting in their holders, and the inverted water-light abaft the port ring buoy. Notice that the aftermost slide on the mizzen has parted its lashing.

possible at major points of stress. Also, wherever possible, all cleats and other fittings should be through-bolted. Inspect very carefully the spreaders and the masthead. See that the spreaders are securely fastened and that wire halyards cannot possibly jump out of their sheaves. Double check the spinnaker halyard blocks and swivels, because these take tremendous strain. It is always wise to have spare halyards rigged in case one parts from chafe. See that all stays and shrouds are fitted with toggles. Also see that most halyards or at least the essential ones are fitted with downhauls (light lines attached to the halyard ends so that they can be pulled down in case a halyard shackle breaks or the head pulls out of a sail and leaves the halyard end aloft).

An important aspect of inspecting the boat that relates to speed rather than safety is an inspection of the bottom surface. The hull should be as smooth and fair as possible. Slime and marine growth on the bottom, especially barnacles, are disastrous to boat speed. A foul bottom can make a difference of many hours on a distance race. Before racing in a major ocean race, the boat should be hauled and her bottom cleaned. Particular attention should be given to the bottom of the keel as this is an area that is

often neglected. If the boat cannot be hauled, the crew should go overboard and scrub her bottom with stiff brushes. Before starting the race, don't fail to see that the two blades of the propeller are lined up directly behind the keel, in the position of least drag. The shaft should be marked so that the propeller position for sailing can be noted by looking at the shaft from aboard the boat. Quite often this position can be noted by looking at the shaft keyways. If the propeller is out of position, it can be corrected by turning the shaft by hand. Once in position, the shaft must be locked (with the gear shift or shaft lock) to prevent inadvertent turning.

Emergencies

If an ocean racer is properly inspected and equipped, and if her crew take common-sense safety precautions, it is not likely that emergency situations will arise, but nevertheless, certain emergencies should be prepared for.

Every crew member should be given instruction on what to do if a man falls overboard, and if possible, a man overboard drill or two should be practiced before the start of an offshore race. In most cases, a boat under sail should be jibed when returning to a man who has fallen overboard. This is usually the quicker, more effective maneuver, and the reason for this is shown in Figure 115. Of course, if the boat were running dead before the wind when the man fell overboard, there would be an option between jibing or tacking, and the latter might be easier and safer. Another exception to the jibing rule might be if a boat were running or reaching with a spinnaker, a boom vang, and/or a mizzen staysail set. Of course, these should quickly be removed before jibing. Still another exception is in a strong breeze and rough sea, when care must be taken that the boat does not get too far to leeward of the man.

When a man falls overboard, whoever sees him first should shout, "Man overboard," at the top of his lungs to alert the rest of the crew. The nearest man to the life ring should immediately throw it over the side near the man, but must take care not to hit him. Another crew member should keep his eyes on the man (or water light at night) and point to him continuously. All hands should come on deck, and other crew members should make the boat ready for jibing, especially taking care to slack the running backstay, or for tacking, as the case may be. The helmsman should note his compass course and the time of the accident so that a return course to the victim can be figured, if this becomes necessary.

The man overboard should be approached as shown in the diagram at a slow speed with luffing sails. Notice that the man is pulled aboard on the boat's leeward side so that the boat's hull forms a lee and so that the boat will drift toward the man, rather than away from him. Lines looped and hung over the side can assist the man to reboard the boat. A crew member with a boat hook and another with a heaving line should stand by. Other crew members can stand by to back the sails to slow the boat as the man is brought aboard. If he needs artificial respiration, use the mouth-to-mouth method. This is now almost universally accepted as the best method.

Of course during a race, you will be under sail when the man goes overboard, but you may wish to start the engine to help maneuver.

Figure 115 MAN OVERBOARD

1 Shout "man overboard!" to your crew.
2 Throw life buoy.
3 Have a crew member keep eyes on victim.
4 Jibe in most cases.

A CORRECT MANEUVER UNDER SAIL

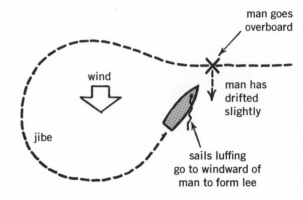

Hang looped or knotted lines or ladder over lee side to assist man getting aboard.

B ALTERNATE MANEUVER FOR HEAVY WEATHER

C ALTERNATE MANEUVER FOR HEAVY WEATHER

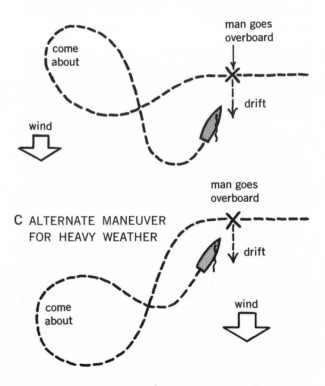

If under power, throw gear into neutral temporarily and swing stern away from victim so that he will not be cut by prop. When picking him up go close to windward of him, put gear in neutral, and drift down to him.

146

Don't forget to remove the propeller lock, and be careful not to let lines that may have been trailed overboard foul the propeller. When picking up the man, you must be careful to keep the propeller away from him. Go to windward and drift down on him with the engine in neutral.

Some thought should be given to fire at sea. Of course, the Navy yawls are relatively safe in this respect with their diesel engines. Fuel for these engines does not have an explosion potential as has gasoline, but nevertheless a close check should be kept to see that there are no drips or leaks in the fuel lines or tanks. Bilges ought to be clean. Do not allow grease and oil to accumulate in the bilge, as this can become a definite fire hazard.

A potential fire hazard on many boats is the galley stove. The Navy yawls are equipped with very safe, gimbled alcohol stoves, but certain precautions should be taken. Garments and towels should not be hung too close to open flames, woodwork and painted surfaces around the stove must be protected or insulated from flames, the stove should be kept clean and grease-free, and care must be taken when filling or priming not to spill fuel. A dry chemical fire extinguisher is hung near the stove. Minor fires can be smothered with a towel or by pouring salt on the flames. Some people advocate pouring water on flaming alcohol, but this could be dangerous when the boat is heeled, because the water may float the burning alcohol and the fire may flow to a new location. If the cook has a good harness to hold him in his cooking location, there will be less chance of his spilling foods or being thrown against the stove in rough weather.

Obviously, precautions should be taken against smoking around flammable materials, against smoking in bunks, and so forth. A fire at sea is usually a lot more dangerous than a fire in one's home.

Another potential emergency for which the crew of an ocean racer should prepare is the breaking of vital rigging. At sea when sailing continuously for days at a time, rigging gets a lot more wear than one would ordinarily think. Metals can become fatigued from the constant motion, and lines that are rubbed can soon chafe through. Chafe is a major enemy at sea, and chafing gear must be applied to any running rigging where it touches a spar or life line, etc. Chafing gear must be checked and adjusted continually.

If the head stay should part while beating, bear off immediately so that you are running dead before the wind. Don't lower the jib right away because its wire luff will help hold the mast forward. Set up the forestay at once, if it is not already rigged. Fasten one or two masthead halyards to the stem head, and tighten these halyards so that they pull the masthead forward. Lower the mainsail and reef it to the point where its head is no higher than the forestay's point of attachment to the mast. If a spare head stay is carried then this may be rigged when the weather permits. Otherwise, perhaps the wire jib halyard can be rigged as a *jury* (makeshift) head stay. The upper end of the halyard might be held to the masthead with wire clamps, and in moderate or light weather a large jib could be hoisted with a spinnaker halyard. Needless to say, spares of every size turnbuckle should be carried because these will often break before the wire stay breaks.

If any of the main shrouds should break on the boat's windward side, tack immediately so that the strain will be put on the opposite shrouds. This maneuver, quickly done, might save the mast. If the mast should happen to break (a very unlikely occurrence if the rigging is regularly inspected), the mast will usually fall over the side. In this case the broken spar should be hauled aboard as soon as possible because in rough seas, it can pound a hole in the hull. This is where the required rigging cutters will come in handy. At sea in heavy weather it is always a good idea to glance at the lee shrouds immediately before tacking to see that none are loose. Masts have been lost needlessly because of failure to check the lee rigging before tacking.

Should the permanent backstay break, round up into the wind at once. Simultaneously set up the running backstays and haul the mainsail in flat. Then lower the jib to take the strain off the head of the mast. If a jury backstay is rigged, don't set the spinnaker, as this can put a great strain on the backstays.

The chance of breaking a stay is rather remote if the rigging is thoroughly inspected. It is not enough to do this before going to sea. Inspections should also take place regularly while at sea. Every few days, when weather permits, a man should be hauled up to the head of the mast in a bosun's chair so that he can check stays, mast sheaves, blocks, pins, tangs, splices, swages, halyards, etc. Hauling a man up the mast at sea when the boat is rolling can be a dangerous operation. Every precaution should be taken. It is important that the man going aloft is lashed in his seat in such a way that he cannot possibly fall even if he is knocked unconscious.

A chafed rope halyard should be replaced long before it has a chance to chafe through. It is often possible to replace a halyard without going aloft by *marrying* the new halyard to the old one. (This is done by placing the ends of the two halyards together, end-to-end, and sewing them together in that position.) Then the old halyard can be unrove from the deck, and the new halyard will follow the old one through the block.

Spinnaker halyards are particularly susceptible to chafe aloft but this chafe can be reduced

by taking the hauling part of the halyard to leeward of the head stay so that the halyard will not cross the head stay and chafe on it.

Regulations and Lights

On most ocean races, contestants are governed by the NAYRU racing rules until they reach International waters, at which time Part IV of the NAYRU rules is replaced by the International Rules of the Road. Of course, exact rule stipulations of a particular race will be stated in the race circular. The International Rules are quite similar to the racing rules. Rule 17 of the International Rules reads:

"(a) When two sailing vessels are approaching one another, so as to involve risk of collision, one of them shall keep out of the way of the other as follows:

"(i) When each has the wind on a different side, the vessel which has the wind on the port side shall keep out of the way of the other.

"(ii) When both have the wind on the same side, the vessel which is to windward shall keep out of the way of the vessel which is to leeward.

"(b) For the purposes of this rule the windward side shall be deemed to be the side opposite to that on which the mainsail is carried or, in the case of a square-rigged vessel, the side opposite to that on which the largest fore-and-aft sail is carried."

All boats, over the size of a row boat, are required to carry navigation or running lights when under way between dusk and dawn, in order that they may be seen by other vessels. Racing boats have been known, on rare occasions, to extinguish their lights for the purpose of deceiving covering competitors, but this is forbidden by law. Even if the main batteries go dead, some sort of jury lights, perhaps powered by flashlight batteries, should be improvised. Running lights are colored red, green, or white; and they have definite sectors or arcs of visibility which are shown in Figure 116. Most ocean racers, including the Navy yawls, are fitted with lights that meet the requirements of the International Rules. Boats meeting these requirements have proper lights for the high seas, and also their lights are legal on all U. S. waters. Fig-

Figure 116   ARCS OF VISIBILITY FOR RUNNING LIGHTS

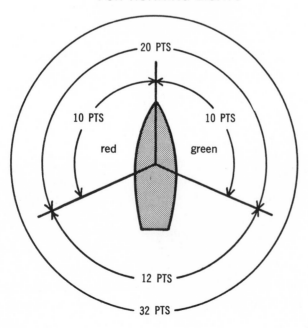

ure 117 shows International Rule lighting for motorboats and sailboats. Notice that when the engine is running on an auxiliary sailboat, the 20-point white light forward must be turned on, but when under sail alone, this light must be turned off.

Under International Rules, there is a lighting option that enables a sailing vessel under sail to carry (in addition to her normal side lights and 12-point stern light) a 20-point red light over a 20-point green light at the masthead, sufficiently separated so as to be clearly distinguished and visible for two miles. This option has been added because normal side lights are often obscured by sails. The rule also says that a vessel may, if necessary in order to attract attention, in addition to the lights which she is required to carry, show a flare-up light. In other words, it is often wise to shine a flashlight on the sails when converging with another vessel at night.

If you are in shallow water and decide to anchor at night, you must turn off the running lights and display an anchor light (except if under 65 feet L.O.A. in special anchorage areas). An anchor light or riding light is a white, 32-point light displayed on the forward part of the vessel.

A careful lookout should be kept at night, even in uncongested waters. When you spot another vessel, her approximate course can usually be determined by looking at her lights. If the after white light can be seen, she is moving away from you. If her red and green lights show simultaneously, she is headed directly toward you. If only one red or green light can be seen, you are looking at her side or at her starboard or port bow as she approaches you at an angle. The course of a large ship can be determined with further accuracy by looking at her masthead and range lights which are white mast lights, one forward and one aft with the after light being higher than the forward one. If these lights are widely separated, the ship is not headed very close to you; but if they are close together, the ship is headed toward you. When the masthead light and range light line up vertically, then obviously the ship is headed directly toward you.

When the lights of a distant vessel are

Figure 117 REQUIRED LIGHTS FOR MOTORBOATS & AUXILIARY SAILBOATS UNDER INTERNATIONAL RULES
required on the high seas and may be shown on U. S. waters

POWER OR POWER & SAIL (65 ft. or less) less than 40 gross tons

AUXILIARY (65 ft. or less) any tonnage UNDER SAIL ALONE

ALSO FOR SAILBOATS (NO POWER) Internat. Rules

WHITE LIGHT FORWARD OFF

12 PT. WHITE STERN LIGHT VISIBLE 2 MILES SEPARATE RED & GREEN SIDE LIGHTS 10 PTS. EACH VISIBLE 1 MILE 20 PT. WHITE LIGHT FORWARD VISIBLE 3 MILES

OR

12 PT. WHITE STERN LIGHT VISIBLE 2 MILES SEPARATE RED & GREEN SIDE LIGHTS 10 PTS. EACH VISIBLE 2 MILES

OR

If vessel is less than 20 gross tons, (under 40 ft. after Sept. 1, 1965)

(STERN LIGHT & WHITE LIGHT FORWARD ARE SAME AS ABOVE)

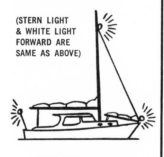

(STERN LT. SAME AS ABOVE)

WHITE LIGHT FORWARD OFF

COMBINATION RED AND GREEN BOW LIGHT, 20 PT., VIS. 1 MI. MAY BE USED IN LIEU OF SIDE LIGHTS

COMBINATION RED AND GREEN BOW LIGHT, 20 PT., VIS. 1 MI. MAY BE USED IN LIEU OF SIDE LIGHTS

A RED & GREEN BOW LIGHT MUST BE MOUNTED AT LEAST 3 FEET BELOW 20 POINT WHITE LIGHT FORWARD.

spotted, the possibility of collision should be determined by taking bearings on her. If the bearing holds steady and the light becomes more and more distinct, then you are on a collision course. When you are the burdened vessel, naturally you must change course; and if you are privileged, you hold your course, but make certain that the other boat sees you by shining a light on your sail. In close passing situations, it

Figure 118 THE WHEEL, BINNACLE, AND COMPASS ON A LUDERS FIBERGLASS YAWL

Notice that the compass is clearly marked in degrees as well as points. Courses
may be referred to by points, as for example, South East (SE), or by degrees, as
135°, which is the more customary. The black knob on the fore side of the glass
dome is the light. The thin white line on the after side of the compass bowl
is the after lubber's line. The knob on the starboard side of the binnacle
locks the wheel when screwed in clockwise.

is a good idea to be prepared to use a sound signal (one which cannot be mistaken for any
other signal authorized in the rules).

All racing boats should be equipped with not
only the NAYRU Racing Rules, but also the
complete International and Inland Rules of the
Road. These are reproduced in Appendixes A,
B, and C. Learn the fog signals. Poor visibility
is often encountered on distance races.

Helmsmanship at Night

One of the keys to successful distance racing
is the ability to keep a boat moving at her best
at night. This is not easy. In the dark, some
competent daytime helmsmen become disoriented, and sail trimming is often neglected.

On downwind courses at night, steering is
done by the compass primarily. In this case, the
helmsman usually tries to steer the straightest
course; at least he should not let his heading
wander excessively. It is not easy to steer a
straight compass course with a following or
quartering sea, when the boat has a tendency to
yaw. The helmsman must attempt to "catch"
the boat before she swings past her proper
heading. The common mistake of beginners is
to turn the helm too late and to overcorrect.

This kind of steering takes practice and the helmsman's full attention.

Beginners often become disoriented when steering with a compass at night, because of a lack of distant visible reference points. On a clear night it is sometimes wise to pick out a star somewhere ahead that can be lined up with the mast or rigging for a check point. Sometimes a beginner becomes almost hypnotized by the compass so that it seems as though the compass card moves while the boat remains stationary. However, it must always be kept in mind that the card stands still and the *lubber line* (the mark or thin post on the compass bowl which corresponds to the boat's heading) is what really moves. (See Figure 118.)

It is important that the binnacle light not be too bright, because this can be blinding to the helmsman when he has to look away from the compass. Red binnacle lights are the least damaging to night vision. Those crew members in the cabin should be careful to use a minimum of light so as not to blind the helmsman (and of course so that they won't disturb off-watch sleepers or use more electrical power than necessary).

When sailing to windward at night, the helmsman must depend to a lesser degree on his sense of sight and to a greater degree on some of the senses discussed in Chapter 4, sound, feel, balance, and the helm touch. He must determine when the boat is moving at her best to windward by listening to the bow wave, sensing the liveliness of the boat, and feeling the balance of the helm. He senses when to bear off or head up by listening to the rattling of the sail slides, by feeling any wind changes on his face, and by using his sense of balance in detecting any changes in the angle of heel.

Although there is less emphasis on the visual aspects of helmsmanship when sailing at night, the sense of sight should not be discounted altogether. When there is a moon, sails can often be seen fairly well. Also the luff of a sail can be occasionally checked with a flashlight that is not overly bright. White ribbon telltales should be substituted for those of light thread. Although the compass is not used as much when beating, it should constantly be consulted to see that you are sailing the generally proper course close-hauled and to detect wind shifts. If you were headed southeast on the starboard tack, for example, you should be sailing roughly southwest on the port tack, barring any permanent wind shift. Also, of course, the navigator is usually interested in your "average" heading for his *dead reckoning* (the figuring of the boat's position by recording or estimating the distance over a known course). There is a normal tendency to pinch a boat at night because the boat's speed usually sounds and feels greater than it actually is, and heavy night air can cause the misjudging of wind strength.

When one helmsman relieves another, the new man, just going on watch, should have plenty of time to get oriented and to let his eyes become adjusted to the dark. The new helmsman should watch the one he is relieving for several minutes before taking the wheel to see how the boat is being steered and to study how the compass heading averages. The helmsman to be relieved should give the new man all pertinent information, such as the course he is trying to make good, the location of other boats, the steering characteristics, what sails are set, what preventers are rigged, or any special problems that might be met.

Sails should constantly be trimmed at night just as they are in the daytime. It is easy to become complacent in this respect after dark, but boat speed will suffer far more than one might think from apathetic attention to trim. Sails can be checked by stationing a man forward to check the headsails (when weather permits), by occasionally shining a dim flashlight on the sails, or by use of the spreader lights once in a while, and by noting the proper daylight trim points and lead positions. It is often a help to mark the sheets with pieces of white tape at proper positions of trim for various points of sailing.

When carrying the spinnaker at night, keep the wind well on the quarter, so there is little danger of the sail being blanketed by the mainsail. On this point of sailing in a good breeze the sheet should be trimmed a little more than usual to guard against the sail collapsing at the luff. A man should be standing by the sheet at all times, ready to give it a quick pull in the event of collapse. Naturally, the helmsman should be ready to bear off when the sail first begins to break at the luff. The Navy yawls carry striped spinnakers and these are relatively easy to see or at least to interpret in the dark. When these sails begin to break, one can see a distortion in the contrasting striped pattern.

The Crew

Although all racing is a team effort, in short races the skipper is the most important member of the crew. His start has a great bearing on the outcome, strategy is largely based on his quick tactical decisions, and he usually has the helm for most of the time. In distance racing, however, other members of the crew gain importance. There is less emphasis on the start, most members of the crew must take their trick at the helm; and although strategy is the skipper's responsibility, other members of the crew are conferred with and consulted before major decisions are made. In fact, it is usually the judgment of the weather expert or the navigator that influences the skipper's decisions.

Signing on a qualified crew is vital to the success of a distance race. A few inexperienced crew members may be taken if there are an ample number of veterans aboard. However, the novices should be thoroughly investigated for susceptibility to seasickness, and they should be given ocean racing instruction and training before the race. All new crew members, whether experienced or not, should be thoroughly familiarized with every aspect of the boat. An attempt should be made to acquire a number of good helmsmen, because no one helmsman, regardless of his skill, should be allowed to steer for too long a period of time. If so, he will become fatigued and lose judgment and effectiveness.

Certain of the crew have definite specialities, for example the navigator and the cook. Other members should be able helmsmen, sail handlers, and seamen; but even these men should have knowledge of, or should be encouraged to specialize in, one or more useful subjects. For instance, there should be a weather specialist, a medic, or one with a good knowledge of first aid, at least one member with mechanical and electrical aptitude, a carpenter, an expert on marlinspike seamanship, and so forth. Of course, the perfect crew is hard to find, but regardless of experience and skills the single most important ingredient for an ocean racing crew is probably enthusiasm.

When there are not other competitors around, it often helps to build up a sort of competition between watches to see which watch can log the greater number of miles or keep above a certain speed. Of course, such contests are not really meaningful and are contrived, to a large extent, in the spirit of fun, but often they do help keep the crew on their toes.

On most ocean races, the deck watch is on duty four hours and off four hours. This is commonly referred to as the "two-watch" or "watch-and-watch" system. In order to avoid the rotation sequence that would bring the same watch on duty at the same times each day, one of the four-hour periods is divided into two *dog watches*. These are two-hour watches, customarily from 1600 to 1800 and from 1800 to 2000, for the specific purpose of alternating watch hours each day. Another popular watch schedule is the *Swedish system*, which divides the day into five watches: 0200-0600, 0600-1200, 1200-1800, 1800-2200, and 2200-0200.

This method gives six-hour watches during daylight, four-hour watches at night, and automatically alternates watches daily. Quite often the navigator is not required to stand watches, and in some cases the skipper does not stand regular watches. Each watch should have a capable watch officer.

Soon after the start of a long distance race, although excitement is high, it is a good idea to settle down into a regular routine. It is important from the outset to combat fatigue. This is the ever present enemy of the ocean racing sailor. Fatigue causes carelessness, poor judgment, and laziness which can lose races, cause accidents, and even endanger lives. An adequate crew should be carried so that the boat can be tacked and her headsails changed without rousing out the watch below. It is important that the crew get plenty of rest and sleep. If anyone has trouble sleeping, he might try using ear plugs or an eye mask or perhaps even a mild sedative. Ample food, sweets, and vitamin B1 pills provide energy.

Another enemy of the offshore sailor is seasickness. As said before, any person particularly prone to this malady should not be allowed on an ocean race, but most sailors, even veterans, can expect to be at least mildly afflicted at times. Many sailors are subject to stomach queasiness the first day or so at sea, and then they become accustomed to the boat's motion and feel well for the rest of the passage, unless exceptionally rough weather is encountered. It is generally agreed that greasy and acid foods as well as excessive use of alcoholic beverages should be avoided a week or ten days before the beginning of an offshore race. If you should begin to feel mildly seasick or queasy, stay as much as possible on deck in the fresh air, try nibbling on dry soda crackers or biscuits, do not use your eyes excessively for close work such as compass or chart reading, and keep warm and dry. In rough weather, smoking in the cabin, especially cigar smoking, should be forbidden. Care should be taken to see that odorless alcohol is used in the galley stove. The galley should be ventilated as much as possible commensurate with safety. There will be the least amount of motion in the aftermost bunks. Certain seasickness remedies such as Dramamine and Bonamine are a real help, but they should be taken before rough weather is encountered. Also, they are apt to make some people very drowsy.

The most valuable personal gear for the offshore crew is good oilskins. These not only keep him dry, but warm. They should be of medium weight and colored bright yellow for best visibility. It is generally agreed that the jacket should open at the front with snaps. This type is the easiest to put on and take off in rough weather and to doff if you should fall overboard. Boots are a great comfort in bad weather, but they should be short, light, have skidproof soles, and be designed so that they can be kicked off easily. There is a great tendency for the crew to peel off their clothes in fair weather, but over-exposure to the sun should be avoided. This can not only produce bad burns, but it can be enervating. It is important for any sailor to carry a knife and wear nonskid deck shoes, but it is doubly important for the offshore sailor.

Distance Racing Strategy

The strategy and tactics involved in a distance race are basically similar to those of a short race, but there are subtle differences. The start of a distance race is, of course, very important, but it is not as crucial as in a short, closed-course race around the buoys. In long ocean races there is a greater dependence on general weather forecasts. Navigation plays a greater role in the distance race, and there is less boat-for-boat racing and emphasis on covering tactics. By and large, each skipper sails his own race.

Although the start is not as vital in a 600-mile race as in one 20 miles long, the start is always important. Distance races have been won and lost by minutes and even seconds. However, it seems ridiculous to attempt a split second start at the risk of fouling (as happened to one famous ocean racer) when there are perhaps four or five days of racing to come. The important thing is to start in clear air. More often than not, a distant point-to-point race will have a reaching start. In such a case, the smaller boats or late starters will often be subjected to the disturbed wind of the leaders. Don't follow in the wakes of those boats ahead unless they are far ahead. It is usually best to drive off or head up until you reach clear air. Quite often when there is a long starting line with competitors bunched at the windward end, it pays to try a leeward-end start with a "full head of steam." In this way, perhaps you can get a safe leeward position, and if you are overtaken by a large boat close to windward, you can usually bear off below her wind shadow. It seldom pays to split tacks on a reaching start. Even if your wind is disturbed temporarily, boats will soon disperse.

The general weather picture certainly must be carefully considered in a distance race. Weather maps should be meticulously studied before the race. Most ocean racers do not have the facilities, nor their crew the inclination, to pick up the vast number of radio weather reports (some of which are in code) necessary to draft their own complete daily weather maps during the progress of a race. However, forecasts based on the information available just before the start can predict weather over the following few days with reasonable accuracy. These predictions can be substantiated or modified by tuning in, as often as possible, to the regular forecasts on commercial stations or reports from airports.

On many long ocean races, contestants can benefit greatly from passing cyclones or barometric lows which move in a general west-to-east direction in the middle latitudes. In the northern hemisphere, the winds rotate counterclockwise around a low and blow inward towards its center. Lows usually follow more or less definite tracks, and by staying in the favorable quadrant of a low, of course, a boat can get the benefit of its favoring winds. Keeping a continuous record of wind direction and barometer readings can help determine where your boat is located with respect to the low. Of course, natural signs of the weather such as the color of the sky at dawn and dusk and especially the clouds should be studied.

Everyone knows that weather reports are not entirely reliable, and therefore they should not be absolutely depended on. Don't make a drastic alteration in a normally sensible course to gamble on a probable weather change. If the risk is such that a predicted change which fails to materialize costs you only few miles or even hours, it may pay to take the risk. However, if the non-materialization could seriously damage your chances of doing well in the race, don't take the risk. In other words, where the weather is concerned, don't climb out on a limb. Make slight alterations in the course in an attempt to take advantage of weather predictions, but don't risk everything.

Any course alterations on the *rhumb line* (the straight line course on a Mercator chart) will not amount to any great change in the total distance to be covered if you are far from your destination, but a similar course alteration close to your destination will add considerably to the total distance remaining. Another thing to keep in mind if you are attempting to follow a rhumb line course, is that your *present* rhumb line is a straight line from where you are, at the moment, to the finish line. Don't feel that you necessarily have to get back to the original (start to finish) rhumb line. This original course may have been the shortest one at the time of the start, but it is not later on in the race if you are not located on that line.

With some skippers, the desire to stick to the rhumb line becomes almost an obsession. Don't become overly concerned with a straight-line course especially in the early stages of the race. The important thing is to keep your boat moving even if it is not in the exact direction of the finish line. If, for example, you have a close-hauled course to the finish and you pinch up in an attempt to fetch, a competitor near you who cracks sheets and sails full and bye on a non-fetching course will almost always beat you. The reason for this is that there will probably be a general wind shift later on that will either lift and allow your competitor to fetch, or else will head you both allowing neither of you to fetch. In the latter case, this shift will put you directly astern of your competitor, because (as you will recall from the last chapter) a heading shift favors the leeward leading boat. The same principle often applies when you are reaching or running. If you are sailing a course which gives you an effective angle with the wind, especially when the spinnaker is set, don't worry about straying from the rhumb line, because the chances are that the wind will shift or change velocity later on. Use the wind you have to best advantage while you have it.

One of the keys to successful distance racing is the maintaining of the best possible speed, not only through choosing the right course, but through continual attention to such factors as sail trim and helmsmanship. It is easy to let down on these matters when there are not other competitors in sight, but an attempt should be made to sail the boat just as though she were racing around the buoys. Not only should sheets be adjusted for every wind change, but also outhauls, downhauls, and leads should be adjusted. It is of the utmost importance that the

Figure 119 UNDER REDUCED SAIL

The skippers of the four Luders yawls shown in this photo have all decided on different reduced sail combinations. From left to right these are: No. 2 Genoa, reefed main and mizzen; No. 2 Genoa and mizzen; No. 1 Genoa and trysail; and No. 3 Genoa and full main. The extreme left and right boats have the more effective rigs for beating to windward, and they seem to be sailing a bit faster than the other two boats.

boat be reefed when there is a need for it and that appropriate headsails are carried. There is a common tendency to procrastinate when it comes to sail changes. Sails are usually reefed and unreefed too late, and headsails are not changed with enough frequency. (See Figure 119.)

When the wind moderates while you are carrying a Number 3 Genoa, it is easy to be lazy and rationalize that the wind will freshen again after a while, but in most cases the Number 1 Genoa should be set. If properly done, a headsail change does not waste much time. On a Navy yawl, or any boat with a double head rig, the forestaysail is set as an interim sail to prevent excessive speed loss while the jib is down.

Before the original jib is lowered, its two lower hanks are unsnapped and the substitute jib is hanked onto the head stay beneath the original jib. A new set of sheets are bent to the substitute jib, and of course they are properly led. Then the original jib is lowered, and its hanks are unsnapped as it comes down. The halyard is quickly shifted to the substitute jib and this is immediately hoisted. In a strong breeze, it sometimes pays to stop the substitute jib with light thread, similar to the way a spinnaker is stopped. Then after the jib is hoisted, the stops can be broken by hauling back on the sheet. Of course, after the new jib has been hoisted and sheeted, the forestaysail may be lowered if so desired. On a short closed-course race, it is

155

often not advisable to change jibs, because the time wasted is too great when compared with the time spent on a course leg; but on a distance race, the best sails for the conditions of the moment should be used, and this often means reasonably frequent sail changes.

One sail change that is important, even though it is not often required, is a change from a reefed mainsail to the storm trysail, or vice versa. Slides on the luff of the trysail are fitted into a separate track alongside the track for the mainsail. The trysail track connects into the main track on the mast via a switch about four feet above the gooseneck. This arrangement allows the trysail to be bent onto its track while the mainsail is still set, and then to be hoisted as soon as the mainsail is lowered below the switch, and the main halyard has been shackled onto the head of the trysail. On three of the fiberglass yawls, the separate trysail track runs up the mast alongside the main track far enough so that the trysail can be set on its own

track. The wooden yawls have no separate track, so that the mainsail must be unbent before the trysail may be bent on.

The trysail has a tack line that is shackled into the gooseneck fitting and allows the tack of the sail to ride up the mast about six feet when the sail is set.

Sheets are attached permanently to the trysail. The sail is normally sheeted like a headsail, with one sheet led on each side. The lead is through a block shackled into the base of the stanchion just forward of the forward mizzen shroud. Alternatively, the clew of the trysail may be lashed to the main boom after the mainsail has been lowered and the sail trimmed by using the mainsheet. In this case, the clew of the trysail must be lashed strongly aft, as well as down. Also, the main topping lift should be set up to take some of the weight of the boom.

The questions of how hard to drive a boat and how long to carry on in bad weather are

Figure 120 **HEAVING TO (UNDER SAIL)**

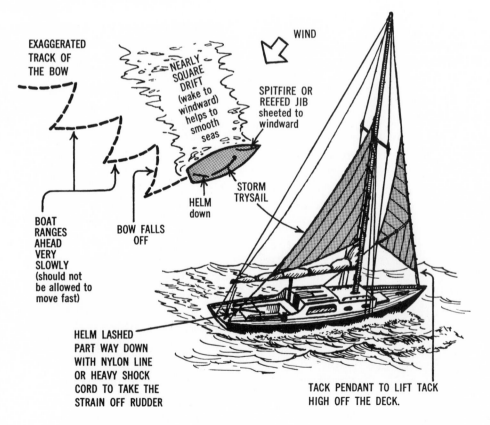

EXAGGERATED TRACK OF THE BOW

WIND

NEARLY SQUARE DRIFT (wake to windward) helps to smooth seas

SPITFIRE OR REEFED JIB sheeted to windward

STORM TRYSAIL

HELM down

BOAT RANGES AHEAD VERY SLOWLY (should not be allowed to move fast)

BOW FALLS OFF

HELM LASHED PART WAY DOWN WITH NYLON LINE OR HEAVY SHOCK CORD TO TAKE THE STRAIN OFF RUDDER

TACK PENDANT TO LIFT TACK HIGH OFF THE DECK.

very difficult to answer. When these questions arise the skipper must carefully consider: the trend of the weather, the behavior of his boat, the condition of the boat and her equipment, and the ability of his crew. If the weather appears to be growing worse, the boat is becoming difficult to manage, and there have been a number of gear failures and jury repairs; and/or if some of the crew are sick, tired or inexperienced, then it is time to reduce sail drastically. As weather conditions get worse, sail should be reduced accordingly. At first you might shift to a smaller Genoa, then to a double head rig, with working jib, and forestaysail, then take in the mizzen and reef the mainsail. A further wind increase might call for the storm trysail with the forestaysail, storm jib, and mizzen. If it blows even harder, you might reduce sail further to the double head rig and mizzen. This is the smallest rig under which the boat will perform well to windward. If even further sail reduction is necessary, you would have the choice of either trysail and forestaysail, or forestaysail and mizzen. The boat will handle well under either of these minimum rigs, but cannot be expected to drive to windward with so little sail.

Under conditions that would warrant such sail reduction, the boat should be eased along and held as near as possible on course. However, if she shows any alarming tendencies to bury the lee rail, or broach to when running or reaching, or frequently to take solid green water on deck, she should be put on the easiest, most comfortable course, and her speed should be further slowed.

In gale force winds, the boat might be run before the wind under a storm jib trimmed flat or, in extreme conditions, under bare poles with lines and cables towed astern to slow her speed. If a running course should take you away from the direction of the finish line, then you might try *heaving to* (stopping speed under counteracting sails with the bow near the wind). This might be done under a storm trysail and a storm jib backed (trimmed to windward) with the helm lashed all the way down. Finding the best means of heaving to will take a little experimentation. The boat should lie reasonably comfortably, and she should not be allowed to *fore-reach* (move ahead) with any speed (see Figure 120).

Get ready for bad weather early; the simplest task on deck becomes extraordinarily difficult in a gale, and an undone rigging chore may lead to a serious casualty.

CHAPTER ELEVEN

Sailboats Under Power

All sailboats equipped with inboard propulsion engines are referred to as *auxiliaries*. The six fiberglass Luders yawls in the Naval Academy fleet are auxiliary yawls; eventually, all will be, as the older wooden Luders yawls continue to be replaced by new, fiberglass boats. Sailing an auxiliary adds an entirely new dimension to the responsibilities of the skipper. He must be able to handle the boat under power as well as under sail. He must know how to operate the power plant and all its associated electrical circuits and piping systems, be conversant with the minimum daily maintenance needs of the engine, and have a knowledge of basic troubleshooting procedures. He has to be aware of all safety precautions.

There are still today a few sailors who remain purists and refuse to have engines in their boats. These seamen have to be admired for their tenacity. While the fiberglass Luders yawls do have engines, it must be remembered that sail training is the purpose of these vessels; the engine should be used sparingly and difficult maneuvers under sail alone should become routine.

While the vast majority of sailboats do have power, engines remain for many seamen a continual source of trouble. This stems from the fact that to many sailors, engines constitute an unpleasant necessity and are not adequately understood. When the skipper does not really know his sailboat engine, it becomes a liability, because of the inherent dangers that exist when adequate safety precautions are not followed, or when the engine is not kept in good running order. An unreliable engine is worse than none at all, for it leads to a false sense of security, and the skipper can count on neither a reliable engine, nor the absolute certainty that all his maneuvers must be carried out under sail.

Handling Under Power

In handling a sailboat under power, many of the principles learned about handling her under sail can be put to good use. In particular, the effects of wind and tide on the hull, the speed required for adequate steerage way, and an appreciation for the amount the boat will forereach under varying conditions are important. There are, however, forces that affect a sailboat only when she is under power. The effects of these forces must be understood in order to handle the boat properly. Most important is the force of ahead *propeller wash*, water forced astern when the engine is going ahead. This wash, when deflected by the rudder, will move the stern of the boat in the opposite direction to that of the rudder (see Figure 121). Astern propeller wash has much less maneuvering potential, since it is not deflected by the rudder.

This lateral force created by ahead propeller wash against the rudder can be used to pivot a sailboat in restricted waters. This maneuver is accomplished by rapidly shifting the engine from ahead to reverse, so that the boat gains very little headway or sternway. In a turn to starboard, each time the engine is put ahead, right rudder is used; the surge of water from the propeller forces the stern to port, and consequently the bow to starboard. Before the boat gathers much headway, the engine is reversed and the rudder is shifted. This operation is repeated until the boat is headed in the direction desired. A turn in like manner to port necessitates just the opposite rudder action. The same force is also used to good advantage to spring away from the windward side of a dock, as will be explained in detail later.

A second force that affects a sailboat under power is that of *torque*. Briefly, it is a force that

Figure 121 EFFECTS OF PROPELLER WASH ON RUDDER OF STATIONARY BOAT

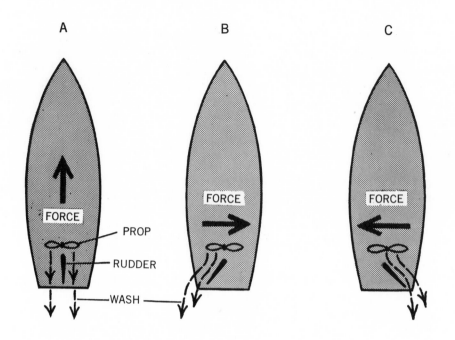

A   B   C

FORCE

FORCE

FORCE

PROP

RUDDER

WASH

IN ALL 3 CASES ENGINE IS GOING AHEAD.
IN CASE B AND C THERE IS AN AHEAD
COMPONENT IN ADDITION TO THE LATERAL ONE.

tends to *walk* (move slowly sideways) the stern of a boat in the direction toward which the propeller is turning. As most propellers rotate clockwise (when viewed from astern) when going ahead and counter-clockwise when going astern, torque forces the stern to starboard when going ahead and to port when going astern. Propeller torque has more effect on shallow-draft boats than on those with deep draft, because of the greater lateral resistance of the latter's underwater body. With ample steerage way, torque is of little importance, except that, when going ahead, the boat will tend to steer to port with the rudder amidships. With little or no way on, however, the rudder has very little effect when the engine is first put in reverse and the torque cannot be counteracted. With no wind, the stern will back to port with the rudder amidships, but a moderate, or stronger, breeze adds another factor. A sailboat nearly always will back into the wind. The reasons for this are that the center of effort of the spars and rigging is located forward of the center of later-

al resistance and that the underwater shape is more cut away forward than aft, and consequently the bow falls off to leeward. In a light breeze, the rudder can be used to counteract this tendency, but with more breeze the bow will fall off faster than the stern can be turned and the boat will almost *always* end up stern to the wind.

When docking under power, some basic rules must be taken into consideration. Maneuver the boat slowly, surely, and with minimum risk of damage; speed is not a seamanlike objective in handling a boat alongside a dock or another boat. Always know the precise direction and strength of the wind and the current. Knowing these, when possible choose the most advantageous docking situation, that is, moving into the wind and current. Wind and current often will not be from the same direction, and in such cases it is best to dock *into* the dominating force. For example, in a 10-knot breeze, you should dock into a 2-knot current, and, conversely, in a 25-knot breeze with a slight current of 1 knot or less, the docking should be made into the wind, if possible. The reason for docking into the forces affecting the boat whenever possible is that a sailboat is very hard to stop when under power due to her large forward momentum and the inefficiency of her propeller. Most sailboats use propellers with minimum drag when stopped, so that the propeller slows the boat down as little as possible when she is under sail. These propellers, usually two-bladed or *feathering* (with blades that can rotate to a vertical position for minimum drag), are not very efficient for backing down. Also, with a head current, steerage way is maintained to the end of the maneuver, while with a fair current steerage is lost while the boat is still making way over the bottom.

When the wind and current are perpendicular to the pier, instead of parallel to it, another choice presents itself. The maneuver is more difficult when the approach is made on the side of the pier toward which the stronger force is moving. In this case, the wind or current (or both, if they have the same direction) will set the boat against the dock, and the danger is that of not allowing enough room for leeway when making the initial approach, with the result that the boat may be set against the dock hard enough to damage her. With strong forces setting onto the only available pier, it may be necessary to drop an anchor to control the boat's motion toward the pier. If the water is rough alongside the pier, such an anchor can also be used to hold the boat off the pier after the landing, so that she will not be damaged.

Experienced seamen prefer the leeward or into-the-current approach. This maneuver has the advantage that during the approach and once alongside, wind or current tend to keep the boat away from the pier. An approach to the leeward side of a pier should be made with decisiveness and adequate steerage way. The boat should be brought into the pier at a slight angle, so that the leeward setting effects of the wind and current can be compensated for. The stronger the leeward set, the faster the approach should be. At very nearly the last moment, the boat is swung parallel to the pier and the engine is reversed smartly to kill headway.

The first line over should be the bow spring line (a line leading from the bow to a point well aft on the pier), which can be used both to check forward motion and to spring the boat in to the pier. (See Figure 122 for explanation of docking lines.) The second and third lines over should be the bow line (a line leading from the bow forward to the pier) and stern line (a line leading from the stern aft to the pier); lastly, the quarter spring line (a line leading from the quarter to a point well forward on the pier) may be made up.

Landing in all possible combinations of wind and current cannot be explained within the confines of a book. If the beginner remembers that the deeper the draft of the boat, the more current affects the hull in relation to wind, he has the basic principle on which to decide the approach in each situation. He should also remember that it is easy to overestimate the effect of wind and to underestimate the effect of current, perhaps because wind strength is much easier to sense than is current strength. It is recommended that docking evolutions be practiced often under varying conditions, not just when you need to dock.

Figure 122 DOCK LINES

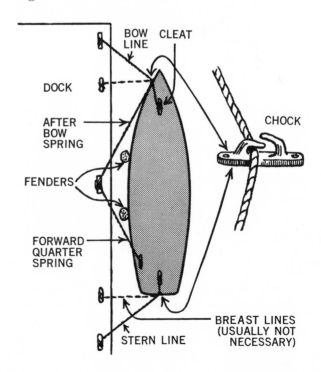

161

In preparation for a docking maneuver, it is important that the entire evolution be worked out in your own mind *ahead of time*, including an alternative plan to be used if the initial approach fails at any point in its execution. *The seaman tries never to get himself into a situation from which he cannot recover.* He makes elaborate preparations even for a simple maneuver. An anchor should always be ready for use in any situation where engine failure would endanger or embarrass the boat. Under some circumstances, a ready stern anchor may also be necessary. In every case, dock lines should be ready and led. Fenders should be out, but preferably not over the side until near the pier. Most important, the crew should be briefed on the skipper's plan and exactly what their individual jobs will be. Confusion at the last minute is the cause of most unseamanlike docking maneuvers. The crew, once briefed, should keep out of the skipper's way, *and out of his line of vision.*

When getting under way, the same detailed preparations should be made. It is worth emphasizing again that it is care in preparation that separates the seaman from the landlubber. If the boat is on the leeward side of the pier, the maneuver is relatively simple. (This is another reason for landing on the lee side of a dock.) Spring lines are taken in, coiled, and stowed. Then bow and stern lines are taken in together. Remember that the bow will swing faster than the stern and a strong breeze could cause the stern to walk toward the pier before clearing. For this reason, it is best to cast off the stern line first in a strong breeze then cast off the bow line, and then go ahead when clear.

When leaving the windward side of the pier, the maneuver is more complex. If the wind or current is very strong, the only solution is to row out an anchor to weather (if one was not dropped during the landing) and warp the boat around head to wind or current. If, however, the forces setting onto the pier are not too strong, the boat may be gotten under way under power alone. This is accomplished by springing the stern away from the pier. First, the bow line, stern line, and quarter spring are taken in, then a fender is positioned forward

and a crewman is stationed forward to fend off the bow. The engine is put ahead slowly and the rudder put over toward the pier. The boat pivots slowly against the bow spring. Power is kept on until the bow comes in against the forward fender and the stern swings away from the pier. When the stern is well away from the pier, the engine is reversed smartly, the rudder is shifted, and the bow spring is taken in. If the wind is not too strong, the boat can be backed rapidly away from the pier. When the wind is strong, there is the danger that the bow will scrape along the pier before the boat can be backed clear. If this is the case, the rudder should *not* be shifted immediately, allowing the boat to back in a direction more parallel to the pier until the bow is well clear. In this maneuver, it should be remembered that torque effect tends to walk the stern to port. In *all* cases the boat should be backed clear smartly to avoid being blown back against the pier. Again, practice is essential.

When mooring to a buoy or anchoring, it is most important to determine whether the wind or the current will have the greater effect on the boat's heading, once she is stopped. Simply, after anchoring or mooring, will the boat lie head to wind or head to current? Observation of other craft in the anchorage is a good indication. Beware, however, of using power boats as a guide, because their large windage and shallow draft tend to make them lie head to wind when a deep-draft sailboat with opposite characteristics may lie head to current. Once this determination has been made, the approach should be in the direction that the boat will assume when stopped. Care should be taken when picking up a mooring to retain at least bare steerage way until just before the mooring line is picked up. If this is not done, the bow may blow off before the mooring line can be taken on board. When anchoring, care should be taken to ensure that *all* forward way is off the boat before the anchor is let go. If the boat overrides her anchor, the line may foul the anchor or even foul the propeller. Once the anchor is down and has been given adequate scope, it should be *set* (dug into the bottom) by reversing the engine while the anchor line is *snubbed* (held taut). This procedure is especially important when using the Danforth anchor.

When weighing anchor under power, heave in to straight up-and-down, belay, and ease ahead on the engine to break out the anchor. Then stop the boat until the anchor has been brought aboard.

In coming alongside an anchored or moored boat, the problem is simplified in one respect in that the direction of approach is dictated. When possible, one should come alongside to starboard of the moored boat. The point where the bow will lie when secured alongside should be determined. Then an angled approach toward the point is made. The bow spring and bow line are put over. With the engine reversed, the torque effect will tend to bring the stern to port, parallel to the anchored boat. Of course, fenders should be rigged on both boats before the maneuver is begun. *Remember to look aloft when going alongside another sailboat.* It is distressing to have a nice landing spoiled by the sound from aloft of spreader crunching against spreader.

Occasionally when under power it will be necessary to render assistance to boats becalmed or in distress. Towing is a very delicate maneuver and must be very well planned before being attempted. There are no hard and fast rules. Each situation must be analyzed before action is taken, however, it can safely be said that a capsized boat should not be towed. Assisting capsized boats will be discussed in more detail in the next chapter. If the vessel requiring assistance is *not* aground, she may be approached from either her windward or leeward side. When approaching from the windward side, a lee is provided for the disabled boat which may be helpful, but the boats will tend to be blown together while the tow line is passed. Usually the better approach is from the leeward side. The approach is made at an angle across the bow of the disabled vessel. The tow line is passed as the vessel's bow is crossed. In both cases, the tow line should be made fast, properly led, and be ready for passing before the approach is begun. Once the tow line has been passed, it should be payed out slowly, allowing the towing vessel enough slack to come up into the wind before taking a strain.

Coming head to wind is important, because it allows the towing vessel to maintain her position while waiting for the tow line to be secured on the disabled vessel. Great care must be taken while paying out the tow line not to let it foul the propeller.

If the tow line should foul the propeller, put the clutch in neutral immediately and try reversing the engine slowly. If this fails, the line will have to be cleared by a man diving to the propeller where he can unwrap, or cut away, if necessary, the fouled line. Another tow line will have to be passed, and it may be desirable to anchor while the old tow line is being cleared.

When the tow line has been secured on the disabled vessel, strain should be taken very slowly. It is at this point, when the inertia of the towed vessel is greatest, that the greatest danger of parting the tow line exists. Speed should be increased slowly until both vessels have adequate steerage way. Maximum towing speed will be determined by wind and sea conditions and by the size of the vessels, but it should always be *moderate*. Remember that towing another vessel puts a double load on the engine and severely reduces the maneuverability of your boat.

The amount of tow line will vary with the sea condition. In calm water, several boat lengths should separate the boats, but in a rough sea, considerably more scope should be used. The more scope, the more spring and the less sudden strain on the tow line and towed boat. Although it is desirable to have the two boats in the same position relative to crests and troughs, the sea is seldom regular enough to achieve this condition.

Assisting a vessel that has gone aground presents many additional problems. First, it must be determined how hard she is aground. If she is high and dry, any efforts to dislodge her will end in parted tow lines or damaged gear. Offer to set an anchor to windward and let the tide take care of the rest. If, however, she is not too hard aground, towing assistance may be rendered with caution. Most often, the grounded vessel will be on a lee shore, with the wind pushing her farther on the shoal. In this situation, the approach must be made directly down wind, and great care must be taken not to be run aground in the process. The best precaution against that occurrence is to set an anchor well to windward and ease back towards the grounded vessel, using the anchor to hold the bow into the wind. Once the tow line has been passed, strain can be increased gradually while still using the anchor to keep from being blown broadside to the wind. After the grounded vessel has been freed, the anchor may be picked up. If the vessel can proceed under her own power, cast her off when she is ready. If not, take her in tow, remembering the precautions mentioned in the preceding section.

If the situation is reversed and you have run aground, there is an excellent chance that you will be able to get off if you act quickly enough. If the boat has power, it should be used whether the boat is under sail or power at the instant of grounding. If under sail, take down the sails. Initially, an attempt should be made to back the boat off in the direction from which she came, as there is always good water astern. The engine should be put in full reverse and the entire crew, perhaps even including the helmsman, should move to the bow. As most sailboats are deepest aft, this tends to lessen the draft. The wash from the reversed engine will tend to free the keel from mud or sand. The crew can help by rhythmically jumping in unison on the bow. If this procedure does not free the boat in a few minutes, do not continue it, because prolonged running of the engine in full reverse will

overheat it. Whether this action gets the boat off or not, be sure to check the salt-water cooling system intake strainer for weeds and sand before proceeding.

If the boat has not been freed by the above method, other steps, such as those described in Chapter 2, will have to be taken. Two points should be re-emphasized. If you accept help from another boat, you must remain in charge of the situation as it affects your boat, and must be ready to take immediate action to avoid having a would-be rescuer inadvertently damage your boat. In this regard, it is well to convey your exact intention to the boat rendering assistance before any maneuvering starts, as once engines begin to strain, communications may be difficult. Secondly, it is much better to wait for the tide than to damage a boat getting her off.

Rules of the Road

When operating under power, whether or not sails are set, a sailboat must comply with those regulations governing motor vessels. She is no longer a sailboat. The applicable International Rules of the Road and Inland Rules of the Road are in Appendixes B and A. Therefore, explanation here will be brief.

In addition to knowing which boat has the right of way in meeting, overtaking, and crossing situations, the skipper of a sailboat under power must be familiar with the maneuvering whistle signals prescribed by International and Inland rules.

Figure 123 INLAND PILOT RULES (for motorboats or sailboats under power)

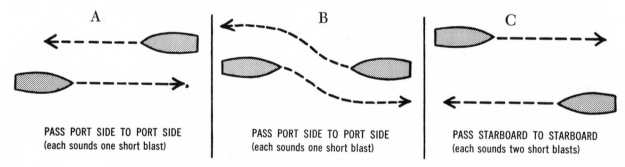

A	B	C
PASS PORT SIDE TO PORT SIDE (each sounds one short blast)	PASS PORT SIDE TO PORT SIDE (each sounds one short blast)	PASS STARBOARD TO STARBOARD (each sounds two short blasts)

When vessels meet head on or nearly so, each vessel passes on the
port side of the other unless the courses of such vessels are so far
to starboard of each other as not to be considered meeting head and head.

The diagrams in Figure 123 A-F illustrate the six basic situations encountered by vessels under power under Inland Rules, the rules that apply in Chesapeake Bay. The proper reaction to each situation should be, or become, instinctive to the skipper.

In Figure 123A, both vessels are evidently passing to port of each other, which is preferable in this situation. Each had signified his intent by one short blast of the whistle. Both are burdened, while neither is obliged to change course. At night the masthead light and red (port) side light would be visible to each.

In Figure 123B, both vessels were headed directly toward each other. In this situation, the rule is that each shall turn to starboard and pass on the port side of the other. Each has signified his intent to do so by one short blast of the whistle. Both are burdened and both are obliged to alter course. At night, both side lights (red and green) and the masthead light would be visible to each before altering course, and the red side light and masthead light remain visible after course alteration.

In Figure 123C, the vessels are going to pass to starboard of each other. Each has signified this to be his intent by two short blasts of the whistle. Both are burdened, but neither has to alter course. At night, the masthead light and green (starboard) side light would be visible to each.

Figures 123D and 123E illustrate overtaking situations. (To be considered an overtaking, rather than a crossing, situation, the overtaking vessel must be at least two points or more abaft the beam of the overtaken vessel.) In both cases the overtaken vessel (b) is privileged and must maintain course and speed, while the overtaking vessel (a) is burdened and must alter course. In Figure 123D, vessel (a) should signify intent to pass to port of vessel (b) by sounding two short blasts. If such a passage is clear, and acceptable to vessel (b), she should answer two short blasts and the passing will be effected. In Figure 123E, vessel (a) should signify intent to pass to starboard of vessel (b) by sounding one short blast. If the passage is clear and acceptable to vessel (b), she should answer with one short blast. If, in either case, the initially proposed passage is dangerous, vessel (b) would sound the Inland Rules danger signal of four or more short blasts. After the passage is clear, vessel (b) would sound the proper answering signal.

In the crossing situation, diagrammed in Figure 123F, two vessels are approaching each other at right angles or obliquely in such a manner that there is a risk of collision. Vessel (a), which holds the other to starboard, is burdened and should maneuver to keep clear either by altering course to starboard, slowing, or both. She may signify this to be her intent by sounding one short blast. Vessel (b), which holds the other to port, is the privileged vessel and is obliged to maintain course and speed. This intent should be signified by one short blast. Whistle signals are not mandatory, however, in the crossing situation under Inland Rules. At night, vessel (a) would see the masthead light and red (port) side light of vessel (b), while (b) would see the masthead light and green (starboard) side light of (a). In studying these situations, see

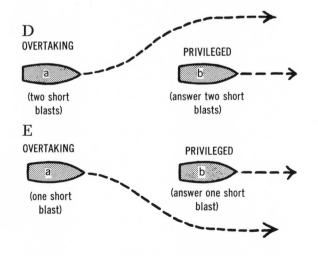

D
OVERTAKING

PRIVILEGED

a

b

(two short blasts)

(answer two short blasts)

E
OVERTAKING

PRIVILEGED

a

b

(one short blast)

(answer one short blast)

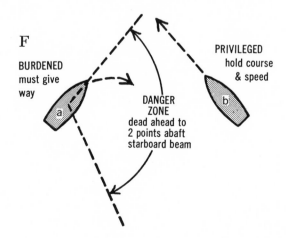

F

BURDENED must give way

a

DANGER ZONE
dead ahead to 2 points abaft starboard beam

PRIVILEGED hold course & speed

b

Sections 80.4-80.7 of the Inland Rules (Appendix A).

The navigational lights required by both International and Inland Rules for a sailboat under sail were described in Chapter 10. When under power, sailboats are required to carry the same lights, plus a single, white, twenty-point, masthead light at least three feet above the side lights on the forward mast. This light should be visible for a distance of at least two miles on a clear, dark night.

Electrical and Water Systems of the Wooden Luders Yawl

The wooden yawls remaining in the Naval Academy fleet are without auxiliary power. Nonetheless, it is appropriate to describe here their electrical, and fresh- and salt-water systems, since detailed knowledge of these systems is required of any wooden-yawl skipper.

The electrical system of the wooden yawl utilizes two 6-volt wet-cell batteries connected in series to obtain 12 volts. These batteries are located in a lead or fiberglass battery box (to protect the boat from acid) abaft the companionway ladder. These batteries provide power for cabin lights, running lights, spreader lights, the binnacle, and a Kenyon light (in boats where Kenyon speed indicators are installed). The cabin lights are controlled by switches on the fixtures, in addition to switches on the control panel located abaft the companion ladder. The appropriate switch on the control box must be turned on before the fixture switches will work. The other lights are controlled solely by the switch on the control panel. On deck, two electrical jacks are provided for connecting emergency running lights and spot lights. When not in use, these jacks should be capped to ensure that salt water does not short the circuit.

The fresh-water system has two 50-gallon tanks, located under the lower bunks amidships. Connecting valves are located beneath the cabin sole and are reached by removing a portable section of the cabin sole. The tanks are filled from the deck. The fresh-water fill pipe deck plate is on the port side amidships. The boat's tool kit should include a spanner wrench

for removing the plate. Each tank has a vent on its top. There are two fresh-water pumps in the boat, one at the galley sink and one at the head sink. The head sink drains into the toilet bowl. The galley sink drains via a globe valve, pump, and sea cock overboard through the hull. The ice box drains via a separate valve into this same drain line, so that the pump below the ice box can be used to empty either the ice box or the sink. To do so, the appropriate valve must be open, and the valve not in use should be shut. Both these valves are in the locker next to the ice box.

Before using any pump, check that both intake and discharge valves are open. If the intake valve is shut, useless effort is expended merely, but if the discharge valve is shut, *pumping can rupture the pump or discharge line.*

Included in the salt-water system is the piping for the bilge pumps, cockpit scuppers, and the head. On all the boats there are two bilge pumps. One is located just aft of the head, to starboard of the companionway. The other is beneath the cockpit and is operated from the cockpit. The intake strainers for both these pumps are in the bilge beneath the companionway. Both these pumps discharge through the hull through sea cocks, which should be opened for use and shut immediately afterwards. A sea cock is opened by paralleling the handle with the piping; when the handle is perpendicular to the piping, the valve is shut. All through-hull fittings on the Luders yawls are equipped with sea cocks, and familiarity with their location and use is a must. If a bilge pump seems hard to operate, first check to make certain that the discharge valve is open. Second, check the intake strainer in the bilge to see if it has been clogged. For this very reason, it is important to keep all foreign matter out of the bilge. On some of the wooden yawls, a third bilge pump is installed. It is a high-capacity diaphragm pump located beneath the cabin sole. The intake for this pump is beneath it in the bilge, and it discharges over the side via a length of fire hose led out through the hatch. This length of fire hose and the handle needed to operate the pump should be stowed with the pump. If they are misplaced, the pump cannot be operated.

The head has two sea cocks, one at the hull on the intake side (this one is the smaller of the two), the other at the hull on the discharge side. The intake (hull) valve is beneath the cabin sole next to the head, and the discharge valve is in the locker just outboard of the head. Both must be open to use the head. To operate the head, open the valves, depress the pedal on the foot-operated intake valve, and pump. This action pumps water both in and out. After the head has been pumped clear, pump ten more strokes to clear the discharge line, then release the foot pedal and continue to pump until most of the water has been removed from the bowl. In a rough sea, remove all water from the bowl. Before leaving, *shut the valves. Never* put solid objects or large quantities of paper in a marine toilet, as they will not fit through the rubber diaphragms. These rules apply to most marine toilets, but if there is any question about operation, ask before using one.

The cockpit scuppers drain overboard through pipes located beneath the cockpit. These pipes are fitted with sea cocks at the through-hull fittings which are aft of the ice box on the port side and under the quarter berth on the starboard side. These valves should always be left *open* so that the cockpit will drain.

As has been mentioned, it is good practice to shut sea cocks that are below the water line, if not after every use, at least when securing the boat. The reason for this is that pumps and the head often will siphon water back into the boat after use. Occasionally a boat has sunk while the owner was ashore because the head or bilge pump discharge sea cock had been left open.

All of the Luders yawls are equipped with alcohol-burning galley stoves. To the uninitiated, these stoves are hard to operate and very dangerous. An alcohol stove must be filled before it is operated. Be very careful not to spill the alcohol while filling the stove. Once the tank is filled and the cap secured, the tank must be pressurized. There is a pump for this purpose and a pressure gauge which is very clearly marked. When the tank is full, it is very easy to *over*-pressurize the tank. Be sure to watch the gauge while pumping. Also, remember that pressure must be maintained during use. This will require occasional pumping while the stove is in use.

After the stove has been filled it must be primed. First some alcohol must be collected in the small basins below the burners. This is done by opening the burner valves *very* briefly. About three seconds will be all that is necessary. If the valves are left open too long, raw alcohol will spill onto the tray under the stove and when the stove is lighted there will be a conflagration. If alcohol has spilled, wait for it to evaporate before lighting. If a flash fire does occur, as it will whenever excess alcohol is allowed to collect on the tray beneath the burners, it can often be put out by smothering with a towel or garment. Do not use the dry-chemical fire extinguisher unless it is necessary, because it will cover the galley with a white powder that takes hours to clean up.

The alcohol in the basins under the burners is lighted to heat the burners. After the burners have been adequately pre-heated, when the valves are opened, the alcohol will vaporize before reaching the burner and will burn as a gas.

If a proper gas flame cannot be obtained, turn off the valves and start the whole process of priming again.

Auxiliary Engine of the Fiberglass Luders Yawl

The fiberglass yawls are equipped with a four-cylinder Westerbeke Model Four-107 diesel engine (see Figure 124). These engines are direct drive and have hydraulic transmissions. The engines are controlled from the cockpit by Morse single-lever controls (see Figure 125). These engines are reliable and easy to operate, as are the controls, but there are a number of *essential* checks that must be made prior to operation in order to ensure continued reliability. Remember, the more you know about the operation of the auxiliary, the less likely it is to give you trouble. The checks that are necessary for the Westerbeke are similar to checks required before getting under way with any auxiliary. In every case, the cooling system, oil level

Figure 124 THE WESTERBEKE MODEL FOUR-107 DIESEL

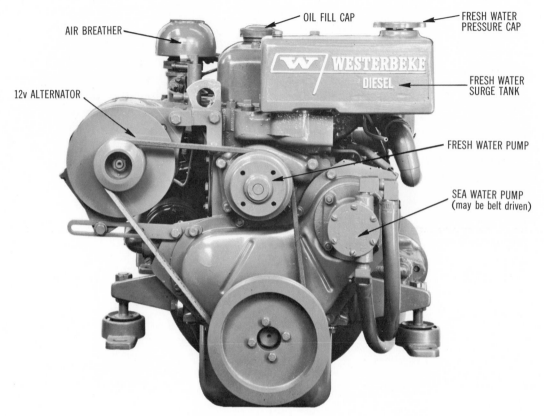

AIR BREATHER

OIL FILL CAP

FRESH WATER PRESSURE CAP

12v ALTERNATOR

WESTERBEKE DIESEL

FRESH WATER SURGE TANK

FRESH WATER PUMP

SEA WATER PUMP (may be belt driven)

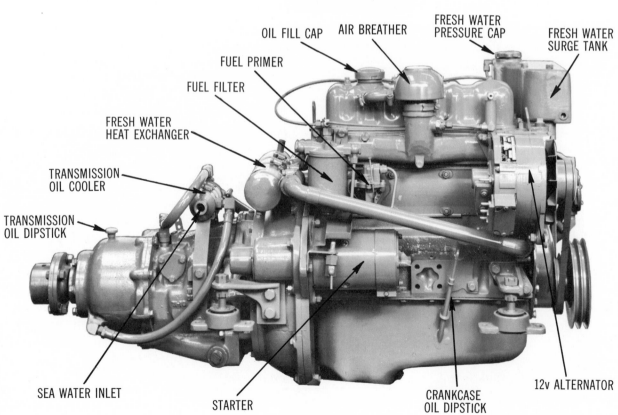

OIL FILL CAP

AIR BREATHER

FRESH WATER PRESSURE CAP

FRESH WATER SURGE TANK

FUEL PRIMER

FUEL FILTER

FRESH WATER HEAT EXCHANGER

TRANSMISSION OIL COOLER

TRANSMISSION OIL DIPSTICK

SEA WATER INLET

STARTER

CRANKCASE OIL DIPSTICK

12v ALTERNATOR

168

in the engine, fuel supply, and shaft lock, if there is one, should be checked.

The Westerbeke engine has a self-contained fresh-water cooling system. The fresh-water tank is atop the forward end of the engine and must be checked before starting. It should be filled to three-quarters of an inch below the opening. The fresh water, which recirculates, is kept cool by a heat exchanger on the after end of the engine, which in this system uses salt water. In addition, the salt water cools the lubricating oil heat exchanger and the exhaust pipe. The salt-water cooling system has two valves, an intake and a discharge, and *both must be open when the engine is running*. The salt-water intake valve is abaft the engine shaft coupling on the port side. The discharge valve is in the exhaust line and is in the lazarette. The discharge valve should always be shut when under sail in a seaway, because it then keeps salt water from entering the engine via the exhaust line. Both valves are shown in Figure 126.

The lubricating oil sump on the Westerbeke has a maximum capacity of five pints of oil. For proper engine operation the oil level in the sump must be kept between four and five pints. The engine sump dipstick must be pulled and inspected to ensure that the lubricating oil is at the required level. The dipstick on the Westerbeke is on the starboard side of the engine, down quite low. Be sure to push it all the way into the sump when checking the oil level. As already mentioned, the engines are equipped with hydraulic reverse gears. Because of this, the reverse gear has a separate oil sump which must also be checked. The reverse gear dipstick is on top of the gear box at the after end of the engine on the port side. If oil is needed in the main sump, only Navy symbol 9250 oil or a high-quality, heavy-duty, 30-weight detergent oil should be used. The gear box uses special, light, hydraulic oil, and *only* this should be used if oil is needed. These dipsticks are located as shown in Figure 124.

Fuel is supplied by one 40-gallon tank, which is amidships below the cabin sole. As indicated in Figure 126, it is the forward one of the two tanks in this area. It is reached by lifting the

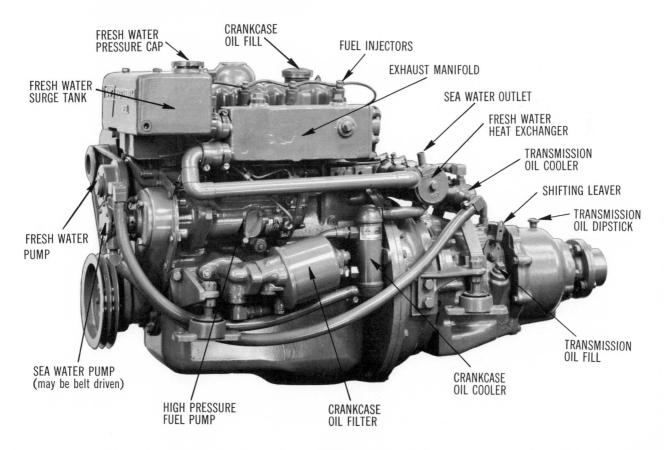

169

Figure 125 ENGINE CONTROLS
ON THE LUDERS YAWL

The lever with the white knob is a combination throttle and gearshift. The button to the right of the lever is a clutch; when the button is pulled out, the gears are disengaged and the lever acts as a throttle only. The lever below the instructions turns in either direction to shut off the engine. The rotary switch is for lights on the binnacle and instrument panel; the nearer button below it is the engine starter; the further button is the pre-heater (see also Figure 127).

forward removable section of the sole in the main cabin. The fuel gauge is on top of the tank. The fuel tank is filled from the deck. The fill pipe deck plate is forward in the cockpit. As a general rule, the cockpit floor is a poor location for a fuel fill fitting, because there is often water on it and some is apt to leak into the fuel tank. The valve in the fuel supply line is on the bulkhead aft of the companionway just forward of the first fuel strainer; it should be left open. On boats with a gasoline auxiliary, because of the very explosive nature of the fuel, it is good practice to shut the gasoline supply valve when leaving the boat. More on this subject will be discussed at the end of this chapter in the section on safety precautions.

One last item remains on the check-off list. This is the shaft lock, which is used to keep the propeller in a vertical position for minimum drag when sailing. It must be released before the engine is run. It is on the shaft beneath the cockpit. Once these items, (1) fresh-water tank,

(2) salt-water exhaust and intake valves, (3) oil supply in sump and reverse gear, (4) fuel gauge, and (5) shaft lock, have been checked, you are ready to start the engine.

The first step in starting the engine is to energize the electrical system. This is done by switching the battery selector switch from "off" to position "1" or "2." The battery selector switch is abaft the companionway. It is a Perko circular switch, and it determines which of the yawl's two 12-volt batteries is going to be used for power. The switch is illustrated in Figure 127. One should note that between positions "1" and "2" on the switch is a position marked "ALL." When the switch is moved to this position, power is drained from both batteries simultaneously. The "ALL" position should not be used unless neither battery has sufficient power by itself to start the engine. If both batteries must be used to start the engine, switch to position "1" or "2" immediately after starting, as any short circuit in the electrical system will discharge both batteries if the selector switch is left on "ALL."

The next step is to prime the engine. This is done by lifting the hand prime pump shown in Figure 124 three or four times. A diesel cannot be flooded, so over-prime rather than under-prime.

The rest of the starting operation is conducted from the cockpit. The engine is put in neutral, by putting the Morse control handle in the vertical position. This control is both gear shift and throttle. It is on the starboard side of the cockpit and is illustrated in Figure 125. Once in neutral, the knob below the handle must be pulled out to disengage the gear shift, and then the throttle is advanced forward about one-half speed. After this has been done, turn the starter switch clockwise to start the engine. On some yawls, the starter is a button which must be depressed. The starter switch is on the panel at the after end of the cockpit, or on the starboard side of the cockpit. This panel is illustrated in Figure 127. As soon as the engine starts, move the throttle back to the idle position and let the engine warm up for at least five minutes. Remember to push in the knob below the handle to engage the gear shift. To start the engine in

170

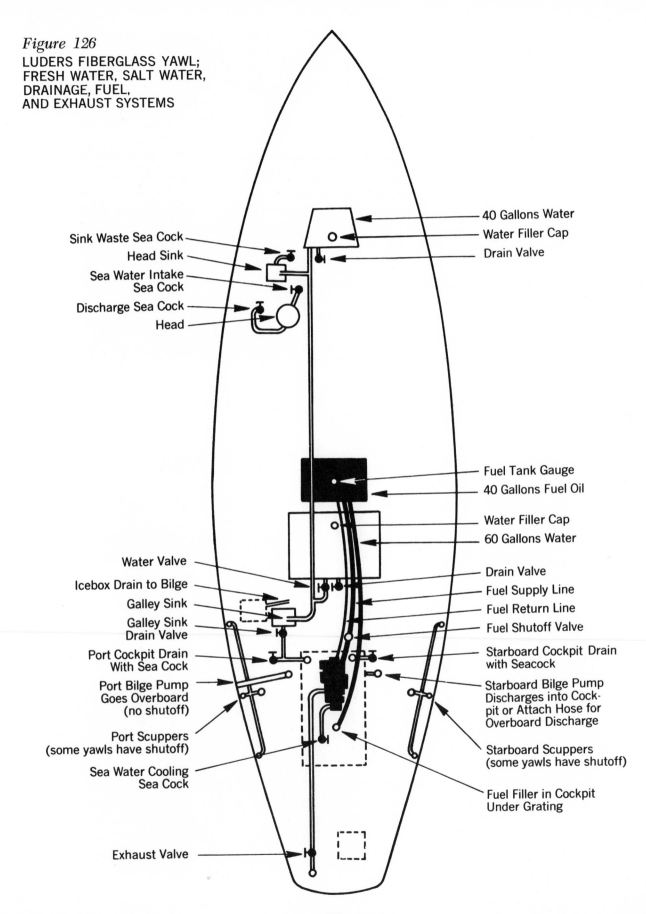

Figure 126
LUDERS FIBERGLASS YAWL;
FRESH WATER, SALT WATER,
DRAINAGE, FUEL,
AND EXHAUST SYSTEMS

Sink Waste Sea Cock
Head Sink
Sea Water Intake
Sea Cock
Discharge Sea Cock
Head

40 Gallons Water
Water Filler Cap
Drain Valve

Fuel Tank Gauge
40 Gallons Fuel Oil

Water Filler Cap
60 Gallons Water

Water Valve
Icebox Drain to Bilge
Galley Sink
Galley Sink
Drain Valve
Port Cockpit Drain
With Sea Cock
Port Bilge Pump
Goes Overboard
(no shutoff)
Port Scuppers
(some yawls have shutoff)
Sea Water Cooling
Sea Cock

Drain Valve
Fuel Supply Line
Fuel Return Line
Fuel Shutoff Valve
Starboard Cockpit Drain
with Seacock
Starboard Bilge Pump
Discharges into Cock-
pit or Attach Hose for
Overboard Discharge
Starboard Scuppers
(some yawls have shutoff)
Fuel Filler in Cockpit
Under Grating

Exhaust Valve

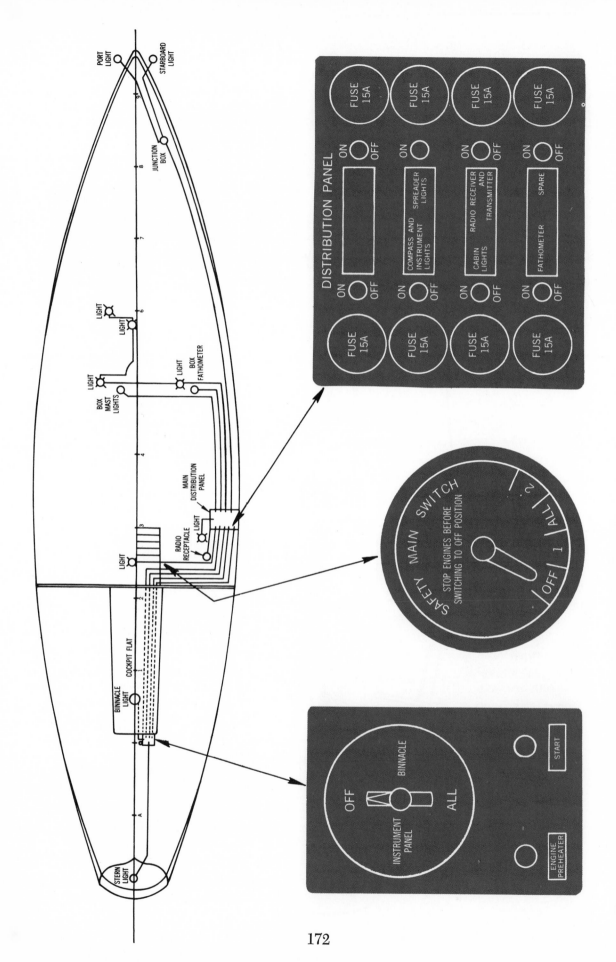

Figure 127 LUDERS FIBERGLASS YAWL, ELECTRICAL SYSTEM

cold weather, it must be preheated. This is done by pushing in the button labeled "preheat" and holding it in for about 15 seconds. After the engine is heated, start in the normal manner. In each yawl, there are starting instructions posted in the cockpit near the starting panel.

Once the engine has started, check the oil pressure. The gauge is in the instrument panel at the forward end of the cockpit, and should read 30 pounds or more. Then check over the stern to see if water is coming out of the exhaust. If it is not, the salt-water cooling system is not working properly. If the oil pressure is low, or if water is not being pumped out the exhaust, shut down the engine immediately.

While running the engine, periodically check the oil pressure and the water temperature. The water temperature gauge is beside the oil pressure gauge. The oil pressure should never go below 30 pounds, and the water temperature should never go higher than 190°F. *Never run the engine faster than 3,000 RPM.* Proper cruising speed for the Luders yawls is six knots at about 1,800 RPM. It should be noted in Table 1, that for engine RPMs greater than 1,800, fuel consumption goes up much faster than speed. When running the engine for several hours or more, shut it down periodically, and check the oil and fresh-water levels.

To secure the engine, put the throttle in neutral and pull out the engine "STOP" button. Remember to push the stop button back in, because it cuts off engine fuel and unless it is reset, the engine cannot be restarted. Once the engine has stopped and when power is no longer needed, switch the battery selector switch to the "OFF" position. Check fuel, oil, and fresh water to ensure that the engine will be ready for use when next desired.

Table 2 has been included to help troubleshoot the Westerbeke diesel engine. It does, however, offer many suggestions for the owner of any auxiliary trying to determine the cause of engine malfunction. It is for use primarily by trained mechanics, but also includes probable faults that can be checked by even the most inexperienced operator. The most common causes of engine failure, low battery, loss of cooling water, and dirty fuel (dirt or water in

Table 1 LUDERS FIBERGLASS YAWL, PERFORMANCE CHARACTERISTICS UNDER POWER.

Engine RPM	Speed in Knots	Fuel Consumed in Gallons Per Hour
1,000	3.0	0.39
1,500	4.5	0.48
1,750	5.5	0.57
2,000	6.0	0.66
2,250	6.3	0.75
2,500	6.5	0.82
2,750	6.6	1.00

the fuel), have been underlined.

On the Westerbeke engine, overheating is often a problem. Overheating can be caused by closed salt-water cooling system valves or an empty fresh-water tank. Often overheating is caused by the malfunction of either the fresh or the salt-water pump. These pumps are mounted on the front of the engine and are belt-driven. If the drive belts are too loose, they will not function. There are adjustments on both pumps which can be altered to increase tension.

Electrical and Water Systems of the Fiberglass Luders Yawl

In addition to knowing how to run the engine on the fiberglass yawls, the skipper and crew must know the location of the valves in the fresh- and salt-water systems and the switches in the electrical system (see Figures 126 and 127). The fiberglass yawls carry 100 gallons of fresh water in two tanks, one in the forepeak with a capacity of 40 gallons, and one amidships in the main cabin aft of the fuel tank under the cabin sole with a capacity of 60 gallons. On some boats both tanks are filled via the tank in the main cabin and are vented on the bulkhead over the starboard berth in the main cabin. The tanks are interconnected by opening both valves on the supply line. These valves are at each tank. They must be open when filling the tanks, or the forward tank will not fill. On other boats, the forward tank must be filled separately from a fill pipe on top of the tank. Each tank has a drain at the bottom which must be shut to prevent the water from running into the bilge. The system has two pumps, one at the head sink and one at the galley sink. Both these sinks drain overboard through a sea cock in the hull. The valve in the head is below the sink. The valve for the galley sink is located in the port cockpit locker and is also the valve for the port cockpit scupper. For this reason it must be left open. To keep sea water from backing up into the galley sink when under sail, there is an additional stop valve in the sink drain line in the locker just below the sink. This valve should be shut when the sink is not in use.

The icebox drains into a 5-gallon plastic container located beneath the after removable section in the cabin sole. This container should be checked frequently to ensure that it does not overflow. Of course, it should be emptied when securing.

The fiberglass yawls have two bilge pumps, both located in the cockpit. The intake strainers for each are in the bilge beneath the companionway ladder. The pump on the port side discharges overboard above the water line, so it has no sea cock. The pump on the starboard side discharges into the cockpit, but has a hose

attachment which allows it to be discharged over the side.

The marine toilet in the head is installed with sea cocks on both intake and discharge lines. The intake valve is beneath the sink, and the discharge is in the locker behind the toilet. The operating procedure for the head is the same as that for the wooden yawls. It should be noted that the fiberglass yawl heads have a hand-, rather than a foot-operated intake valve.

Power for the electrical instruments and lights aboard the fiberglass yawls is supplied by two 12-volt storage batteries located aft and to starboard of the engine. The engine is equipped with a 60-amp, 14-volt, battery-charging alternator-rectifier system. This system rapidly charges the batteries until they reach capacity and then shuts itself down and provides only a trickle charge to keep them fully charged. All control switches and fuses are installed in the control panel above the navigator's chart table on the starboard side of the main cabin, with the exception of the engine starter, binnacle, and engine panel light switches, which are in the cockpit.

Battery-powered equipment aboard the fiberglass yawls includes cabin lights, running lights, spreader lights, masthead lights, stern light, an-

Table 2 TROUBLESHOOTING THE WESTERBEKE DIESEL

174

Figure 128 GAS TANK INSTALLATION

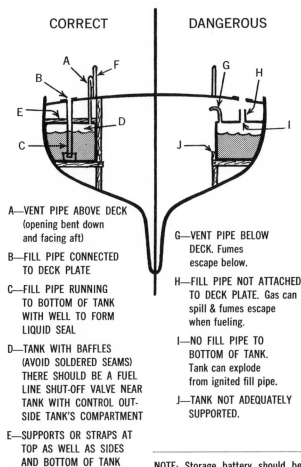

CORRECT | DANGEROUS

A—VENT PIPE ABOVE DECK (opening bent down and facing aft)

B—FILL PIPE CONNECTED TO DECK PLATE

C—FILL PIPE RUNNING TO BOTTOM OF TANK WITH WELL TO FORM LIQUID SEAL

D—TANK WITH BAFFLES (AVOID SOLDERED SEAMS) THERE SHOULD BE A FUEL LINE SHUT-OFF VALVE NEAR TANK WITH CONTROL OUT-SIDE TANK'S COMPARTMENT

E—SUPPORTS OR STRAPS AT TOP AS WELL AS SIDES AND BOTTOM OF TANK

F—VENT FASTENED TO COAMING, CABIN SIDE, OR INSIDE WINCH BASE

G—VENT PIPE BELOW DECK. Fumes escape below.

H—FILL PIPE NOT ATTACHED TO DECK PLATE. Gas can spill & fumes escape when fueling.

I—NO FILL PIPE TO BOTTOM OF TANK. Tank can explode from ignited fill pipe.

J—TANK NOT ADEQUATELY SUPPORTED.

NOTE: Storage battery should be in ventilated lead-lined box with a cover to prevent metal objects falling on battery terminals

chor light, binnacle light, fathometer, and radio. The entire system is diagrammed in detail in Figure 127.

Safety Precautions

Fire is an ever-present danger on any auxiliary, whether gasoline- or diesel-powered. At sea, fire is a most dangerous emergency. Bilges should be kept clean. Never allow gasoline, diesel oil, or lubricating oil to accumulate. The engine room should be ventilated properly in accordance with the latest Coast Guard regulations. When the engine is running for long periods, inspect it frequently for fuel and lubricating oil leaks. To guard against broken fuel lines caused by engine vibration, flexible hose should be used between the engine and any unflexible connection.

The boats are equipped with at least two fire extinguishers placed in widely separated parts of the cabin, preferably near the companionway and the forward hatch for easy accessibility. If you have a fire, shut down the engine and head off the wind to minimize relative wind velocity.

With a gasoline auxiliary, the times for *extra* caution are when fueling and when starting, especially starting after fueling or after a prolonged absence from the boat. (Figure 128 indicates proper and improper fuel tank installations.) Before fueling, shut off all power, extinguish fires, and cease smoking. Attempt to fuel with the boat heading so that the tanks are to leeward of the companionway. Then the gasoline fumes will be blown away from the boat, *not* down below. Remember that gasoline fumes are heavier than air and will displace the air in the cabin and engine room. When fueling, keep the nozzle of the gasoline hose in contact with the fill pipe to prevent a possible static electric spark. A static electric spark can also be caused by running water, so do not fill water tanks at the same time or immediately after filling fuel tanks. Do not spill fuel, and be very careful not to overflow the tank. After fueling, air the boat and run the engine room blower for at least five minutes before starting the engine. The higher the humidity and the lighter the breeze, the greater the danger from accumulated gasoline fumes. Open the engine compartment and smell for fumes *in the bilge* before starting.

When securing gasoline engines prior to leaving the boat, shut off the fuel at the tank. This ensures that there will be no leakage from the carburetor into the bilge while the boat is at the mooring.

When starting engines after a long absence, open the engine room hatch and smell for gasoline fumes in the bilge before energizing any of the systems. Most important of all, incorporate these precautions into a routine that is *never* varied. Over-confidence and haste are the most usual causes of boat explosions and fires.

CHAPTER TWELVE

Single-Screw Powerboats

Learning to handle a small, single-screw powerboat is important, because midshipmen often have occasion to run such boats at the Naval Academy and on summer cruises with the Fleet. Moreover, the midshipman or young ensign assigned to a ship for training or duty will soon find himself designated "Boat Officer," or, in effect, Officer-in-Charge of a boat, a position of great responsibility that requires detailed knowledge of small powerboat seamanship and safety precautions.

Naval Academy Single-Screw Powerboats

The two powerboats illustrated in Figure 129 are used at the Naval Academy to assist larger vessels, in patrolling sailing areas, ferrying people, and for general utility work. One is a 20-foot line-handling boat, the other, a 22-foot utility boat. Both are diesel-powered and of fiberglass construction. These two boats have a helm that is a bit awkward to use, at first. This helm is an upright lever connected to the rudder by a bar and yoke. The rudder is put to the left by pulling the lever aft, and to the right by pushing it forward. It is well to spend some time practicing with this type of helm before maneuvering in restricted waters.

Both these boats steer somewhat sluggishly at slow speeds due to their small rudders. This is particularly true of the 20-foot line handler, because she has a cylindrical rudder that encloses the propeller. This rudder, designed to keep lines out of the propeller, is rather inefficient at slow speeds and makes the boat somewhat hard to handle.

The capacity of the 20-foot line handler is 6 men, including the crew; the 22-foot utility boat will carry 16, including crew. These boats, of course, should never be loaded beyond their capacity. Life jackets for each passenger are carried under the seats or in the *forepeak* (the space beneath the foredeck). Each carries a 15-pound, CO_2 fire extinguisher, and has running lights and a horn. All of the 22-foot utility boats are equipped with high-capacity bilge pumps for pumping out knockabouts and other craft.

Illustrated in Figure 130 is a 33-foot utility boat. These craft are used at the Naval Academy primarily as tenders for the yawls and for ferrying people. They may be used to carry cargo. They are diesel-powered, built of fiberglass, and are capable of carrying up to 45 men, including crew. The crew usually consists of three men: a *coxswain* (man in charge who steers the boat and runs the engine), and a *bow hook* and *stern hook* (men in the bow and stern to handle lines). These boats are equipped with a horizontal steering wheel and hydraulic clutch-and-throttle control. This arrangement gives the coxswain good visibility and adds to the boat's maneuverability. Life jackets are located under the seats and in the forepeak. A 15-pound CO_2 fire extinguisher is mounted near the engine box.

The two motorboats used primarily for midshipman small-boat training are illustrated in Figure 131. These two, the 50-foot motor launch and the 50-foot utility boat, are used extensively in the Fleet as liberty launches and thus provide the midshipmen with very realistic Boat Officer training.

The 50-foot motor launch is diesel-powered and of carvel-planked, round-bottom construction. She normally carries a crew of four and has a maximum capacity of 150 men. Life jackets are located beneath the after seats and in the forepeak. She is equipped with two 15-pound CO_2 fire extinguishers.

The motor launch is steered with a tiller. The

coxswain handling the motor launch stands on the afterdeck. The engine is controlled by an engineer at the engine, amidships. The boat's bell is used by the coxswain to relay orders to the engineer. This signal system will be described in detail later in the chapter. Wooden motor launches with this type of control are being phased out of service in the Navy and replaced by the newer utility boats, all of which give the coxswain direct engine control.

The 50-foot utility boat is also diesel-powered and of round-bottom, wooden construction. She has a maximum capacity of 150 men, including the crew of 4: coxswain, engineer, bow hook and stern hook. There are two 15-pound CO_2 fire extinguishers on board. This utility boat, like the 33-foot utility boat, is steered by a horizontal wheel on the port side, amidships. The clutch is a foot-operated mechanical model, and the throttle control is on the steering column.

Both these boats have very large propellers, turning at a relatively low speed, which adds to their maneuverability at slow speeds. The utility boat has a great deal more power than the motor launch: 165 horsepower, compared to 60 horsepower. She also has a faster hull. For these reasons she is capable of a top speed of 11 knots fully loaded, while the motor launch will make only 8 knots. Both these boats carry life jackets for the crew and passengers beneath the seats and in the forepeak. They are equipped with electric horns and navigational lights. Each boat has at least two bilge pumps, and two 15-pound CO_2 fire extinguishers installed. For extra

equipment, they should normally carry magnetic compasses, harbor charts, oars, boat hooks, dock lines, and an anchor and rode.

Another type of small boat used at the Naval Academy by sailing coaches is the gasoline outboard-motor powered Boston Whaler. She is illustrated in Figure 132. These boats have a planing hull and with their engines are capable of speeds up to 30 knots. All are equipped with a compass, navigational lights, fire extinguisher, and floatable cushions. They are steered with a wheel and have a single-lever clutch and throttle control. The maximum capacity of these boats is eight. They are of double-hull, fiberglass construction and have flotation foam between the hulls, which makes them unsinkable. They are extremely maneuverable, but because the outboard shaft and propeller extend well below the bottom of the hull, they are very vulnerable to damage caused by running over floating objects. Great care must be taken to keep the propeller clear of debris and mooring lines, especially when running at high speeds.

Single-Screw Shiphandling

In the last chapter, the forces that affect the handling of a single-screw auxiliary were discussed in detail. These same forces, of course, affect the handling of a single-screw powerboat, though on a different scale. In general, a small powerboat is more maneuverable than an auxiliary, because she has more power in a smaller hull.

Figure 129

20-FOOT LINE HANDLER AND 22-FOOT UTILITY BOAT

The line handler is shown at full speed. Note the vertical steering lever on both boats.

One of these forces, torque, has a much greater effect on the handling of a shallow-draft powerboat than it has on a deep-draft auxiliary, since the former has much less lateral resistance. It will be remembered that torque effect is a force that tends to walk the stern in the direction toward which the propeller is turning, that is if the propeller is turning ahead (clockwise when viewed from astern), the stern will walk to starboard. The reason for this is that the sideways thrust of the propeller blades is at a maximum at the bottom of the swing (thrusting to starboard with the propeller turning ahead) and at a minimum at the top of the swing (thrusting to port with the propeller turning ahead). The difference in thrust is caused by the difference in sea pressure and turbulence at the bottom and top of the propeller's swing.

The major significance of the torque effect is that the powerboat will back very noticeably to port, and will make a much tighter turn to port than to starboard when accelerating ahead. Landings made port-side-to will always be easier than those starboard-side-to, because the backing action will tend to swing the stern toward, rather than away from, the pier. When leaving a pier, if tied up port-side-to, the stern must be swung clear by going ahead slowly against the bow line with left rudder before backing down, because the stern will tend to swing back toward the pier as soon as the engine is reversed. Full right rudder will help to compensate for this once the boat gathers sternway.

Often small powerboats are used for tenders to larger vessels, and the coxswain will be required to go alongside another boat or ship. Gangways are customarily on the starboard side, and the starboard side should be approached unless special circumstances dictate otherwise. This approach allows the landing to be made port-side-to.

It is important that the approach be as straight as possible and at just the right angle to allow the stern to swing parallel while backing to kill headway. Any movement of the vessel approached around her mooring must be studied carefully and compensated for. Approaches should always be made as slowly as possible. Sometimes speed will be required to

Figure 130 **33-FOOT UTILITY BOAT**
This boat is shown running at full speed.

keep steerage way and maneuverability, but landings made at a greater speed than necessary are not seamanlike, even if well executed. The possibility of engine failure must always be kept in mind. If the engine fails during a high-speed landing requiring a lot of backing power, damage to one or both vessels is inevitable. Mooring lines and fenders should of course always be rigged before going alongside.

Small powerboats may be used to assist capsized or swamped sailboats. If the crew of the distressed boat have been in the water for some time or appear to be fatigued, they must be picked up *first*. They should usually be approached from the windward side and the clutch must be kept in neutral while alongside until they are aboard. Nearby loose gear should be collected next. Be careful not to hit the disabled boat, and beware of fouling floating lines in your propeller. The sailboat should be righted, sails doused, and loose gear secured (see Chapter 2). She should be bailed out before towing. The towline should be made fast around the mast and led forward through a bow chock. Great care must be taken not to get the towline wrapped in your propeller when making the final approach. The towline should never be made fast to the quarter of the towing boat, because this will make her exceedingly difficult to steer and cause her to turn toward the quarter on which the line is belayed. When possible, belay the towline amidships well forward of the stern. The 20-foot-line-handling boats

179

Figure 131

50-FOOT MOTOR LAUNCH AND 50-FOOT UTILITY BOAT

Note the horizontal steering wheel on the utility boat and the tiller on the motor launch.

have a towing bit in this position specifically for this purpose. It is well to have a helmsman aboard the boat being towed; he should follow in the wake of the towing boat.

Once the towline is belayed, a strain should be taken gradually. The tow should be begun from ahead. Once the towline takes a strain and the boat begins to get way on, power can be increased steadily. All turns should be made gradually. Tow slowly, never at greater than the hull speed of the boat being towed.

Man overboard procedures on a small power-boat are similar to those on a larger vessel. These are described in the next chapter.

Engine Order Bells

It was mentioned that on the 50-foot motor launch, engine orders are given on the boat's bell. This is done because the engineer is unable to hear verbal commands when the engine is running. Four signals are used to control the engine. One bell means put the engine *ahead slow*. Two bells means idle the engine in *neutral*. Three bells means *back slow*, and four bells means to use full throttle in whichever direction the engine is running when the signal is given. For example, the sequence, 2 bells, 1 bell, 4

bells, means idle, go ahead slow, increase to full speed ahead. Remember that when the bells are used to give engine orders there will always be some time lag. The engine orders must always be anticipated.

Boat Crew Duties

The number of men in a boat crew will differ with the size of the boat. The normal crew size of the larger personnel boats will be four. Each crew will consist of a coxswain, an engineer, a bow hook, and a stern hook. The safety of the passengers embarked and the smartness of the boat depend to a great extent on how well these crewmen do their jobs.

The coxswain is in charge of the boat and is the helmsman, subject to supervision and possible relief by the Boat Officer or the senior line officer aboard the boat. It should be noted here that although the boat coxswain and assigned Boat Officer share in the responsibility for any mishap, Navy Regulations make it very clear that the final responsibility rests with the senior line officer aboard, even if he is only a passenger. *United States Navy Regulations*, Article 1331, "Authority in a Boat," states: "When embarked in a boat the senior line officer (includ-

180

ing commissioned warrant and warrant officers), eligible for command at sea, has authority over all persons embarked therein, and is responsible under all circumstances for the safety and management of the boat."

The coxswain is responsible for making certain that all necessary gear is aboard the boat and that it is in proper working order. It is also his responsibility to enforce safety precautions and supervise the loading and unloading of the boat. He must ensure that the boat is never loaded beyond capacity. The posted capacity prescribes the maximum number of persons allowed aboard during good weather in a protected anchorage. When the weather is questionable and sea conditions become hazardous, this capacity must be reduced. In addition to these duties, the coxswain is responsible for the proper helmsmanship and safe navigation of his boat. He must obey the rules of the road, pilot carefully, and use common sense in handling his boat near piers, anchored vessels, and crowded channels.

The engineer is responsible for the operation and maintenance of the engine. On the motor launches, he controls the clutch and throttle in response to the bell orders given by the coxswain. In all cases, he is responsible for fueling the boat.

The bow hook is the forward line handler and, as such, handles the bow boat hook, from which he derives his title, bow line, sea painter, and forward fenders. He also acts as forward lookout while under way and should always be stationed in the forward part of the boat.

Figure 132 BOSTON WHALERS

The whaler's nearly flat bottom gives her a high degree of initial stability and allows her to plane very easily.

The stern hook handles stern lines, stern fenders, the stern boat hook, and acts as an after lookout.

The boat crew should always be in the uniform of the day, wear boat sneakers and, when conditions warrant them, life jackets.

Boat Officer Responsibilities

The Boat Officer has a very delicate job, for he must supervise the coxswain and his crew and make certain that safety precautions are followed and the boat safely navigated without interfering needlessly with the coxswain's control of the boat, passengers, and crew. The Boat Officer is a safety observer and should only take charge of the boat personally when absolutely necessary. In such a case, he should formally relieve the coxswain.

Navy small-boat safety precautions result from years of experience. They should be obeyed by the passengers and crew and enforced by the coxswain. The Boat Officer is responsible for seeing that safety precautions are carried out.

A *Summary of Small-Boat Safety Precautions*

• All safety equipment, including life jackets, lights, and bilge pump, should be inspected regularly.

• The smoking lamp is always out.

• Passengers must always remain seated on thwarts and seats, with hands and fingers inside the gunwales.

• Boat crews must keep their stations, especially when weather conditions are unpleasant, for it is usually during these times that vigilance is most needed.

• Boats must always be properly loaded for the sea state. In heavy weather, the boat should be loaded slightly down by the stern and the passengers and crew kept in life jackets.

• Bilges should be kept free of oil.

• Shafts and engine equipment should be kept covered.

• All passengers should be kept clear of the boat while refueling.

• Boats should be loaded and unloaded in a safe, orderly fashion.

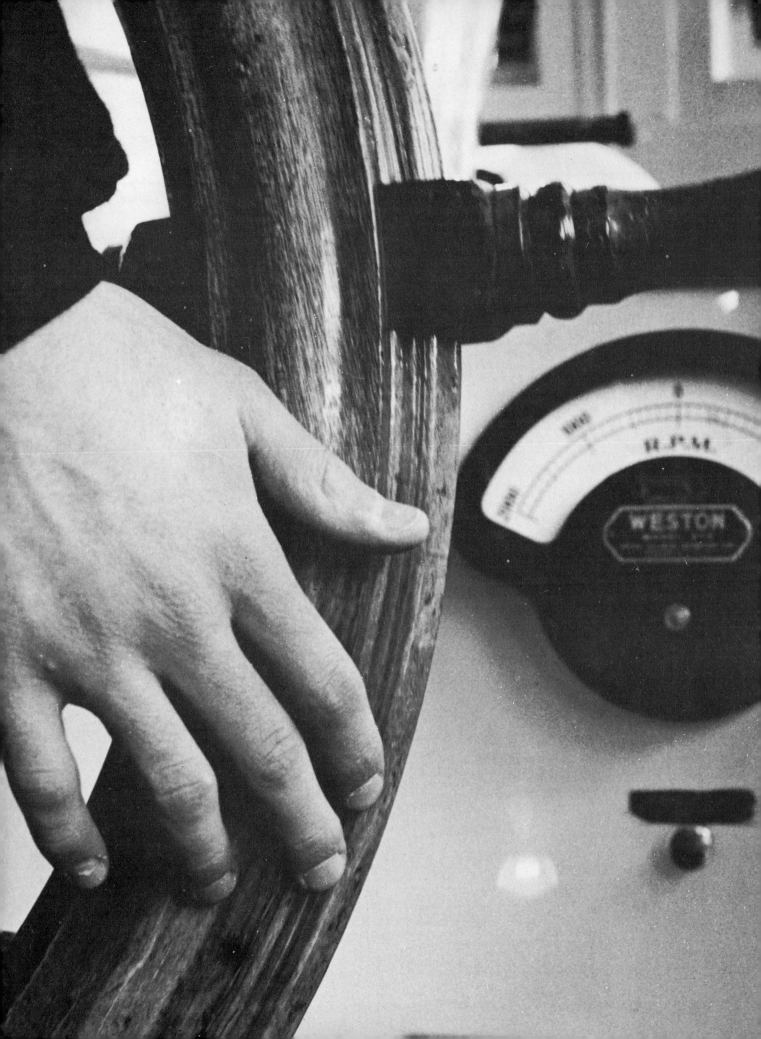

CHAPTER THIRTEEN

Yard Patrol Craft

The 80-foot twin-screw, wooden yard patrol craft (YP) used at the U.S. Naval Academy closely resemble in handling characteristics and equipment many of the ships in the Fleet (see Figure 133A, B, and C). They provide advanced seamanship training under conditions approximating those that will be encountered by the newly commissioned ensign at sea.

Professionally, YP training provides every midshipman with experience in seamanship, shiphandling, navigation, naval tactics and communications, naval phraseology, and standard shipboard procedures.

YP Characteristics

The Naval Academy has 14 yard patrol craft. All are of the 654 Class, and while some of the newer vessels have slightly different equipment, they all have identical characteristics and tactical data. Table 3 lists their important characteristics. Many of these facts are required only occasionally, and this table can be referred to when necessary. Some, however, must be remembered, for they are essential to proper shiphandling. Length, draft, "masthead" height, and rudder angles should be memorized.

Also important to the shiphandler are the YP's performance characteristics. These include turning circle (see Figure 134 for explanation of turning circle), acceleration and deceleration figures, and the relationship between engine

rpm and hull speed. Table 4 indicates the hull speed in knots compared to engine rpm. The speeds of 5 knots and 5.6 knots are achieved by turning only one shaft. For all other speeds, both shafts are required. The EOT (engine order telegraph) settings are also indicated. The EOT will be explained later in the section of ship's control equipment.

Also included in Table 4 is data essential to shiphandling in a formation. This "tactical data" standardizes speeds and distances used in formation maneuvering.

Turning and deceleration data for the 654-Class YP is found in Table 5. Of all the statistics in this table, the most important to remember are the tactical diameters for standard and full rudder at 8 and 10 knots (200 yards and 125 yards), and the deceleration time and distance covered when going from full ahead to stop by backing full (8 seconds and 57 feet). The YP will accelerate from 7 to 10 knots in 22 seconds. The surge rate when changing speed is 9 yards for each knot of speed differential. This factor is very important when station-keeping in formation. For example, a YP making 10 knots to maintain station alongside one making 7 knots must slow to 7 knots when 27 yards from station ($3 \times 9 = 27$).

Ship Control Equipment

The main propulsion engines aboard the 654-Class YPs are four 165-horsepower General Motors 6-71 diesels. These engines are installed two to a shaft with a hydraulic clutch and 2:1 reduction gear. The maximum forward speed is 1,800 rpm and the maximum reverse speed is 1,500 rpm. The throttle control and clutch are in a control booth in the engine room, and are controlled manually from this station by an engineer. Engine orders are transmitted to him by the Engine Order Telegraph (EOT) system. This is a mechanical system which links a signal device in the pilot house to one in the engine room (see Figure 135). The master, called simply the EOT, is to port of the helm in the pilot house. It has one handle for each bank of engines. The port and starboard shafts are controlled by the port and starboard handles. Be-

Figure 133 YARD PATROL CRAFT-654; OUTBOARD PROFILE, INTERIOR ARRANGEMENT, AND DECK PLAN

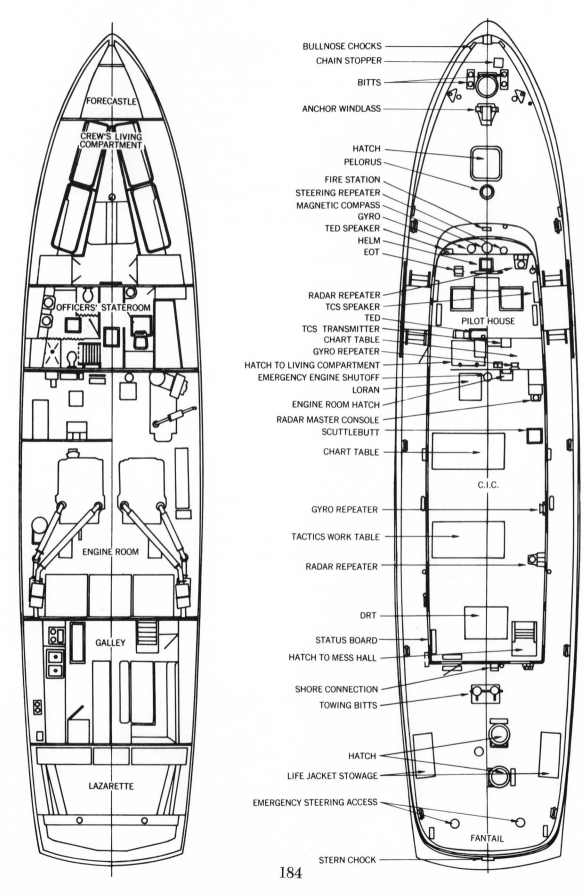

FORECASTLE

CREW'S LIVING COMPARTMENT

OFFICERS' STATEROOM

ENGINE ROOM

GALLEY

LAZARETTE

BULLNOSE CHOCKS
CHAIN STOPPER
BITTS
ANCHOR WINDLASS

HATCH
PELORUS

FIRE STATION
STEERING REPEATER
MAGNETIC COMPASS
GYRO
TED SPEAKER
HELM
EOT

RADAR REPEATER
TCS SPEAKER
TED
TCS TRANSMITTER
CHART TABLE
GYRO REPEATER
HATCH TO LIVING COMPARTMENT
EMERGENCY ENGINE SHUTOFF
LORAN
ENGINE ROOM HATCH
RADAR MASTER CONSOLE
SCUTTLEBUTT
CHART TABLE

PILOT HOUSE

C.I.C.

GYRO REPEATER

TACTICS WORK TABLE

RADAR REPEATER

DRT

STATUS BOARD

HATCH TO MESS HALL

SHORE CONNECTION
TOWING BITTS

HATCH

LIFE JACKET STOWAGE

EMERGENCY STEERING ACCESS

FANTAIL

STERN CHOCK

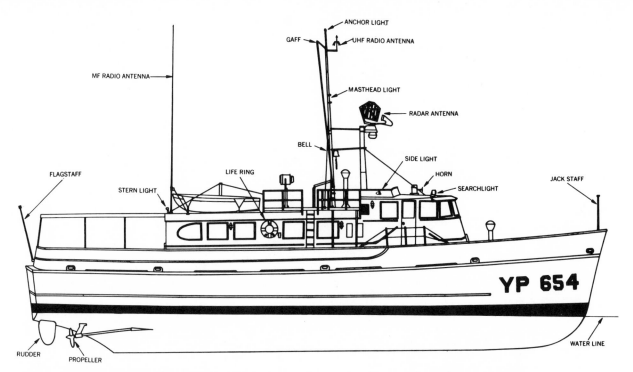

Photograph shows the
YP-662 running in
a smooth sea.

Table 3 YP-654 CLASS CHARACTERISTICS

Length Over-All	80'5"	Rudder angles (twin rudders)	
Extreme Beam	18'9"	Standard	13½°
Draft (light load)	5'4"	Full	25°
Displacement	69.5 tons	Hard	35°
Main propulsion	(4) GM-6-71 diesels, 165 horsepower each	Heights	
		Top of mast to boot top	37'10"
Generator	(1) 120-volt, 20-kilowatt, A.C. generator	Yard arm to boot top	35'6" (doubled for use with stadimeter)
Propellers	(2) 3-bladed, 36"-diameter screws	Radar antenna to boot top	28'
		Vertical distance between sidelights and masthead light	13'1"
Fuel Oil Capacity	2,070 gallons		
Lubricating Oil Capacity	15 gallons	Height of eye (6-foot man)	
Fresh water	420 gallons	Main deck (forward)	12.8'
Maximum Speed	13.5 knots	Main deck (aft)	11.6'
Cruising Speed	10 knots	Signal bridge	19.6'
Maximum Safe Capacity	60 people		

Figure 134   SHIP TURNING CIRCLE

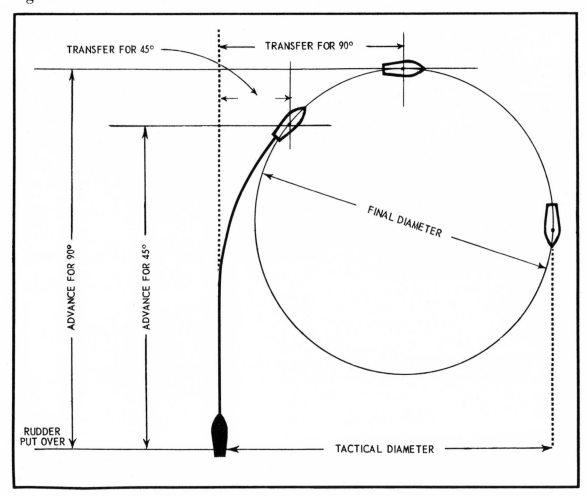

neath each handle the telegraph face is divided into the following positions: Ahead Flank, Ahead Full, Ahead Standard, Ahead ⅔, Ahead ⅓, Stop, Back ⅓, Back ⅔, Back Full.

As engine speeds are ordered, they are answered manually by the engineer in the control booth. When they have been answered, a follow-up pointer under the handle will so indicate. It should be noted that to shift from forward to reverse or vice versa, the engine must be slowed to idling speed in order to shift into and out of reverse gear. This takes several seconds. For this reason, unless an emergency exists, Stop should always be ordered before changing the direction of shaft rotation. Engine speeds other than normal (those indicated in Table 4) may be ordered by calling the engineer on the 1JV sound-powered telephone, located next to the EOT.

The 654-Class YPs have two rudders, one astern of each propeller, for added maneuverability. The rudders are linked together and controlled mechanically by the helm in the pilot house. A rudder angle indicator is located forward of the steering wheel on the steering stand. The full throw of the rudders is 70 degrees, from 35 degrees port to 35 degrees starboard. Hard rudder, 35 degrees, should be avoided except in an emergency, because the mechanical linkage is likely to jam in this position. The maximum rudder angle used under normal circumstances should be 30 degrees. When backing at speeds greater than ⅔, never use more than 10 degrees rudder. Care must be taken when backing to hold the steering wheel firmly. If it is let go, it will spin hard over and the rudders will jam in the stops.

Emergency steering on the YP is effected by

connecting tiller extensions through deck fittings on the *fantail* (afterdeck) to the starboard rudder post, which is located in the lazarette. The rudder posts are linked so that both rudders respond to tiller movements from the fantail.

For ground tackle the YP-654 Class carries two Danforth anchors, one of 75 pounds and one of 150 pounds, and 70 *fathoms* (six feet to a fathom) of one-half-inch chain. The anchor windlass pictured in Figure 136 is a power-driven, nonreversible, single-speed (20 feet per minute) model which can only be used to heave in. It can, in an emergency, be operated manually. The windlass is activated by a button on its after side. The *wildcat* (drum) over which the chain is heaved in, is engaged by a handwheel friction clutch on the starboard side of the windlass (see Figure 136). This wheel is turned clockwise to engage the wildcat. In addition to the clutch there is a handbrake. The *gypsy head*

(see Figure 136) operates continuously and can be used independently from the wildcat by disengaging the wildcat and setting the brake. The anchoring procedure will be discussed in a later section of this chapter.

The navigation equipment aboard the 654-Class YP is extensive. Each YP has one standard 6½-inch magnetic compass installed immediately forward of the helm. To port of the helm, a Sperry gyro compass Mark 22, Model O is mounted. This master gyro provides an input for six gyro repeaters located in the pilot house (2), the combat information center (CIC), forecastle, and the bridge (2). In addition the Mark 22 gyro supplies true ship's head to the master radar console, both radar repeaters, the dead reckoning tracer (DRT), and the dead reckoning analyzer (DRA). The control panel that connects these stations with the master gyro is located in the pilot house beneath the gyro.

Table 4 **SPEED AND RPM**

EOT Setting	Speed in Knots	RPM
Starboard (or Port) Engine Ahead ⅓	5	680 (one shaft)
Starboard (or Port) Engine Ahead ⅓	5.6	810 (one shaft)
All Engines Ahead ⅓	6	680
All Engines Ahead ⅓	7	810
All Engines Ahead ⅔	8	940
All Engines Ahead Standard	9	1,070
All Engines Ahead Full	10	1,200
All Engines Ahead Flank	11	1,400
(Speeds above Flank must be ordered on	12	1,700
the 1JV sound-powered telephone)	13.5	1,800
All Engines Back ⅓	....	600
All Engines Back ⅔	....	1,000
All Engines Back Full	....	1,500

Tactical Data

Tactical Speeds
    Normal speed............... 7 knots
    Stationing speed............. 10 knots
    Operational speed.......... 11 knots
Tactical Diameters
    Standard diameter..........200 yards. Standard rudder (13½ degrees)
    Reduced diameter..........125 yards. Full rudder (25 degrees)
Distances
    Standard distance..........100 yards
    Circle spacing..............100 yards

Table 5 TURNING AND DECELERATION DATA—YP 654 CLASS

Time to Turn (Min.-Sec.)

Speed (Knots)	Rudder Angle (Standard 13½° Full 25°)	30°	60°	90°	180°	270°	360°
6	Standard	0–27	0–41	0–57	1–40	2–24	3–10
6	Full	0–13	0–23	0–34	1–04	1–33	2–02
7	Standard	0–22	0–36	0–50	1–27	2–04	2–40
7	Full	0–12	0–21	0–30	0–56	1–20	1–45
8	Standard	0–20	0–32	0–43	1–14	1–45	2–16
8	Full	0–12	0–18	0–26	0–49	1–09	1–31
9	Standard	0–18	0–28	0–37	1–04	1–31	1–57
9	Full	0–11	0–17	0–23	0–44	1–01	1–20
10	Standard	0–17	0–25	0–33	0–56	1–20	1–43
10	Full	0–10	0–16	0–20	0–39	0–54	1–12
11	Standard	0–15	0–23	0–30	0–51	1–12	1–32
11	Full	0–10	0–15	0–19	0–34	0–50	1–05
12	Standard	0–15	0–22	0–27	0–47	1–06	1–23
12	Full	0–10	0–14	0–18	0–31	0–46	1–00

Advance and Transfer (Yards)

	30° Adv.	30° Tr.	60° Adv.	60° Tr.	90° Adv.	90° Tr.
Standard Rudder	75	15	112	57	130	112
Full Rudder	51	6	70	32	80	66

Diameter (Feet)

	Tactical	Final
Standard Rudder	200	190
Full Rudder	125	120

Deceleration to Dead in Water

Speed (Knots)	Backing Speed	Reach Ahead (Feet)	Time (min.-sec.)
6	Full	24	0–6
6	⅔	31	0–11
6	⅓	69	0–27
6	0	160	2–11
7	Full	31	0–8
7	⅔	41	0–12
7	⅓	74	0–28
7	0	194	2–36
8	Full	39	0–8
8	⅔	49	0–13
8	⅓	81	0–28
9	Full	47	0–8
9	⅔	57	0–14
9	⅓	87	0–29
10	Full	49	0–8
10	⅔	66	0–16
10	⅓	97	0–30
11	Full	54	0–8
11	⅔	72	0–17
11	⅓	99	0–31
12	Full	57	0–8
12	⅔	77	0–18
12	⅓	103	0–31

Figure 135   YP PILOT HOUSE
Notice the Engine Order Telegraph to port of the steering wheel. A fire extinguisher
is against the bulkhead. A sound-powered telephone is above the EOT. Forward and to
port of the helm is the Sperry gyro compass. Directly forward of the helm is the
magnetic compass. To starboard of the wheel is the radar.

The YP-654 Class carry as navigational lights one white 20-point masthead light, one white 12-point stern light, one white 32-point anchor light, one 10-point green starboard sidelight and one 10-point red port sidelight.

There are three 20-point white lights arranged vertically on the mast as towing lights and two 32-point red lights for breakdown lights. The control panel for the navigational lights is in the pilot house over the chart table. The ship's horn is electric and is atop the pilot house. It is operated by a push button located to the right of the helm. The ship's bell is on the mast. A 7-inch, sealed-beam navigational searchlight is installed atop the pilot house and is controlled from within the pilot house.

The YP has three *peloruses* (rotatable circles with sights mounted on the gyro compass repeaters on the bridge wings and on the forecastle for taking visual bearings). Each YP carries at least one *stadimeter,* an optical ranging device with which to obtain visual ranges using known masthead heights. Each vessel also carries a depth recorder, loran, and radar. These navigational devices will be discussed in the section on electronic equipment.

Figure 136 YP ANCHOR WINDLASS
The wildcat is shown with the chain around it. The handwheel on the wildcat is the wildcat clutch. The after handwheel is the brake, and the gypsy head is on the top of the windlass. Note the winch drum on the far side of the windlass, and the bitts atop it for belaying a line.

189

Communications Equipment

The communications equipment on the YP-654 Class falls into two basic categories, internal and external. Internal communication aboard the YP is accomplished by voice tubes and *sound-powered telephone* (a telephone that generates its own power by the sound vibrations of the voice) circuits. The voice tubes connect the bridge with the pilot house and CIC, the pilot house with the captain's stateroom, the pilot house chart table with the forward pelorus, and the pilot house with the signal bridge. Of these, the voice tubes most commonly used are those located on each wing of the bridge connecting the bridge with the helmsman in the pilot house.

There are five sound-powered telephone circuits installed aboard the YP. These circuits and their stations are listed in Table 6. The sound-powered telephone jack boxes for the bridge, engine room, forecastle, and pilot house stations (with one exception) are clearly labeled by circuit designators. The jack boxes for the CIC stations (with one exception) can be patched into any of the five circuits. These jack boxes, labeled JX1 through JX6, are controlled by a master control panel on the starboard bulkhead in CIC. Outlet JX7, in the pilot house, is also controlled by this panel.

For external communication, the 654-Class YP is equipped with two radios, one 12-inch signal searchlight, and two sets of standard Navy

signal flags. The ultra high frequency (UHF) radio consists of a TED-7 transmitter and an AN/URR-35 receiver, both installed in the pilot house. This transmitter-receiver combination gives line-of-sight radio communication in the frequency range of 225-400 megacycles. The UHF is the primary ship-to-ship tactical communications system. Both transmitter and receiver have crystal frequency control. The transmitter has a capacity for four crystals and the receiver for one. There are three speakers for the UHF radio, one in CIC, one on the bridge, and one in the pilot house. There is one remote transmitting station on the bridge.

There is also one medium frequency (MF) radio installed in the pilot house. This radio, a TCS, has a longer range than the UHF. The TCS frequency range is between 1,500 and 12,000 kilocycles. There are speakers for the TCS in the pilot house and in CIC. A remote transmitting station is also located in CIC.

Electronic Equipment

The 654-Class YP, in addition to the radios, carries a radar fathometer, and loran. YPs 654 through 663 are equipped with AN/SPS-35 radar, YPs 664 and 665 with AN/SPS-21, and the latest YPs, 666 and 667, with AN/SPS-53 radar. Although differing in model number, these radars are all similar, and all are excellent at relatively short range. The master console in all installations is located in the forward starboard

Table 6 **SOUND-POWERED PHONE CIRCUITS**

Circuit		Stations				
		Pilot House	Forecastle	Engine Room	Bridge	CIC
JA	Captain's Battle Circuit	1			2	JX4
JW	Navigation Circuit	1	1		2	JX5
1JV	Engineering Circuit	1 (handset)		1 (handset)		
21JS	Radar Information Circuit No. 1					1 JX1, JX2, JX6
22JS	Radar Information Circuit No. 2	1				

Note: As mentioned in the text the seven outlets JX1–JX7 may be used with any of the circuits except the 1JV. They are usually used as listed above.

Table 7 **DAMAGE CONTROL EQUIPMENT**

EQUIPMENT	LOCATION	QUANTITY
15 pound portable CO_2 extinguishers	Crew's living compartment	1
	Officers' stateroom	1
	Engine Room	2
	Galley	1
	Pilot House	1
	CIC	2
	Lazarette	1
5 gallon cans of liquid foam	Lazarette	5
1½ inch mechanical foam nozzle with pick-up tube	Lazarette	1
Fire stations (Firemain outlet, 4-ft. fog applicator, 1½ inch fire hose, all purpose nozzle, spanner wrench)	Forecastle (50 feet of hose)	1
	Fantail (50 feet of hose)	1
	Engine Room (25 feet of hose)	1
Fire Axe	Lazarette	1
Damage control plugs and wedges	Lazarette	1 bag
Pipe patching kit	Lazarette	1 bag

Note: The CO_2 extinguisher is a general purpose fire extinguisher and specifically intended for electrical (Class C) fires.

corner of CIC. In addition there are two repeaters, one located aft in CIC and the other in the pilot house.

The fathometer, an AN/UQN-1, is located in CIC. This fathometer is capable of recording depth up to 36,000 feet. The depth indicated is measured from the transducer, which is approximately 3′6″ below the waterline. For this reason 3′6″ must be added to the sounding to get the actual depth.

The AN/UPN-12 loran is installed against the forward bulkhead in CIC. This equipment is installed primarily for training. Interference in the Chesapeake Bay area makes it quite unreliable for actual navigation. In this area reception is limited to stations 1H4 and 1H6.

The dead reckoning tracer (DRT) is an electro-mechanical device used primarily for tracking surface contacts and secondarily for navigation. The DRT and its associated equipment, the dead reckoning analyzer (DRA), are located in the after part of CIC, the DRA on the after bulkhead and the DRT just forward of the bulkhead. The DRA, using inputs of ship's course and speed fed to it by the gyro and a dummy log, breaks down the ship's movement into north-south and east-west components. North-south and east-west signals move a *bug* (small, moving light) in the DRT which simu-

lates the ship's track by continuously displaying the ship's position from beneath a tracing paper. The scale of the DRT is adjustable between 500 and 32,000 yards per inch, and there is a 200-yard-per-inch scale for use in man-overboard plotting. A parallel motion protractor is positioned atop the DRT for use in plotting surface contacts.

Safety Equipment

For life saving, the 654-Class YP carries 30 life preservers, 25 inflatable and 5 kapok, and one 12-foot *wherry* (small rowboat). All of the life preservers are stowed in a deck box on the fantail. The wherry is stowed in chocks on the house above CIC. The procedure for lowering the wherry will be discussed in a later section. Two 24-inch life rings with attached float lights are positioned on deck amidships, one on each side. Six aircraft *smoke floats* (floating markers that emit smoke) are stowed in racks on the bulkhead abaft the pilot house, three to port and three to starboard. A first aid kit is located on the mess deck.

The fire fighting and damage control equipment carried aboard the 654-Class YP is listed in Table 7. The use of this equipment will be covered in a later section.

191

Shiphandling

Shiphandling characteristics of single-screw, single-rudder powerboats have been described in the preceding two chapters. The 654-Class YP with twin screws and twin rudders adds an entirely new dimension to shiphandling under power.

Twin-screw propulsion makes available to the shiphandler a type of slow-speed turning maneuver that is not available to the handler of a single-screw vessel. The twin-screw vessel may be turned with minimum headway or sternway, or even with no way on whatsoever, and this type of maneuver is often most useful in getting under way from or landing at a pier or for putting the vessel alongside any more-or-less stationary object in the water, such as a disabled boat or a man overboard.

Turning the twin-screw vessel with a minimum of way on can be accomplished by twisting (going ahead on one screw while backing the other).

Three different kinds of turning forces are available when twisting (see Figure 137 and Figure 138).

The primary turning force is the twisting moment applied to the vessel by off-the-centerline propellers pushing in opposite directions. Thus with the port engine going ahead and the starboard engine backing, the ship will twist to the right, and with starboard ahead and port backing, she will twist to the left. If a stationary twist is desired, simply apply equal power on both screws; and, of course, if a little headway is wanted, order more power on the ahead screw than on the backing screw, and for sternway, more power on the backing screw than on

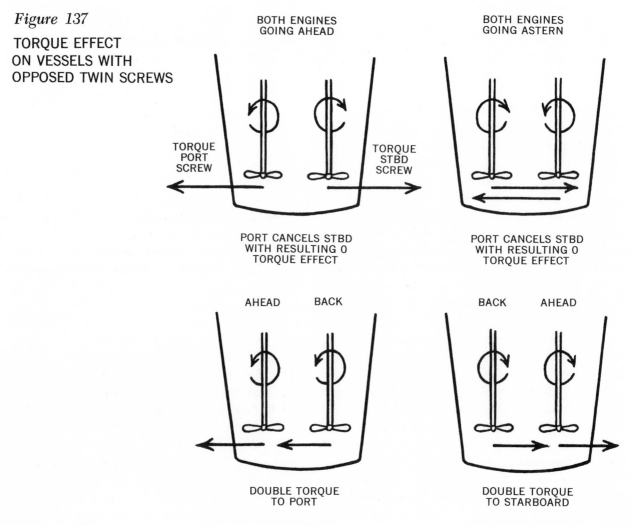

Figure 137

TORQUE EFFECT
ON VESSELS WITH
OPPOSED TWIN SCREWS

BOTH ENGINES
GOING AHEAD

BOTH ENGINES
GOING ASTERN

TORQUE
PORT
SCREW

TORQUE
STBD
SCREW

PORT CANCELS STBD
WITH RESULTING 0
TORQUE EFFECT

PORT CANCELS STBD
WITH RESULTING 0
TORQUE EFFECT

AHEAD   BACK

BACK   AHEAD

DOUBLE TORQUE
TO PORT

DOUBLE TORQUE
TO STARBOARD

192

Figure 138 **WASH EFFECT COMBINED WITH TORQUE EFFECT**

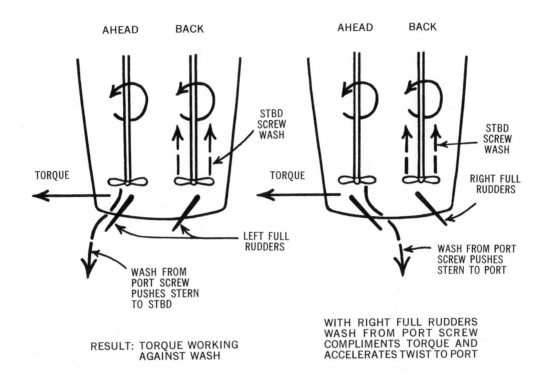

AHEAD BACK

STBD SCREW WASH

TORQUE

LEFT FULL RUDDERS

WASH FROM PORT SCREW PUSHES STERN TO STBD

RESULT: TORQUE WORKING AGAINST WASH

AHEAD BACK

STBD SCREW WASH

TORQUE

RIGHT FULL RUDDERS

WASH FROM PORT SCREW PUSHES STERN TO PORT

WITH RIGHT FULL RUDDERS WASH FROM PORT SCREW COMPLIMENTS TORQUE AND ACCELERATES TWIST TO PORT

the ahead screw. The specific engine orders to give desired amounts of headway or sternway or to keep the ship dead in the water must be learned by experience, and, of course, wind and current are variables that must be estimated and compensated for.

A single combination of ahead and backing engine orders seldom gives exactly the twist desired, and as too much way comes on the vessel, the engines must be jockeyed to compensate for it. For example, with the combination of one engine ahead ⅓ and the other back ⅓, the YP will gather headway. As soon as headway is sensed, the ahead screw should be slowed or stopped, but then the ahead power must be applied again as soon as any sternway is sensed. By thus varying the engine orders, the vessel can be kept twisting as desired.

A secondary turning force that affects twisting is ahead propeller wash against the affected rudder. When twisting to the right with the port engine going ahead, the wash from the port screw against the port rudder can be used to increase the amount of turning force being

applied to the ship. If the rudder is right, the wash will tend to throw the stern to port, thus increasing the twist to the right. Normally, the maximum twist is desired, so that the rudder should be put over in the direction in which it is desired to twist, just as if the shiphandler were merely turning his vessel, that is right rudder to twist to the right, and vice versa.

A third turning force involved with twisting is the torque effect of the propellers. The propellers on the YP, as on most twin-screw vessels, rotate in opposite directions when both screws are going ahead. Viewed from astern, with both screws going ahead, the port screw rotates counterclockwise and the starboard screw rotates clockwise. Thus the torque effect is cancelled out. When twisting, however, with one engine going ahead and the other astern, both screws are rotating in the same direction so that their torque effect is in the same direction. Thus, when twisting to the right, with the port engine going ahead and the starboard engine backing, the torque effect of both propellers tends to walk the stern to port and augment the

193

Figure 139 USE OF MOORING LINES WHEN MANEUVERING ALONGSIDE

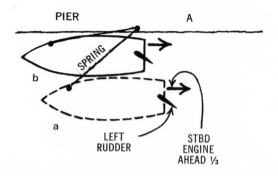

PIER   A

LEFT RUDDER   STBD ENGINE AHEAD ⅓

A BOW SPRING CAN BE USED TO BRING A VESSEL ALONGSIDE, IN THIS CASE BY GOING AHEAD ON THE STARBOARD SCREW WHILE USING LEFT RUDDER.

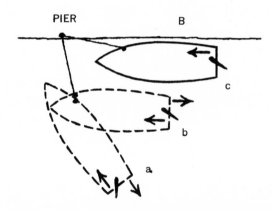

PIER   B

TWISTING AGAINST A BOW LINE WITH STARBOARD AHEAD, PORT BACKING, AND LEFT RUDDER, ONCE ALONGSIDE, STOP THE TWIST AND BACK STARBOARD.

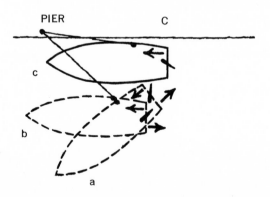

PIER   C

TWISTING AGAINST A QUARTER SPRING IS MUCH LESS EFFICIENT, SINCE THE PIVOT POINT IS AFT NEAR THE SCREWS.

(Arrows show screw wash)

twist. When twisting to port, of course, the torque is in the opposite direction and also increases the turning force. This rule notwithstanding, twisting a vessel in confined waters is a complicated maneuver, and a great deal of practice is required before the engine and rudder orders to achieve the amount of twist and headway or sternway desired become second nature.

Another factor essential to the proper handling of a vessel under power is an understanding of the location and movement of the vessel's pivot point. All vessels have a point around which they will turn. This pivot point moves forward and aft as the forces controlling the ship are changed. In general, it is located between 15 per cent and 40 per cent of the length of the ship abaft the bow. The more the forward speed, the further ahead the pivot point will be, and the more the sternway, the further aft the pivot point. When a ship is being twisted while dead in the water, one engine ahead and the other back with equal power, the pivot point is usually very near a point one-third of the ship's length abaft the bow. The pivot point on the 654-Class YP when twisting dead in the water is just forward of the bridge. When moving ahead it is near the forward pelorus. It is important to know the location of this point, because it determines how much of the vessel will swing in which direction.

When handling close enough to a pier so that a mooring line can be put ashore, the position of the pivot point can be controlled exactly. If the vessel can be made to twist around a single mooring line, the point at which that line is belayed aboard the vessel will be the pivot point. Some examples of this kind of maneuvering are shown in Figure 139.

Line handling requires a detailed knowledge of the forces involved in mooring a vessel, proper phraseology, and safety precautions. The *conning officer* (the officer doing the shiphandling), when directing the line handlers, must use standard commands, if he is to get the desired results. It is also necessary to ensure that gear is not *parted* (broken) and that the crew is not endangered. Bow and stern lines are referred to by name or number while the other lines are referred to by number. The lines are numbered from forward to aft. Standard YP mooring lines are illustrated in Figure 140.

Safety must always be foremost in the conning officer's mind, safety of the vessel and safety of the crew. Line handling on a large vessel is always dangerous because lines are often put under considerable strain. Unless basic safety precautions are observed, injuries can result. The YP Officer of the Deck (OOD) should always ensure that all line handlers are briefed, and he should supervise their actions closely when alongside the pier.

The primary rule in line handling is never to position yourself in the *bight* of a line (slack or loop in the middle part of a line which will come taut when the line is put under strain). Also, when a mooring line parts, anyone in line with it is very likely to be hit. Line handlers must keep their hands and feet out of coils of loose line to avoid being caught when tension is applied. Docking lines should never be held without taking a turn or two on a bitt or cleat, as raw hands, and possibly more serious injury, may result if the line comes under strain. On the YPs when coming alongside, all members of the crew should stay inboard of the bulwarks until way is off the boat. Line handlers should never jump ashore with a mooring line, but rather should jump ashore empty-handed and then have the line heaved ashore by another crewman. The crew must be alert to keep stern lines from fouling in the propellers when the lines are heaved too short, and must be retrieved and heaved again.

An anchor can often be used as a shiphandling tool. It can be set to windward and used to move the pivot point forward to the hawse hole in order to twist into the wind, and it can be held *under foot* (on the bottom just below the bow) with just enough scope to allow it to drag without catching. When under foot, the anchor will keep the bow from blowing to leeward faster than the stern in a strong breeze.

The YP, because of her small size and exceptional maneuverability, should very seldom need to use an anchor alongside a pier. Larger vessels, especially single-screw vessels, often will use an anchor.

Figure 140

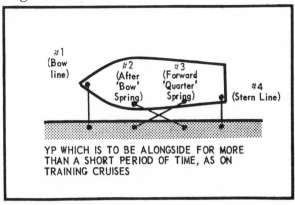

YP WHICH IS TO BE ALONGSIDE FOR MORE THAN A SHORT PERIOD OF TIME, AS ON TRAINING CRUISES

We have now discussed the forces affecting the handling of a vessel which can be controlled by the conning officer. There remain those factors not under his control. These are the same factors mentioned in an earlier chapter: wind, current, and maneuvering room. While these factors cannot be controlled, they must be known and understood. In Chapters 3 and 9, the methods of determining the directions of wind and current were discussed. The importance of determining which of the two, wind or current, will have the greater effect on the vessel in any specific situation was emphasized. Because of the YP's high freeboard and deckhouse and small underbody, wind will usually be the controlling force in her case. Still, no hard and fast rules can be given and experience and practice remain the best method for developing a "feel" for any given situation.

The phrase "conning officer" has been used in the preceding section. The term was defined as the person on board the vessel who is handling her. Often this person will actually be steering and controlling the engines. When this is the case, conning is analogous to driving a car, the person conning has the "feel" of the boat in his own hands and decisions can be translated directly into actions. The YPs can be conned in this manner from the pilot house. On large ships, however, the conning officer does not handle the helm or engine order telegraph, for he must be free to move about on the open bridge to have the visibility necessary to do the job. When this is the case, a new dimension is added to the conning problem, because the conning officer must translate his decisions into commands to the helmsman or *lee helmsman* (man operating the engine order telegraph and standing by to assist the helmsman) rather than carry them out himself. A different sense of timing is needed by the conning officer when he is controlling the ship through others, rather than by his own action. This is a skill that requires a great deal of practice. It is also a skill that is essential for all officers who go to sea in surface ships or submarines. It is for this reason that the YP, while on drills, is always conned from the open bridge.

With regard to steering, there are two distinctly different methods for conning a vessel from the bridge. The first, which can be called positive control, is recommended in all maneuvering situations when the conning officer wants direct control over rudder angle. For this method of conning, all steering commands relate to the positioning of the rudder. There is no reference to the compass or ship's head and, in fact, the compass is not required. This method of conning comes as close as possible to actually steering oneself. The standard commands for

Table 8 A **STANDARD COMMANDS FOR POSITIVE CONTROL CONNING**

Commands	Meaning
"Left (Right) _____ Degrees Rudder."	Put on the left (right) rudder ordered.
"Left (Right) Standard Rudder."	Put on the previously specified amount of left (right) rudder required to turn the ship in her "standard tactical diameter."
"Left (Right) Full Rudder."	Put on the previously specified amount of left (right) rudder to turn the ship in her "reduced tactical diameter."
"Hard Left (Right) Rudder."	Use maximum left (right) rudder.
"Ease the Rudder to _____ Degrees."	Decrease the rudder angle to _____ degrees.
"Shift the Rudder."	Change from left to right rudder (or vice versa) an equal amount.
"Rudder amidships."	Put the rudder amidships (to decrease the rate of swing).
"How is your rudder?"	Report the rudder's position.

Table 8 B **STANDARD COMMANDS FOR CONNING BY COMPASS HEADING**

Commands	Meaning
"Steady on course _____."	Steady on course _____, using the amount of rudder previously ordered.
"Come left (right) to _____."	Put the rudder left (right), and steady on new course _____.
"Come left (right) handsomely to _____."	Use a small amount of rudder and come to course _____ (used when a very small course change is desired).
"Nothing to the left (right) of _____."	Do not steer to the left (right) of ordered heading.
"Steady," or "Steady as she goes."	Steer the course on which the ship is heading when the command is received. The helmsman's reply is "Steady as she goes; course _____, Sir."
"Meet her."	Use rudder as necessary to check the swing.
"Mind your rudder."	Steer more carefully.
"How does she head?" or	
"Mark your head."	What is the ship's heading?
"Keep her so."	Steer the course that has just been reported as ship's heading.

this method are listed with their meanings in Table 8A.

In the second method, a certain amount of helm control is relinquished by the conning officer to the helmsman, and commands relate to ship's head and compass courses. Once given a course—and courses must always be given when using this method—the helmsman will use the rudder required to keep the vessel on the ordered course. This second method is recommended for normal conning in channels and in formation. The standard commands for this method are listed in Table 8B.

There are some general rules that apply to all standard conning commands. The most important is that *only* standard commands may be used. For this reason, the prospective conning officer must learn the commands and their meanings verbatim. Orders to the lee helmsman are always given in the following format: engine, direction, speed. The word "engine" or "engines" is always used, and the words "port" and "starboard," not "left" and "right" are used to indicate to which engine the order applies. The engine speeds that are available on standard Navy engine order telegraphs were discussed in a preceding section. Emergency orders are indicated on the EOT by ordering Ahead Flank or Back Full several times in rapid succession.

All commands given by the conning officer to either the helmsman or lee helmsman should be repeated verbatim by the helmsman or lee helmsman. If the order has been heard and repeated correctly the conning officer should answer with a "Very well." Once the engine order has been answered by the engine room or the helm order accomplished by the helmsman, the lee helmsman should so inform the conning officer with a "Port engine answers Back ⅓," or "All engines answer Ahead Full," and the helmsman with "My rudder is Right Standard," or "steady, zero six zero," etc. The proper response from the conning officer is again, "Very well." The helmsman and lee helmsman should continue to repeat the information until answered by the conning officer.

Engine direction should never be changed except in an emergency without first ordering Stop. This allows the engine to idle before clutching. When conning by compass heading, a course order should always follow a rudder order. This ensures that the vessel will not swing past the desired course. Course changes up to 15 degrees should be ordered by giving the direction of turn followed by the new course. For example, when steadied on 050 degrees, the proper order of a change to 055 degrees would be, "Come right to zero five five." For course changes greater than 15 degrees, a rudder order may be given, followed by the new course. For example, to change course from 050 degrees to 090 degrees, the conning officer might say, "Right Standard Rudder. Come to course zero nine zero." Rudder orders may be given in degrees or by the commands, standard, full, and hard. Hard rudder should be used only in an emergency, because in this position the rudder is apt to jam in the stops.

Remember that the helmsman always goes by the last order given, and a change in rudder order will supercede a previous course given. Finally, the terms "belay my last," "negate my last," and "disregard" are never used. When an incorrect order has been given, simply correct it with a proper one.

Typical Maneuvers

In this section specific shiphandling situations that occur frequently on the YP's, such as mooring and getting under way, station keeping, maneuvering alongside while under way, and anchoring will be examined in full detail.

The preparation and planning for making a landing in a YP is essentially the same as is required for the auxiliary or motor launch. A berth must be selected, conditions evaluated, and the crew briefed. The landing should be made at the *flattest* (smallest) angle to the pier possible (with the vessel nearly parallel to the pier) to minimize the risk of collision with the pier. Under perfect conditions, with no wind or current, a 15-degree angle of approach and a course directly for the berth is recommended. This angle, while quite flat, still leaves room to maneuver until the ship is alongside. (See Track A, Figure 141.) If conditions are such that the YP

Figure 141 LANDING APPROACHES

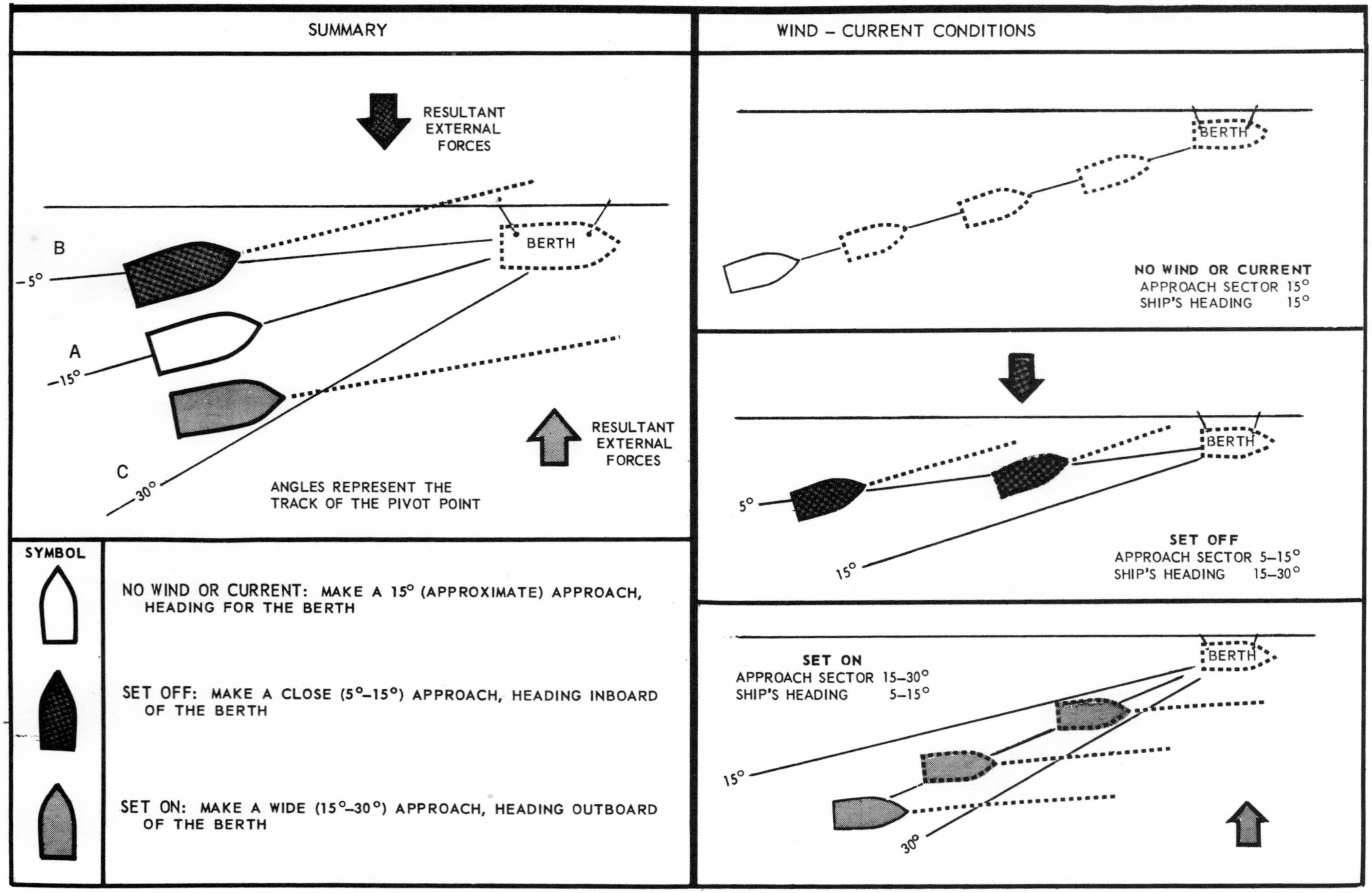
SUMMARY
RESULTANT EXTERNAL FORCES
BERTH
B
-5°
A
-15°
C
30°
RESULTANT EXTERNAL FORCES
ANGLES REPRESENT THE TRACK OF THE PIVOT POINT
SYMBOL
NO WIND OR CURRENT: MAKE A 15° (APPROXIMATE) APPROACH, HEADING FOR THE BERTH
SET OFF: MAKE A CLOSE (5°–15°) APPROACH, HEADING INBOARD OF THE BERTH
SET ON: MAKE A WIDE (15°–30°) APPROACH, HEADING OUTBOARD OF THE BERTH
WIND – CURRENT CONDITIONS
BERTH
NO WIND OR CURRENT
APPROACH SECTOR 15°
SHIP'S HEADING 15°
BERTH
5°
15°
SET OFF
APPROACH SECTOR 5–15°
SHIP'S HEADING 15–30°
BERTH
SET ON
APPROACH SECTOR 15–30°
SHIP'S HEADING 5–15°
15°
30°

is being set off the pier, an even flatter angle and a course inboard of the berth are required to keep the YP from being set wide of the berth. (See Track B, Figure 141.) To minimize the effects of the set, a slightly higher than normal approach speed is used. When conditions are such that the YP is being set onto the pier, a slow approach and a course outboard of the berth are required to keep the YP from fetching up against the pier before reaching her berth. This outboard course should not be overdone, because if the YP is stopped opposite her berth, but some distance off it, and the set onto the pier is strong, considerable leeway will be built up. This leeway cannot be controlled and may result in damage to the YP when she fetches up against the pier.

When the set is parallel to the pier, the landing should be made into the set, if possible. A landing in this situation is similar to Track C in Figure 141, with the wind or current acting on the outboard bow tending to set the YP onto the pier. There are times, however, when a landing must be made with the set. A flat approach, as in Track B of Figure 141, should be made, as the wider the approach angle, the more the YP's stern will be set off the pier. While the approach should be rather fast, it is important to remember that in addition to the vessel's speed through the water, the set will have to be overcome when backing down. Always back harder with the outboard screw, as this tends to swing the stern toward the pier.

Under normal conditions a speed greater than 7 knots (All Ahead ⅓) should never be used in a landing approach. With no wind and no current, All Engines Stop should be ordered about 100 yards from the pier. If a landing is not proceeding as planned, the vessel should be backed clear, and the whole maneuver started again. A situation requiring last-minute action to avoid ramming the pier should never arise.

Once alongside with way off, the bow line is put over and the boat twisted, using proper rudder and engine orders, to get the stern alongside the pier. Remember that proper orders must be given the line handlers.

Getting under way from a pier in the YP is more conducive to a planned procedure than is making a landing. Wind and current can be observed closely and their effect on the YP, once under way, can be estimated rather accurately. The position of other craft, both tied up and under way, should be checked. Lastly, lines and fenders should be checked to be sure that none of them are fouled or jammed.

The YP should always leave the berth stern first. By backing away from the berth the chances of scraping the ship's side or damaging a screw are minimized. If the set is off the pier, the stern line can be taken in, and when the stern has swung out, the bow line is taken in, and the vessel backed clear smartly. When the set is onto the pier, the stern line is taken in, the bow line is held or checked, and the stern swung out by twisting, going ahead on the outboard screw, backing the inboard screw, and using full rudder in the direction of the twist. The stronger the set onto the pier, the more power required to twist. A fender should be positioned forward whenever twisting away from the pier. Once the stern has been swung well clear, the bow line should be taken in and the YP backed clear smartly. It must be remembered to bring the rudder amidships or shift it, otherwise the YP will back toward the pier, especially if the wind is blowing off the pier, as the YP tends to back into the wind. As soon as the pier has been cleared, the conning officer has two options. He can stop both engines, then come ahead on one or both, and turn to the desired course; or he can keep one engine backing, stop the other, then come ahead on it and twist until the ship is headed in the desired direction. The latter method takes much less room and should be used in a restricted space.

If the YP is getting under way from a berth and proceeding into a blind channel, the Inland Rules change-of-status signal, one long blast (8–10 seconds—see Appendix A) should be sounded. This is seldom necessary when getting under way from Dewey sea wall. If, while the YP is backing clear, a danger of collision exists, then the Inland Rules backing signal of three short blasts, or the danger signal of four or more short blasts, should be sounded (see Appendix A). These signals should *not* be sounded if there is no danger of collision.

Once under way, colors must be shifted (this will be described in a later section of this chapter) and all fenders rigged in. While in the channel, the conning officer must be continually anticipating the next move; wind and current are checked and rechecked, channel marks located, bearings taken, and, most important, the helmsman given timely course changes to keep the YP on the proper (righthand) side of the channel at all times.

Anchoring is often required on the YPs. The anchors are stowed on deck on the forecastle and are *not* connected to the anchor chain. To ready the anchor for use, first the handbrake and the clutch on the windlass must be released. Then enough chain to reach through the starboard hawse hole, over the bulwarks, and

Figure 142 YP ANCHOR DAVIT AND FALL
The Danforth anchor is secured to the bulwark abaft the davit, where it is stowed when not in use.

back to the anchor on deck must be hauled by hand from the chain locker. When the anchor chain and anchor buoy line have been bent onto the anchor, the *anchor davit fall* (tackle on a small crane for handling the anchor) is hooked onto the anchor (see Figure 142). The anchor is then hoisted, swung out over the bulwarks, and lowered to the rub rail. The wildcat is then engaged and the slack taken out of the chain. The anchor should remain just outboard of the starboard hawse hole until dropped. After the anchor is in position, the handbrake is set up, the wildcat disengaged, and the anchor davit fall slacked and unhooked. The anchor is then ready for letting go.

The conning procedure for anchoring a YP is the same as it is for the auxiliary (see Chapter 11). The forecastle crew should be informed when 1,000 yards and 500 yards from the anchorage. When the YP is head to wind, or current as the case may be, with all way off, the anchor is let go by releasing the windlass handbrake. When the anchor is on the bottom, sternway should be made to pay the chain out of the chain locker and finally to set the anchor. During this process, the forecastle crew should be reporting to the bridge the amount of chain at the water's edge, the direction it is tending, and the amount of strain (slack, or light, moderate, or heavy strain). When the chain is snubbed, the report that the anchor is holding or dragging should be made.

When weighing anchor, it is usually "heaved around" to a short stay first, that is the scope is shortened as much as possible without breaking out the anchor. Once the command to "heave on in" is given, the forecastle crew weighs anchor, reporting when it is "up and down" (the chain is vertical), "aweigh" (the anchor is broken out and lifted clear of the bottom), "in sight," "clear," or, "foul," "clear of the water," and "to the hawse hole." While anchored, the proper signals under Inland Rules must be observed; a black anchor ball hoisted at the yardarm by day, and a white, 32-point light shown by night.

The YP's 12-foot fiberglass wherry has been mentioned. When stowed for sea, the wherry is *griped* (strapped down) to the chocks on deck above CIC abaft the signal bridge on the port side. The wherry davit is rigged inboard. Before launching, the cover and gripes are removed, the chain bridle, attached fore and aft in the wherry, is connected to the davit fall, and a *sea painter* (long, heavy, tending line attached to the bow of a small boat that is to be launched at sea) is made fast to the wherry. The sea painter must be led outboard and well forward, especially if the wherry is to be launched while the YP is underway, as it is this line which controls the wherry once she is in the water.

When the preparations are complete, a strain is taken on the fall, and the wherry is lifted clear of the boat chocks. The davit and wherry are then swung aft and out over the side. The davit has fore and aft guys with which to swing and control it. The guys should be belayed to hold the davit in place once the wherry has been swung outboard. The wherry can then be lowered into the water. The crew should board the wherry by the *Jacob's ladder* (a rope or chain ladder with wooden or iron rungs, which is secured over the bulwarks).

Usually the wherry will be launched while the YP is at anchor or dead in the water. Because of the maneuverability of the YP, there is seldom a need to launch the wherry in the open sea. If she did have to be launched in a seaway, the YP should be turned so that the wherry is on the lee side. When launching in a seaway, it is usually best to keep a little headway on.

When the wherry is picked up, the launching sequence is reversed. In a seaway the wherry should always be picked up to leeward.

Formation Shiphandling

Operating with other ships in a formation presents the Officer of the Deck (OOD) with many problems not encountered when conning a ship which is maneuvering independently. In addition to a knowledge of basic shiphandling, a familiarity with formation shiphandling is required, particularly as described in Allied Tactical Publication, ATP 1 (A), Volumes I and II. Also essential to the OOD maneuvering in formation is a thorough understanding of relative motion and the ability to work a maneuvering board. It is beyond the scope of this book to

present a detailed explanation of Navy tactical publications or to attempt to teach the *maneuvering board* (a printed polar coordinate plotting sheet with convenient scales and a nomogram and logarithmic scale used to solve relative motion problems). It is possible and pertinent, however, to point out some of the problems encountered in formation shiphandling and their solutions.

When ships are operating in a formation, they are all assigned specific positions relative to each other. One ship, usually the largest and when possible the one in the center, is designated the "Guide." This ship is always assumed to be *on station* (in the correct position) and to be making precisely the signaled course and speed. All other ships keep their stations with reference to the Guide. It is therefore essential that the OOD keep track of base course and speed and the range and bearing to the Guide when maintaining station.

It is up to the OOD to keep his ship on station. Staying within 3 degrees in bearing and 50 yards in range is usually acceptable on the YP. The standard maneuvering board scale used on the YPs is 100 yards per circle.

Station keeping is quite simple, as Figure 143 indicates, but takes *constant* attention, requiring continual alteration of course and speed.

When stationed ahead of the Guide, as in Situation A in Figure 143, changes of speed affect range, and course changes alter bearing. When stationed on the beam, as in Situation B of Figure 143, the effect is opposite, with course alterations changing range, and speed changes affecting bearing. Usually, as in Situation C of Figure 143, the station is neither directly ahead nor abeam of the Guide, in which case station keeping is a function of combined course and speed changes. For example, if, in Situation C, the OOD wanted to keep the bearing to the Guide constant, but decrease the range, he would have to alter course to the left to close the Guide and thereby decrease the range, and at the same time increase speed in order not to fall behind while closing, and thereby change the bearing.

The best advice for station keeping is to work out a solution and then take action, using common sense backed up by a maneuvering board

201

Figure 143 STATION KEEPING (Course versus Speed)

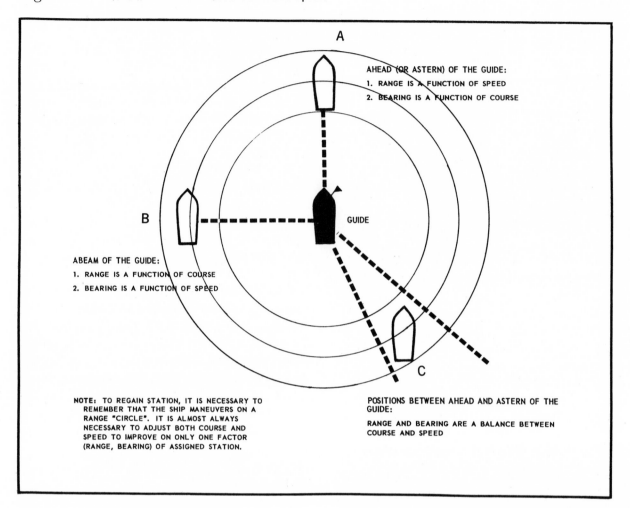

A

AHEAD (OR ASTERN) OF THE GUIDE:
1. RANGE IS A FUNCTION OF SPEED
2. BEARING IS A FUNCTION OF COURSE

B

GUIDE

ABEAM OF THE GUIDE:
1. RANGE IS A FUNCTION OF COURSE
2. BEARING IS A FUNCTION OF SPEED

C

NOTE: TO REGAIN STATION, IT IS NECESSARY TO REMEMBER THAT THE SHIP MANEUVERS ON A RANGE "CIRCLE". IT IS ALMOST ALWAYS NECESSARY TO ADJUST BOTH COURSE AND SPEED TO IMPROVE ON ONLY ONE FACTOR (RANGE, BEARING) OF ASSIGNED STATION.

POSITIONS BETWEEN AHEAD AND ASTERN OF THE GUIDE:

RANGE AND BEARING ARE A BALANCE BETWEEN COURSE AND SPEED

solution to choose a course and speed to produce the desired relative motion to move the ship from her actual to her desired position with respect to the Guide. Course and speed changes should be gradual and a constant check kept on the resulting change in position relative to the Guide. An attempt to regain station should never be made by radical course and speed changes, for when wrong, this type of solution is *very* wrong, and when right, before base course and speed can be resumed, the ship often will be as far from station as before, but in the opposite direction.

When station keeping, a constant check may be kept on the range to the Guide by using the *stadimeter* (an optical range-finding device that computes distance to an object of known height

once the angle between the bottom and top of the object is measured). The masthead height of the Guide must be set on the stadimeter before accurate ranges can be determined. It should be remembered that the masthead height of the 654-Class YP is 35 feet, 6 inches. Since the masthead height scale on the stadimeter cannot be set this low, a setting of 71 feet (twice 35 feet, 6 inches) is therefore used, and all ranges read from the stadimeter must be halved to obtain the true ranges.

To stay on station, all movements of the Guide must be followed precisely. All turns, unless otherwise indicated, should be executed when the Guide turns and with standard rudder. The use of standard rudder ensures that all ships turn with the same tactical diameter, in this case 200 yards, and thus the range to the Guide from each ship remains the same. When full rudder is prescribed, the result is the same, except that all ships turn with reduced tactical diameter, 125 yards for the YP. (See Table 5.)

The safety of the ship is the paramount responsibility of the OOD. The OOD should never assume that all ships will act on a given signal correctly. For this reason, a constant check should always be kept on other ships in the formation, especially those toward which the ship is turning, to ensure that they are turning in the same direction.

When ordered to move from one station in a formation to another, the OOD at the earliest possible moment should acquaint himself with the new station number, the range and bearing to the Guide from the new station, and the initial direction of turn if it has been prescribed. From this information, the OOD should be able to work out a rough course and speed solution to get to the new station. As soon as the maneuvering board solution for the problem is available, it should be checked against this initial rough calculation.

It must be remembered that the maneuvering board will often show on paper, solutions that in reality are not practical. For instance, a speed increase from 7 knots to a stationing speed of 10 knots is not a practical solution for moving ahead 150 yards. In this case, the *three-minute rule* (speed, or relative speed, in knots times 100 equals distance travelled, or relative distance if relative speed was used, in yards in three minutes) would indicate that at 3 knots relative speed, it would only take 1½ minutes to travel the required relative distance of 150 yards. When it is remembered that it will take 22 seconds to accelerate from 7 knots to 10 knots, and that the 7-knot formation speed should be resumed when 27 yards from station, it will be realized that the 10-knot speed could only be kept on for about one minute. Although this solution may at first be indicated on the maneuvering board, common sense would suggest a more moderate solution.

If a signal is executed before the precise course and speed solution to station is known, the best action is to turn in the correct direction and use the estimated rough course and speed. Course and speed can always be refined on the way to station.

The straight maneuvering board solution does not allow for other ships that may be obstructing the direct route from one station to another. A YP should not be passed by another closer than 100 yards, and an attempt should be made to pass under the stern whenever possible. This is especially true when maneuvering close to the Guide. While proceeding to station a constant check must be kept on range and bearing to the guide. If the range and bearing is not changing as it should be, a return to base course and speed will at least maintain the status quo until the proper solution can be determined.

When proceeding to a new station, the number of the station should be indicated by an information signal flown from the yardarm. The proper signal is the Designation pennant followed by the numeral flag (never pennant unless out of flags) of the new station. This signal is flown *at the dip* (two or three feet below the yardarm) as soon as the new station is assigned. It is *closed up* (hoisted to the yardarm) while proceeding to station, and hauled down when on the new station. Station indicators are used to determine where other ships are going. If another YP is flying the same station number you are flying, assignments should be rechecked.

When maneuvering in formation:

• Always know the base course and speed of the formation.

• Know your ship's course and speed.

• Know the proper range and bearing of the Guide.

• Know the actual range and bearing to the Guide and check it continually.

• Always look before maneuvering and don't count on correct action from other vessels.

• Using all available information and a good deal of common sense, make decisions promptly and then take action.

• Most important, keep in mind that at all times the OOD's primary responsibility is the safety of the ship and only a constant vigil will keep the ship out of danger. This is particularly important when operating in close company.

Maneuvering Alongside: Replenishment

The YP OOD will occasionally be required to maneuver alongside another YP while under way, either in a replenishment drill or to transfer a piece of equipment. In most cases, the delivering ship will act as control ship and Guide. A replenishment course should be chosen that is into both wind and sea. When wind and sea are not from the same direction, the course should be into whichever element is the more significant. Replenishment speed should be the minimum speed required for responsive shiphandling. For the YPs, 7 knots is a good replenishment speed. Once signalled, the control ship should maintain replenishment course and speed. The ship designated to go alongside should, prior to her approach, steady on replenishment course and speed astern of the control ship. This gives the OOD an opportunity to check for gyro error and speed difference. On the YP, these differences, especially the gyro, can be significant.

Flag hoist procedures used in Navy replenishment operations are found in ATP 1 (A), Volume II, page 2-5, and are used during YP drills. Before an approach, fenders should be rigged along the appropriate sides of the delivering and receiving ships. On each ship, the most experienced helmsman and lee helmsman should be on watch. A helm error on either ship while alongside can cause a collision.

In making the approach, the OOD of the receiving ship should use a speed differential of from 3 to 5 knots. Three knots is recommended for the YPs. It should be kept in mind that surge for the 654-Class YP is 9 yards per knot. This dictates that with a 3-knot speed advantage, the OOD should reduce speed when 27 yards from station alongside. A much higher speed advantage combined with an appropriate backing bell is often used in the Fleet, but is not required or recommended for the YP.

The approach should be made from astern on the appropriate quarter. By the time the receiving ship begins to overlap the delivering ship, the approach course should be within two or three degrees of, or the same as, replenishment course. The separation between the two vessels at this point should never be less than the eventual desired separation. For the YPs this is not less than 20 feet. For the separation to be greater is merely to err on the safe side. It is during the approach and breakaway phases of the replenishment operation that the greatest danger of collision exists. The bow shape of the two ships as they come together acts to form a funnel. The water forced into this funnel increases in velocity as it passes between the two ships. As the velocity of the water between the ships increases, the pressure on their inboard sides is reduced relative to the pressure on their outboard sides. In effect, there is a force tending to pull them together (see illustration of Bernoulli's Principle, Figure 32). During the approach and breakaway phases of the operation, any rudder action that ends to swing the stern of the receiving ship towards the delivering ship causes an increase in this force which can result in the vessels being drawn together. This is why a near-parallel approach course is recommended. The same is true for breaking away. Speed should be increased to clear the side of the delivering ship, but course should not be altered significantly until the receiving ship is clear ahead. If, while alongside, the replenishment course must be changed, it should be changed very gradually, in 5-degree increments, and with great caution.

Safe Navigation

Safe navigation dictates that all aspects of good seamanship and navigation be used to keep a vessel safe from harm, whether at anchor or under way. It is important here to detail those rules of safe navigation not previously mentioned and to explain briefly the use of the YP navigational equipment listed earlier in this chapter.

Besides determining the vessel's position, the navigator should provide the OOD with ranges and bearings to the nearest shoal water and timely recommendations for course changes. This is especially important, of course, when in restricted water, such as a channel.

The navigator's table on the YP is in the pilot house. Here the navigator has a radar repeater

204

for obtaining ranges and bearings (remember that radar bearings are never as accurate as radar ranges) for navigational use. This repeater normally operates on a 0-5,000 yard scale, and when ranges in excess of this are desired, the range scale must be turned to the 50,000-yard position. The range is read from a three-digit counter. In addition, there are two zeros that light up when they should be used for the different scales. When operating on the 0-5,000 yard scale, one zero must be added to the counter reading; two zeros are added when the 50,000 yard scale is being used. The minimum readable range for both scales is approximately 100 yards. The model radar used on the 654-Class YP can be oriented to true north or ship's head. For ease in navigation, it should always be set on true. This setting can only be controlled on the console in CIC.

The YP has a depth recorder in CIC, and she should never be navigated in water less than 10 feet deep without its soundings or those of a leadsman stationed forward with a lead line marked in fathoms. The markings on a proper lead line are specific (see Figure 144). These markings enable the user to "read" the line at night without benefit of a light. The OOD and the navigator should never hesitate to use a lead line when entering shoal water. All the YPs have one or more lead lines aboard as standard gear.

The navigator should use visual bearings when possible. For normal YP drills a bearing taker is stationed on the bridge to assist the navigator. He can use the bridge wing peloruses and communicate with the navigator on the JW circuit.

The OOD is responsible for safe navigation,

Figure 144 LEAD LINE

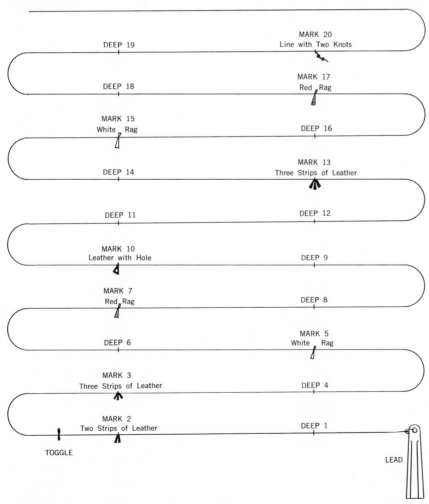

Figure 145 METHODS OF MAN OVERBOARD RECOVERY

METHOD AND PRIMARY USE	DIAGRAM (SHIP ON COURSE 090; NUMBERS REFER TO THE EXPLANATION)	EXPLANATION	ANALYSIS	
			ADVANTAGES	DISADVANTAGES
WILLIAMSON TURN 1. USED IN REDUCED VISIBILITY BECAUSE IT MAKES GOOD THE ORIGINAL TRACK. 2. USED WHEN IT IS BELIEVED THAT A MAN FELL OVERBOARD SOME TIME PREVIOUSLY AND HE IS NOT IN SIGHT.	① ⊗ = MAN	1. PUT THE RUDDER OVER FULL IN THE DIRECTION CORRESPONDING TO THE SIDE OVER WHICH THE MAN FELL. STOP THE INBOARD ENGINE. 2. WHEN CLEAR OF THE MAN, GO AHEAD FULL ON ALL ENGINES, CONTINUE USING FULL RUDDER. 3. WHEN HEADING IS 60° BEYOND THE ORIGINAL COURSE, SHIFT THE RUDDER WITHOUT HAVING STEADIED ON A COURSE. 60° IS PROPER FOR MANY SHIPS, HOWEVER, THE EXACT AMOUNT MUST BE DETERMINED THROUGH TRIAL AND ERROR (50° FOR YPs). 4. COME TO THE RECIPROCAL OF THE ORIGINAL COURSE, USING FULL RUDDER. 5. USE THE ENGINES AND RUDDER TO ATTAIN THE PROPER FINAL POSITION (SHIP UPWIND OF THE MAN AND DEAD IN THE WATER WITH THE MAN ALONGSIDE, WELL FORWARD OF THE PROPELLERS).	1. SIMPLICITY, THE REASON WHY IT IS TAUGHT ON YP DRILLS. 2. MAKES GOOD THE ORIGINAL TRACK IN THE OPPOSITE DIRECTION, EXCEPT FOR THE EFFECTS OF WIND AND CURRENT.	1. SLOW 2. TAKES THE SHIP A RELATIVELY GREAT DISTANCE FROM THE MAN, WHEN SIGHT MAY BE LOST.
ONE TURN ("ANDERSON") USED BY DESTROYERS, SHIPS WHICH HAVE CONSIDERABLE POWER AVAILABLE AND RELATIVELY TIGHT TURNING CHARACTERISTICS.		1. PUT THE RUDDER OVER FULL IN THE DIRECTION CORRESPONDING TO THE SIDE OVER WHICH THE MAN FELL. STOP THE INBOARD ENGINE. 2. WHEN CLEAR OF THE MAN, GO AHEAD FULL ON THE OUTBOARD ENGINE ONLY. CONTINUE USING FULL RUDDER. 3. WHEN ABOUT TWO-THIRDS OF THE WAY AROUND, BACK THE INBOARD ENGINE 2/3 OR FULL. ORDER ALL ENGINES STOPPED WHEN THE MAN IS WITHIN ABOUT 15 DEGREES OF THE BOW, THEN EASE THE RUDDER AND BACK THE ENGINES AS REQUIRED TO ATTAIN THE PROPER FINAL POSITION (AS FOR THE OTHER METHODS). 4. MANY VARIATIONS OF THIS METHOD ARE USED, DIFFERING PRIMARILY IN RESPECT TO THE USE OF ONE OR BOTH ENGINES, AND THE TIME WHEN THEY ARE STOPPED AND BACKED TO RETURN TO THE MAN AND TIGHTEN THE TURN. THE VARIATION USED SHOULD REFLECT INDIVIDUAL SHIP'S CHARACTERISTICS, SEA CONDITIONS, PERSONAL PREFERENCES, ETC.	THE FASTEST RECOVERY METHOD.	1. REQUIRES A RELATIVELY HIGH DEGREE OF PROFICIENCY IN SHIPHANDLING BECAUSE OF THE LACK OF A STRAIGHT-A-WAY APPROACH TO THE MAN. 2. OFTEN IMPOSSIBLE FOR A SINGLE PROPELLER SHIP.
RACETRACK TURN (TWO 180° TURNS) USED IN GOOD VISIBILITY WHEN A STRAIGHT FINAL APPROACH LEG IS DESIRED.	②	1. A VARIATION OF THE ONE TURN METHOD WHICH PROVIDES A DESIRABLE STRAIGHT FINAL APPROACH TO THE MAN. 2. PUT THE RUDDER OVER FULL IN THE DIRECTION CORRESPONDING TO THE SIDE OVER WHICH THE MAN FELL. STOP THE INBOARD ENGINE. 3. WHEN CLEAR OF THE MAN, GO AHEAD FULL ON ALL ENGINES, CONTINUE USING FULL RUDDER TO TURN TO THE RECIPROCAL OF THE ORIGINAL COURSE. 4. STEADY FOR A DISTANCE WHICH WILL GIVE THE DESIRED RUN FOR A FINAL STRAIGHT APPROACH. 5. USE FULL RUDDER TO TURN TO THE MAN. 6. USE THE ENGINES AND RUDDER TO ATTAIN THE PROPER FINAL POSITION (SHIP UPWIND OF THE MAN AND DEAD IN THE WATER WITH THE MAN ALONGSIDE WELL FORWARD OF THE PROPELLERS).	1. THE STRAIGHT FINAL APPROACH LEG FACILITATES A MORE CALCULABLE APPROACH. 2. THE SHIP WILL BE RETURNED TO THE MAN IF HE IS LOST FROM SIGHT. 3. REASONABLY FAST. 4. EFFECTIVE WHEN THE WIND WAS FROM ABEAM ON THE ORIGINAL COURSE.	SLOWER THAN THE ONE TURN METHOD.
DELAYED TURN USED WHEN WORD IS RECEIVED THAT A MAN FELL OVERBOARD, MAN IN SIGHT AND CLEAR ASTERN OF THE SHIP.		1. A VARIATION OF THE ONE TURN METHOD. 2. PUT THE RUDDER OVER FULL IN THE DIRECTION CORRESPONDING TO THE SIDE OVER WHICH THE MAN FELL. GO AHEAD FULL ON ALL ENGINES. 3. HEAD TOWARDS THE MAN. 4. USE THE ENGINES AND RUDDER TO ATTAIN THE PROPER FINAL POSITION (SHIP UPWIND OF THE MAN AND DEAD IN THE WATER WITH THE MAN ALONGSIDE, WELL FORWARD OF THE PROPELLERS).	1. THE FASTEST METHOD WHEN THE MAN IS IN SIGHT AND ALREADY CLEAR ASTERN OF THE SHIP. 2. PROVIDES A STRAIGHT RUN IN THE CRITICAL FINAL PHASE. 3. EFFECTIVE WHEN THE WIND IS FROM AHEAD OR ASTERN OF THE SHIP ON THE ORIGINAL COURSE.	1. DOES NOT ENSURE RETURN TO THE MAN. 2. REQUIRES GOOD VISIBILITY. 3. TAKES THE SHIP FARTHER FROM THE MAN THAN THE OTHER METHODS.
Y BACKING USED BY SUBMARINES BECAUSE THE SHIP (LOW HEIGHT OF EYE) REMAINS COMPARATIVELY CLOSE TO THE MAN.	③	1. PUT THE RUDDER OVER FULL IN THE DIRECTION CORRESPONDING TO THE SIDE OVER WHICH THE MAN FELL. STOP THE INBOARD ENGINE. 2. WHEN CLEAR OF THE MAN, BACK THE ENGINES WITH FULL POWER, USING OPPOSITE RUDDER. 3. GO AHEAD. USE THE ENGINES AND RUDDER TO ATTAIN THE PROPER FINAL POSITION (SHIP UPWIND OF THE MAN AND DEAD IN THE WATER WITH THE MAN ALONGSIDE, WELL FORWARD OF THE PROPELLERS).	THE SHIP REMAINS COMPARATIVELY CLOSE TO THE MAN.	MOST SHIPS BACK INTO THE WIND/SEA, RESULTING IN POOR CONTROL OF THE SHIP WHILE BACKING.
BOAT RECOVERY 1. USED BY SHIPS LACKING SUFFICIENT MANEUVERABILITY TO MAKE A GOOD APPROACH FOR A SHIP RECOVERY. 2. USED WHEN THE SHIP IS DEAD IN THE WATER WITH THE MAN CLOSE ABOARD BUT NOT ALONGSIDE. 3. CAN BE USED IN CONJUNCTION WITH ANY OF THE METHODS SHOWN ABOVE.	BASIC BOAT RECOVERY METHOD:	BASIC BOAT RECOVERY METHOD: 1. PUT THE RUDDER OVER FULL IN THE DIRECTION CORRESPONDING TO THE SIDE OVER WHICH THE MAN FELL. STOP THE INBOARD ENGINE. 2. WHEN THE MAN IS CLEAR, BACK ALL ENGINES FULL TO NEARLY STOP THE SHIP. USE RUDDER TO THE SIDE OF THE READY LIFEBOAT TO PROVIDE A SLICK IN WHICH THE BOAT CAN BE LOWERED. STOP THE ENGINES WHILE THE SHIP STILL HAS VERY SLIGHT HEADWAY TO PERMIT BETTER CONTROL OF THE BOAT AND TO KEEP IT OUT OF THE PROPELLER WASH.	BASIC BOAT RECOVERY METHOD: 1. SIMPLE 2. FOR ANY GIVEN TYPE OF SHIP, THE SHIP WILL REMAIN CLOSER TO THE MAN THAN BY ANY OF THE OTHER METHODS. 3. DOES NOT REQUIRE THAT A PARTICULAR FINAL POSITION BE ATTAINED.	BASIC BOAT RECOVERY METHOD: 1. THE MAN MUST BE IN SIGHT. 2. SEA AND WEATHER CONDITIONS MUST BE SATISFACTORY FOR LOWERING AND RECOVERING THE LIFEBOAT AND FOR SMALL BOAT OPERATIONS.

and he should take bearings himself, referring when necessary to a chart kept on the open bridge. He must also be familiar with the navigational aids in the area and with, of course, the applicable rules of the road. The lookout, as has been mentioned, will normally be stationed on the forecastle deck. He should be instructed in his duties, should perform no other duties, and should be able to communicate directly with the bridge. The OOD, however, remains his own best lookout.

Ultimate responsibility aboard the YP rests with the Officer-in-Charge, usually a drill instructor or YP Squadron Safety Officer. These officers should strive to give the midshipmen the maximum amount of freedom in conning and navigation, consistent with safety. Should the safety of the crew or vessel be endangered, however, they must not hesitate to take charge. If there is no Officer-in-Charge or Safety Officer assigned, the midshipman Commanding Officer acts in this capacity.

There are some rules prescribed by the Head of the Naval Science Department that apply specifically to the YPs. In particular, the YPs shall proceed at a speed not greater than 8 knots between Dewey seawall and Nun No. 14 in Annapolis Roads, both leaving and entering the Severn River. When the boat crane at the Small Craft Facility is in use, a speed of not greater than 6 knots will be maintained. The yawl mooring area off Trident Light will be avoided by the YPs. If this area must be traversed, caution must be exercised not to run over the mooring lines which often will trail the mooring buoys with the current by 20 feet.

Emergency Procedures

Emergencies can occur on any vessel at any time, but the watch officer who makes a habit of thinking ahead can visualize many emergencies and prevent them, or at least be prepared to meet them. The only way to prepare for emergencies is to be alert always and to know in advance exactly what action must be taken in a given situation. It is good practice for the watch officer, when conditions permit, to discuss emergency procedures with other members of the watch and all hands whenever possible.

While not the only emergencies possible, man overboard, breakdown, collision, fire, and grounding are the most likely emergencies and pose the greatest threat to the YP or any other vessel. At a minimum, the proper procedures to cope with these emergencies must be known by the OOD. It is also his responsibility to keep the Officer-in-Charge of the YP informed of emergency situations and casualties, but action should precede reporting. It is obvious that this discussion is as pertinent to the skipper of a small auxiliary as it is to the OOD of a YP or the Captain of a destroyer. All must know how to deal immediately with an emergency situation when it occurs.

Man Overboard

There are a number of man overboard recovery methods. The three most common are: (1) Williamson turn for night or low visibility, (2) race track for fastest recovery when proceeding at high speed in clear weather, and (3) Y-backing, for ships with large turning circles and great backing power, proceeding at slow speeds. These three methods are illustrated in Figure 145. Very large ships often use a small boat to recover a man from the water. Smaller vessels will use the boat recovery method as well when the sea is very rough and the possibility of getting the man close alongside the ship small. The principles mentioned earlier about launching a small boat in a seaway would apply if this method were used on the YP.

Regardless of which recovery method is used, the same basic principles and required action apply. Initially a life ring, life jacket, floating light, or smoke float is thrown overboard to provide flotation for the man and to mark his position. At the same time, the report is made to the OOD, "Man overboard, starboard (port) side." The OOD swings the stern away from the man with full rudder. If it is possible to stop the shaft on the side toward the man before he reaches the screws, this should be done. If it is not, which is likely, continue the recovery without attempting to stop the screw. CIC must be informed immediately, in order that the man on the DRT can mark the ship's position when the man went overboard, shift the DRT scale to 200 yards to the inch, and provide continual ranges and bearings to the man. The word must be passed throughout the ship, so that all man overboard stations can be manned. These stations should be manned by one or more strong swimmers, line tenders, and a man with a first-aid kit. On the bridge, as many men as can be spared should be detailed to *keep the man overboard in sight*. Visual bearings and approximate ranges should be sent to CIC for cross-checking with the DRT plot.

Other ships in company must be informed of the emergency and be kept informed of recovery progress. Voice radio is the best method. In addition, six short blasts should be sounded at frequent intervals. As time permits, the Oscar flag should be hoisted during daylight, or the two, vertical, red, 32-point lights turned on and pulsated at night.

The man should be recovered in the shortest possible time. For the YPs, in good weather this means the race track method and at night or in low visibility, the Williamson turn, though not the fastest recovery method, must be used to bring the ship back along her track. For any method, the desired final position is beam to the wind slightly to windward of the man with all way off. When in this position a lee is provided for the man, and since the ship will make more leeway than will the man, she will drift toward, rather than away from him. As has been mentioned, swimmers with life jackets and tending lines donned should be ready to go into the water.

Man overboard maneuvering instructions for naval vessels involved in tactical evolutions can be found in ATP 1(A), Volume I, Chapter 5. Of specific importance to the YP OOD are the instructions for man overboard recovery from a column formation. In this situation, the ship that loses the man takes action to avoid him, and others do as well, with odd-numbered ships in the column clearing to starboard, and even-numbered ships clearing to port. The ship in the best position to recover the man does so, keeping the other vessels informed of her actions. All ships resume stations when clear.

In summary, when a man falls overboard, the following actions should be taken as rapidly as possible:
- Drop a life ring or jacket, light, or smoke float.
- Swing stern away from man.
- Inform CIC and ship's company.
- Keep man in sight.
- Inform other ships by radio, sound, and visual signals.
- Maneuver to recover man using race-track, Y-backing, or Williamson-turn method.
- Always put your ship to windward of the man.
- Assist the recovery with swimmers.

Breakdown

Breakdowns that prevent the YP from maneuvering do not occur very frequently, because there are two engines to each shaft and a direct mechanical linkage for rudder control. When a breakdown occurs, the immediate reaction must always be to try to maintain control of the vessel. If there is a rudder casualty, the ship may be steered with the engines.

All ships in company should be notified of the casualty by voice radio. Six short blasts should be sounded and during daylight the Five flag should be hoisted. At night, the six blasts should be sounded, the breakdown lights turned on, and the running lights turned off. The vessel should be anchored, if necessary.

When the nature of the breakdown has been determined, the senior officer present should be notified and given an estimate of repair time. If the casualty cannot be repaired and the YP is without power, preparations for towing should be made.

It will occasionally be necessary for the YP to tow another vessel, and infrequently one may have to accept a tow. There are no hard and fast rules for towing or being towed, because wind and sea conditions and the size of the vessels involved are variable. Each situation must be evaluated before decisions are made. In a seaway, it may often be important to provide a lee for the disabled vessel, in which case a parallel approach to windward would be best. If the disabled vessel makes less leeway than the towing vessel, however, and a windward approach is made, the towing vessel will be blown down onto the disabled vessel. Under these circumstances a parallel approach to leeward would be best. In every towing situation, a heaving line with a towline attached must be passed to the disabled vessel. The YPs each have a 2¾-inch, nylon, 300-fathom towline. The towline is made up to the anchor chain of a large vessel being towed, and this chain is veered to provide a shock absorbing catenary in the towline. For smaller vessels, the chain is not required.

The critical point in the towing operation, regardless of the size of the towed vessel, is taking the strain. The towing ship must increase speed very gradually and overcome the inertia of the other vessel slowly in order to keep the towline from parting. Once under way, speed may be increased gradually to hull speed of the vessel under tow, conditions permitting. Being towed at greater than hull speed can do considerable damage to a vessel.

When towing at night, the YP should carry on her mast, in addition to her masthead light, her two, white, 20-point, towing lights. (If towing in International waters, and the length of the two is less than 600 feet, measured from the YP's stern to the stern of the tow, then only one of the towing lights should be carried in addition to the masthead light.)

Collision

Collisions do not "just happen." They can usually be prevented by prudent, timely action on the part of the OOD. Even when timely action is not taken, a collision involving a YP should never occur because of the vessel's great backing power and maneuverability. If the OOD of a YP does find himself *in extremis* with another vessel (in a situation where action by both vessels is required to avoid collision), then both are burdened to take action, and emergency shiphandling procedures must be used in order to avoid collision. There are three important factors that must be considered by the OOD when choosing an emergency shiphan-

dling course of action. What action will best avoid a collision? What action will the other vessel probably take? Where will the collision occur if it cannot be avoided? There are no set rules, especially for the YP with her maneuverability and power. The decision must be rapid and action immediate. If a collision occurs, an inspection of damage should be made at once, the bilge pumps started, and, if possible, the YP returned to the Small Craft Facility.

Fire

As has been mentioned, fires at sea must be fought quickly, because limited fire fighting equipment is available, and escape is difficult. All crew members must know the location of the fire fighting equipment and its use.

In the Navy, fires are classified according to the type of combustible material involved. There are three classes of fire: Alpha, solid combustibles, such as wood, rags, or canvas; Bravo, petroleum products; and Charlie, electrical. There is equipment aboard the YP for combating each of these types of fires (See Table 7). The proper equipment must be used for each type of fire. A solid stream of water often is the most effective means of combating a class Alpha fire, but may enlarge a class Bravo fire, because the burning oil may be spread by the water. If a stream of water is used against a class Charlie fire, the fire fighter could be electrocuted, because water will conduct electricity.

Special equiment available for fighting class Bravo and Charlie fires consists of fog spray nozzles and foam extinguishers for Bravo fires, and CO_2 extinguishers for Charlie fires. The water spray can be used on an oil fire because it cools a large area without disturbing the burning surface. The foam and CO_2 smother, rather than cool, a fire.

If a fire occurs in a YP the Officer-in-Charge should be notified immediately. The O-in-C is responsible for notifying the engineers so that the fire pump and bilge pump can be started, and electrical power to the applicable section of the vessel turned off. Leading a fire party at the scene, the O-in-C can promptly fight the fire with the proper equipment. In order to ensure that the YP fire fighting gear is properly maintained and in working order, it should be checked frequently.

Grounding

With the array of navigational gear aboard the YP, it should certainly be possible to keep her in deep water. The use of this gear has already been mentioned in the section on safe navigation. If a YP should run aground, the reaction should be exactly the same as it would be on any power vessel. (See the section on grounding in Chapter 11.)

An attempt should be made to back the grounded YP off, but the engines should not be run full astern for long. The YP should make use of the advantage of being a twin-screw vessel. A twist can often be used alternatively with full astern to break the YP free of the bottom. If the engines alone are not sufficient to free the YP, the wherry should be lowered and the anchor put out for a kedge. With the anchor windlass taking a strain on the kedge anchor forward and the engines twisting at full power, the YP should be able to free herself. If these efforts are unsuccessful remember that a little higher tide will help the vessel off. If, however, it is already high tide, or if the vessel is being damaged, towing assistance should be requested.

Basic Communications Procedures

INTERNAL COMMUNICATIONS: SOUND-POWERED TELEPHONE

Internal communications between the many stations in a YP are essential to the smooth running and safe handling of the ship. These internal communications are conducted for the most part over sound-powered telephones that connect the various stations. (See Table 6 for the YP sound-powered telephone circuits.) On sound-powered telephones, the button on the mouthpiece must be depressed before speaking.

There will often be many stations on the circuit, and for this reason precise phone talking procedure and specific message format must be used by the telephone talkers in order to eliminate confusion and ensure efficient communications. Messages should never be transmitted while the circuit is busy. When the line is clear, the station originating the message does so using the following format: station called, station calling, message. For example, if the CIC officer wants the OOD on the bridge to know the range and bearing to the Guide, the transmission on the JA circuit would be "Bridge, Combat, Guide bears 030, 620 yards." The bridge talker would then answer if he received the message, "Bridge aye." If he had not received the message, he would say, "Combat, Bridge, say again," and the CIC talker would send the message again. The primary advantage of this type of format is brevity and a degree of familiarity that can come about only through the repetitive use of a format that never varies.

This brief format used on the sound-powered telephone always takes concentrated attention on the part of the talkers and, initially, considerable practice. Familiarity with the general subject matter usually transmitted on a particular circuit is also a help to the talker. Telephone talkers should be briefed on the standard format and expected subject matter and nomenclature before being assigned to a circuit. Sound-powered telephone talkers must not interpret messages they are given to send, or that they receive. Rather, these messages should be sent and relayed verbatim. When vital messages between stations are so transmitted, there is little chance of misinterpretation.

EXTERNAL COMMUNICATIONS

External communications, or ship-to-ship and ship-to-shore communications, are accomplished in the YP by the use of the radio telephone, flashing light, and signal flag hoists. Of these three, the radio telephone and signal flag hoists are used to send the majority of messages.

To send tactical signals, the code in ATP 1(A), Volume II is used. This code, which breaks messages into two-letter groups and associated numbers, is intended primarily for brevity and only secondarily for secrecy. It also allows Allied, non-English speaking navies to use the code, as the alphabet is always spoken phonetically. (See Table 9 for phonetic alphabet.) Signals encoded from ATP 1(A), Volume II may be sent by radio, flashing light, or flag hoist.

Non-naval vessels use the *International Code of Signals* (Hydrographic Office Publication No. 103) to encode and decode messages. This publication contains one, two, and three-letter groups with standard meanings to simplify the sending of messages. The single-letter groups are the most frequently used, for they have either very urgent or very common meanings. The meanings of the single-letter signals are set forth in Table 10. When these signals are flown by a naval vessel, they are always preceded by the special pennant, Code. Flags and flag hoist procedures will be explained in a later section.

Radio Telephone Communications

The radio telephone is used for rapid, short-range, tactical communications between ships, as well as for long-range, ship-to-shore communication. Specific procedures are prescribed for each type of communication in the *Director of Naval Communications Publication No. 5* (DNC-5). These procedures will merely be summarized here. Frequent reference should be made to DNC-5 to ensure correctness of format, phraseology, and procedure. *Communication Instructions Radiotelephone Procedure* (ACP 125 series) prescribes specific details with regard to radiotelephone voice procedures.

Proper radio telephone format and procedure is as important to the proper functioning of a group of naval ships as is proper internal communication procedure to the individual ship.

Table 9 ALLIED PHONETIC ALPHABET

A	Alfa	J	Juliet	S	Sierra
B	Bravo	K	Kilo	T	Tango
C	Charlie	L	Lima	U	Uniform
D	Delta	M	Mike	V	Victor
E	Echo	N	November	W	Whiskey
F	Foxtrot	O	Oscar	X	X-Ray
G	Golf	P	Papa	Y	Yankee
H	Hotel	Q	Quebec	Z	Zulu
I	India	R	Romeo		

Table 10 SINGLE LETTER SIGNALS FROM THE INTERNATIONAL CODE OF SIGNALS

A	I am undergoing a speed trial.
B	I am taking in or discharging explosives.
C	Yes (Affirmative).
D	Keep clear of me—I am maneuvering with difficulty.
E	I am directing my course to starboard.
*F	I am disabled. Communicate with me.
G	I require a pilot.
H	I have a pilot on board.
I	I am directing my course to port.
J	I am going to send a message by semaphore.
*K	You should stop your vessel instantly.
*L	You should stop. I have something important to communicate.
M	I have a doctor on board.
N	No (Negative).
*O	Man overboard.
*P	IN HARBOR ("Blue Peter")—All persons are to repair on board as the vessel is about to proceed to sea. (Note—To be hoisted at the foremast head.) AT SEA—Your lights are out, or burning badly.
Q	My vessel is healthy and I request free pratique.
*R	The way is off my ship; you may feel your way past me.
S	My engines are going full speed astern.
T	Do not pass ahead of me.
*U	You are standing into danger.
*V	I require assistance.
*W	I require medical assistance.
X	Stop carrying out your intentions and watch for my signals.
Y	I am carrying mails.
*Z	To be used to address or call shore stations.

* These signals only may be sent by flashing light.

Specific message headings are used on the radio telephone. On tactical circuits, "call signs" are used. Call signs are words of two or more syllables used for identifying ships, groups of ships, and ship-group commanders. On non-tactical circuits and ship-to-shore circuits, call signs are replaced by YP hull numbers. Hull numbers and call signs are never used on the same circuit. Table 11 lists the standard YP organization call signs. Table 12 lists international call signs for the individual YPs.

As has been mentioned, the phonetic alphabet is always used to identify any letter of the alphabet. Numbers are spoken digit by digit, except for multiples of hundreds and thousands, which may be spoken normally. For example, 10 is spoken "one zero," while 100 is

Table 11 STANDARD YP ORGANIZATION CALL SIGNS

	Command	Collective
O & C	Antagonize	Peso
Division 1	Floating Rib	Teakettle
Division 2	Sugar Tree	Brown Bread
Screen	Magnify	Kirkland
Main Body	Adjoin	Dehydrate

Ship Call Signs			
p1	Aimwell	p9	Repairman
p2	Beerfoam	p10	Stickpin
p3	Drexel	p11	Turbojet
p4	Enjoyment	p12	Tuxedo Junction
p5	Geraldine	p13	Virginia
p6	Holywreath	p14	White Owl
p7	Openstock	p15	Yorktown
p8	Plastered		

spoken "one hundred." Procedure words, or prowords, are used to simplify radio telephone format. These prowords have standard meanings that cannot be varied. Table 13 lists some common prowords and their meanings. Note in this table the use and meaning of the proword "say again." A very common error on the radio telephone is to use the word "repeat," instead of "say again." Also note that all transmissions must be ended with either "over" or "out."

There are two methods for executing tactical signals over the radio telephone. One, called the non-executive method, is used for information signals and emergency signals. In this method, the signal is executed as soon as it is understood. If a signal is an emergency signal, the word "emergency" is included in the text of the message, and the text is repeated. (See Table 14 for the precise format used in transmitting non-executive signals. Call signs from Table 11 have been used therein.)

The second method, called the executive method, prescribes a precise moment for the execution of each signal. There are two formats that can be used with this method, the delayed executive and the immediate executive. Examples of each will be found in Table 14. The delayed executive format is used for signals that must be executed simultaneously by all ships, but need not be executed immediately. The initial signal is sent and acknowledged, and then another signal is sent at the time of execution. This is the preferred format, because it allows time to decode the signal between receipt and execution. The immediate executive format is used for readily understood signals that require simultaneous, immediate execution, as the name implies. Note that with the immediate executive format, the text must be repeated before it is executed. Signals sent by the immediate executive method should be in plain language or limited to commonly used signals, because there is no opportunity for verification, repetition, or acknowledgment between receipt and execution.

It should be noted in Table 14 that for both methods of execution, the same message format is used. This format consists of a heading, the call sign of the ship or unit signaled, and that of the ship or unit signalling. The heading indicates precisely whom the signal is to and whom it is from. The heading is separated from the text by the proword, "break." The proword, "break," is used again to separate the text from the ending. The call signs in the ending indicate which ships should acknowledge the signal. This assignment of responsibility for acknowledgment must not be confused with the heading

Table 12 INTERNATIONAL CALL SIGNS FOR THE 654-CLASS YPS

YP Hull Number	International Call Sign
654	NOSE
655	NHVC
656	NRCE
657	NJOE
658	NNAZ
659	NOTA
660	NRBC
661	NNCJ
662	NJQO
663	NOTN
664	NYTG
665	NPSS
666	NSGH
667	NSVV

Table 13 **COMMON NAVY PROWORDS**

PROWORD	EXPLANATION
MESSAGE FOLLOWS	A message which requires recording is about to follow. Transmitted immediately after the call.
SIGNALS FOLLOW	The groups which follow are taken from a signal book. Not used on nets primarily employed for conveying signals. Intended for use when signals are passed on non-tactical nets such as the CI Net.
BREAK	I hereby indicate the separation of the text from other portions of the message.
CORRECTION	An error has been made in this transmission. Transmission will continue with the last word correctly transmitted.
DISREGARD THIS TRANSMISSION	This transmission is in error; disregard it, not used to cancel any message that has been completely transmitted and for which receipt or acknowledgement has been received.
NEGATIVE	Not received. No.
AFFIRMATIVE	Yes. Permission granted.
SAY AGAIN	Repeat all (or portion indicated) of your last transmission.
I SAY AGAIN	I am repeating transmission or portion indicated.
VERIFY	Verify entire message (or portion indicated) with the originator and send correct version.
I VERIFY	That which follows has been verified at your *request* and is repeated.
I SPELL	I shall spell the next word phonetically.
EXECUTE TO FOLLOW	Action on the message or signal which follows is to be carried out upon receipt of the proword "EXECUTE."
EXECUTE	Carry out the purport of the message or signal to which this applies.
ROGER	I have *received* your last transmission *satisfactorily*.
ACKNOWLEDGE	Let me know that you have received and understand this message.
WILCO	Reply to "ACKNOWLEDGE," meaning "I have received your message, understand it, and will comply." Must be authorized by the Commanding Officer (Officer-in-Charge).
OVER	This is the end of my transmission to you and a response is necessary. Go ahead; transmit. (Note: All transmissions must end with OVER or OUT.)
OUT	This is the end of my transmission to you and no answer is required or expected.
WORD AFTER	The word of the message to which I have reference is that which follows _____.
WORD BEFORE	The word of the message to which I have reference is that which precedes _____.

that indicates which ships are to take action on the signal. The ending is used by the originator to ensure that the transmission has been received. If no specific call sign is used in the ending, all units called in the heading answer by call sign in alphabetical order.

Frequencies normally used aboard the YP and the uses for each frequency are indicated in Table 15.

Visual Signaling

There are three methods of visual communication: flag hoist, flashing light, and semaphore.

The YPs use the flag hoist method extensively and flashing light only occasionally, usually in conjunction with a flag hoist to attract attention to it, or to relay the signal to a ship from which the flags cannot be seen. Semaphore is seldom used. Midshipmen are required to learn signal flags, flag hoist procedures, and the Morse code for use in flashing light, but they are not required to learn semaphore.

Flag hoist signaling is a rapid, accurate, and secure system for handling tactical and informational signals during daylight. The signals must be as brief as possible, and ships must be within easy visual range. For flag hoist signal-

Table 14 TACTICAL SIGNAL EXECUTION

Methods of Execution As Spoken on Tactical Nets
NON-EXECUTIVE METHOD Peso, this is Antagonize, break, (signal), break, Beerfoam, over. This is Beerfoam, roger, out.
EMERGENCY SITUATION Peso, this is Antagonize, break, *emergency* turn niner, I say again, *emergency* turn niner, break, Aimwell, Beerfoam, over. This is Aimwell, roger, out. This is Beerfoam, roger, out.
EXECUTIVE METHOD *Delayed Executive* Peso, this is Antagonize, *execute to follow*, break, turn niner, break, Drexel, over. This is Drexel, roger, out. Peso, this is Antagonize, turn niner, standby, *execute*, break, Enjoyment, over. This is Enjoyment, roger, out. *Immediate Executive* Peso, this is Antagonize, *immediate execute*, break, turn niner, *I say again*, turn niner, standby, execute, break, Geraldine, over. This is Geraldine, roger, out. *Note: Commas as used above signify pauses.*

ing, the Navy uses standard international alphabet flags and numeral pennants, and also numeral flags and special flags and pennants. Figure 146 shows flag nomenclature and the various flag types. A complete Navy flag bag is shown inside the back cover. When learning the signal flags, it may be helpful to divide them into groups by function. This breakdown is given in Table 16.

In addition to the flags and pennants, tack lines are used in visual signaling. A tack line is a length of halyard about three feet long and is used between signals or groups of numerals to avoid ambiguity and to indicate a break. It is also used when specified by the signal book. When a signal to be flown is so long that it cannot be bent onto one hoist, it should be broken where a tack line would normally occur and flown from more than one halyard.

Multiple hoists must be hoisted in the order in which they are to be read. Signals on the YP are flown from either the port or starboard yard-

arm and are read from top to bottom, and from outboard to inboard on each side.

Flag Hoist Procedure

The ship originating a flag hoist will hoist signals *close up* (with the top of the hoist touching the block on the yardarm). All ships respond by hoisting the identical signal, flag for flag, and fly it *at the dip* (three-fourths of the way up). Small vessels or vessels without a required flag may hoist the answering pennant at the dip instead of the entire hoist. The hoist should remain at the dip until the signal is understood. When understood, the signal is closed up. The signal is executed when the originator hauls down his signal. Normally, this will not be done until all vessels have the signal closed up. When the signal is executed, all vessels haul down the signal. Some signals may prescribe a certain time for execution. Signals preceded by the emergency pennant are executed as soon as understood.

Flag hoists originated by the *OTC* (Officer in Tactical Command) are considered to be addressed to all ships unless a specific ship or ships are indicated in the heading. Ships are indicated by their visual call, a one-letter, type-of-ship designator and a numeral pennant. The numeral pennant will be the last digit of the ship's hull number. For example, the usual call for YP-658 would be: Y8. Numeral pennants, not numeral flags, are used in these visual calls.

When ships are positioned so that the originator cannot be seen from all of them, such as in a column, a signal relay system is used. Ships nearest the originator have "visual responsibility" for those further away in the same direction. The signal closed up on the originator is hoisted at the dip on the nearest ships. It is not closed up by them until the signal is both understood on board and the correct signal has been closed up on the next ship in line away from the originator. In this manner the originator knows that when the adjacent ship or ships close up the signal, it is ready for execution on all ships. If the originator should execute the signal before all ships have acknowledged, those ships which have answered should close up and execute the signal and then relay the signal by

Table 15 **RADIO FREQUENCY PLAN**

FREQ.	PURPOSES FOR WHICH USED				GUARDED BY*	CALLS USED	REMARKS
	GENERAL	DRILL	YP SQDN.	MISC.			
2792 kcs	SCF** admin., Ship-Shore, Alternate Maneuvering	Ship-Shore Note #1	Ship-Shore 2nd Alt. Man.	Ship-Shore 1st Alt. Man.	"(Small craft) Control" (Ops. Office, SCF). Others as appropriate.	Plain language	Note #2
2252 kcs	Local drills	Note #1			Drill units as directed	Tactical and voice call signs	Note #3
2716 kcs	Harbor communications				"(Annapolis) Control" (Ops. Office, SCF)	Plain language	Note #4
284.4 mcs	Drills and tactics	Note #1	Pri. Man.	2nd Alt. Man.	Drill/cruise units as directed	Tactical and voice call signs	Note #5
304.2 mcs	Drills and tactics	Note #1	1st Alt. Man.	Pri. Man.	Drill/cruise units as directed	Tactical and voice call signs	Note #5
277.8 mcs	Drills and tactics			3rd Alt. Man.	Units as directed	Tactical and voice call signs	Note #5
359.4 mcs	Ship-Shore				Units as directed	Plain language	
2670 kcs	Marine Info. and weather				USCG on Chesapeake Bay (see Note #6)	Plain language	Weather every half-hour
2182 kcs	Distress				USCG on Chesapeake Bay (see Note #7)	Plain language	
162.55 mhz	Weather forecasts				Washington, D.C. Forecast Center	Plain language	Continuous 24 hours

* Calls enclosed in parentheses are not used unless essential for clarity or to avoid ambiguity.
** Small Craft Facility.

NOTES

1. (Primary/Alternate) Tactical, Maneuvering, and Warning Net as directed.
2. May be used outside the local operating area. Tactical and voice call signs may be used within the local operating area only.
3. May not be used outside the local operating area. Plain language calls may be used but not mixed with tactical voice call signs.
4. Used only when directed by SOPA or in an emergency.
5. May be used outside the local operating area.
6. Baltimore CG Radio, Piney Pt. Lt., and Thomas Pt. Lt. continuously; Sandy Point Lt. periodically.
7. Baltimore CG Radio and Piney Point Lt. continuously; Sandy Pt. Lt. periodically.

other means to the ships for which they are responsible.

Acknowledging ships may question a signal by hoisting Interrogative while leaving the questioned signal at the dip. Flag hoists are cancelled by the originator by hoisting Negative on an adjacent halyard. If only one of many signals is to be cancelled it must be repeated and preceded by Negative. When all ships have acknowledged the cancellation, the hoists are cleared.

When proceeding independently in or out of port, naval ships are obliged to fly speed information signals indicating the speed that they are making through the water. Speed is always indicated by two numeral flags (never pen-

Figure 146   FLAG NOMENCLATURE & FOUR BASIC SHAPES

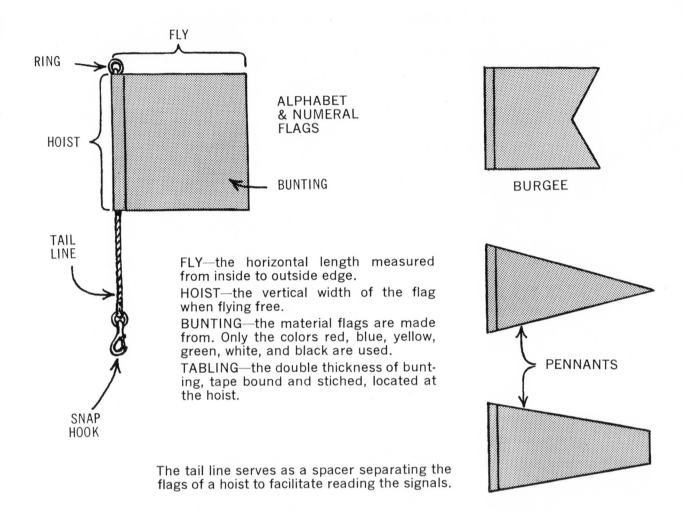

RING

FLY

HOIST

ALPHABET
& NUMERAL
FLAGS

BUNTING

TAIL
LINE

SNAP
HOOK

FLY—the horizontal length measured from inside to outside edge.
HOIST—the vertical width of the flag when flying free.
BUNTING—the material flags are made from. Only the colors red, blue, yellow, green, white, and black are used.
TABLING—the double thickness of bunting, tape bound and stiched, located at the hoist.

The tail line serves as a spacer separating the flags of a hoist to facilitate reading the signals.

BURGEE

PENNANTS

nants) flown at the dip. The special pennant, Speed, is never flown in conjunction with these speed indicator flags.

All ships that are designated as radio transmitting and receiving stations are assigned international radio call signs by the federal government. These call signs are flown by Navy ships from the outboard port signal halyard while under way in Inland waters. YPs hoist these international call signs smartly as soon as all lines are cast off when getting underway, and lower them leaving Annapolis Roads when red flashing bell buoy No. 8 comes in line with the fixed light of Greenbury Point (see chart inside front cover). When entering Annapolis Roads,

they will be hoisted at this same point and lowered when the first mooring line is put ashore. The international call signs for the 654-Class YPs are listed in Table 12.

The flashing light is used aboard the YP primarily as a back-up communication system. Nonetheless, international Morse code symbols and elementary flashing light procedures must be learned. For ease of learning, the Morse code has been broken down into five groups in Table 17.

For recording both flag hoist and flashing light messages, a specific format is used in the Navy. This format must be followed to avoid confusion. Recording format is given in Table 18.

216

Table 16 BREAKDOWN OF SIGNAL FLAGS AND PENNANTS BY FUNCTION

SPECIAL FLAGS AND PENNANTS	
PREP INT NEGAT	GOVERNING PENNANTS
FORM STATION TURN CORPEN SPEED	SPECIAL PENNANTS FOR MANEUVERING SIGNALS
SUBDIV DIV SQUAD FLOT	UNIT INDICATORS
CODE OR ANS BLACK DESIG EMERG PORT STBD	ATP 1 (A) VOL II DESCRIBES THE USE OF THESE SPECIAL PENNANTS

Honors and Ceremonies

The national ensign is flown from the gaff of the YP at all times while under way. When not under way, the national ensign and union jack are flown between 0800 and sunset from the flagstaff aft and jack staff forward, respectively. A ship changes status from under way to not under way when the first mooring line is put over or the anchor let go. At this moment colors are shifted with ceremony. Men are stationed at the flagstaff, jack staff, and the signal bridge. One blast on a hand whistle is sounded when the status is shifted, for example from under way to not under way, and the command, "shift colors," is given. At this command, the national ensign is lowered from the gaff and the international call sign from the yardarm. At the same time, the national ensign is run up on the flagstaff and the union jack raised on the jack staff. If the ship moors before 0800 or after sunset, the national ensign and the union jack are not raised, of course.

The ceremonial raising and lowering of the national ensign and union jack in port at 0800 and sunset is referred to as morning and evening colors. The procedure for carrying out morning and evening colors aboard the YP and other naval vessels is standard. All ships follow the timing of the Senior Officer Present. Five minutes before the ceremony, Prep is hoisted by all vessels. Prep is hauled down and attention sounded (one long blast on the hand whistle) precisely at 0800 and at sunset. All hands face the national ensign and salute. When men are formed in ranks, only the officer or petty officer in charge salutes, while the rest remain at attention. The ensign and jack are hoisted smartly and lowered slowly. They are never hoisted and then broken out. After the colors ceremony, "carry on" is sounded by three short blasts on a hand whistle.

When boarding a naval vessel between the hours of 0800 and sunset, naval officers face and salute the national ensign and then turn and salute the OOD. Civilians should face the national ensign before facing the OOD to ask permission to board. The reverse order is used when disem-

Table 17 INTERNATIONAL MORSE CODE SYMBOLS

Group 1		Group 2		Group 3		Group 4		Group 5	
•	E	• —	A	— •	N	—	T	• — — — —	1
• •	I	• — —	W	— • •	D	— —	M	• • — — —	2
• • •	S	• — — —	J	— • • •	B	— — —	O	• • • — —	3
• • • •	H	• — •	R	— • —	K	— — •	G	• • • • —	4
• • —	U	• — • •	L	— • — •	C	— — • •	Z	• • • • •	5
• • — •	F	• — — •	P	— • — —	Y	— — • —	Q	— • • • •	6
• • • —	V			— • • —	X			— — • • •	7
								— — — • •	8
								— — — — •	9
								— — — — —	0

Table 18 **RECORDING FORMAT FOR FLAGHOIST MESSAGES**

ABCDEFGHIJKLM
NOPQRSTUVWXYZ
1234567890
p1 p2 p3 p4 p5 p6 p7 p8 p9 p0
ANS/CODE BLACK CORPEN DESIG DIV
EMERG FLOT FORM INT NEGAT
PREP PORT SPEED SQUAD STBD
STATION SUBDIV TURN TACK
1ST 2ND 3RD 4TH

Some of the most common recording errors are

- Flags written out phonetically.
- Letters not capitalized for flags.
- Numerals not in arabic script.
- Numeral 1 not recorded with horizontal foot.
- Numeral 0 not recorded with slant line.
- Letter Z not recorded with cross bar.
- Numeral pennants not recorded with prefix "p."

Note: Special flags and pennants are correct if PRINTED in CAPS, incorrect if written in longhand or lower case.

Table 19 **PASSING HONOR PROCEDURES**

OOD OF JUNIOR SHIP	OOD OF SENIOR SHIP	HAND WHISTLE SIGNAL
1. Sound "attention to (port/starboard)"		1 whistle for attention to starboard 2 whistles for attention to port
	2. Sound "attention to (port/starboard)"	
3. Sound "hand salute"	4. Sound "hand salute"	1 short whistle
	5. (after approximately 3 seconds) sound "two"	2 short whistles
6. Sound "two"	7. Sound "carry on"	3 short whistles
8. Sound "carry on"		

barking. The OOD returns the salute to both the national ensign and himself.

Salutes are rendered to naval vessels by private vessels under way by *dipping* (lowering halfway) the national ensign. When these salutes are received from vessels under the registry of nations formally recognized by the United States, naval vessels will return the salute, dip for dip. To return a dip, the ensign is lowered halfway, held momentarily, and then re-hoisted. When the dip has been answered, the saluting ship re-hoists her colors. Naval vessels never initiate dips; they only return them.

Appropriate honors are rendered to other naval vessels, both United States and foreign, and to embarked high-ranking naval officers and civilians when they are passed close aboard. These *passing honors,* as they are called, are accomplished by calling the crew to attention on the appropriate side and having them render a hand salute. This salute is then answered by the honored ship, and then both ships carry on. The precise steps in this procedure together with the proper hand whistle signals are found in Table 19. Passing honors are not rendered before 0800 or after sunset, and they are not exchanged by YPs engaged in drills. Procedures for dressing ship, half-masting colors, and other points of etiquette afloat will be covered in the next chapter.

CHAPTER FOURTEEN

Etiquette Afloat

To most seamen, a love of boats and the sea is accompanied by a profound respect for and admiration of those age-old traditions long associated with the sea. These often unwritten customs and traditions provide the basis of etiquette afloat.

When entering and leaving port, particular attention should be paid to the appearance of the vessel. Lines should never be left trailing over the side, at any time, of course, but such sloppiness is particularly noticeable in harbor. Fenders and fender boards when entering port should be left on deck until nearing the dock. They should be taken aboard immediately after clearing the dock when leaving. There are few things that spoil the sight of a beautiful boat more than three or four fenders hanging over the side.

When entering harbor in a sailboat under power, sails should be furled neatly, sheets and halyards belayed and coiled properly, and loose gear, including clothes and towels, should be put below. Leave no *Irish pennants* (dangling rope ends). The importance of presenting a most seamanlike appearance when entering and leaving harbor cannot be overemphasized.

Once in the harbor, don't anchor too close to other boats already moored. Always allow for shifts in the wind and current, leaving room to swing a full 360 degrees around the anchor. It must also be kept in mind that deep draft sailboats will often swing to the current while shallow draft boats swing to the wind. This means extra care and foresight when anchoring a sailboat in a harbor with many powerboats, and vice versa.

Often in a crowded anchorage there will be guest moorings provided by the community or local yacht club for visiting vessels. These moorings should not be picked up without first checking with the yacht club or harbor master. This is not only a courtesy, but also a precaution, since the mooring may be in disrepair or not heavy enough for your vessel.

When anchored or moored in a crowded anchorage, keep in mind that sound travels easily over the water. Late gatherings in the cockpit should be kept reasonably quiet. Boisterousness lasting until the early hours of the morning is not appreciated by others in the anchorage. Tying halyards away from aluminum masts will eliminate an objectionable source of noise on a windy evening. Keep radios turned low.

Trash should never be thrown overboard in harbors or inland waters. The rule definitely applies to the Chesapeake Bay, since a Maryland law prohibits such pollution of its waters. All trash and garbage should be disposed of ashore or saved until well clear of the land when going offshore.

When under power, always respect the rights of boats under sail, and remember the effect that a large wake will have on a sailboat, slowing whenever possible when passing a sailboat and giving her a wide berth. Often the ignorant or rude sailboat skipper will needlessly interfere with a powerboat navigating in a channel. This discourteous conduct must be taken in stride by the powerboat man and the sailboat allowed to proceed without interference. Sailboats racing should be given an especially wide berth, because wakes and wind interference left by powerboats or other sailboats can seriously effect the outcome of the race. This is especially true in light weather. When maneuvering around racing sailboats reduce speed to minimize wake and always pass astern and to leeward of them, so their wind is not disturbed. Don't anchor near racing marks or starting or finish lines.

Channels, like roads, have two sides. Don't be

Table 20 **SEQUENCE OF BUNTING FOR FULL DRESS SHIP**

a. U.S. Navy FLAG BAG: *(starting from bow)*
3, 4, p1, S, 1st, A, Prep, C, M, Speed, J, p5, R, p9, Z, Corpen, 8, U, 6, X, Negat, 2, Port, N, p2, T, 2nd, B, D, Turn, 5, Station, K, p6, W, p0, 1, 0, 3rd, H, E, Emerg, L, p7, 0, Int, Div, p4, 9, 4th, P, Form, V, G, Stbd, I, F, Q, p8, Y, Desig, 7, p3, Squad, Ans.

b. Standard FLAG BAG: *(starting from bow)*
AB 2, UJ 1, KE 3, GH 6, IV 5, FL 4, DM 7, PO 3rd, RN 1st, ST 0, CX 9, WQ 8, ZY 2nd

a channel hog, keep to the right, and remember the proper whistle signals.

When in harbor, always proceed at a very slow speed, leaving little or no wake. In many areas, a maximum speed of five knots is allowed by law and will be posted. Whether posted or not, this rule of courtesy should be observed.

When proceeding under sail, never interfere with a power vessel just to emphasize a sailboat's right of way. Attempt not to harass powerboats negotiating a crowded channel, and do not interfere with large steam vessels in restricted waters. Such prudent respect for size is common sense and also law under both International and Inland Rules of the Road.

Flag Etiquette

The flying of flags or *colors* (the term may include all of the flags flown by a vessel or it may refer only to the national or yacht ensign) on sailing and power vessels is a subject governed primarily by custom and tradition. The right of private vessels to fly national colors stems indirectly from the Navy's long traditional use of the stars and stripes. When the Continental Congress established a national flag in June, 1777, it was immediately thereafter flown from naval vessels. As the Navy then and for some time thereafter was supplemented by large numbers of privateersmen, it became customary for these privately owned naval vessels to fly the national standard as well.

The yacht ensign, a Betsy Ross flag with a fouled anchor inside the circle of thirteen white stars, is flown from yachts instead of the national flag (see inside back cover). It was designed by the New York Yacht Club and adopted in 1849 by the Secretary of the Navy as a signal to be flown by certain merchantmen, exempting them from entering and clearing at customs houses. Because of its similarity to the national flag, it has become the yacht ensign and is today the customary ensign for yachts to fly. All U.S. Naval Academy vessels fly the national ensign, as they are naval vessels, rather than private yachts, of course.

Colors are flown aboard yachts, as they are in naval vessels, from 0800 until sunset while in port. Under way, entering or leaving port, they may be flown whenever there is enough light to distinguish them, but before 0800 or after sunset, they should be hauled down immediately after anchoring. When under way offshore, colors may be flown whenever required, such as when meeting other vessels. They may also be flown as needed when approaching lightships or nearing foreign shores.

When making colors in the morning, if shorthanded, the ensign is raised first, then the *yacht club burgee* (flag, usually triangular, designating a specific yacht club). At sunset, colors are executed in the reverse order, if shorthanded. Whenever possible, however, all colors should be raised and lowered simultaneously. The Senior Officer Present should initiate morning and evening colors, all others following his timing and example.

If the ensign is to be flown at half-mast, it must first be mastheaded and then lowered to half-mast (actually about two-thirds of staff height). Before lowering from half-mast, colors should first be mastheaded and then lowered.

At anchor, all yachts should fly the yacht ensign from a staff aft. It should be noted that members of the *U.S. Power Squadrons* (an educational organization dedicated to safety afloat and good seamanship) are entitled to fly the U.S. Power Squadron ensign in place of the yacht ensign. The Power Squadron ensign is pictured inside the back cover. Under way the ensign is flown from a staff aft on a powerboat or a sailboat under power.

Under sail, the Luders yawls fly the ensign

sewn onto the mizzen leech, two-thirds of the way up.

The yacht club *burgee* is flown both at anchor and under way from a bow staff on powerboats.

On the Luders yawls, the U.S. Naval Academy Sailing Squadron burgee (see inside back cover) is flown from the mainmast head while under way (except when racing outside Chesapeake Bay) or at anchor.

Sailing Squadron members holding the ranks of commodore, vice commodore, and rear commodore, should display the flag of their rank at the mizzen masthead in the Luders yawls, except when racing. These flags should be flown day and night.

On national holidays, at regattas, and when ordered or on other special occasions, a vessel

Figure 147

THE FEARLESS IN FULL DRESS

Notice that the signal flags extend below the rail at the bow and stern. The Union Jack is shown at the bow, the Naval Academy Sailing Squadron burgee at the masthead, and the Tango signal flag (launch requested) below the starboard lower spreader.

223

may "dress ship" with signal flags and pennants of the International Code of Signals. In order to achieve the most colorful sequence of flags and pennants, the Navy method of two signal flags to one pennant is recommended. Table 20 gives the order of flags for dressing ship. The ship should be dressed at 0800 and should remain dressed until sunset. The signal flags should reach from the water line forward to the heads of all masts, and down to the water line aft (see Figure 147).

When visiting in foreign waters, the national ensign of the host country should be displayed from the starboard, lower main spreader between 0800 and sunset.

Regatta Protocol

There are many rules of etiquette afloat that are peculiar to regattas and sailboat racing in general. Entry forms required for most regattas must be filled in accurately. They often provide the basis for handicapping the entrants, and all information contained on them is assumed to be correct. These entry forms often stipulate conditions of the race or regatta (for example, rules governing the shifting of ballast, required safety equipment, etc.). These stipulations are honored without question. By the same unwritten rule of gentlemanly conduct, the skipper of the yacht racing under a handicap system is honor bound to race his boat loaded as nearly as possible as she was when measured. Particularly important in this regard is ballast of any type or heavy deck gear, such as the dinghy.

If after entering a race, the skipper finds he will not be able to race his boat, he should try to notify the race committee of his change in plans before the date of the race.

Before starting a race, it is courteous conduct (and required by the racing rules) to keep clear of the starting area while other classes start. The same principle applies after finishing. It is also expected that boats that have not started or are not racing will keep clear of boats that are racing, regardless of who may have the right of way.

When racing, keep clear whenever possible of other racing classes. It is considered poor sportsmanship to use racing tactics such as covering, blanketing, and luffing against boats of other classes that are not actual competitors.

When racing, all boats should seek to avoid collision. A boat with the right of way must hold course until in extremis, but must then maneuver to avoid collision, just as must the other boat. If the skipper of a racing yacht feels that another skipper is in danger of violating the racing rules, he should so inform him. If the rules are violated and a protest results, the protesting skipper should try to inform the protested skipper immediately. The racing rules require that the red protest flag be flown and the race committee be informed of the protest when finishing, if not sooner.

Whenever a skipper of a boat being protested realizes that he is in fact guilty of an infraction of the rules, he should immediately withdraw from the race. If, however, he elects to continue to sail in the vicinity of the course for practice or just for the sail, he must keep well clear of all racing yachts. The skipper of a boat that fouls a mark or rounds a buoy the wrong way and cannot correct his mistake should immediately withdraw, regardless of whether or not any other boats are aware of his error.

It is not ethical to drop a protest just because the protested boat is eventually beaten in the race. If an infraction of the rules occurred, the case should be protested and decided. Information given to the members of the protest committee should be as accurate as possible.

By way of summarizing this chapter, it may be sufficient to note that, interestingly enough, most rules of etiquette afloat are also good rules of safety afloat.

Appendixes

Inland Rules of the Road

I. ENACTING CLAUSE, SCOPE, AND PENALTY

Whereas the provisions of chapter eight hundred and two of the laws of eighteen hundred and ninety, and the amendments thereto, adopting regulations for preventing collisions at sea, apply to all waters of the United States connected with the high seas navigable by seagoing vessels, except so far as the navigation of any harbor, river, or inland waters is regulated by special rules duly made by local authority; and

Whereas it is desirable that the regulations relating to the navigation of all harbors, rivers, and inland waters of the United States, except the Great Lakes and their connecting and tributary waters as far east as Montreal and the Red River of the North and rivers emptying into the Gulf of Mexico and their tributaries, shall be stated in one act: Therefore,

Be it enacted by the Senate and House of Representatives of the United States of America in Congress assembled, That the following regulations for preventing collisions shall be followed by all vessels upon the harbors, rivers, and other inland waters of the United States, except the Great Lakes and their connecting and tributary waters as far east as Montreal, and the waters of the Mississippi River between its source and the Huey P. Long Bridge and all of its tributaries emptying thereinto and their tributaries, and that part of the Atchafalaya River above its junction with the Plaquemine-Morgan City alternate waterway, and the Red River of the North; and are hereby declared special rules duly made by local authority.

SEC. 2. (a) The Secretary of the Department in which the Coast Guard[2] is operating shall establish such rules to be observed, on the waters described in section 1 of this Act, by steam vessels in passing each other and as to the lights and day signals to be carried on such waters by ferryboats, by vessels and craft of all types when in tow of steam vessels or operating by hand power or horsepower or drifting with the current, and by any other vessels not otherwise provided for, not inconsistent with the provisions of this Act, as he from time to time may deem necessary for safety, which rules are hereby declared special rules duly made by local authority. A pamphlet containing such Act and regulations shall be furnished to all vessels and craft subject to this Act. On vessels and craft over sixty-five feet in length the pamphlet shall, where practicable, be kept on board and available for ready reference.

(b) Except in an emergency, before any rules or any alteration, amendment, or repeal thereof are established by the Secretary under the provisions of this section, the said Secretary shall publish the proposed rules, alterations, amendments, or repeals, and public hearings shall be held with respect thereto on such notice as the Secretary deems reasonable under the circumstances.

SEC. 3. Every licensed and unlicensed pilot, engineer, mate, or master of any vessel[3] who violates the provisions of this Act or the regulations established pursuant hereto shall be liable to a penalty of not exceeding $500, and for all damages sustained by any passenger, in his person or baggage, as a result of such violation: Provided, That nothing herein shall relieve any vessel, owner, or corporation from any liability incurred by reason of such violation.

SEC. 4. Every vessel which is navigated in violation of any of the provisions of this Act or the regulations established pursuant hereto shall be liable to a penalty of $500, one-half to go to the informer, for which sum such vessel may be seized and proceeded against by action in any district court of the United States having jurisdiction of the offense.

PRELIMINARY DEFINITIONS

In the following rules every steam vessel which is under sail and not under steam is to be considered a sailing vessel, and every vessel under steam, whether under sail or not, is to be considered a steam vessel.

The words "steam vessel" shall include any vessel propelled by machinery.

A vessel is "under way," within the meaning of these rules, when she is not at anchor, or made fast to the shore, or aground.

II. LIGHTS, AND SO FORTH

The word "visible" in these rules, when applied to lights, shall mean visible on a dark night with a clear atmosphere.

ART. 1. The rules concerning lights shall be complied with in all weathers from sunset to sunrise, and during such time no other lights which may be mistaken for the prescribed lights shall be exhibited.

ART. 2.[4] A steam vessel when under way shall carry—(a) On or in the front of the foremast, or if a vessel without a foremast, then in the fore part of the vessel, a bright white light so constructed as to show an unbroken light over an arc of the horizon of twenty points of the compass, so fixed as to throw the light ten points on each side of the vessel, namely, from right ahead to two points abaft the beam on either side, and of such a character as to be visible at a distance of at least five miles.

STEAM VESSELS—SIDE LIGHTS

(b) On the starboard side a green light so constructed as to show an unbroken light over an arc of the horizon of ten points of the compass, so fixed as to throw the light from right ahead to two points abaft the beam on the starboard side, and of such a character as to be visible at a distance of at least two miles.

(c) On the port side a red light so constructed as to show an unbroken light over an arc of the horizon of ten points of the compass, so fixed as to throw the light from right ahead to two points abaft the beam on the port side, and of such a character as to be visible at a distance of at least two miles.

(d) The said green and red side lights shall be fitted with inboard screens projecting at least three feet forward from the light, so as to prevent these lights from being seen across the bow.

STEAM VESSELS—RANGE LIGHTS

(e) A seagoing steam vessel when under way may carry an additional white light similar in construction to the light mentioned in subdivision (a). These two lights shall be so placed in line with the keel that one shall be at least fifteen feet higher than the other, and in such a position with reference to each other that the lower light shall be forward of the upper one. The vertical distance between these lights shall be less than the horizontal distance.

(f) All steam vessels (except seagoing vessels and ferryboats), shall carry in addition to green and red lights required by article two (b), (c), and screens as required by article two (d), a central range of two white lights; the after light being carried at an elevation at least fifteen feet above the light at the head of the vessel. The headlight shall be so constructed as to show an unbroken light through twenty points of the compass, namely, from right ahead to two points abaft the beam on either side of the vessel, and the after light so as to show all around the horizon.

STEAM VESSELS—WHEN TOWING OR PUSHING

ART. 3. (a) A steam vessel when towing another vessel or vessels alongside or by pushing ahead shall, in adition to her side lights, carry two bright white lights in a vertical line, one over the other, not less than three feet apart, and when towing one or more vessels astern, regardless of the length of the tow, shall carry an additional bright white light three feet above or below such lights. Each of these lights shall be of the same construction and character, and shall be carried in the same position as the white light mentioned in article 2 (a) or the after range light mentioned in article 2 (f).

(b) A steam vessel carrying towing lights the same as the white light men-

[1] 30 Stat. 96-103; 31 Stat. 30; 38 Stat. 381; 47 Stat. 415; 1417; 49 Stat. 669, 1367, 1380; 54 Stat. 150; 60 Stat. 1097; 61 Stat. 501; 62 Stat. 249; 63 Stat. 496, 561; 67 Stat. 497; 33 U.S.C. 154-159, 171-183, 191, 192, 201-222, 231, 232.

[2] By Reorganization Plan No. 26 of 1950, effective July 31, 1950 (15 F. R. 4935) the functions formerly vested in the Commandant, U. S. Coast Guard, were transferred to the Secretary of the Treasury with certain exceptions. The Secretary, however, by an order dated July 31, 1950 (15 F. R. 6521), delegated to the Commandant the functions formerly performed by him under Reorganization Plan No. 3 of 1946.

[3] For a definition of the word "vessel," see Rule 1 (c)(i), International Rules.

[4] Article 2 is amended by an act of Congress approved April 25, 1940, describing lights required to be carried by every vessel propelled by machinery and not more than 65 feet in length except tugboats and towboats propelled by steam. See p. 104.

tioned in article 2 (a), when pushing another vessel or vessels ahead, shall also carry at or near the stern two bright amber lights in a vertical line, one over the other, not less than three feet apart; each of these lights shall be so constructed as to show an unbroken light over an arc of the horizon of twelve points of the compass, so fixed as to show the light six points from right aft on each side of the vessel, and of such a character as to be visible at a distance of at least two miles. A steam vessel carrying towing lights the same as the white light mentioned in article 2 (a) may also carry, irrespective of the position of the tow, the after range light mentioned in article 2 (f); however, if the after range light is carried by such a vessel when pushing another vessel or vessels ahead, the amber lights shall be carried in a vertical line with and at least three feet lower than the after range light. A steam vessel carrying towing lights the same as the white light mentioned in article 2 (a), when towing one or more vessels astern, may also carry, in lieu of the stern light specified in article 10, a small white light abaft the funnel or aftermast for the tow to steer by, but such light shall not be visible forward of the beam.

LIGHTS FOR SAILING VESSELS AND VESSELS IN TOW

ART. 5. A sailing vessel under way and any vessel being towed, except barges, canal boats, scows, and other vessels of nondescript type, when in tow of steam vessels, shall carry the same lights as are prescribed by article 2 for a steam vessel under way, with the exception of the white lights mentioned therein, which they shall never carry.

LIGHTS FOR SMALL VESSELS IN BAD WEATHER

ART. 6. Whenever, as in the case of vessels of less than ten gross tons under way during bad weather, the green and red side lights cannot be fixed, these lights shall be kept at hand, lighted and ready for use; and shall, on the approach of or to other vessels, be exhibited on their respective sides in sufficient time to prevent collision, in such manner as to make them most visible, and so that the green light shall not be seen on the port side nor the red light on the starboard side, nor, if practicable, more than two points abaft the beam on their respective sides. To make the use of these portable lights more certain and easy the lanterns containing them shall each be painted outside with the color of the light they respectively contain, and shall be provided with proper screens.

LIGHTS FOR ROWING BOATS

ART. 7. Rowing boats, whether under oars or sail, shall have ready at hand a lantern showing a white light which shall be temporarily exhibited in sufficient time to prevent collision.

LIGHTS FOR PILOT VESSELS

ART. 8. Pilot vessels when engaged on their stations on pilotage duty shall not show the lights required for other vessels, but shall carry a white light at the masthead, visible all around the horizon, and shall also exhibit a flare-up light or flare-up lights at short intervals, which shall never exceed fifteen minutes.

On the near approach of or to other vessels they shall have their side lights lighted, ready for use, and shall flash or show them at short intervals, to indicate the direction in which they are heading, but the green light shall not be shown on the port side nor the red light on the starboard side.

A pilot vessel of such a class as to be obliged to go alongside of a vessel to put a pilot on board may show the white light instead of carrying it at the masthead, and may, instead of the colored lights above mentioned, have at hand, ready for use, a lantern with a green glass on the one side and a red glass on the other, to be used as prescribed above.

Pilot vessels, when not engaged on their station on pilotage duty, shall carry lights similar to those of other vessels of their tonnage.

A steam pilot vessel, when engaged on her station on pilotage duty and in waters of the United States, and not at anchor, shall in addition to the lights required for all pilot boats, carry at a distance of eight feet below her white masthead light a red light, visible all around the horizon and of such a character as to be visible on a dark night with a clear atmosphere at a distance of at least two miles, and also the colored side lights required to be carried by vessels when under way.

228

When engaged on her station on pilotage duty and in waters of the United States, and at anchor, she shall carry in addition to the lights required for all pilot boats the red light above mentioned, but not colored side lights. When not engaged on her station on pilotage duty, she shall carry the same lights as other steam vessels.

LIGHTS, ETC., OF FISHING VESSELS

ART. 9. (a) Fishing vessels of less than ten gross tons, when under way and when not having their nets, trawls, dredges, or lines in the water, shall not be obliged to carry the colored side lights; but every such vessel shall, in lieu thereof, have ready at hand a lantern with a green glass on one side and a red glass on the other side, and on approaching to or being approached by another vessel such lantern shall be exhibited in sufficient time to prevent collision, so that the green light shall not be seen on the port side nor the red light on the starboard side.

(b) All fishing vessels and fishing boats of ten gross tons or upward, when under way and when not having their nets, trawls, dredges, or lines in the water, shall carry and show the same lights as other vessels under way.

(c) All vessels, when trawling, dredging, or fishing with any kind of drag nets or lines, shall exhibit, from some part of the vessel where they can be best seen, two lights. One of these lights shall be red and the other shall be white. The red light shall be above the white light, and shall be at a vertical distance from it of not less than six feet and not more than twelve feet; and the horizontal distance between them, if any, shall not be more than ten feet. These two lights shall be of such a character and contained in lanterns of such construction as to be visible all around the horizon, the white light a distance of not less than three miles and the red light of not less than two miles.

LIGHTS FOR RAFTS OR OTHER CRAFT NOT PROVIDED FOR

(d) Rafts, or other water craft not herein provided for, navigating by hand power, horse power, or by the current of the river, shall carry one or more good white lights, which shall be placed in such manner as shall be prescribed by the Commandant of the Coast Guard.

LIGHTS FOR AN OVERTAKEN VESSEL

ART. 10. (a) A vessel when under way, if not otherwise required by these rules to carry one or more lights visible from aft, shall carry at her stern a white light, so constructed that it shall show an unbroken light over an arc of the horizon of twelve points of the compass, so fixed as to show the light six points from right aft on each side of the vessel, and of such a character as to be visible at a distance of at least two miles. Such light shall be carried as nearly as practicable on the same level as the side lights.

(b) In a small vessel, if it is not possible on account of bad weather or other sufficient cause for this light to be fixed, an electric torch or a lighted lantern shall be kept at hand ready for use and shall, on the approach of an overtaking vessel, be shown in sufficient time to prevent collision.

ANCHOR LIGHTS

ART. 11. A vessel under one hundred and fifty feet in length when at anchor shall carry forward, where it can best be seen, but at a height not exceeding twenty feet above the hull, a white light in a lantern so constructed as to show a clear, uniform, and unbroken light visible all around the horizon at a distance of at least one mile: Provided, That the Secretary of the Army may, after investigation, by rule, regulation, or order, designate such areas as he may deem proper as "special anchorage areas"; such special anchorage areas may from time to time be changed, or abolished, if after investigation the Secretary of the Army shall deem such change or abolition in the interest of navigation: Provided further, That vessels not more than sixty-five feet in length when at anchor in any such special anchorage area shall not be required to carry or exhibit the white light required by this article.

A vessel of one hundred and fifty feet or upward in length when at anchor, shall carry in the forward part of the vessel, at a height of not less than twenty and not exceeding forty feet above the hull, one such light, and at or near the stern of the vessel, and at such a height that it shall be not less than fifteen feet lower than the forward light, another such light.

The length of a vessel shall be deemed to be the length appearing in her certificate of registry.

SPECIAL SIGNALS

ART. 12. Every vessel may, if necessary, in order to attract attention, in addition to the lights which she is by these rules required to carry, show a flare-up light or use any detonating signal that cannot be mistaken for a distress signal.

NAVAL LIGHTS AND RECOGNITION SIGNALS

ART. 13. Nothing in these rules shall interfere with the operation of any special rules made by the Government of any nation with respect to additional station and signal lights for two or more ships of war or for vessels sailing under convoy, or with the exhibition of recognition signals adopted by shipowners, which have been authorized by their respective Governments, and duly registered and published.

STEAM VESSEL UNDER SAIL BY DAY

ART. 14. A steam vessel proceeding under sail only, but having her funnel up, may carry in daytime, forward, where it can best be seen, one black ball or shape two feet in diameter.

III. SOUND SIGNALS FOR FOG, AND SO FORTH

PRELIMINARY

ART. 15. All signals prescribed by this article for vessels under way shall be given:

1. By "steam vessels" on the whistle or siren.

2. By "sailing vessels" and "vessels towed" on the fog horn.

The words "prolonged blast" used in this article shall mean a blast of from four to six seconds' duration.

A steam vessel shall be provided with an efficient whistle or siren, sounded by steam or by some substitute for steam, so placed that the sound may not be intercepted by any obstruction, and with an efficient fog horn; also with an efficient bell. A sailing vessel of twenty tons gross tonnage or upward shall be provided with a similar fog horn and bell.

In fog, mist, falling snow, or heavy rain storms, whether by day or night, the signals described in this article shall be used as follows, namely:

STEAM VESSEL UNDER WAY

(a) A steam vessel under way shall sound, at intervals of not more than one minute, a prolonged blast.

SAIL VESSEL UNDER WAY

(c) A sailing vessel under way shall sound, at intervals of not more than one minute, when on the starboard tack, one blast; when on the port tack, two blasts in succession, and when with the wind abaft the beam, three blasts in succession.

VESSEL AT ANCHOR OR NOT UNDER WAY

(d) A vessel when at anchor shall, at intervals of not more than one minute, ring the bell rapidly for about five seconds.

VESSELS TOWING OR TOWED

(e) A steam vessel when towing, shall, instead of the signals prescribed in subdivision (a) of this article, at intervals of not more than one minute, sound three blasts in succession, namely, one prolonged blast followed by two short blasts. A vessel towed may give this signal and she shall not give any other.

RAFTS, OR OTHER CRAFT NOT PROVIDED FOR

(f) All rafts or other water craft, not herein provided for, navigating by hand power, horse power, or by the current of the river, shall sound a blast of the fog horn, or equivalent signal, at intervals of not more than one minute.

ART. 16. Every vessel shall, in a fog, mist, falling snow, or heavy rain storms, go at a moderate speed, having careful regard to the existing circumstances and conditions.

A steam vessel hearing, apparently forward of her beam, the fog signal of a vessel the position of which is not ascertained shall, so far as the circumstances of the case admit, stop her engines, and then navigate with caution until danger of collision is over.

IV. STEERING AND SAILING RULES

PRELIMINARY—RISK OF COLLISION

Risk of collision can, when circumstances permit, be ascertained by carefully watching the compass bearing of an approaching vessel. If the bearing does not appreciably change, such risk should be deemed to exist.

SAILING VESSELS

ART. 17. When two sailing vessels are approaching one another, so as to involve risk of collision, one of them shall keep out of the way of the other as follows, namely:

(a) A vessel which is running free shall keep out of the way of a vessel which is closehauled.

(b) A vessel which is closehauled on the port tack shall keep out of the way of a vessel which is closehauled on the starboard tack.

(c) When both are running free, with the wind on different sides, the vessel which has the wind on the port side shall keep out of the way of the other.

(d) When both are running free, with the wind on the same side, the vessel which is to the windward shall keep out of the way of the vessel which is to the leeward.

(e) A vessel which has the wind aft shall keep out of the way of the other vessel.

APPROACHING STEAM VESSELS

ART. 18. RULE I. When steam vessels are approaching each other head and head, that is, end on, or nearly so, it shall be the duty of each to pass on the port side of the other; and either vessel shall give, as a signal of her intention, one short and distinct blast of her whistle, which the other vessel shall answer promptly by a similar blast of her whistle, and thereupon such vessels shall pass on the port side of each other. But if the courses of such vessels are so far on the starboard of each other as not to be considered as meeting head and head, either vessel shall immediately give two short and distinct blasts of her whistle, which the other vessel shall answer promptly by two similar blasts of her whistle, and they shall pass on the starboard side of each other.

The foregoing only applies to cases where vessels are meeting end on, or nearly end on, in such a manner as to involve risk of collision; in other words, to cases in which, by day, each vessel sees the masts of the other in a line, or nearly in a line, with her own, and by night to cases in which each vessel is in such a position as to see both the side lights of the other.

It does not apply by day to cases in which a vessel sees another ahead crossing her own course, or by night to cases where the red light of one vessel is opposed to the red light of the other, or where the green light of one vessel is opposed to the green light of the other, or where a red light without a green light or a green light without a red light, is seen ahead, or where both green and red lights are seen anywhere but ahead.

RULE III. If, when steam vessels are approaching each other, either vessel fails to understand the course or intention of the other, from any cause, the vessel so in doubt shall immediately signify the same by giving several short and rapid blasts, not less than four, of the steam whistle.

RULE V. Whenever a steam vessel is nearing a short bend or curve in the channel, where, from the height of the banks or other cause, a steam vessel approaching from the opposite direction can not be seen for a distance of half a mile, such steam vessel, when she shall have arrived within a half a mile of such curve or bend, shall give a signal by one long blast of the steam whistle, which signal shall be answered by a similar blast given by any approaching steam vessel that may be within hearing. Should such signal be so answered by a steam vessel upon the farther side of such bend, then the usual signals for meeting and passing shall immediately be given and answered; but, if the first alarm signal of such vessel be not answered, she is to consider the channel clear and govern herself accordingly.

When steam vessels are moved from their docks or berths, and other boats are liable to pass from any direction toward them, they shall give the same signal as in the case of vessels meeting at a bend, but immediately after clearing the berths so as to be fully in sight they shall be governed by the steering and sailing rules.

RULE VIII. When steam vessels are running in the same direction, and the vessel which is astern shall desire to pass on the right or starboard hand of the vessel ahead, she shall give one short blast of the steam whistle, as a signal of such desire, and if the vessel ahead answers with one blast, she shall direct her course to starboard; or if she shall desire to pass on the left or port side of the vessel ahead, she shall give two short blasts of the steam whistle as a signal of such desire, and if the vessel ahead answers with two blasts, shall direct her course to port; or if the vessel ahead does not think it safe for the vessel astern to attempt to pass at that point, she shall immediately signify the same by giving several short and rapid blasts of the steam whistle, not less than four, and under no circumstances shall the vessel astern attempt to pass the vessel ahead until such time as they have reached a point where it can be safely done, when said vessel ahead shall signify her willingness by blowing the proper signals. The vessel ahead shall in no case attempt to cross the bow or crowd upon the course of the passing vessel.

RULE IX. The whistle signals provided in the rules under this article, for steam vessels meeting, passing, or overtaking, are never to be used except when steamers are in sight of each other, and the course and position of each can be determined in the day time by a sight of the vessel itself, or by night by seeing its signal lights. In fog, mist, falling snow or heavy rain storms when vessels can not see each other, fog signals only must be given.

TWO STEAM VESSELS CROSSING

ART. 19. When two steam vessels are crossing, so as to involve risk of collision, the vessel which has the other on her own starboard side shall keep out of the way of the other.

STEAM VESSEL SHALL KEEP OUT OF THE WAY OF SAILING VESSEL

ART. 20. When a steam vessel and a sailing vessel are proceeding in such directions as to involve risk of collision, the steam vessel shall keep out of the way of the sailing vessel. This rule shall not give to a sailing vessel the right to hamper, in a narrow channel, the safe passage of a steam vessel which can navigate only inside that channel.

COURSE AND SPEED

ART. 21. Where, by any of these rules, one of the two vessels is to keep out of the way, the other shall keep her course and speed.
[See articles 27 and 29.]

CROSSING AHEAD

ART. 22. Every vessel which is directed by these rules to keep out of the way of another vessel shall, if the circumstances of the case admit, avoid crossing ahead of the other.

STEAM VESSEL SHALL SLACKEN SPEED OR STOP

ART. 23. Every steam vessel which is directed by these rules to keep out of the way of another vessel shall, on approaching her, if necessary, slacken her speed, or stop, or reverse.

OVERTAKING VESSELS

ART. 24. Notwithstanding anything contained in these rules every vessel, overtaking any other, shall keep out of the way of the overtaken vessel.

Every vessel coming up with another vessel from any direction more than two points abaft her beam, that is, in such a position, with reference to the vessel which she is overtaking that at night she would be unable to see either of that vessel's sidelights, shall be deemed to be an overtaking vessel; and no subsequent alteration of the bearing between the two vessels shall make the overtaking vessel a crossing vessel within the meaning of these rules, or relieve her of the duty of keeping clear of the overtaken vessel until she is finally past and clear.

As by day the overtaking vessel can not always know with certainty whether she is forward of or abaft this direction from the other vessels she should, if in doubt, assume that she is an overtaking vessel and keep out of the way.

NARROW CHANNELS

ART. 25. In narrow channels every steam vessel shall, when it is safe and practicable, keep to that side of the fairway or midchannel which lies on the starboard side of such vessel. In narrow channels a steam vessel of less than sixty-five feet in length shall not hamper the safe passage of a vessel which can navigate only inside that channel.

RIGHT OF WAY OF FISHING VESSELS

ART. 26. Sailing vessels under way shall keep out of the way of sailing vessels or boats fishing with nets, lines, or trawls. This rule shall not give to any vessel or boat engaged in fishing the right of obstructing a fairway used by vessels other than fishing vessels or boats.

GENERAL PRUDENTIAL RULE

ART. 27. In obeying and construing these rules due regard shall be had to all dangers of navigation and collision, and to any special circumstances which may render a departure from the above rules necessary in order to avoid immediate danger.

SOUND SIGNALS FOR PASSING STEAMERS

[See article 18.]

ART. 28. When vessels are in sight of one another a steam vessel under way whose engines are going at full speed astern shall indicate that fact by three short blasts on the whistle.

PRECAUTION

ART. 29. Nothing in these rules shall exonerate any vessel, or the owner or master or crew thereof, from the consequences of any neglect to carry lights or signals, or of any neglect to keep a proper lookout, or of the neglect of any precaution which may be required by the ordinary practice of seamen, or by the special circumstances of the case.

SUSPENSION OF LIGHTS ON NAVAL AND COAST GUARD VESSELS

ART. 30. The exhibition of any light on board of a vessel of war of the United States or a Coast Guard cutter may be suspended whenever, in the opinion of the Secretary of the Navy, the commander in chief of a squadron, or the commander of a vessel acting singly, the special character of the service may require it.

DISTRESS SIGNALS

ART. 31. When a vessel is in distress and requires assistance from other vessels or from the shore the following shall be the signal to be used or displayed by her, either together or separately, namely:

In the daytime—
A continuous sounding with any fog-signal apparatus, or firing a gun.
At night—
First. Flames on the vessel as from a burning tar barrel, oil barrel, and so forth.
Second. A continuous sounding with any fog-signal apparatus, or firing a gun.

ORDERS TO HELMSMEN

ART. 32. All orders to helmsmen shall be given as follows:
"Right Rudder" to mean "Direct the vessel's head to starboard."
"Left Rudder" to mean "Direct the vessel's head to port."

PART A. PRELIMINARY AND DEFINITIONS

RULE 1

(a) These Rules shall be followed by all vessels and seaplanes upon the high seas and in all waters connected therewith navigable by seagoing vessels, except as provided in Rule 30. Where, as a result of their special construction, it is not possible for seaplanes to comply fully with the provisions of Rules specifying the carrying of lights and shapes, these provisions shall be followed as closely as circumstances permit.

(b) The Rules concerning lights shall be complied with in all weathers from sunset to sunrise, and during such times no other lights shall be exhibited, except such lights as cannot be mistaken for the prescribed lights or do not impair their visibility or distinctive character, or interfere with the keeping of a proper lookout. The lights prescribed by these Rules may also be exhibited from sunrise to sunset in restricted visibility and in all other circumstances when it is deemed necessary.

(c) In the following Rules, except where the context otherwise requires:

(i) the word "vessel" includes every description of water craft, other than a seaplane on the water, used or capable of being used as a means of transportation on water;

(ii) the word "seaplane" includes a flying boat and other aircraft designed to manoeuvre on the water;

(iii) the term "power-driven vessel" means any vessel propelled by machinery;

(iv) every power-driven vessel which is under sail and not under power is to be considered a sailing vessel, and every vessel under power, whether under sail or not, is to be considered a power-driven vessel;

(v) a vessel or seaplane on the water is "under way" when she is not at anchor, or made fast to the shore, or aground;

(vi) the term "height above the hull" means height above the uppermost continuous deck;

(vii) the length and breadth of a vessel shall be her length overall and largest breadth;

(viii) the length and span of a seaplane shall be its maximum length and span as shown in its certificate of airworthiness, or as determined by measurement in the absence of such certificate;

(ix) vessels shall be deemed to be in sight of one another only when one can be observed visually from the other;

(x) the word "visible," when applied to lights, means visible on a dark night with a clear atmosphere;

(xi) the term "short blast" means a blast of about one second's duration;

(xii) the term "prolonged blast" means a blast of from four to six seconds' duration;

(xiii) the word "whistle" means any appliance capable of producing the pre-scribed short and prolonged blasts;

(xiv) the term "engaged in fishing" means fishing with nets, lines or trawls but does not include fishing with trolling lines.

PART B. LIGHTS AND SHAPES

RULE 2

(a) A power-driven vessel when under way shall carry:

(i) On or in front of the foremast, or if a vessel without a foremast then in the forepart of the vessel, a white light so constructed as to show an unbroken light over an arc of the horizon of 225 degrees (20 points of the compass), so fixed as to show the light 112½ degrees (10 points) on each side of the vessel, that is, from right ahead to 22½ degrees (2 points) abaft the beam on either side, and of such a character as to be visible at a distance of at least 5 miles.

(ii) Either forward or abaft the white light prescribed in sub-section (i) a second white light similar in construction and character to that light. Vessels

234

of less than 150 feet in length shall not be required to carry this second white light but may do so.

(iii) These two white lights shall be so placed in a line with and over the keel that one shall be at least 15 feet higher than the other and in such a position that the forward light shall always be shown lower than the after one. The horizontal distance between the two white lights shall be at least three times the vertical distance. The lower of these two white lights or, if only one is carried, then that light, shall be placed at a height above the hull of not less than 20 feet, and, if the breadth of the vessel exceeds 20 feet, then at a height above the hull not less than such breadth, so however that the light need not be placed at a greater height above the hull then 40 feet. In all circumstances the light or lights, as the case may be, shall be so placed as to be clear of and above all other lights and obstructing superstructures.

(iv) On the starboard side a green light so constructed as to show an unbroken light over an arc of the horizon of 112½ degrees (10 points of the compass), so fixed as to show the light from right ahead to 22½ degrees (2 points abaft the beam on the starboard side, and of such a character as to be visible at a distance of at least 2 miles.

(v) On the port side a red light so constructed as to show an unbroken light over an arc of the horizon of 112½ degrees (10 points of the compass), so fixed as to show the light from right ahead to 22½ degrees (2 points) abaft the beam on the port side, and of such a character as to be visible at a distance of at least 2 miles.

(vi) The said green and red sidelights shall be fitted with inboard screens projecting at least 3 feet forward from the light, so as to prevent these lights from being seen across the bows.

(b) A seaplane under way on the water shall carry:

(i) In the forepart amidships where it can best be seen a white light, so constructed as to show an unbroken light over an arc of the horizon of 220 degrees of the compass, so fixed as to show the light 110 degrees on each side of the seaplane, namely, from right ahead to 20 degrees abaft the beam on either side, and of such a character as to be visible at a distance of at least 3 miles.

(ii) On the right or starboard wing tip a green light, so constructed as to show an unbroken light over an arc of the horizon of 110 degrees of the compass, so fixed as to show the light from right ahead to 20 degrees abaft the beam on the starboard side, and of such a character as to be visible at a distance of at least 2 miles.

(iii) On the left or port wing tip a red light, so constructed as to show an unbroken light over an arc of the horizon of 110 degrees of the compass, so fixed as to show the light from right ahead to 20 degrees abaft the beam on the port side, and of such a character as to be visible at a distance of at least 2 miles.

RULE 3

(a) A power-driven vessel when towing or pushing another vessel or seaplane shall, in addition to her sidelights, carry two white lights in a vertical line one over the other, not less than 6 feet apart, and when towing and the length of the tow, measuring from the stern of the towing vessel to the stern of the last vessel towed, exceeds 600 feet, shall carry three white lights in a vertical line one over the other, so that the upper and lower lights shall be the same distance from, and not less than 6 feet above or below, the middle light. Each of these lights shall be of the same construction and character and one of them shall be carried in the same position as the white light prescribed in Rule 2(a) (i). None of these lights shall be carried at a height of less than 14 feet above the hull. In a vessel with a single mast, such lights may be carried on the mast.

(b) The towing vessel shall also show either the stern light prescribed in Rule 10 or in lieu of that light a small white light abaft the funnel or aftermast for the tow to steer by, but such light shall not be visible forward of the beam.

(c) Between sunrise and sunset a power-driven vessel engaged in towing, if the length of tow exceeds 600 feet, shall carry, where it can best be seen, a black diamond shape at least 2 feet in diameter.

(d) A seaplane on the water, when towing one or more seaplanes or vessels, shall carry the lights prescribed in Rule 2(b)(i), (ii), and (iii); and, in addition, she shall carry a second white light of the same construction and character as the white light prescribed in Rule 2(b)(i), and in a vertical line at least 6 feet above or below such light.

(a) A vessel which is not under command shall carry, where they can best be seen, and, if a power-driven vessel in lieu of the lights prescribed in Rule 2(a) (i) and (ii), two red lights in a vertical line one over the other not less than 6 feet apart; and of such a character as to be visible all around the horizon at a distance of at least 2 miles. By day, she shall carry in a vertical line one over the other not less than 6 feet apart, where they can best be seen, two black balls or shapes each not less than 2 feet in diameter.

(b) A seaplane on the water which is not under command may carry, where they can best be seen, and in lieu of the light prescribed in Rule 2(b)(i), two red lights in a vertical line, one over the other, not less than 3 feet apart, and of such a character as to be visible all round the horizon at a distance of at least 2 miles, and may by day carry in a vertical line one over the other not less than 3 feet apart, where they can best be seen, two black balls or shapes, each not less than 2 feet in diameter.

(c) A vessel engaged in laying or in picking up a submarine cable or navigation mark, or a vessel engaged in surveying or underwater operations, or a vessel engaged in replenishment at sea, or in the launching or recovery of aircraft when from the nature of her work she is unable to get out of the way of approaching vessels, shall carry, in lieu of the lights prescribed in Rule 2(a)(i) and (ii), or Rule 7(a)(i), three lights in a vertical line one over the other so that the upper and lower lights shall be the same distance from, and not less than 6 feet above or below, the middle light. The highest and lowest of these lights shall be red, and the middle light shall be white, and they shall be of such a character as to be visible all round the horizon at a distance of at least 2 miles. By day, she shall carry in a vertical line one over the other not less than 6 feet apart, where they can best be seen, three shapes each not less than 2 feet in diameter, of which the highest and lowest shall be globular in shape and red in colour, and the middle one diamond shape and white.

(d)(i) A vessel engaged in minesweeping operations shall carry at the fore truck a green light, and at the end or ends of the fore yard on the side or sides on which danger exists, another such light or lights. These lights shall be carried in addition to the light prescribed in Rule 2(a)(i) or Rule 7(a)(i) as appropriate, and shall be of such a character as to be visible all round the horizon at a distance of at least 2 miles. By day she shall carry black balls, not less than 2 feet in diameter, in the same position as the green lights.

(ii) The showing of these lights or balls indicates that it is dangerous for other vessels to approach closer than 3000 feet astern of the minesweeper or 1500 feet on the side or sides on which danger exists.

(e) The vessels and seaplanes referred to in this Rule, when not making way through the water, shall show neither the coloured side lights nor the stern lights, but when making way they shall show them.

(f) The lights and shapes prescribed in this Rule are to be taken by other vessels and seaplanes as signals that the vessel or seaplane showing them is not under command and cannot therefore get out of the way.

(g) These signals are not signals of vessels in distress and requiring assistance. Such signals are contained in Rule 31.

RULE 5

(a) A sailing vessel under way and any vessel or seaplane being towed shall carry the same lights as are prescribed in Rule 2 for a power-driven vessel or a seaplane under way, respectively, with the exception of the white lights prescribed therein, which they shall never carry. They shall also carry stern lights as prescribed in Rule 10, provided that vessels towed, except the last vessel of a tow, may carry, in lieu of such stern light, a small white light as prescribed in Rule 3(b).

(b) In addition to the lights prescribed in section (a), a sailing vessel may carry on the top of the foremast two lights in a vertical line one over the other, sufficiently separated so as to be clearly distinguished. The upper light shall be red and the lower light shall be green. Both lights shall be constructed and fixed as prescribed in Rule 2(a)(i) and shall be visible at a distance of at least 2 miles.

(c) A vessel being pushed ahead shall carry, at the forward end, on the starboard side a green light and on the port side a red light, which shall have the same characteristics as the lights prescribed in Rule 2(a)(iv) and (v) and shall be screened as provided in Rule 2(a)(vi), provided that any number of vessels pushed ahead in a group shall be lighted as one vessel.

(d) Between sunrise and sunset a vessel being towed, if the length of the tow exceeds 600 feet, shall carry where it can best be seen a black diamond shape at least 2 feet in diameter.

Rule 6

(a) When it is not possible on account of bad weather or other sufficient cause to fix the green and red sidelights, these lights shall be kept at hand lighted and ready for immediate use, and shall, on the approach of or to other vessels, be exhibited on their respective sides in sufficient time to prevent collision, in such manner as to make them most visible, and so that the green light shall not be seen on the port side nor the red light on the starboard side, nor, if practicable, more than 22½ degrees (2 points) abaft the beam on their respective sides.

(b) To make the use of these portable lights more certain and easy, the lanterns containing them shall each be painted outside with the colour of the lights they respectively contain, and shall be provided with proper screens.

Rule 7

Power-driven vessels of less than 65 feet in length, vessels under oars or sails of less than 40 feet in length, and rowing boats, when under way shall not be required to carry the lights prescribed in Rules 2, 3 and 5, but if they do not carry them they shall be provided with the following lights:

(a) Power-driven vessels of less than 65 feet in length, except as provided in sections (b) and (c), shall carry:

(i) In the forepart of the vessel, where it can best be seen, and at a height above the gunwale of not less than 9 feet, a white light constructed and fixed as prescribed in Rule 2(a)(i) and of such a character as to be visible at a distance of at least 3 miles.

(ii) Green and red sidelights constructed and fixed as prescribed in Rule 2(a) (iv) and (v), and of such a character as to be visible at a distance of at least 1 mile, or a combined lantern showing a green light and a red light from right ahead to 22½ degrees (2 points) abaft the beam on their respective sides. Such lantern shall be carried not less than 3 feet below the white light.

(b) Power-driven vessels of less than 65 feet in length when towing or pushing another vessel shall carry:

(i) In addition to the side lights or the combined lantern prescribed in section (a)(ii) two white lights in a vertical line, one over the other not less than 4 feet apart. Each of these lights shall be of the same construction and character as the white light prescribed in section (a)(i) and one of them shall be carried in the same position. In a vessel with a single mast such lights may be carried on the mast.

(ii) Either a stern light as prescribed in Rule 10 or in lieu of that light a small white light abaft the funnel or aftermast for the tow to steer by, but such light shall not be visible forward of the beam.

(c) Power-driven vessels of less than 40 feet in length may carry the white light at a less height than 9 feet above the gunwale but it shall be carried not less than 3 feet above the sidelights or the combined lantern prescribed in section (a)(ii).

(d) Vessels of less than 40 feet in length, under oars or sails, except as provided in section (f), shall, if they do not carry the sidelights, carry, where it can best be seen, a lantern showing a green light on one side and a red light on the other, of such a character as to be visible at a distance of at least 1 mile, and so fixed that the green light shall not be seen on the port side, nor the red light on the starboard side. Where it is not possible to fix this light, it shall be kept ready for immediate use and shall be exhibited in sufficient time to prevent collision and so that the green light shall not be seen on the port side nor the red light on the starboard side.

(e) The vessels referred to in this Rule when being towed shall carry the sidelights or the combined lantern prescribed in sections (a) or (d) of this Rule, as appropriate, and a stern light as prescribed in Rule 10, or, except the last vessel of the tow, a small white light as prescribed in section (b)(ii). When being pushed ahead they shall carry at the forward end the sidelights or combined lantern prescribed in sections (a) or (d) of this Rule, as appropriate, provided that any number of vessels referred to in this Rule when pushed ahead in a group shall be lighted as one vessel under this Rule unless the overall length of the group exceeds 65 feet when the provisions of Rule 5(c) shall apply.

(f) Small rowing boats, whether under oars or sail, shall only be required to have ready at hand an electric torch or a lighted lantern, showing a white light, which shall be exhibited in sufficient time to prevent collision.

(g) The vessels and boats referred to in this Rule shall not be required to carry the lights or shapes prescribed in Rules 4(a) and 11(e) and the size of their day signal may be less than is prescribed in Rules 4(c) and 11(c).

RULE 8

(a) A power-driven pilot-vessel when engaged on pilotage duty and under way:

(i) Shall carry a white light at the masthead at a height of not less than 20 feet above the hull, visible all round the horizon at a distance of at least 3 miles and at a distance of 8 feet below it a red light similar in construction and character. If such a vessel is of less than 65 feet in length she may carry the white light at a height of not less than 9 feet above the gunwale and the red light at a distance of 4 feet below the white light.

(ii) Shall carry the sidelights or lanterns prescribed in Rule 2(a)(iv) and (v) or Rule 7(a)(ii) or (d), as appropriate, and the stern light prescribed in Rule 10.

(iii) Shall show one or more flare-up lights at intervals not exceeding 10 minutes. An intermittent white light visible all round the horizon may be used in lieu of flare-up lights.

(b) A sailing pilot-vessel when engaged on pilotage duty and underway:

(i) Shall carry a white light at the masthead visible all round the horizon at a distance of at least 3 miles.

(ii) Shall be provided with the sidelights or lantern prescribed in Rules 5(a) or 7(d), as appropriate, and shall, on the near approach of or to other vessels, have such lights ready for use, and shall show them at short intervals to indicate the direction in which she is heading, but the green light shall not be shown on the port side nor the red light on the starboard side. She shall also carry the stern light prescribed in Rule 10.

(iii) Shall show one or more flare-up lights at intervals not exceeding 10 minutes.

(c) A pilot-vessel when engaged on pilotage duty and not under way shall carry the lights and show the flares prescribed in sections (a)(i) and (iii) or (b) (i) and (iii), as appropriate, and if at anchor shall also carry the anchor lights prescribed in Rule 11.

(d) A pilot-vessel when not engaged on pilotage duty shall show the lights or shapes for a similar vessel of her length.

RULE 9

(a) Fishing vessels when not engaged in fishing shall show the lights or shapes for similar vessels of their length.

(b) Vessels engaged in fishing, when under way or at anchor, shall show only the lights and shapes prescribed in this Rule, which lights and shapes shall be visible at a distance of at least 2 miles.

(c) (i) Vessels when engaged in trawling, by which is meant the dragging of a dredge net or other apparatus through the water, shall carry two lights in a vertical line, one over the other, not less than 4 feet nor more than 12 feet apart. The upper of these lights shall be green and the lower light white and each shall be visible all round the horizon. The lower of these two lights shall be carried at a height above the side lights not less than twice the distance between the two vertical lights.

(ii) Such vessels may in addition carry a white light similar in construction to the white light prescribed in Rule 2(a)(i) but such light shall be carried lower than and abaft the all-round green and white lights.

(d) Vessels when engaged in fishing, except vessels engaged in trawling, shall carry the lights prescribed in section (c)(i) except that the upper of the two vertical lights shall be red. Such vessels if of less than 40 feet in length may carry the red light at a height of not less than 9 feet above the gunwale and the white light not less than 3 feet below the red light.

(e) Vessels referred to in sections (c) and (d), when making way through the water, shall carry the sidelights or lanterns prescribed in Rule 2(a)(iv) and (v) or Rule 7(a)(ii) or (d), as appropriate, and the stern light prescribed in Rule 10. When not making way through the water they shall show neither the sidelights nor the stern light.

(f) Vessels referred to in section (d) with outlying gear extending more than 500 feet horizontally into the seaway shall carry an additional all-round white light at a horizontal distance of not less than 6 feet nor more than 20 feet away from the vertical lights in the direction of the outlying gear. This additional white light shall be placed at a height not exceeding that of the white light prescribed in section (c)(i) and not lower than the sidelights.

(g) In addition to the lights which they are required by this Rule to carry, vessels engaged in fishing may, if necessary in order to attract the attention of an approaching vessel, use a flare-up light, or may direct the beam of their searchlight in the direction of a danger threatening the approaching vessel, in such a way as not to embarrass other vessels. They may also use working lights but fishermen shall take into account that specially bright or insufficiently screened working lights may impair the visibility and distinctive character of the lights prescribed in this Rule.

(h) By day vessels when engaged in fishing shall indicate their occupation by displaying where it can best be seen a black shape consisting of two cones each not less than 2 feet in diameter with their points together one above the other. Such vessels if of less than 65 feet in length may substitute a basket for such black shape. If their outlying gear extends more than 500 feet horizontally into the seaway vessels engaged in fishing shall display in addition one black conical shape, point upwards, in the direction of the outlying gear.

Note.—Vessels fishing with trolling lines are not "engaged in fishing" as defined in Rule 1(c)(xiv).

RULE 10

(a) Except where otherwise provided in these Rules, a vessel when under way shall carry at her stern a white light, so constructed that it shall show an unbroken light over an arc of the horizon of 135 degrees (12 points of the compass), so fixed as to show the light 67½ degrees (6 points) from right aft on each side of the vessel, and of such a character as to be visible at a distance of at least 2 miles.

(b) In a small vessel, if it is not possible on account of bad weather or other sufficient cause for this light to be fixed, an electric torch or a lighted lantern showing a white light shall be kept at hand ready for use and shall, on the approach of an overtaking vessel, be shown in sufficient time to prevent collision.

(c) A seaplane on the water when under way shall carry on her tail a white light, so constructed as to show an unbroken light over an arc of the horizon of 140 degrees of the compass, so fixed as to show the light 70 degrees from right aft on each side of the seaplane, and of such a character as to be visible at a distance of at least 2 miles.

RULE 11

(a) A vessel of less than 150 feet in length, when at anchor, shall carry in the forepart of the vessel, where it can best be seen, a white light visible all round the horizon at a distance of at least 2 miles. Such a vessel may also carry a second white light in the position prescribed in section (b) of this Rule but shall not be required to do so. The second white light, if carried, shall be visible at a distance of at least 2 miles and so placed as to be as far as possible visible all round the horizon.

(b) A vessel of 150 feet or more in length, when at anchor, shall carry near the stem of the vessel, at a height of not less than 20 feet above the hull, one such light, and at or near the stern of the vessel and at such a height that it shall be not less than 15 feet lower than the forward light, another such light. Both these lights shall be visible at a distance of at least 3 miles and so placed as to be as far as possible visible all round the horizon.

(c) Between sunrise and sunset every vessel when at anchor shall carry in the forepart of the vessel, where it can best be seen, one black ball not less than 2 feet in diameter.

(d) A vessel engaged in laying or in picking up a submarine cable or navigation mark, or a vessel engaged in surveying or underwater operations, when at anchor, shall carry the lights or shapes prescribed in Rule 4(c) in addition to those prescribed in the appropriate preceding sections of this Rule.

(e) A vessel aground shall carry the light or lights prescribed in sections (a) or (b) and the two red lights prescribed in Rule 4(a). By day she shall carry, where they can best be seen, three black balls, each not less than 2 feet in diameter, placed in a vertical line one over the other, not less than 6 feet apart.

(f) A seaplane on the water under 150 feet in length, when at anchor, shall carry, where it can best be seen, a white light, visible all round the horizon at a distance of at least 2 miles.

(g) A seaplane on the water 150 feet or upwards in length, when at anchor, shall carry, where they can best be seen, a white light forward and a white light aft, both lights visible all round the horizon at a distance of at least 3 miles; and, in addition, if the seaplane is more than 150 feet in span, a white light on each side to indicate the maximum span, and visible, so far as practicable, all round the horizon at a distance of 1 mile.

(h) A seaplane aground shall carry an anchor light or lights as prescribed in sections (f) and (g), and in addition may carry two red lights in a vertical line, at least 3 feet apart, so placed as to be visible all round the horizon.

RULE 12

Every vessel or seaplane on the water may, if necessary in order to attract attention, in addition to the lights which she is by these Rules required to carry, show a flare-up light or use a detonating or other efficient sound signal that cannot be mistaken for any signal, authorized elsewhere under these Rules.

RULE 13

(a) Nothing in these Rules shall interfere with the operation of any special rules made by the Government of any nation with respect to additional station and signal lights for ships of war, for vessels sailing under convoy, for fishing vessels engaged in fishing as a fleet or for seaplanes on the water.

(b) Whenever the Government concerned shall have determined that a naval or other military vessel or waterborne seaplane of special construction or purpose cannot comply fully with the provisions of any of these Rules with respect to the number, position, range or arc of visibility of lights or shapes, without interfering with the military function of the vessel or seaplane, such vessel or seaplane shall comply with such other provisions in regard to the number, position, range or arc of visibility of lights or shapes as her Government shall have determined to be the closest possible compliance with these Rules in respect of that vessel or seaplane.

RULE 14

A vessel proceeding under sail, when also being propelled by machinery, shall carry in the daytime forward, where it can best be seen, one black conical shape, point downwards, not less than 2 feet in diameter at its base.

PART C. SOUND SIGNALS AND CONDUCT IN RESTRICTED VISIBILITY

(Preliminary)

1. The possession of information obtained from radar does not relieve any vessel of the obligation of conforming strictly with the Rules and, in particular, the obligations contained in Rules 15 and 16.

2. The Annex to the Rules contains recommendations intended to assist in the use of radar as an aid to avoiding collision in restricted visibility.

RULE 15

(a) A power-driven vessel of 40 feet or more in length shall be provided with an efficient whistle, sounded by steam or by some substitute for steam, so placed that the sound may not be intercepted by any obstruction, and with an efficient fog horn to be sounded by mechanical means, and also with an efficient bell. A sailing vessel of 40 feet or more in length shall be provided with a similar fog horn and bell.

240

(b) All signals prescribed in this Rule for vessels under way shall be given:

(i) by power-driven vessels on the whistle;

(ii) by sailing vessels on the fog-horn;

(iii) by vessels towed on the whistle or fog-horn.

(c) In fog, mist, falling snow, heavy rainstorms, or any other condition similarly restricting visibility, whether by day or night, the signals prescribed in this Rule shall be used as follows:

(i) A power-driven vessel making way through the water, shall sound at intervals of not more than 2 minutes a prolonged blast.

(ii) A power-driven vessel under way, but stopped and making no way through the water, shall sound at intervals of not more than 2 minutes two prolonged blasts, with an interval of about 1 second between them.

(iii) A sailing vessel under way shall sound, at intervals of not more than 1 minute, when on the starboard tack one blast, when on the port tack two blasts in succession, and when with the wind abaft the beam three blasts in succession.

(iv) A vessel when at anchor shall at intervals of not more than 1 minute ring the bell rapidly for about 5 seconds. In vessels of more than 350 feet in length the bell shall be sounded in the forepart of the vessel, and in addition there shall be sounded in the after part of the vessel, at intervals of not more than 1 minute for about 5 seconds, a gong or other instrument, the tone and sounding of which cannot be confused with that of the bell. Every vessel at anchor may in addition, in accordance with Rule 12, sound three blasts in succession, namely, one short, one prolonged, and one short blast, to give warning of her position and of the possibility of collision to an approaching vessel.

(v) A vessel when towing, a vessel engaged in laying or in picking up a submarine cable or navigation mark and a vessel under way which is unable to get out of the way of an approaching vessel through being not under command or unable to manoeuvre as required by these Rules shall, instead of the signals prescribed in subsections (i), (ii) and (iii) sound, at intervals of not more than 1 minute, three blasts in succession, namely, one prolonged blast followed by two short blasts.

(vi) A vessel towed, or, if more than one vessel is towed, only the last vessel of the tow, if manned, shall, at intervals of not more than 1 minute, sound four blasts in succession, namely, one prolonged blast followed by three short blasts. When practicable, this signal shall be made immediately after the signal made by the towing vessel.

(vii) A vessel aground shall give the bell signal and, if required, the gong signal, prescribed in subsection (iv) and shall, in addition, give 3 separate and distinct strokes on the bell immediately before and after such rapid ringing of the bell.

(viii) A vessel engaged in fishing when under way or at anchor shall at intervals of not more than 1 minute sound the signal prescribed in sub-section (v). A vessel when fishing with trolling lines and under way shall sound the signals prescribed in sub-sections (i), (ii) or (iii) as may be appropriate.

(ix) A vessel of less than 40 feet in length, a rowing boat, or a seaplane on the water, shall not be obliged to give the above-mentioned signals but if she does not, she shall make some other efficient sound signal at intervals of not more than 1 minute.

(x) A power-driven pilot-vessel when engaged on pilotage duty may, in addition to the signals prescribed in sub-sections (i), (ii) and (iv), sound an identity signal consisting of 4 short blasts.

(a) Every vessel, or seaplane when taxi-ing on the water, shall, in fog, mist, falling snow, heavy rainstorms or any other condition similarly restricting visibility, go at a moderate speed, having careful regard to the existing circumstances and conditions.

(b) A power-driven vessel hearing, apparently forward of her beam, the fog-signal of a vessel the position of which is not ascertained, shall, so far as the circumstances of the case admit, stop her engines, and then navigate with caution until danger of collision is over.

(c) A power-driven vessel which detects the presence of another vessel forward of her beam before hearing her fog signal or sighting her visually may take early and substantial action to avoid a close quarters situation but, if this cannot be avoided, she shall, so far as the circumstances of the case admit, stop her engines in proper time to avoid collision and then navigate with caution until danger of collision is over.

241

PART D. STEERING AND SAILING RULES

(Preliminary)

1. In obeying and construing these Rules, any action taken should be positive, in ample time, and with due regard to the observance of good seamanship.

2. Risk of collision can, when circumstances permit, be ascertained by carefully watching the compass bearing of an approaching vessel. If the bearing does not appreciably change, such risk should be deemed to exist.

3. Mariners should bear in mind that seaplanes in the act of landing or taking off, or operating under adverse weather conditions, may be unable to change their intended action at the last moment.

4. Rules 17 to 24 apply only to vessels in sight of one another.

RULE 17

(a) When two sailing vessels are approaching one another, so as to involve risk of collision, one of them shall keep out of the way of the other as follows:

(i) When each has the wind on a different side, the vessel which has the wind on the port side shall keep out of the way of the other.

(ii) When both have the wind on the same side, the vessel which is to windward shall keep out of the way of the vessel which is to leeward.

(b) For the purposes of this Rule the windward side shall be deemed to be the side opposite to that on which the mainsail is carried or, in the case of a square-rigged vessel, the side opposite to that on which the largest fore-and-aft sail is carried.

RULE 18

(a) When two power-driven vessels are meeting end on, or nearly end on, so as to involve risk of collision, each shall alter her course to starboard, so that each may pass on the port side of the other. This Rule only applies to cases where vessels are meeting end on, or nearly end on, in such a manner as to involve risk of collision, and does not apply to two vessels which must, if both keep on their respective courses, pass clear of each other. The only cases to which it does apply are when each of two vessels is end on, or nearly end on, to the other, in other words, to cases in which, by day, each vessel sees the masts of the other in a line, or nearly in a line, with her own, and by night, to cases in which each vessel is in such a position as to see both the sidelights of the other. It does not apply, by day, to cases in which a vessel sees another ahead crossing her own course; or, by night, to cases where the red light of one vessel is opposed to the red light of the other or where the green light of one vessel is opposed to the green light of the other or where a red light without a green light or a green light without a red light is seen ahead, or where both green and red lights are seen anywhere but ahead.

(b) For the purposes of this Rule and Rules 19 to 29 inclusive, except Rule 20(c) and Rule 28, a seaplane on the water shall be deemed to be a vessel, and the expression "power-driven vessel" shall be construed accordingly.

RULE 19

When two power-driven vessels are crossing, so as to involve risk of collision, the vessel which has the other on her starboard side shall keep out of the way of the other.

RULE 20

(a) When a power-driven vessel and a sailing vessel are proceeding in such directions as to involve risk of collision, except as provided for in Rules 24 and 26, the power-driven vessel shall keep out of the way of the sailing vessel.

(b) This Rule shall not give to a sailing vessel the right to hamper, in a narrow channel, the safe passage of a power-driven vessel which can navigate only inside such channel.

(c) A seaplane on the water shall, in general, keep well clear of all vessels and avoid impeding their navigation. In circumstances, however, where risk of collision exists, she shall comply with these Rules.

RULE 21

Where by any of these Rules one of two vessels is to keep out of the way, the other shall keep her course and speed. When, from any cause, the latter vessel finds herself so close that collision cannot be avoided by the action of the giving-way vessel alone, she also shall take such action as will best aid to avert collision (see Rules 27 and 29).

RULE 22

Every vessel which is directed by these Rules to keep out of the way of another vessel shall, so far as possible, take positive early action to comply with this obligation, and shall, if the circumstances of the case admit, avoid crossing ahead of the other.

RULE 23

Every power-driven vessel which is directed by these Rules to keep out of the way of another vessel, shall on approaching her, if necessary, slacken her speed or stop or reverse.

RULE 24

(a) Notwithstanding anything contained in these Rules, every vessel overtaking any other shall keep out of the way of the overtaken vessel.

(b) Every vessel coming up with another vessel from any direction more than 22½ degrees (2 points) abaft her beam, i.e., in such a position, with reference to the vessel which she is overtaking, that at night she would be unable to see either of that vessel's sidelights, shall be deemed to be an overtaking vessel; and no subsequent alteration of the bearing between the two vessels shall make the overtaking vessel a crossing vessel within the meaning of these Rules, or relieve her of the duty of keeping clear of the overtaken vessel until she is finally past and clear.

(c) If the overtaking vessel cannot determine with certainty whether she is forward of or abaft this direction from the other vessel, she shall assume that she is an overtaking vessel and keep out of the way.

RULE 25

(a) In a narrow channel every power-driven vessel when proceeding along the course of the channel shall, when it is safe and practicable, keep to that side of the fairway or mid-channel which lies on the starboard side of such vessel.

(b) Whenever a power-driven vessel is nearing a bend in a channel where a vessel approaching from the other direction cannot be seen, such power-driven vessel, when she shall have arrived within one-half (½) mile of the bend, shall give a signal by one prolonged blast on her whistle which signal shall be answered by a similar blast given by any approaching power-driven vessel that may be within hearing around the bend. Regardless of whether an approaching vessel on the farther side of the bend is heard, such bend shall be rounded with alertness and caution.

(c) In a narrow channel a power-driven vessel of less than 65 feet in length shall not hamper the safe passage of a vessel which can navigate only inside such channel.

RULE 26

All vessels not engaged in fishing, except vessels to which the provisions of Rule 4 apply, shall, when under way, keep out of the way of vessels engaged in fishing. This Rule shall not give to any vessel engaged in fishing the right of obstructing a fairway used by vessels other than fishing vessels.

RULE 27

In obeying and construing these Rules due regard shall be had to all dangers of navigation and collision, and to any special circumstances, including the limitations of the craft involved, which may render a departure from the above Rules necessary in order to avoid immediate danger.

PART E. SOUND SIGNALS FOR VESSELS
IN SIGHT OF ONE ANOTHER
RULE 28

(a) When vessels are in sight of one another, a power-driven vessel under way, in taking any course authorized or required by these Rules, shall indicate that course by the following signals on her whistle, namely:

One short blast to mean "I am altering my course to starboard."

Two short blasts to mean "I am altering my course to port."

Three short blasts to mean "My engines are going astern."

(b) Whenever a power-driven vessel which, under these Rules, is to keep her course and speed is in sight of another vessel and is in doubt whether sufficient **action is** being taken by the other vessel to avert collision, she may indicate such doubt by giving at least five short and rapid blasts on the whistle. The giving of such a signal shall not relieve a vessel of her obligations under Rules 27 and 29 or any other Rule, or of her duty to indicate any action taken under these Rules by giving the appropriate sound signals laid down in this Rule.

(c) Any whistle signal mentioned in this Rule may be further indicated by a visual signal consisting of a white light visible all round the horizon at a distance of at least 5 miles, and so devised that it will operate simultaneously and in conjunction with the whistle sounding mechanism and remain lighted and visible during the same period as the sound signal.

(d) Nothing in these Rules shall interfere with the operation of any special rules made by the Government of any nation with respect to the use of additional whistle signals between ships of war or vessels sailing under convoy.

PART F. MISCELLANEOUS
RULE 29

Nothing in these Rules shall exonerate any vessel, or the owner, master or crew thereof, from the consequences of any neglect to carry lights or signals, or of any neglect to keep a proper look-out, or of the neglect of any precaution which may be required by the ordinary practice of seamen, or by the special circumstances of the case.

RULE 30

Nothing in these Rules shall interfere with the operation of a special rule duly made by local authority relative to the navigation of any harbour, river, lake, or inland water, including a reserved seaplane area.

RULE 31
Distress Signals

(a) When a vessel or seaplane on the water is in distress and requires assistance from other vessels or from the shore, the following shall be the signals to be used or displayed by her, either together or separately, namely:

(i) A gun or other explosive signal fired at intervals of about a minute.

(ii) A continuous sounding with any fog-signalling apparatus.

(iii) Rockets or shells, throwing red stars fired one at a time at short intervals.

(iv) A signal made by radiotelegraphy or by any other signalling method consisting of the group · · · – – – · · · in the Morse Code.

(v) A signal sent by radiotelephony consisting of the spoken word "Mayday."

(vi) The International Code Signal of distress indicated by N.C.

(vii) A signal consisting of a square flag having above or below it a ball or anything resembling a ball.

(viii) Flames on the vessel (as from a burning tar barrel, oil barrel, etc.).

(ix) A rocket parachute flare or a hand flare showing a red light.

(x) A smoke signal giving off a volume of orange-coloured smoke.

(xi) Slowly and repeatedly raising and lowering arms outstretched to each side.

Note:—Vessels in distress may use the radiotelegraph alarm signal or the radiotelephone alarm signal to secure attention to distress calls and messages. The radiotelegraph alarm signal, which is designed to actuate the radiotelegraph auto alarms of vessels so fitted, consists of a series of twelve dashes, sent in 1 minute, the duration of each dash being 4 seconds, and the duration of the interval between 2 consecutive dashes being 1 second. The radiotelephone alarm signal consists of 2 tones transmitted alternately over periods of from 30 seconds to 1 minute.

(b) The use of any of the foregoing signals, except for the purpose of indicating that a vessel or seaplane is in distress, and the use of any signals which may be confused with any of the above signals, is prohibited.

ANNEX TO THE RULES

Recommendations on the use of radar information as an aid to avoiding collisions at sea.

(1) Assumptions made on scanty information may be dangerous and should be avoided.

(2) A vessel navigating with the aid of radar in restricted visibility must, in compliance with Rule 16(a), go at a moderate speed. Information obtained from the use of radar is one of the circumstances to be taken into account when determining moderate speed. In this regard it must be recognized that small vessels, small icebergs and similar floating objects may not be detected by radar. Radar indications of one or more vessels in the vicinity may mean that "moderate speed" should be slower than a mariner without radar might consider moderate in the circumstances.

(3) When navigating in restricted visibility the radar range and bearing alone do not constitute ascertainment of the position of the other vessel under Rule 16(b) sufficiently to relieve a vessel of the duty to stop her engines and navigate with caution when a fog signal is heard forward of the beam.

(4) When action has been taken under Rule 16(c) to avoid a close quarters situation, it is essential to make sure that such action is having the desired effect. Alterations of course or speed or both are matters as to which the mariner must be guided by the circumstances of the case.

(5) Alteration of course alone may be the most effective action to avoid close quarters provided that:

(a) There is sufficient sea room.

(b) It is made in good time.

(c) It is substantial. A succession of small alterations of course should be avoided.

(d) It does not result in a close quarters situation with other vessels.

(6) The direction of an alteration of course is a matter in which the mariner must be guided by the circumstances of the case. An alteration to starboard, particularly when vessels are approaching apparently on opposite or nearly opposite courses, is generally preferable to an alteration to port.

(7) An alteration of speed, either alone or in conjunction with an alteration of course, should be substantial. A number of small alterations of speed should be avoided.

(8) If a close quarters situation is imminent, the most prudent action may be to take all way off the vessel.

Appendix C* *Racing Rules*

Parts I and IV of the 1965 Yacht Racing Rules of the International Yacht Racing Union as adopted by the North American Yacht Racing Union

PART I
DEFINITIONS

When a term defined in Part I is used in its defined sense it is printed in italic type. All definitions and italicized notes rank as rules.

Racing—A yacht is *racing* from her preparatory signal until she has either *finished* and cleared the finishing line and finishing *marks* or retired, or until the race has been *cancelled, postponed* or *abandoned*, except that in match or team races, the sailing instructions may prescribe that a yacht is racing from any specified time before the preparatory signal.

Starting—A yacht *starts* when, after her starting signal, any part of her hull, crew or equipment first crosses the starting line in the direction of the first *mark*.

Finishing—A yacht *finishes* when any part of her hull, or of her crew or equipment in normal position, crosses the finishing line from the direction of the last *mark*.

Luffing—Altering course towards the wind until head to wind.

Tacking—A yacht is *tacking* from the moment she is beyond head to wind until she has *borne away*, if beating to windward, to a *close-hauled* course; if not beating to windward, to the course on which her mainsail has filled.

Bearing Away—Altering course away from the wind until a yacht begins to jibe.

Jibing—A yacht begins to *jibe* at the moment when, with the wind aft, the foot of her mainsail crosses her centerline and completes the *jibe* when the mainsail has filled on the other *tack*.

* *This appendix is reprinted from* The 1965 Yacht Racing Rules of the International Yacht Racing Union as Adopted by the North American Yacht Racing Union, *published by the North American Yacht Racing Union, 1965.*

On a Tack—A yacht is *on a tack* except when she is *tacking* or *jibing*. A yacht is on the *tack* (*starboard* or *port*) corresponding to her *windward* side.

Close-hauled—A yacht is *close-hauled* when sailing by the wind as close as she can lie with advantage in working to windward.

Leeward and **Windward**—The *leeward* side of a yacht is that on which she is, or, if *luffing* head to wind, was, carrying her mainsail. The opposite side is the *windward* side.

When neither of two yachts on the same *tack* is *clear astern*, the one on the *leeward* side of the other is the *leeward yacht*. The other is the *windward yacht*.

Clear Astern and **Clear Ahead; Overlap**—A yacht is *clear astern* of another when her hull and equipment are abaft an imaginary line projected abeam from the aftermost point of the other's hull and equipment. The other yacht is *clear ahead*. The yachts *overlap* if neither is *clear astern;* or if, although one is *clear astern,* an intervening yacht *overlaps* both of them. The terms *clear astern, clear ahead* and *overlap* apply to yachts on opposite *tacks* only when they are subject to rule 42—Rounding or Passing Marks and Obstructions.

Proper Course—A *proper course* is any course which a yacht might sail after the starting signal, in the absence of the other yacht or yachts affected, to *finish* as quickly as possible. The course sailed before *luffing* or *bearing away* is presumably, but not necessarily, that yacht's *proper course*. There is no *proper course* before the starting signal.

Mark—A *mark* is any object specified in the sailing instructions which a yacht must round or pass on a required side.

Obstruction—An *obstruction* is any object, including craft under way, large enough to require a yacht, if not less than one overall length away from it, to make a substantial alteration of course to pass on one side or the other, or any object which can be passed on one side only, including a buoy when the yacht in question cannot safely pass between it and the shoal or object which it marks.

Cancellation—A *cancelled* race is one which the Race Committee decides will not be sailed thereafter.

Postponement—A *postponed* race is one which is not started at its scheduled time and which can be sailed at any time the Race Committee may decide.

Abandonment—An *abandoned* race is one which the Race Committee declares void at any time after the starting signal, and which can be resailed at its discretion.

PART IV
SAILING RULES WHEN YACHTS MEET

Helmsman's Rights and Obligations Concerning Right of Way

The rules of Part IV apply only between yachts which either are intending to **race** *or are* **racing** *in the same or different races, and, except when rule 3.2(k) applies, replace the International Regulations for Preventing Collisions at Sea or Government Right-of-Way Rules applicable to the area concerned, from the time a yacht intending to* **race** *begins to sail about in the vicinity of the starting line until she has either* **finished** *or retired and has left the vicinity of the course.*

SECTION A—RULES WHICH ALWAYS APPLY

31—Disqualification

1. A yacht may be disqualified for infringing a rule of Part IV only when the infringement occurs while she is *racing*, whether or not a collision results.

2. A yacht may be disqualified before or after she is *racing* for seriously hindering a yacht which is *racing*, or for infringing the sailing instructions.

32—Avoiding Collisions

A right-of-way yacht which makes no attempt to avoid a collision resulting in serious damage may be disqualified as well as the other yacht.

33—Retiring from Race

A yacht, which realizes she has infringed a racing rule or a sailing instruction, should retire promptly; but, if she persists in *racing*, other yachts shall continue to accord her such rights as she may have under the rules of Part IV.

34—Misleading or Balking

1. When one yacht is required to keep clear of another, the right-of-way yacht shall not (except to the extent permitted by rule 38.1, *Luffing after Starting*), so alter course as to:
   (*a*) prevent the other yacht from keeping clear; or
   (*b*) mislead or balk her while she is keeping clear.

2. A yacht is not misleading or balking another if she alters course by *luffing* or *bearing away* to conform to a change in the strength or direction of the wind.

35—Hailing

A right-of-way yacht, except when *luffing* under rule 38.1, *Luffing after Starting*, should hail before or when making an alteration of course which may not be foreseen by the other yacht or when claiming room at a *mark* or *obstruction*.

SECTION B—OPPOSITE TACK RULE

36—Fundamental Rule

A *port-tack* yacht shall keep clear of a *starboard-tack* yacht.

SECTION C—SAME TACK RULES

37—Fundamental Rules

1. A *windward yacht* shall keep clear of a *leeward yacht*.

2. A yacht *clear astern* shall keep clear of a yacht *clear ahead*.

3. A yacht which establishes an *overlap* to *leeward* from *clear astern* shall allow the *windward yacht* ample room and opportunity to keep clear, and during the existence of that *overlap* the *leeward yacht* shall not sail above her *proper course*.

38—Right-of-Way Yacht Luffing after Starting

1. **Luffing Rights and Limitations.** After she has *started* and cleared the starting line, a yacht *clear ahead* or a *leeward yacht* may *luff* as she pleases, except that:

A *leeward yacht* shall not sail above *her*

proper course while an *overlap* exists if, at any time during its existence, the helmsman of the *windward yacht* (when sighting abeam from his normal station and sailing no higher than the *leeward yacht*) has been abreast or forward of the mainmast of the *leeward yacht*.

2. **Overlap Limitations.** For the purpose of this rule: an *overlap* does not exist unless the yachts are clearly within two overall lengths of the longer yacht; and an *overlap* which exists between two yachts when the leading yacht *starts*, or when one or both of them completes a *tack* or *jibe*, shall be regarded as a new *overlap* beginning at that time.

3. **Hailing to Stop or Prevent a Luff.** When there is doubt, the *leeward yacht* may assume that she has the right to *luff* unless the helmsman of the *windward yacht* has hailed "Mast Abeam," or words to that effect. The *leeward yacht* shall be governed by such hail, and, if she deems it improper, her only remedy is to protest.

4. **Curtailing a Luff.** The *windward yacht* shall not cause a *luff* to be curtailed because of her proximity to the *leeward yacht* unless an *obstruction*, a third yacht or other object restricts her ability to respond.

5. **Luffing Two or More Yachts.** A yacht shall not *luff* unless she has the right to *luff* all yachts which would be affected by her *luff*, in which case they shall all respond even if an intervening yacht or yachts would not otherwise have the right to *luff*.

39—Sailing Below a Proper Course after Starting

A yacht which is on a free leg of the course after having *started* and cleared the starting line shall not sail below her *proper course* when she is clearly within three of her overall lengths of either a *leeward yacht* or a yacht *clear astern* which is steering a course to pass to *leeward*.

40—Right-of-Way Yacht Luffing before Starting

Before a yacht has *started* and cleared the starting line, any *luff* on her part which affects another yacht shall be carried out slowly. A *leeward yacht* may so *luff* only when the helmsman of the *windward yacht* (sighting abeam from his normal station) is abaft the mainmast of the *leeward yacht*. However, after her starting signal the *leeward yacht* may *luff* slowly to assume her *proper course* even when, because of her position, she would not otherwise have the right to *luff*. Rules 38.3, Hailing to Stop or Prevent a Luff; 38.4, Curtailing a Luff; and 38.5, Luffing Two or More Yachts, also apply.

SECTION D—CHANGING TACK RULES

41—Tacking or Jibing

1. A yacht which is either *tacking* or *jibing* shall keep clear of a yacht *on a tack*.

2. A yacht shall neither *tack* nor *jibe* into a position which will give her right of way unless she does so far enough from a yacht *on a tack* to enable this yacht to keep clear without having to begin to alter her course until after the *tack* or *jibe* has been completed.

3. A yacht which *tacks* or *jibes* has the onus of satisfying the Race Committee that she completed her *tack* or *jibe* in accordance with Rule 41.2.

4. When two yachts are both *tacking* or both *jibing* at the same time, the one on the other's *port* side shall keep clear.

SECTION E—RULES OF EXCEPTION AND SPECIAL APPLICATION

When a rule of this section applies, to the extent to which it explicitly provides rights and obligations, it overrides any conflicting rule of Part IV which precedes it, except the rules of Section A—Rules Which Always Apply.

42—Rounding or Passing Marks and Obstructions

When yachts either on the same *tack* or, after *starting* and clearing the starting line, on opposite *tacks*, are about to round or pass a *mark* on the same required side or an *obstruction* on the same side:

When Overlapped

1. (a) An outside yacht shall give each yacht *overlapping* her on the inside room to round or pass it, except as provided in Rules 42.1(c), (d) and (e). Room includes room to *tack* or *jibe* when either is an integral part of the rounding or passing maneuver.

(b) When an inside yacht of two or more *overlapped* yachts on opposite *tacks* will have to *jibe* in rounding a *mark*, in order most directly to assume a *proper course* on the next leg, she shall *jibe* when she has obtained room.

(c) When two yachts on opposite *tacks* are either on a beat or when one of them will have to *tack* either to round the *mark* or to avoid the *obstruction*, as between each other Rule 42.1(a) shall not apply and they are subject to Rules 36, Opposite Tack Fundamental Rule, and 41, Tacking or Jibing.

(d) An outside *leeward yacht* with luffing rights may take an inside yacht to windward of a *mark* provided that she hails to that effect and begins to *luff* before she is within two of her overall lengths of the *mark* and provided that she also passes to windward of it.

(e) When approaching the starting line to *start*, a *leeward yacht* shall be under no obligation to give any *windward yacht* room to pass to leeward of a starting *mark* surrounded by navigable water; but, after the starting signal, a *leeward yacht* shall not deprive a *windward yacht* of room at such *mark* either:

(i) by heading above the first *mark*; or

(ii) by *luffing* above *close-hauled*.

When Clear Astern and Clear Ahead

2. (a) A yacht *clear astern* shall keep clear in anticipation of and during the rounding or passing maneuver when the yacht *clear ahead* remains on the same *tack* or *jibes*.

(b) A yacht *clear ahead* which *tacks* to round a *mark* is subject to Rule 41, Tacking or

Jibing, but a yacht *clear astern* shall not *luff* above *close-hauled* so as to prevent the yacht *clear ahead* from *tacking*.

Restrictions on Establishing and Breaking an Overlap

3. (a) A yacht *clear astern* shall not establish an inside *overlap* and be entitled to room under Rule 42.1(a) when the yacht *clear ahead*:

(i) is within two of her own lengths of the *mark* or *obstruction*, except as provided in Rule 42.3(b); or

(ii) is unable to give the required room.

(b) A yacht *clear astern* may establish an *overlap* between the yacht *clear ahead* and a continuing *obstruction* such as a shoal or the shore, only when there is room for her to do so in safety.

(c) A yacht *clear ahead* shall be under no obligation to give room before an *overlap* is established. The onus will lie upon the yacht which has been *clear astern* to satisfy the Race Committee that the *overlap* was established in proper time.

(d) When an *overlap* exists at the time the outside yacht comes within two of her lengths of the *mark*, she shall nevertheless be bound by Rule 42.1(a), even though the *overlap* may thereafter be broken.

43—Close-Hauled, Hailing for Room to Tack at Obstructions

1. **Hailing.** When safe pilotage requires one of two *close-hauled* yachts on the same *tack* to make a substantial alteration of course to clear an *obstruction*, and if she intends to *tack*, but cannot *tack* without colliding with the other yacht, she shall hail the other yacht for room to *tack*.

2. **Responding.** The hailed yacht at the earliest possible moment after the hail shall either:

(a) *tack*, in which case, the hailing yacht shall begin to *tack* either:

(i) before the hailed yacht has completed her *tack*, or

(ii) if she cannot then *tack* without colliding with the hailed yacht, immediately she is able to *tack,* or

(b) reply "You *tack,*" or words to that effect, if in her opinion she can keep clear without *tacking* or after postponing her *tack.* In this case:

(i) the hailing yacht shall immediately *tack* and

(ii) the hailed yacht shall keep clear.

(iii) the onus shall lie on the hailed yacht which replied "You *tack*" to satisfy the Race Committee that she kept clear.

3. Limitation on Right to Room

(a) When the *obstruction* is a *mark* which the hailed yacht can fetch, the hailing yacht shall not be entitled to room to *tack* and the hailed yacht shall immediately so inform the hailing yacht.

(b) If, thereafter, the hailing yacht again hails for room to *tack,* she shall, after receiving it, retire immediately.

(c) If, after having refused to respond to a hail under Rule 43.3(a), the hailed yacht fails to fetch, she shall retire immediately.

44—Yachts Returning to Start

1. (a) A premature starter when returning to *start,* or a yacht working into position from the wrong side of the starting line or its extensions, when the starting signal is made, shall keep clear of all yachts which are *starting,* or have *started,* correctly, until she is wholly on the right side of the starting line or its extensions.

(b) Thereafter, she shall be accorded the rights under the rules of Part IV of a yacht which is *starting* correctly; but if she thereby acquires right of way over another yacht which is *starting* correctly, she shall allow that yacht ample room and opportunity to keep clear.

2. A premature starter while continuing to sail the course and until it is obvious that she is returning to *start,* shall be accorded the rights under the rules of Part IV of a yacht which has *started.*

45—Anchored, Aground or Capsized

1. A yacht under way shall keep clear of another yacht *racing* which is anchored, aground or capsized. Of two anchored yachts, the one which anchored later shall keep clear, except that a yacht which is dragging shall keep clear of one which is not.

2. A yacht anchored or aground shall indicate the fact to any yacht which may be in danger of fouling her. Unless the size of the yachts or the weather conditions make some other signal necessary, a hail is sufficient indication.

3. A yacht shall not be penalized for fouling a yacht in distress which she is attempting to assist nor a yacht which goes aground or capsizes immediately ahead of her.

Appendix D

U.S. Naval Academy Regulations for Sailing Craft and YP's

(This appendix is identical to Chapter 19, U.S. Naval Academy Regulations.)

1901 Categories of Sailing at the Naval Academy

1. Basic sailing instruction, and qualification in knockabouts, Luders yawls and Class "A" yachts.

2. Recreational sailing in knockabouts, Luders yawls and Class "A" yachts.

3. Intra-Brigade knockabout competition.

4. Competitive sailing of knockabouts, dinghies, Shields sloops, Luders yawls, and Class "A" yachts.

5. Knockabouts and smaller sailing craft will normally be referred to as "boats." Shields sloops and larger sailing craft will normally be referred to as "yachts."

1902 Responsibilities for Sailing

1. The Commanding Officer, Naval Station, has full responsibility for the operations, custody and maintenance of all boats except as otherwise designated in these regulations. He will administer recreational and competitive sailing in accordance with USNA Instruction 1710.7 series. In addition, as Commodore, Naval Academy Sailing Squadron (NASS), he is responsible directly to the Superintendent for all Naval Academy liaison with other military and civilian yacht sailing organizations. He is specifically responsible for all details of planning, coordination, and execution incident to Naval Academy participation in military and civilian Chesapeake Bay and ocean sailing events.

2. The Head of the Naval Science Department is responsible for:

a. Basic sailing instruction in knockabouts and basic sailing instruction of midshipmen in Luders yawls. This responsibility includes the instruction and qualification of midshipmen and others eligible for instruction in knockabouts. Instruction in Luders yawls is carried on by the Naval Science Department during Plebe Summer as part of the basic curriculum only.

b. Administering the Intra-Brigade Knockabout competition.

3. The Director of Athletics is responsible for all inter-collegiate sailing competition in dinghies. The administration of dinghies will be coordinated between the Director of Athletics and the Commanding Officer, Naval Station.

4. Midshipmen who participate in recreational and competitive sailing are responsible to the Commandant of Midshipmen for complying with these and other duly promulgated regulations and procedures concerning sailing. The Officer Representative of the Midshipmen Sailing Squadron assists the Commandant of Midshipmen in coordinating midshipmen participation in sailing activities.

5. Midshipmen in charge of sailing craft are responsible for the safety of their assigned craft and their crew and passengers. They will assure that these regulations and other instructions applicable to sailing in Naval Academy sailing craft are complied with by their crew and passengers. They will meet commitments and scheduled times for returning to moorings. Midshipmen in charge of sailing craft and their midshipmen crew will report to the Officer of the Watch, Bancroft Hall, immediately upon securing when they have returned late and missed a formation or scheduled event.

1903 Responsibility of Those Who Use Sailing Craft

1. Maintaining sailing craft in proper condition is the duty of those using them as well as a function of the Commanding Officer, Naval Station. To facilitate maintenance:

a. Only shoes with white rubber soles will be worn when embarked in sailing craft.

b. Personal belongings and trash will not be left on board.

c. Sailing craft will be secured to their assigned moorings and left in a shipshape condition.

d. Check-off lists for securing are posted in sailing craft and will be complied with before disembarking.

e. When a Midshipman Sailing Master is assigned to an ocean racing yacht, he is responsible for its cleanliness and routine upkeep.

1904 Rules of the Road

1. Rules of the Nautical Road and all laws for the prevention of collision in rivers, harbors, and inland waters will be obeyed by personnel in charge of Naval Academy craft. The current racing rules of the North American Yacht Racing Union will apply between competitors in races unless otherwise specified. Customs and courtesies of the sea will be

observed and a good example will always be set in sea manners.

2. Men of war and other large vessels will be given a wide berth. The draft of such vessels restricts their ability to maneuver to avoid collision. The intended action should be indicated to the larger ship as early as possible.

3. Boats and yachts will remain clear of all races in progress in which they are not competing.

1905 Damage to Boats

1. Discrepancies in the condition of sailing craft will be reported as follows:

   a. For dinghies, knockabouts, and Shields—in the discrepancy log maintained for each type at the dinghy and knockabout check-out booths.

   b. For larger sailing craft—in the discrepancy log maintained aboard each yacht.

   c. In the event a discrepancy log cannot be located, discrepancies will be telephoned to Head, Department of Small Craft, extension 603.

2. Serious damage to sailing craft, collisions, and groundings will be made the subject of a written report to the Commanding Officer, Naval Station, explaining all the circumstances of the incident. Such reports are due within two working days after the incident.

3. Failure to make proper and timely reports may result in loss of sailing privileges and other disciplinary action.

1906 Sailing Season

1. The normal season for all Naval Academy sailing craft will be from the last week in March through the second week in November. Subject to weather conditions and availability of sailing craft, the Commanding Officer, Naval Station, may extend or curtail the sailing season for all or some types of sailing craft.

2. Personnel directly concerned with organized sailing (the head coach of the Midshipman Sailing Squadron, the coach of the dinghy team and the Head of the Naval Science Department) who desire to commence sailing activities prior to the last week in March will submit a letter stating their plans to the Commanding Officer, Naval Station, by 1 December to permit planning overhaul schedules to accommodate their requirements.

1907 Recreational Sailing Periods

1. Midshipmen knockabouts recreational sailing periods are as follows:

Monday–Friday	1515-1800
Saturday & Sunday	1300-1530 (first period)
	1530-1800 (second period)
Holidays	0900-1200
	1300-1530
	1530-1800

2. Knockabout recreational sailing periods for all other qualified persons will include those times set forth for midshipmen and an additional morning period from 0900-1200 on Saturdays and Sundays. During Fourth Class Summer there will be no recreational sailing on Saturday mornings. The Recreational Sailing Supervisory Watch, and all midshipmen watches, will be posted only during midshipmen recreational sailing hours.

3. Recreational sailing in dinghies (skipjack class only) may be permitted for qualified persons during the above periods at the discretion and with the approval of the Sailing Center Watch Officer.

4. Recreational sailing in yachts may be conducted by qualified persons during daylight hours when the yachts are not required for instruction, organized sailing, or maintenance.

   a. Subject to the approval of the Commodore, NASS, and the Commandant of Midshipmen for midshipmen concerned, yachts may sail at night. This permission will be obtained by the individual concerned, and appended to the request form submitted to the Sailing Center. Special permission is not required to sail at night in an authorized race or other event.

5. In the event the Commandant of Midshipmen grants midshipmen permission to sail at times other than noted above, the Commanding Officer, Naval Station (Sailing Center Watch Officer) will be notified so that he will assure that the required watches are posted.

6. Authority to permit commencement of recreational sailing and the responsibility for termination of sailing in event of unusual circumstances rests with the Commanding Officer, Naval Station. During Naval Station working hours this responsibility is delegated to the Sailing Officer and after working hours, Saturdays, Sundays, and holidays to the Command Duty Officer, Naval Station. The responsible authority will be stationed in the Sailing Center.

1908 Races

1. The permission of the Superintendent is required prior to entry of any Naval Academy sailing craft in any race except those races under auspices

of the Naval Academy Sailing Squadron.

2. The Commanding Officer, Naval Station, may authorize the use of such craft as necessary for special purposes and races.

1909 Safety Officers

1. Qualification: Safety Officers are designated as such by the Commodore, Naval Academy Sailing Squadron, from the most capable and experienced members of the squadron. A person must hold a knockabout qualification, be a member of the Naval Academy Sailing Squadron, hold a qualification for the yacht involved, and hold a racing command in order to be designated as a Safety Officer.

2. Duties and authority: When embarked in the capacity of a Safety Officer, his responsibility for the safety of the yacht and crew is complete, and he is "in charge" of the craft. A racing crew may regard his tactical or strategic assistance as advice, but any orders affecting the safety of the crew or yacht will be complied with at once.

3. When required: Except as authorized by the Commanding Officer, Naval Station, yachts larger than Shields commanded by midshipmen may not enter an extramural race without a safety officer on board. A list of qualified safety officers will be maintained in the Sailing Center.

1910 Prizes and Awards

1. Permanent prizes won in sailing races are considered the property of the person in command during the race.

2. Awards for outstanding performance to members of the midshipman sailing squadron will be made by the Commodore, Naval Academy Sailing Squadron, conforming to existing awards policies.

1911 Swimming and Emergencies

1. Recreational swimming from knockabouts and dinghies is not permitted. Swimming is permitted from Shields sloops, yawls and larger craft only when hove to with all sails down, except the mizzen in the case of yawls. The mizzen left up on a yawl during swimming, distinguishes it from a yawl grounded or in other trouble.

2. Whenever a USNA boat desires assistance due to groundings, becalming, or for other reason, all sails will be doused. This will be the signal for the safety watch to send assistance.

3. Persons embarked in sailing craft attached to the Naval Academy must be able to swim one hundred yards. Non-swimmers will obtain permission from the Commanding Officer, Naval Station

and, when granted, will wear life jackets when sailing.

1912 Children Embarked

1. Children may not be embarked in U.S. Naval Academy sailing craft unless they are at least ten years of age, except that when the craft is commanded by a NASS safety officer they may be as young as six years.

1913 Uniform for Midshipmen

1. The basic uniform of midshipmen for recreational sailing is gym shorts, gym shirts, and rubber soled shoes. However, midshipmen will be attired in a complete white working uniform with white hat while proceeding to and from Bancroft Hall. Midshipmen engaged in maintenance on yachts may wear dungarees on board. When weather dictates, either reefers or blue parkas may be worn in knockabouts or in the case of yachts this or other appropriate similar outer clothing.

2. Members of the varsity sailing team and the Midshipman Sailing Squadron may wear appropriate athletic attire proceeding between Bancroft Hall and scheduled races or practice sessions as specified by their respective officer representatives.

1914 Guests of Midshipmen

1. When young ladies are embarked in knockabouts at least two must be present.

2. When young ladies are embarked in yawls or larger types, a chaperon will be present. Authorized chaperons are:

    a. Mothers of the midshipmen or of the young ladies embarked.

    b. Wives of USNA faculty members, of officers attached to the Naval Academy, or of members of the Naval Academy Sailing Squadron.

3. Ladies are not permitted on board when sailing craft are participating in sanctioned races.

4. Guests normally will not be embarked in Shields sloops or dinghies.

5. Civilian guests who do not hold a current knockabout qualification are not authorized to be embarked in any knockabout unless the person in command and one other qualified crew member have sailed a knockabout at least once since the beginning of the current sailing season.

1915 Limits of Sailing Areas

1. Small Boats:
    Area One—(knockabouts only)—Severn River

from the automobile bridge to Tolly Point; thence to Tolly Point bell buoy "#33"; thence to buoy "C35"; thence to Greenbury Point.

Area Two—(knockabouts only)—Severn River from the automobile bridge to a line extending from Greenbury Point to Tolly Point through Greenbury Point Light.

Area Three—(knockabouts and dinghies)—Severn River from the automobile bridge to a line from the Marine Engineering Laboratory tangent to the eastern extremity of Horn Point.

2. The recreational sailing area for Shields sloops, Luders yawls and Class "A" yachts is:

The Severn River from the automobile bridge east to the Eastern Shore of Chesapeake Bay and from the Chesapeake Bay Bridge south to a line connecting Thomas Point Light and Kent Point.

3. Yachts will not leave this area except for an authorized race, emergency, or by special authority of the Commanding Officer, Naval Station, and, for midshipmen, the Commandant of Midshipmen.

4. Except in emergencies, or when authorized by the Commandant of Midshipmen, landings by midshipmen will not be made on the shores of Chesapeake Bay.

5. Signals to small boats (knockabouts and dinghies):

a. Flaghoists at starboard yardarm

(1) "One Flag"—Area One may be used for knockabouts.

(2) "Two Flag"—Area Two may be used for knockabouts.

(3) "Three Flag"—Area Three may be used for small boats.

b. Shape Signals, Port yardarm

(1) One shape—General recall. All boats return to moorings.

(2) Two shapes—Small boats come within view of signal hoist on starboard yardarm and sail in area designated.

(3) Three shapes—All small boats reef or douse sails as necessary until a squall has passed.

6. The area in which sailing is permitted will be signalled by the safety watch. If no signal is made, Area Two will be used. Yachts need not obey the signals in paragraph 5 above, but will be recalled by dispatch boat displaying the eight flag.

7. Signals hoisted by the safety watch or dispatch boat will be watched for and promptly obeyed.

8. A signal light will be flashed at individual boats any time one of the above signals is changed.

1916 Eligibility for Use of and Qualification in Sailing Craft

1. Midshipmen are eligible to participate in such sailing as their interests and skill permit. The sailing craft at the Naval Academy are primarily for the instruction of and use by midshipmen.

2. *Dinghies*. Members of the varsity and plebe dinghy teams and such others as may be especially authorized by the dinghy coach or the Commanding Officer, Naval Station.

3. *Knockabouts*
   a. Midshipmen
   b. Military personnel of USNA
   c. Civilian faculty
   d. Regular members of the NASS
   e. Dependents of b, c and d above

4. *Shields and larger yachts*
   a. Midshipman members of the MSS
   b. Regular members of the NASS
   c. Others especially designated by the Commodore, NASS, as a result of their contribution to the Midshipman Sailing Squadron.

5. *Dependents*
   a. Dependents are eligible for qualification in and the use of knockabouts.

   b. They may receive instruction in the yawls and larger yachts at the same time their male sponsor does, but will not receive qualification.

   c. To receive qualification in knockabouts, dependents must be at least 13 years of age and able to swim 100 yards.

1917 Sailing Qualifications and Requirements

1. Knockabout qualification entitles a holder to take command of and to act as a qualified crew member of a knockabout. The prerequisites for this qualification are:

   a. Receive practical sailing instruction provided by the Head of the Naval Science Department.

   b. Pass a practical test given by a Naval Science Department instructor.

   c. Pass a theoretical test administered by the Head of the Naval Science Department. This test is given from 1530-1700 every Wednesday and Friday on the fourth deck of Luce Hall.

   d. Pass the required swimming test (swim 100 yards).

2. The Commanding Officer, Naval Station will prescribe the requirements for qualification in Shields sloops, Luders yawls and Class "A" yachts.

3. The Varsity Dinghy Coach will prescribe the requirements for qualification in dinghies.

1918 *Procedure for Administering Qualification Cards*

1. Knockabout Qualification Cards

a. The Head of the Naval Science Department will issue knockabout qualification cards.

b. He will send these cards to the knockabout check-out booth for use in scheduling knockabouts and for logging on the card each instance wherein the individual sailed as skipper or crew member.

c. The knockabout check-out booth will maintain a complete file of these cards for midshipmen and others who are qualified.

2. The Sailing Officer will maintain in his office qualification cards regarding Shields sloops and larger yachts.

3. A list of persons qualified in dinghies will be maintained by the dinghy coach in the dinghy watch folder.

1919 *Reservation and Check-Out Procedures*

1. The following uses of Naval Academy sailing craft are arranged in order of priority.

a. Instruction of midshipmen (0800-1605 daily and 0800-1200 Saturday in knockabouts and yawls during plebe summer).

b. Organized racing and training (yachts and dinghies: 1515-1800 daily during fall and spring of academic year, weekends throughout the sailing season. Knockabouts: 1610-1900 in spring of academic year, plus miscellaneous events such as the NASS Knockabout Regatta).

c. Recreational sailing for qualified midshipmen.

d. Recreational sailing for other qualified and eligible persons.

2. Reservations are not required by midshipmen participating in instruction or organized sailing.

3. Reservations for recreational sailing are handled as follows:

a. Dinghies: No reservations, qualified persons sail on first-come/first-served basis as designated by the Sailing Center Watch Officer.

b. Knockabouts: Request form properly completed and submitted to the knockabout check-out booth constitutes a request to reserve a knockabout. Persons other than midshipmen may submit their requests via telephone (2055). Midshipmen may turn their request forms in at the Main Office for delivery by messenger to the knockabout check-out booth once daily at 1500. "Advanced reservations for knockabouts are not normally considered necessary. However, they will be accepted up to five days in advance at the knockabout check-out booth. Advanced reservation requests will be honored in the order they are received. Once a reservation is made it will not be cancelled solely because a more senior midshipman makes a later reservation request."

c. Yachts:

(1) A request form properly completed and submitted to the Sailing Officer at least one day in advance constitutes a request to reserve a yacht. During academic year midshipmen of the various classes will have the same reservation privileges as indicated above for knockabouts, except that for weekends yachts will be reserved for regularly assigned midshipmen skippers until the Wednesday noon preceding, and requests for weekend sailing from other persons will be processed in order of receipt after all midshipman requests have been satisfied at 1000 Friday.

(2) At other times during the sailing season requests for yacht reservations will be honored in order of receipt. Coaches and Safety Officers of the Midshipman Sailing Squadron, especially designated by the Commodore, NASS, may reserve yachts up to three weeks in advance. Others may reserve yachts one week in advance.

(a) When checking out and returning a yacht, the boat request form and yacht status board will be completed in the Sailing Center.

(b) Special equipment will be signed out prior to 1800 Friday for weekend use.

4. Unused reservations will be canceled 20 minutes after the scheduled time of the reservation when a waiting line for sailing craft exists. Sailing craft will be assigned to those waiting by the cognizant watch-stander on a first-come/first-served basis.

1920 *Duration of Sailing Qualifications*

1. Naval Academy sailing qualifications are valid through the duration of the individual's tour at the Naval Academy.

2. Everyone must requalify for his sailing qualifications on any subsequent tour of duty.

3. For misuse or abuse of sailing privileges, or for displays of poor seamanship, the Head of the Naval Science Department and the Director of Athletics are authorized to revoke sailing qualifications issued by them. The Commanding Officer, Naval Station, may revoke any sailing qualification, and will

inform the Head of the Naval Science Department or the Director of Athletics of any qualification in knockabouts or dinghies, respectively, which he has suspended or revoked.

1921 Crew Requirements

1. The following minimum and maximum capacities will be observed at all times:

TYPE	MINIMUM	MAXIMUM
Finn Dinghies	1	1
Knockabouts	3*	6
Shields Boats	3	6
Luders Yawls	4	16
Norderney	4	16
Gypsy	4	18
Annie D	4	18
Royono	8	40
Freedom	10	60
Dinghies (except Finn class)	1	2

*At least two must be qualified.

1922 Authority of Person in Charge of Sailing Craft

1. At the Naval Academy, there are frequent occasions wherein the person in charge of a sailboat may be junior to those embarked or may be a civilian. In such cases, the provisions of U. S. Navy Regulations, Article 1329, "Authority of Officers Embarked as Passengers," will apply. In other words, the person designated by the Superintendent as being in charge of a sailing craft will have authority over all others embarked except in cases where the embarked passenger is a flag officer eligible for command at sea.

1923 Small Powerboats

1. Various small power boats are assigned to the Commanding Officer, Naval Station, to enable him to fulfill transportation and other logistics requirements. These are not available for recreational use, but managers of the Midshipman Sailing Squadron and Dinghy Team, and others as required, may be qualified in these small boats in connection with their duties in support of various extracurricular or athletic activities.

1924 Responsibilities for YP's

1. The Commanding Officer, Naval Station, has full responsibility for the operation, custody, maintenance, and administration of all YP craft, except as otherwise designated in these regulations.

2. The Head of the Naval Science Department sponsors the activities of the Midshipmen's YP Squadron and is responsible for the training and qualification of midshipmen operating YP Craft and for YP Squadron operations.

3. Midshipmen who participate in YP Programs are responsible to the Commandant of Midshipmen for complying with these and other duly promulgated regulations and procedures concerning YP Programs. The Officer Representative of the YP Squadron assists the Commandant of Midshipmen in coordinating midshipmen participation in the YP Squadron Program.

4. The midshipman YP Squadron battalion representatives are responsible for the cleanliness and routine upkeep of the YP's assigned to their respective battalion.

1925 Damage to YP's

1. Major casualties, deficiencies, damages, groundings, and incidents which involve other boats or which may result in bad public relations will be reported by radio to the Head, Department of Small Craft. A detailed report will be made by midshipman on the reverse side of the boat slip when the YP is checked in or by other persons by memorandum to the Commanding Officer, Naval Station. When appropriate, he will inform the Commandant of Midshipmen or Head of Department concerned.

2. Failure to make timely and proper reports may result in the loss of qualification and/or other disciplinary action.

1926 Availability of YP's

The priorities for use of the YP's are as follows:
    a. First—Midshipmen drills
    b. Second—Midshipmen's YP Squadron
    c. Third—Other midshipmen activities
    d. Fourth—Other uses

1927 Operating Periods

1. The normal YP operating seasons are as follows:
    a. Summer—from the end of one academic year until the beginning of the next academic year.
    b. Academic Year—same as the Intra-Brigade Sports Program seasons.

2. YP's will be available for drills during the summer and during the academic year between 0730 and 1605, and at such times as scheduled by the Head of the Naval Science Department.

3. Special authorization for use of YP's may be requested as follows:

a. Midshipmen: Boat request to the Commanding Officer, Naval Station, via the Head of Naval Science or his representative.

b. Other than midshipmen: Request to the Commanding Officer, Naval Station.

4. YP's will not be operated in periods of darkness unless a safety officer is on board or in company.

1928 *Limits of the Local Operating Area*

1. Unless otherwise directed by competent authority, YP's will be operated within the "local operating area," which has the following limits:

a. Severn River, below the Severn River Bridge.

b. Annapolis inner harbor below Annapolis Harbor Buoy 1.

c. Chesapeake Bay area south of Chesapeake Bay Bridge and north of the line connecting Thomas Point Light and Kent Point.

1929 *Safety Officers*

1. YP safety officers are officers who have been so designated by the Head of the Naval Science Department or Commanding Officer, Naval Station.

2. YP's commanded by midshipmen must have a safety officer on board or in company, if operating either during darkness or outside of the local operating area, except that the YP Squadron Officer Representative may waive their requirement for exceptionally competent midshipmen commanding officers.

1930 *Swimming*

Swimming from YP's will be permitted when authorized by Safety Officer in company. When conducted, the swimming safety precautions contained in YP SOP will be followed.

1931 *Communications and Emergencies*

1. While operating in Chesapeake Bay, YP's will maintain a continuous watch on 2792 kcs. in order to communicate with the Operations Office, Department of Small Craft. In an emergency, 2716 kcs. may be used. When operating in a task organization, the task organization commander may assign a guard ship for his task organization.

2. When assistance is needed due to breakdown, grounding, or for some other reason, the Department of Small Craft and any other YP in the area will be notified.

3. All YP craft will be alert to render assistance to any boat in difficulty. Naval Academy sailboats douse all sails as a signal that assistance is required.

1932 *Minimum Midshipmen Crew*

While under way, the minimum midshipmen crew for a YP will be comprised of midshipmen qualified in the following grades:

1. Local operating area:

Commanding Officer	1
Officer of the Deck	1
Engineman	1
Deck Seaman	2

2. Outside the local operating area:

Commanding Officer	1
Navigator	1*
Officer of the Deck	1
Communications Officer	1*
Engineman	2
Deck Seaman	3

* This billet may be filled by a non-qualified midshipman at the discretion of the cruise officer in tactical command, subject to the approval of the Officer Representative, YP Squadron or other proper authority.

1933 *Midshipmen YP Qualifications*

1. Midshipmen are eligible for YP qualifications as follows:

QUALIFICATION	CLASSES ELIGIBLE
Commanding Officer	1
Navigator	1, 2
Officer of the Deck	1, 2
Engineering Officer	1, 2, 3
Communications Officer	1, 2, 3
Engineman	1, 2, 3, 4
Deck Seaman	1, 2, 3, 4

2. The requirements for a YP qualification which a midshipman will be eligible for the following class year may be completed during the spring. The qualification will then become effective upon advancement to the eligible class.

3. Procedures for obtaining YP qualifications are as specified by the Head of the Naval Science Department who will maintain status records for midshipmen having YP qualifications. Midshipmen will receive a card for each qualification.

1934 *Procedures for Checking Out YP's*

1. For department drills: YP's are requested through the Operations Office, Department of Small Craft for Naval Science Department drills including YP Squadron activities and preparations therefor.

2. For midshipmen use other than scheduled events:

a. Only those midshipmen who have qualified

as a YP commanding officer may check out a YP.

    b. To check out a YP:

      (1) Fill out and sign a boat request form.

      (2) Submit the boat request form to the Operations Officer, Department of Small Craft for approval via the Head of the Naval Science Department.

      (3) The Operations Officer, Department of Small Craft, will notify the midshipman commanding officer as to the status of the request.

    c. Boat requests are not required for scheduled weekly YP operations or for authorized weekend cruises; however, the cruise officer in tactical command will ensure that an accurate sailing list is in the possession of the Officer of the Watch, Bancroft Hall, prior to departure on these cruises.

    d. In the absence of a qualified midshipman YP commanding officer, a YP Squadron member may check out a YP for YP Squadron operations if accompanied by a safety officer. The name of the safety officer must appear on the boat request.

    3. For officer use: Authorization for use of YP's will be requested in writing from the Commanding Officer, Naval Station, via the appropriate Head of Department (and the Commandant of Midshipmen if midshipmen are involved). The request will include an identification of the group or organization represented, desired date, times, number of YP's, number of persons to be embarked, and designation of the officer-in-charge. If host officers are desired for public relations, they will be requested in advance by contacting the Head of the Naval Science Department. Upon receipt of the authorization, the Department of Small Craft will be contacted to complete arrangements for checking out a YP. If no midshipmen are to be embarked, the YP must load and unload at the Department of Small Craft, unless otherwise specifically authorized by Commanding Officer, Naval Station.

1935   *Embarkation of Civilians in YP's*

1. Embarkation of civilians must be authorized on each occasion by the Commanding Officer, Naval Station except:

    a. Guests of qualified YP safety officers.

    b. Guests of midshipmen who are listed on the boat request form.

      (1) When young ladies are embarked as guests of midshipmen, a chaperon will be present.

2. Children will not be embarked in YP's unless they are at least ten years of age, can swim one hundred yards, and are accompanied by an adult who is responsible for them.

3. "Waiver of Claim and Release from Liability" forms will be executed in accordance with existing directives.

1936   *YP Squadron Organization*

1. The following offices will be filled by those midshipmen designated by the Head of the Naval Science Department:

    Commodore
    Chief of Staff
    Operations Officer
    Engineer Officer
    Logistics Officer
    Administration Officer
    Division Commanders
    Battalion Commanding Officers

    a. The designated midshipmen will have sole responsibility for planning and actuating YP Squadron activities in accordance with its objectives.

Appendix E   *Sea State Codes*

Hydrographic Office		International	
Term and height of waves, in feet	Code	Term and height of waves, in feet	Code
Calm, 0	0	Calm, glassy, 0	0
Smooth, less than 1	1		
Slight, 1–3	2	Rippled, 0–1	1
Moderate, 3–5	3	Smooth, 1–2	2
		Slight, 2–4	3
Rough, 5–8	4	Moderate, 4–8	4
		Rough, 8–13	5

Hydrographic Office		International	
Very rough, 8–12	5	Very rough, 13–20	6
High, 12–20	6		
Very high, 20–40	7	High, 20–30	7
Mountainous, 40 and higher	8	Very high, 30–45	8
Confused	9	Phenomenal, over 45	9

Appendix F *Beaufort Scale*

Beaufort Number	Wind speed		Seaman's Terms	Estimating wind speed	
	Knots	mph		Observations at sea	Observations on land
0	under 1	under 1	Calm	Sea like mirror.	Calm; smoke rises vertically.
1	1–3	1–3	Light air	Ripples with appearance of scales; no foam crests.	Smoke drift indicates wind direction; vanes do not move.
2	4–6	4–7	Light breeze	Small wavelets; crests of glassy appearance, not breaking.	Wind felt on face; leaves rustle; vanes begin to move.
3	7–10	8–12	Gentle breeze	Large wavelets; crests begin to break; scattered whitecaps.	Leaves, small twigs in constant motion; light flags extended.
4	11–16	13–18	Moderate breeze	Small waves, becoming longer; numerous whitecaps.	Dust, leaves, and loose paper raised up; small branches move.
5	17–21	19–24	Fresh breeze	Moderate waves, taking longer form; many whitecaps; some spray..	Small trees in leaf begin to sway.
6	22–27	25–31	Strong breeze	Larger waves forming; whitecaps everywhere; more spray.	Larger branches of trees in motion; whistling heard in wires
7	28–33	32–38	Moderate gale	Sea heaps up; white foam from breaking waves begins to be blown in streaks.	Whole trees in motion; resistance felt in walking against wind.
8	34–40	39–46	Fresh gale	Moderately high waves of greater length; edges of crests begin to break into spindrift; foam is blown in well-marked streaks.	Twigs and small branches broken off trees; progress generally impeded.
9	41–47	47–54	Strong gale	High waves; sea begins to roll; dense streaks of foam; spray may reduce visibility.	Slight structural damage occurs; slate blown from roofs.
10	48–55	55–63	Whole gale	Very high waves with overhanging crests; sea takes white appearance as foam is blown in very dense streaks; rolling is heavy and visibility reduced.	Seldom experienced on land; trees broken or uprooted; considerable structural damage occurs.
11	56–63	64–72	Storm	Exceptionally high waves; sea covered with white foam patches; visibility still more reduced.	
12	64–71	73–82	Hurricane	Air filled with foam; sea completely white with driving spray; visibility greatly reduced.	Very rarely experienced on land; usually accompanied by widespread damage.
13	72–80	83–92			
14	81–89	93–103			
15	90–99	104–114			
16	100–108	115–125			
17	109–118	126–136			

Sailing Fleet of the U.S. Naval Academy

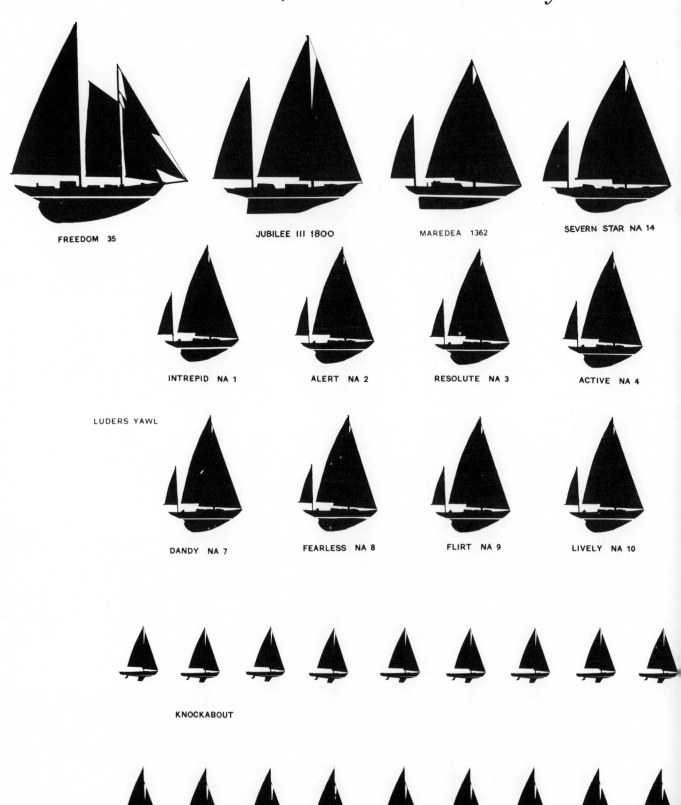

FREEDOM 35

JUBILEE III 1800

MAREDEA 1362

SEVERN STAR NA 14

INTREPID NA 1

ALERT NA 2

RESOLUTE NA 3

ACTIVE NA 4

LUDERS YAWL

DANDY NA 7

FEARLESS NA 8

FLIRT NA 9

LIVELY NA 10

KNOCKABOUT

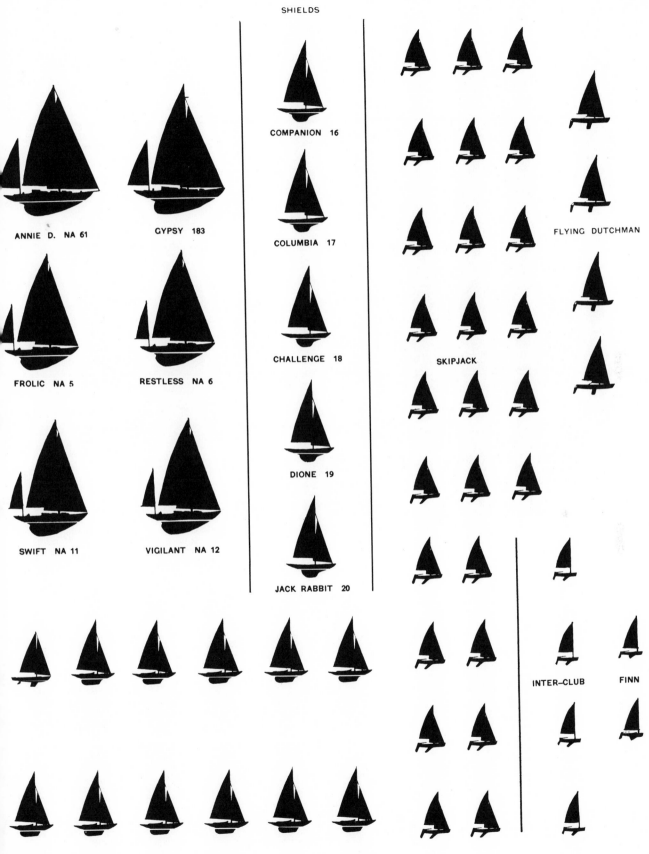

SHIELDS

ANNIE D. NA 61

GYPSY 183

FROLIC NA 5

RESTLESS NA 6

SWIFT NA 11

VIGILANT NA 12

COMPANION 16

COLUMBIA 17

CHALLENGE 18

DIONE 19

JACK RABBIT 20

SKIPJACK

FLYING DUTCHMAN

INTER–CLUB

FINN

FREEDOM, a flush-decked, keel schooner with a diesel auxiliary. Dimensions: 88'2" L.O.A., 66'6" L.W.L., 19'8" beam, 10'0" draft, 3,800 square feet sail area, sail number 35. She ordinarily carries a crew numbering from fifteen to twenty. The **Freedom** was built of wood by the Great Lakes Boat Building Corporation in 1931 from designs by John G. Alden, and she was donated to the Naval Academy by Mrs. Sterling Morton in 1940. She is the largest sailing yacht native to the Chesapeake Bay. Although sailed regularly, she is excluded from many handicap races because she is larger than the rules for most races allow.

ANNIE D., a cruising-racing keel yawl built of wood with a diesel auxiliary. Dimensions: 49'9" L.O.A., 36'4" L.W.L., 12'0" beam, 7'11" draft, 1,177 square feet sail area, sail number 61. She carries a crew of from six to twelve. Formerly named **Windfall II,** the **Annie D.** was built in 1951 by Abeking and Rassmussen in Germany to designs by Philip L. Rhodes. She was donated to the Naval Academy in 1959 by Mr. F. Nichols.

FLYING DUTCHMAN, one of the fastest and most sophisticated of the planing centerboard dinghies. Dimensions: 19'10" L.O.A., 18'0" L.W.L., 5'7" beam, 3'8" draft with centerboard down, 176 square feet sail area, fiberglass construction. Sloop rigged with a Genoa and spinnaker, the Flying Dutchman is fitted with a trapeze (a wire strap attached to the mast which supports the crew) to assist in hiking. This is a Pan American and Olympic class. The Naval Academy has four of these boats.

INTER-CLUB DINGHY, a cat-rigged centerboard dinghy primarily used for Intercollegiate racing and frostbiting (wintertime sailing). The Inter-club was designed by Sparkman and Stephens in 1946. Dimensions: 11'6" L.O.A., 11'6" L.W.L., 4'7½" beam, 3'0" draft with centerboard down, 72 square feet sail area, 195 pounds displacement, fiberglass construction. Four of these boats are currently at the Naval Academy.

262

GYPSY, a cruising-racing yawl built of wood with a diesel auxiliary. She is similar to the **Annie D.** except that **Gypsy** is a keel-centerboarder. Dimensions: 49'11" L.O.A., 36'4" L.W.L., 12'6" beam, 6'5" draft, 1,061 square feet sail area, sail number 183. A Rhodes design, she was built by the same yard as the **Annie D.** in 1951. She is distinguished by her seven-eighths rig. Formerly named **Blue Water,** she was donated to the Naval Academy in 1959.

A new class of KNOCKABOUTS, adopted by the Naval Academy in 1968, will eventually replace the wooden-hulled knockabouts described in Chapter Six. She is a modified **Rainbow**-class sloop, with the cuddy removed and an enlarged cockpit. She is built of fiberglass and has a masthead rig. She was designed by Sparkman and Stephens and is being produced by Tidewater Boats of Annapolis, Maryland. Dimensions: 24'2" L.O.A., 17'3" L.W.L., 6'3" beam and 3'6" draft. She has 1120 pounds of outside ballast in a cast-iron fin keel. Her independent rudder is bronze and fiberglass. She carries 218 square feet of working sail.

DYER DHOW, these dinghies, used primarily as tenders for the Luders yawls and other large boats, and described in detail in Chapter 7, are sometimes used, as shown in this view, for frostbite racing on the Severn River.

FINN MONOTYPE, a planing, cat-rigged, centerboard dinghy intended for singlehanded racing. The class is international and is used in the Olympics. Dimensions: 14'9" L.O.A., 14'6" L.W.L., 5'1" beam, 2'6" draft with centerboard down. 106 square feet sail area, 320 pounds displacement, fiberglass construction. The rig is very simple and extremely flexible. The Naval Academy has two of these boats.

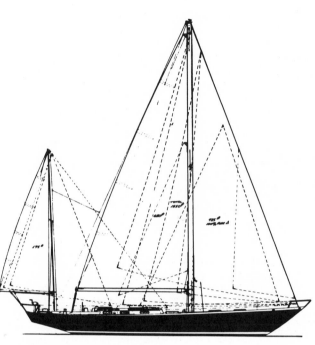

MARADEA, a modern, keel-centerboard, fiberglass yawl with a diesel auxiliary. Dimensions: 60′6″ L.O.A., 41′0″ L.W.L., 14′3″ beam, 5′6″ draft with centerboard up, 28 tons displacement, 1,550 square feet sail area. Donated in 1967 to the Naval Academy by Dr. Homer Denius, the **Maradea** is a very close-winded, competitive ocean-racer, yet has very comfortable accommodations. She was designed by Charles Morgan and built jointly by the Morgan Yacht Corporation and the Eau Gallie Yacht Basin in Florida.

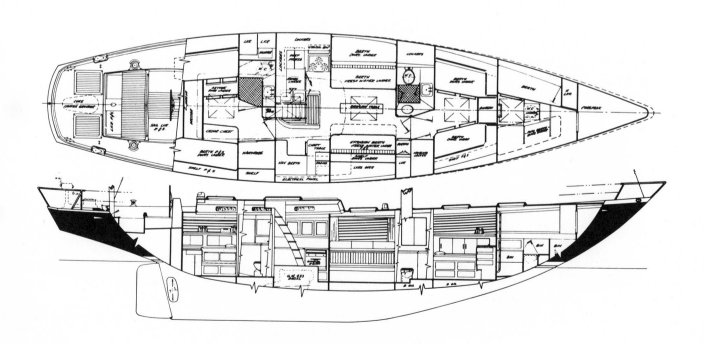

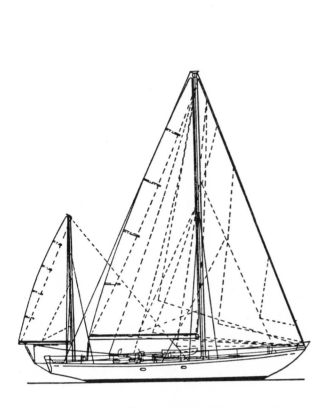

SEVERN STAR, a modern, keel-centerboard, ocean racing yawl with a diesel auxiliary. Dimensions: 57'6" L.O.A., 38'0" L.W.L., 14'1" beam, 8'1" draft (centerboard up), 1,521 square feet sail area, sail number NA 14. Donated to the Naval Academy in 1967 by Sumner A. Long, the **Severn Star** has been sailed in nearly all of the world's major ocean races and has a truly outstanding record. She was built of aluminum by the Jakobsen's Shipyard, Oyster Bay, New York, in 1960 to designs of William H. Tripp. Her small centerboard is intended primarily for balance rather than to supply lateral resistance.

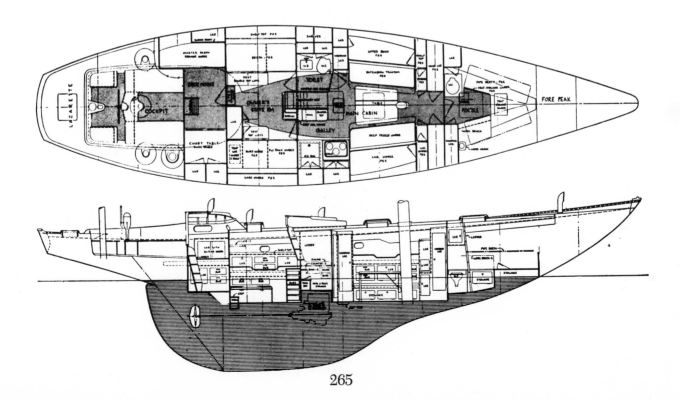

JUBILEE III, an aluminum ketch designed for cruising and ocean racing, with a diesel auxiliary. Dimensions: 73'3" L.O.A., 51'9" L.W.L., 16'4" beam, 8'5" draft, 2,535 square feet sail area. Designed by MacLear and Harris, this boat was donated to the Naval Academy in 1968 by Francis D. Wetherill. Two centerboards increase her draft to 14'1" and give the ability to shift the center of lateral resistance forward or aft in order to achieve balance on various points of sailing under various wind conditions.

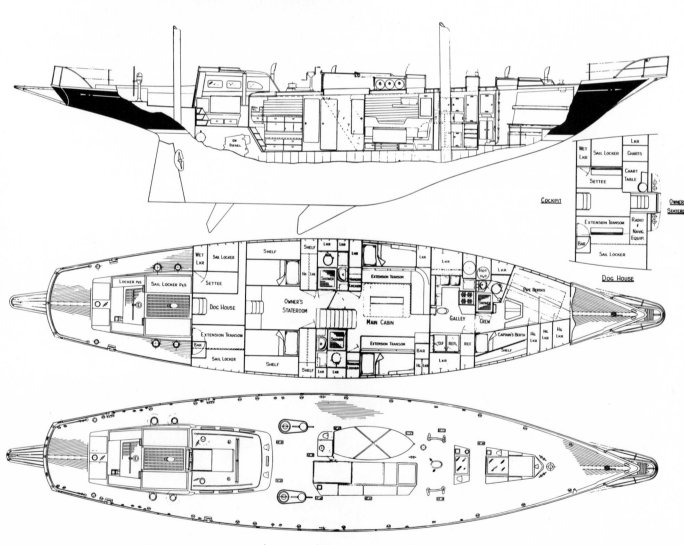

266

Index

Italicized entries indicate a definition or a drawing within the text.

267

268

271

273

Photographic Credits

Robert de Gast: *Frontispiece, 2, 24, 47, 48, 82, 93, 99, 104, 116, 118, 124, 138, 145, 182, 220*. B. Devereux Barker III: *141*. Hugh Whall: *14*. Official U.S. Navy: *10, 71, 77, 79, 80, 83, 84, 95, 97, 101, 123, 155, 176, 179, 180, 185*. David Q. Scott: *100, 114, 150, 158, 170, 178, 181, 189 (3), 200, 223*. K. J. Mierzejewski: *66*. Ed Holm: *32, 142*. Rex Combs: *178*. National Archives: *180*. Courtesy of Westerbeke Corporation: *168-169*. Barrett Gallagher: *91*. Sam Chambliss: *119*. M. Rosenfeld & Sons: *120*.

Notes

Notes

Notes

Notes

ALLIED NAVAL SIGNAL FLAGS AND PENNANTS

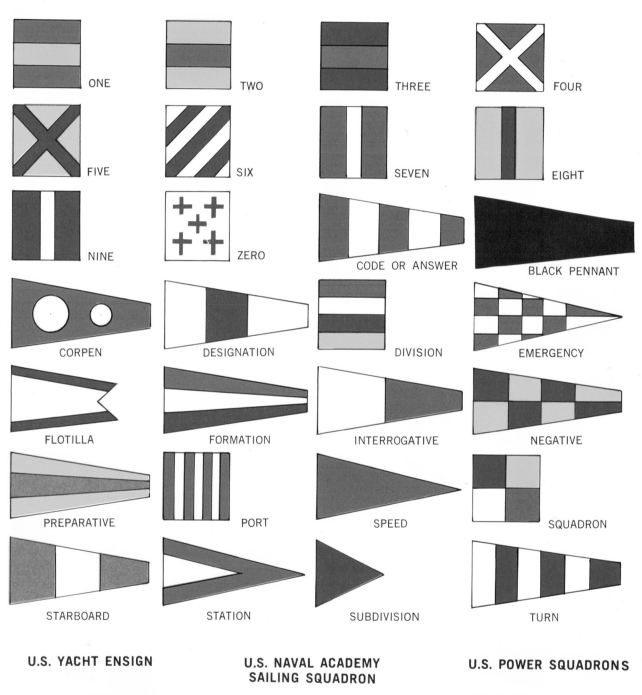

ONE   TWO   THREE   FOUR

FIVE   SIX   SEVEN   EIGHT

NINE   ZERO   CODE OR ANSWER   BLACK PENNANT

CORPEN   DESIGNATION   DIVISION   EMERGENCY

FLOTILLA   FORMATION   INTERROGATIVE   NEGATIVE

PREPARATIVE   PORT   SPEED   SQUADRON

STARBOARD   STATION   SUBDIVISION   TURN

U.S. YACHT ENSIGN

U.S. NAVAL ACADEMY SAILING SQUADRON

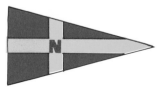

U.S. POWER SQUADRONS

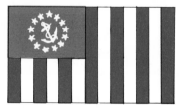

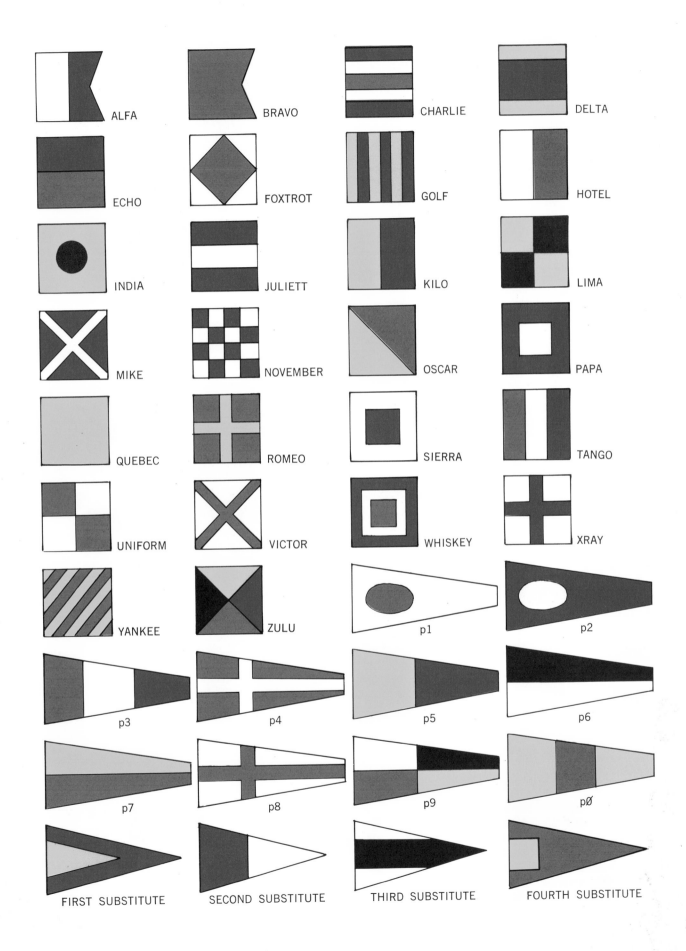

ALFA BRAVO CHARLIE DELTA
ECHO FOXTROT GOLF HOTEL
INDIA JULIETT KILO LIMA
MIKE NOVEMBER OSCAR PAPA
QUEBEC ROMEO SIERRA TANGO
UNIFORM VICTOR WHISKEY XRAY
YANKEE ZULU p1 p2
p3 p4 p5 p6
p7 p8 p9 pØ
FIRST SUBSTITUTE SECOND SUBSTITUTE THIRD SUBSTITUTE FOURTH SUBSTITUTE